Knowing India

NEW PERSPECTIVES ON INDIAN PASTS

THOMAS R. TRAUTMANN
Aryans and British India

A.R. VENKATACHALAPATHY
In Those Days There Was No Coffee:
Writings in Cultural History

DAVID N. LORENZEN
Who Invented Hinduism?
Essays on Religion in History

THOMAS R. TRAUTMANN
Languages and Nations:
The Dravidian Proof in Colonial Madras

HARLAN O. PEARSON
Islamic Reform and Revival in Nineteenth-century India:
The Tarīqah-I Muhammadīyah

THOMAS R. TRAUTMANN
The Clash of Chronologies:
Ancient India in the Modern World

SAURABH DUBE
After Conversion:
Cultural Histories of Modern India

USHA SANYAL
Devotional Islam and Politics in British India:
Ahmad Riza Khan Barelwi and His Movement, 1870–1920 (New Edition)

DAVID N. LORENZEN
The Scourge of the Mission:
Marco della Tomba in Hindustan

BENJAMIN ZACHARIAH
Playing the Nation Game:
The Ambiguities of Nationalism in India (Forthcoming)

Knowing India

Colonial and Modern Constructions of the Past

Essays in Honor of
Thomas R. Trautmann

YODA PRESS

YODA PRESS
268 A/C, Vasant Kunj
New Delhi 110 070
www.yodapress.com

Published in India by YODA PRESS

First Published 2011

ISBN 978-93-80403-03-8

Editor-in-charge: Supriya Nayak
Typeset in Balaram 10.5/14
By Jojy Philip, New Delhi 110 015
Printed at Kaizen Offset Pvt Ltd, New Delhi 110 020
Published by Arpita Das for YODA PRESS

Contents

Illustrations

Foreword

A Return Gift

Essai sur le don, Forme et raison de l'īchange dans les sociītīs archañques—This slim volume, originally penned by the noted French sociologist Marcel Mauss in the journal *L'Annīe sociologique* in 1923–24, is not a book one might expect to find featured so prominently in courses on the early history of South Asia. But it exemplifies the interdisciplinary approach that has infused the teaching and scholarship of Professor Thomas R. Trautmann from the earliest days of his appointment to the Department of History at the University of Michigan in 1968 right down to the present.

Mauss describes the central importance of gift-giving between individuals and societies; that gifts are inseparable from the giver; and that the gift, as part of a system of reciprocal exchange, creates an unbreakable bond between giver and receiver. It is this bond which has linked Professor Trautmann with all of the students that he has trained and all those fortunate enough to know him.

Professor Trautmann has given many gifts to many people over the years, both within the classroom and through his generous spirit to students and colleagues alike. Many of the recipients of these gifts have in return enriched South Asian research and are now training new generations of scholars. Even though it is not possible to repay even a small portion of these gifts, we presented this offering of gratitude on the occasion of a conference held in his honor at the University of Michigan in the fall of 2007. It is a stone inscription, carved into a piece of black granite from India, to commemorate the man who has spent his entire academic career widening the road of South Asian scholarship for all who wish to follow. The inscriptions says:

Figure 1

Hail, prosperity!

We, this great assembly, give this gift of dharma in the 39th 'UM' year of his reign [the 39th year of his tenure at the University of Michigan] to the most eminent scholar, Thomas Raja [Roger] Trautmann, who is the lord of the eastern, southern, western, and northern oceans; who possesses the knowledge of elephants; for imparting everlasting wisdom, sharing knowledge, and providing inspiration to his students and fellow scholars.

This inscription shall last as long as the moon and sun endure.

Thank you, Tom.
Peter Granda

Acknowledgments

The essays in this volume, with one exception, originated as papers presented at "Conceptualizing South Asia's Past at Michigan: A Conference in Honor of Thomas R. Trautmann," held in Ann Arbor, Michigan, on October 5–6, 2007. For the former students, current colleagues, and old friends of Tom Trautmann who participated, it was an opportunity to celebrate his career and express our appreciation. In addition to the contributors to this collection, Peter Granda, Diane Owen Hughes, Barbara Metcalf, Farina Mir, and Andrew Shryock all had roles in the conference, while Stewart Gordon presented a paper—thanks are due to all of them. Only Michael Dodson was not at this gathering—I am grateful to him for generously agreeing to contribute an essay some months later. Many debts were accrued in the course of organizing the conference, most especially to Peter Granda. Immediately senior to me as an ex-student of Tom Trautmann's, Peter cheerfully took care of local hospitality and helped iron out many details relating to the conference. (He has also been a steadfast source of encouragement during the inevitably lengthy process of compiling this book.) The Center for South Asian Studies at the University of Michigan hosted the conference and provided invaluable staff support. My thanks go to several of its Directors—Barbara Metcalf, Sumathi Ramaswamy, and William Glover—as well as Rohit Setty, Cynthia Middleton, and Farina Mir for various kinds of help. The conference was made possible through the financial support not only of the Center for South Asian Studies, but also the University of Michigan's Department of History, Eisenburg Institute for Historical Studies, Horace H. Rackham School of Graduate Studies, and Department of Anthropology.

1

Introduction*

CYNTHIA TALBOT

TRACKING TRAUTMANN'S TRAJECTORY

The standard compartments of academic specialization—the divisions of time periods, geographic areas, or disciplinary and thematic fields into which intellectual activities are typically classified—cannot adequately encapsulate the scholarship of Thomas R. Trautmann, whose writing has spanned disciplinary boundaries and addressed multiple audiences. Among his many fans are historians of the British empire, as well as South Asian Studies scholars, who might be startled to discover that Trautmann is also known among certain circles of Americanists for his contributions to the history of nineteenth-century anthropology or that he has co-edited a volume of essays on conceptions of time. Some sense of his wide-ranging interests can be gleaned from Trautmann's webpage at the University of Michigan's Department of History. With the succinctness and acumen that are so characteristic of his work, Trautmann summarizes his expertise as follows:

> Ancient India; Orientalist scholarship in India; history of anthropology; kinship; ideas of time and history across cultures; anthropology in American culture

* I am grateful to Richard Davis, Peter Granda, Judith Irvine, and Sylvia Vatuk for their comments on an earlier version of this essay.

The words "anthropology," "kinship," and "culture" figure prominently in this intellectual profile of a scholar who started his career studying ancient Indian history with A.L. Basham at the School of Oriental and African Studies, University of London. If Bernard S. Cohn was an anthropologist among the historians, as he described himself in an early essay, then Tom Trautmann has surely been an historian among the anthropologists.[1] Both Cohn and Trautmann represent an interdisciplinarity in scholarly ideas and methods that, although widespread enough today to go largely unremarked, was not only rare but even actively discouraged in earlier decades.

The pioneering aspect of Trautmann's first monograph lay not so much in its traversing of interdisciplinary boundaries, however, as in its employment of a new technology: computers. In *Kautilya and the Arthasastra: A Statistical Investigation of the Authorship and Evolution of the Text* (1971), Trautmann used a mainframe computer to analyze the frequency of certain words, as well as the length of compounds and sentences—this is the "statistical investigation" mentioned in the subtitle. The aim of the word and sentence counts was to determine whether the *Arthasastra* had a single or multiple authors, and whether it had been added to over time. Trautmann did not limit his inquiry into the issue of authorship to the internal evidence of the Sanskrit text. The lengthiest chapter in *Kautilya and the Arthasastra* sifts through a variety of legends about Canakya, the minister of Candragupta Maurya who is often equated with Kautilya, in search of the most reliable information on him. Looking back retrospectively at *Kautilya and the Arthasastra*, we can characterize it as a quest to uncover the author(s) of a path-breaking text. The urge to understand a key text through the person of its author, one of the hallmarks of Trautmann's scholarship, can thus be detected even in this earliest and most Indological of his books.

The anthropological dimension of Trautmann's intellectual disposition came to the forefront in *Dravidian Kinship* (1981;

reprinted in 1995), his second major book. A highly technical (historians might say, arcane) field, kinship was a central topic of study in anthropology for many decades, and Trautmann drew on years of others' fieldwork for the raw data he required to construct an abstract model of Proto-Dravidian kinship. The laborious task of extracting and distilling the kinship terminologies of a variety of south Indian communities was valuable in itself, but Trautmann's real innovation lies in adding another, historical, dimension to the synchronic patterns of Dravidian kinship's structure and extent that he derived from ethnography. Far from being a quintessentially ethnographic phenomenon, Trautmann asserts that "the Dravidian system of kinship is an historical construct, mandating an historical method of study" (1981: 357). In order to more adequately establish what the original Dravidian kinship system had been, Trautmann went back in time to trace the centuries-old distribution and character of this system, or in his words, "to give it, so far as may be possible, a past that is concrete" (1981: 238). He used both literature and inscriptions to ascertain the existence, since ancient times, of a pan-Indian valorization of marriage as a pure gift of the daughter, made to the groom by her father. This ideal led to a preference for matrilateral cross-cousin marriage in the Dravidian sphere, because it differentiated wife-givers from wife-takers. It should also be noted that, despite the exclusive focus on Dravidian kinship suggested by the book's title, Trautmann devotes considerable space to exploring the various Indo-Aryan kinship systems of northern and central India. Thus the work is actually a comprehensive exploration of South Asian kinship systems from the past to the present.

Dravidian Kinship is critical in any consideration of the life of Tom Trautmann's mind, because it was here that questions first arose which he pursued in greater depth in later books. (Disclosure time: I studied with Tom while he was writing *Dravidian Kinship*, and may have been indelibly imprinted by the experience.) In viewing Dravidian kinship as a historical construct, for example,

Trautmann calls attention to the underlying assumption of an actual genetic relationship, not simply a typological similarity among the various Dravidian kinship terminologies observable today, just as in the case of language families in the field of historical linguistics (1981: 3, 20). He points out that both fields employ the metaphor of a family tree, and that South Asian knowledge was seminal in determining their origins: the "discovery" of Sanskrit in the case of historical linguistics and of Dravidian kinship in the case of the comparative study of kinship terminologies (1981: 17, 1). With the benefit of hindsight, Trautmann's progression from the study of kinship to the study of philology thus seems eminently logical.

Most of all, *Dravidian Kinship* serves as a testament to Trautmann's abiding interest in forms of social classification. It concerns itself with a fundamental form of social organization that differs across communities: kinship terminologies and systems. In subsequent research, Trautmann shifted his focus from kinship to the intertwined categories of language, nation (in its older sense of ethnicity), and race which are among the most frequently invoked markers of social identity, along with gender and religion. Kinship, language, ethnicity, and race are all ways of classifying people that have been utilized extensively by social theorists over the past two hundred years—they have been regarded as the basic attributes that differentiate large groups of people, in other words. Trautmann often refers in his writings to ethnology, a term which can be defined as the "attempt to classify globally the great variety of cultures" (Cohn 1987: 24), and it is this ethnological enterprise, as directed at South Asia, that has long aroused Trautmann's curiosity.

The topic of kinship remained central to Trautmann's third monograph, *Lewis Henry Morgan and the Invention of Kinship* (1987). It is a study of the man, an American lawyer from upstate New York, who gave us the idea of Dravidian kinship and, more generally, initiated the modern study of kinship systems. It is not a typical biography, however, in that Trautmann spends only minimal time on Morgan's personal life—it is rather the "biography of a book," *Systems of Consanguinity and Affinity of the Human Family*, published in 1871 (Trautmann 1987: xi). Trautmann first wrote about Morgan in *Dravidian Kinship*; subsequently, he discovered a wealth of archival material that enabled him to carry out a book-length reinterpretation of Morgan's ideas in more philological terms, since "for Morgan, indeed, the whole of the ethnological venture was a continuation of philology by other means" (Trautmann 1987: 158). *Lewis Henry Morgan and the Invention of Kinship*, reissued in 2008, has earned Trautmann an enduring reputation among Americanists and those interested in the history of anthropology. It also provided Trautmann an opportunity to hone his narrative skills, as when (spoiler alert!) he waits until the last few pages to tell us that Morgan was married to his mother's brother's daughter; Morgan's reluctance to bring attention to the closeness of their kin relation may explain why he seems to have willfully overlooked the Dravidian preference for cross-cousin marriage.

For most South Asianists, who are unfamiliar with it, *Lewis Henry Morgan and the Invention of Kinship* constitutes the missing link in the trajectory of Trautmann's scholarly development. It is Trautmann's first lengthy examination of a nineteenth-century Western thinker whose ideas were critical in the characterization and classification of colonized or subjugated peoples—the field of study for which Trautmann is best known among historians of South Asia. As Trautmann explored the inspirations, influences, and innovations in a major social theorist's scholarship in *Lewis Henry Morgan*, the penchant for intellectual biography that was first discernible in *Kautilya and the Arthasastra* became fully manifest. In his subsequent books, Trautmann has continued to concentrate on nineteenth-century ideas and the social context of their creation, most notably the Indo-Aryan concept as formulated by Sir William Jones and others (*Aryans and British India*, 1997) and the comparable Dravidian thesis first advanced by Francis Whyte Ellis (*Languages and Nations,* 2006). All of the men studied by Trautmann generated important theories or insights that remain part of the conventional wisdom on non-Western and/or "primitive" cultures and peoples. Ever since *Lewis Henry Morgan*, Trautmann's focus has been on the ideas born in an imperial and colonial era that have shaped our current views of different peoples and their pasts.

A fascination with social classification, a penchant for biography in the pursuit of a history of ideas, and a concern with the impact of nineteenth-century social theory or colonial knowledge on our present thinking—all three of these characteristics bring coherence to much of the Trautmann corpus. They are brought to bear on conceptions of ancient Indian society, with happy results, in Trautmann's most recent monographs. *Aryans and British India* (1997) began his shift of focus away from kinship to other social markers—primarily language, but also the notions of ethnicity and race that are often associated with language. It is an ambitious book in its scope: tracing the idea of Aryan language and race from its inception by Sir William Jones at the end of the eighteenth century to the emergence of a full-blown race science in the late nineteenth century. In the process, Trautmann chronicles the waning of the Indomania that had flourished in an earlier stage, "killed off" as it was by the Indophobia of the Evangelicals and Utilitarians, and he also reviews the new Orientalism's ethnological classification of the Indian population. By retrieving the earlier meaning of the word "Orientalist" as designating a person who knew Oriental languages and could therefore speak authoritatively about the Orient, Trautmann made it possible to discuss colonial scholarship on India in more nuanced ways.

Languages and Nations: The Dravidian Proof in Colonial Madras, Trautmann tells us, "forms a pair with *Aryans and British India*," since "it is an examination of the same phenomenon from a different perspective and a different local expression" (2006: xiii). The book concentrates on the figure of Francis Whyte Ellis and his circle of associates at the College of Fort St. George in Madras during the early decades of the nineteenth century, as they formulated the notion of a Dravidian language family in opposition to the opinions of their fellow Orientalists in Calcutta. *Languages and Nations* is considerably more restricted than *Aryans and British India* in the span of time and in the range of ideas it surveys, primarily because Trautmann is traversing new terrain that he must introduce at length to the reader. The relatively copious documentation allows Trautmann to identify the Indian assistants who collaborated with Ellis in the creation of knowledge about India; it also enables Trautmann to show that the European languages-and-nations project was so successful in British India precisely because there was a conjuncture of knowledge with the indigenous tradition of language analysis. In its heavy reliance on archival material and its more circumscribed parameters, *Languages and Nations* resembles the standard piece of history-writing more than anything else Trautmann has produced. We might say that the historian, after his long travels and travails among the anthropologists, is returning home in this book; yet Trautmann's thinking defies efforts to categorize it in such simplistic disciplinary terms. His broad field of vision, encompassing a wide sweep of geographic regions, time spans, and types of knowledges, results in insights that are unique and relevant precisely because they exceed the boundaries of academic specialization.

Much more could be said about Trautmann's significance and his body of work than I am able to do here. Fortunately, three scholars have shared with us their personal commentaries on and responses to Trautmann's writing: Tom Fricke on *Dravidian Kinship*, Richard H. Davis on *Aryans and British India*, and Rama Sundari Mantena on *Languages and Nations*. Their short pieces are subsumed under the title "Tributes to Trautmann" toward the end of this volume. Following that is a complete list of Trautmann's publications, so that the reader can get a full picture of his accomplishments and the means to sample all the intellectual delights he has created. Especially noteworthy are two publications from 2009: *The Clash of Chronologies: Ancient India in the Modern World* which gathers together a number of Tom's articles, and *The Madras School of Orientalism*, an edited volume with contributions from numerous scholars on the inter-related projects of Ellis, Colin Mackenzie, and their associates.

ESSAYS IN HONOR OF TRAUTMANN

I now turn our attention away from a direct focus on Trautmann and toward the essays contributed by his friends, colleagues, and admirers, in which the reflections, resonances, and repercussions of his ideas can be witnessed. The essays are arranged in three sets, according to their contents and proximity to Trautmann's recent publications. Those in the first group all engage with one or more of his signature topics—Mosaic ethnology, language study and historical linguistics, or kinship terminologies and systems. The essays in the second set are more varied in subject matter, but all pertain to perceptions of precolonial society or culture by colonial scholars, modern Indian intellectuals, or the modern Indian populace. Moving back from questions relating to the nineteenth and twentieth centuries, the essays in the last group all concern some aspect of the many centuries of earlier Indian history. The diversity of topics and long expanse of time encompassed in these essays is a testament to the breadth of Trautmann's interests and his deep curiosity.

Musings on (Mosaic) Ethnology, Language, and Kinship

The Mosaic ethnology—so central in the work of Sir William Jones and other early Orientalists—surfaces in several of the essays in this volume. In "Language Fields: Robert Needham Cust's Language Map of South Asia, 1878," Judith T. Irvine builds on the discussion of technologies of location in Tom Trautmann's *Languages and Nations: The Dravidian Proof in Colonial Madras*. While the

"Ptolemaic grid of longitude and latitude" was a technology that enabled spatial location, the Mosaic ethnology or Tree of Nations located the relations among different peoples, envisioning them as "branching lineages of the human family tree, as relations near and far" (Trautmann 2006: 6, 11). What had initially been a framework for the classification of peoples gradually got transformed into a classification of languages—that is, into the underlying principles of historical linguistics. Language maps, Irvine suggests, were "one of the means by which language classifications could become understood as the pedigree of nations, as the Biblical model faded from scholarly view." The geographic mapping of languages combined two technologies of location—that for places and that for peoples—and, in the process, replaced the reality of people with the abstraction of language.

Irvine's essay explores the contributions of one British administrator-scholar, Robert Needham Cust, to the geographical mapping of languages. Cust spent almost 25 years in India (1843–1867), much of it in the Punjab while the newly pacified region was being brought under British control. The hands-on style of governance and sympathy for the peasant that characterized the "Punjab school" were shared by Cust, who had extensive experience dealing with land revenue issues. Cust felt that British officials needed to be familiar with local languages, at least to the extent of anticipating what interpreters might be required in court on a given day. He also made frequent use, while in the Punjab, of detailed maps of a settlement's agricultural fields, indispensable for the adjudication of disputes.

These aspects of Cust's background, Irvine believes, help explain his enthusiasm for the mapping of languages, manifested in his *A Sketch of the Modern Languages of the East Indies, Accompanied by Two Language-Maps* (1878), and a few years later in a similar work on African languages. Irvine points out that maps like those produced by Cust—in which swathes of color representing a single language are overlaid onto a topographic map—are problematic in their denial of the co-existence of multiple languages. But Cust discusses the presence of different literary registers and other topics that demonstrate his awareness of the sociolinguistic ambiguities elided on his maps. Irvine argues that Cust's Punjab experience led him to place a premium on the peasantry and their vernacular language, which alone needed to be depicted in his maps. This was in concert with prevailing trends in Europe that viewed the rural population as the true representatives of the "folk" and their language as constituting community. In Irvine's perceptive analysis, we see how language came to stand in for a people, in cartographic representation, as both were increasingly conceptually affixed to a set territory.

Michael S. Dodson, in "Thomas Maurice and Domestic Orientalism, c. 1790–1820," pursues a topic—or more accurately, an intellectual biography—that Tom Trautmann had earlier touched on in passing. Maurice, whose prolific writing Trautmann seems reluctant to describe as scholarship, is just a peripheral figure in *Aryans and British India*, surfacing occasionally in the general discussion on British Indomania. Unlike Sir William Jones, Francis Whyte Ellis, and other Orientalists whom Trautmann has written about, Maurice knew none of the languages of Asia. This is one reason Dodson dubs him a "domestic Orientalist." More importantly, Maurice did not study Asia in and for itself but with the ulterior purpose of verifying the Biblical narrative—"an essentially domestic British agenda," as Dodson puts it.

Maurice's enthusiasm for Sanskrit knowledge—which because of the language's antiquity was presumed to be pure—derived from its ability to stand as independent testimony to the Bible's accuracy. It was seen as a weapon that could be wielded against the deist and atheist critiques that flourished at the end of the eighteenth century. Maurice was by no means alone in this Christian appropriation of Asiatic learning, for he followed in the footsteps of men like Sir William Jones, from whom Maurice borrowed the "whole structure and much of the substance" of his books (Trautmann

1997: 75). Like Jones, Maurice subscribed to the short Biblical chronology, according to which the earth was created in 4004 BC, and also to what Trautmann calls the "Mosaic ethnology," the view that all humans were ultimately descended from the three sons of Noah. Humanity's dispersal from the original homeland in Chaldea explained the similarities in language, temple architecture (for which the Tower of Babel was the prototype), mythology, and astronomical systems that Maurice claimed to have identified in his lengthy treatises. He was particularly taken with the idea that all religions revered a divine triad—thereby validating Christianity's trinity—and also with the belief that past cultures had embedded the truths of astronomy in mythological form.

Dodson observes that Maurice's "mythographical" histories, as he kindly labels them, enjoyed a considerable popularity in their day, as did Maurice's poetry. Today it is all too easy to turn Maurice into a figure of ridicule, a fate that was befalling him as early as the first decade or two of the nineteenth century. Dodson's sympathetic portrayal not only helps us make sense of Maurice intellectually, it also provides an insightful explanation for the rapid decline in his reputation. Citing contemporary reviews of Maurice's work, Dodson argues that the more rational sensibilities of the new imperial age were at odds with Maurice's extravagant excesses and exuberant leaps of logic. By thus contextualizing Maurice's admittedly unusual ideas within the larger intellectual trends of late eighteenth- and early nineteenth-century Britain, Dodson has rescued Maurice from near oblivion in our historiographic consciousness.

Shah Mahmoud Hanifi extends Tom Trautmann's interest in the British languages-and-nations project to the borderlands of the subcontinent, in "Henry George Raverty and the Colonial Marketing of Pashto." He begins with a person and an idea—Sir William Jones and the Mosaic ethnology—that are familiar to us from Trautmann's work. Fragments of documents in the Pashto language had been given to Jones in the 1780s, Hanifi explains, including a text that claimed Afghans were descended from the Lost Tribes of Israel. Jones found the Lost Tribes theory congenial and called for further study of the literature and history of Afghanistan, a region about which very little was known at the time. The idea that Afghans or Pathans might have originated from the Lost Tribes of Israel became sufficiently widespread that European authorities on Afghanistan were compelled to address it up to the time of Sir Olaf Caroe, who served as Governor of the Northwest Frontier Province in 1946. The resilience of this aspect of the Mosaic ethnology is remarkable, even though Mountstuart Elphinstone—the first official British envoy to the Afghan court in 1808—had argued strongly against Jones's suggestion that Pashto was related to the Semitic language Chaldaic (Chaldean) and had thereby refuted the Lost Tribes theory.

At the center of Hanifi's foray into the history of the colonial encounter with Pashto stands the figure of Major H.G. Raverty, a proponent of the Lost Tribes origin of Afghans. Despite his advocacy of this mistaken notion, Raverty was the most accomplished colonial scholar of the Pashto language. A skilled linguist who also knew Hindustani and Persian, he published a grammar of Pashto in 1855 and a Pashto dictionary in 1860, as well as selections from Pashto literature. Raverty contributed to the growing conflation in colonial parlance of the terms Afghan, Pathan, and Pashtun (i.e., Pashto-speaker), a conflation that continues into the present time. His work did not gain much recognition during his lifetime, nor was he successful in selling his language materials for use in training military officers. As a consequence, Raverty is probably best known to South Asianists today for his translation and copious annotation of *Tabaqat-i Nasiri*, a thirteenth-century Indo-Persian chronicle, rather than for his work on the Pashto language. Aside from personality issues, Hanifi explains Raverty's failure to transform his linguistic expertise into a marketable product as the result of his extremely meticulous, even pedantic, approach. For instance, Raverty differentiated 40 characters for transcribing the

Pashto language, while Henry Walter Bellew used only 20 in his grammar—one reason why Bellew's language materials, and not Raverty's, were adopted by the military establishment. In addition to his contribution in bringing Pashto into the dialogue on language knowledge and policy in colonial India, Hanifi opens up a fruitful field of inquiry when he discusses the nineteenth-century market for the teaching of vernacular languages.

Some brief remarks made by Tom Trautmann in *Dravidian Kinship* provide the starting point for Sylvia Vatuk's essay, "Muslim Kinship in the Dravidian Heartland: Kinship Terminology and Close Kin Marriage among Urdu-speaking Nawayats." Trautmann had very little to say about Muslim kinship in his book, except to observe that north Indian Hindus and Muslims closely resembled each other in their kinship terminology, but not in their marriage preferences or patterns of marriage-related gift exchange. While Trautmann's statement is true at the level of normative prescription, Vatuk notes that most South Asian Muslims do not follow Islamic law regarding gift-giving, which requires the groom to present money or valuables to his bride, and have increasingly adopted the Indic custom of offering a dowry. The only significant variation, in practice, are the rules about eligibility for marriage: South Asian Muslims, like those in the Middle East, have a strong preference for marrying a close relative, in diametric opposition to north Indian Hindus, for whom endogamy is prohibited. Muslims differ also from south Indian Hindus in their preference for parallel rather than cross cousins.

In order to flesh out her sketch of Muslim kinship in the subcontinent, Vatuk presents a description of the marriage practices of a large extended family from the Nawayat community, a group of elite Sunni Muslims who served at Muslim courts in south India and adopted the Dakkani Urdu language (and its kinship terminology) in the process. In the past, the Nawayats placed a premium on marrying within the extended family, especially with first cousins. But their kinship terminology is similar to that of north

Indian Hindus and likewise differentiates between consanguineal relatives and affines, as well as paternal from maternal kin. Because the Nawayats are an excellent example of a group whose marriage preferences are at odds with their kinship terminology, Vatuk uses them as a test case of the potential problems arising from the lack of fit between these two aspects of the kinship system. She concludes that the Nawayats circumvent any mismatches between terminology and actual kin relation that result from a marriage by continuing to address each other with the same terms they had used previously.

In her serious engagement with the contents of *Dravidian Kinship*, Vatuk offers a form of homage to it, as well as a salutary corrective to its failure to consider Muslim kinship. Vatuk's ethnography of the Nawayats may not have the range of information necessary to construct a general model for the marriage and kinship systems of South Asian Muslims comparable to what Trautmann has done for Hindus, yet its rich details and attention to practice bring out the personal dimension of kinship studies.

Seeing the Precolonial through Colonial/Modern Eyes

The following essays do not analyze the same issues as does Trautmann, but they all resemble his scholarship in their interest in how colonial thinkers conceptualized some feature of precolonial India. We begin with Bhavani Raman, whose essay relates to the general area of Trautmann's current research, the Madras School of Orientalism. Through their new emphasis on the written signature at the turn of the nineteenth century, the East India Company in Madras caused a major shift in the methods by which documents were validated as authentic. In "Recovering Attestation Practices from the Footnotes of a Colonial History: The *Treatise of Mirasi Right* Revisited," Bhavani Raman recuperates the earlier practices of attestation that the Company was replacing, or more precisely, Francis Whyte Ellis's conception of what those protocols had been. Ellis and his Dravidian proof are the central concern of Tom

Trautmann's *Languages and Nations*, while Ellis's *Treatise of Mirasi Right* is itself the subject of an article by Trautmann, "Riot over Ryotwar" (2009b).

Ellis's objective in *Treatise of Mirasi Right* (1818) was to establish that the form of land tenure known as *mirasi* had existed since ancient times in the Tondaimandalam region of northern Tamil Nadu. (As Trautmann argues convincingly in his article, Ellis's unstated intent was to refute Thomas Munro's claim that *ryotwari* was the prevalent tenure in south India.) Since *mirasi* (Tamil *kaniyatci*) did not figure in any indigenous lawbook or revenue manual, Ellis had no choice but to resort to inscriptions and land deeds from the past several centuries in order to prove that it had been customary usage. First, however, the documents in south Indian languages that he invoked as sources of information had to be authenticated as true records of the past. He did this partly through pointing out continuities with the present day in the vocabulary of land revenue, and also by arguing that the transactions recorded in the older inscriptions and land deeds met the standards of the classical lawbooks for the legal alienation of property.

The heart of Raman's essay lies in her analysis of Ellis's reasoning when confronted with a variety of different formats for land deeds. How had it been possible in the precolonial past to ascertain the validity of a document despite such variation? In short, the credibility of land deeds derived principally from the reputation of the individual who composed and notarized them, the village accountant or *kanakkupillai*. Closely associated with the authority of the accountant was the sanction of elite witnesses, who collectively consented to and vouched for the transaction being recorded. Raman notes the presence of classical legal norms on the identity of acceptable witnesses, which restricted the category to men of wealth and high birth, emphasizing the importance once again of personal credibility. While Raman looks at the same material as Trautmann, even this brief summary exposes the marked difference in the questions they pose to it. Raman's pioneering work on attestation protocols promises not only to uncover changes that occurred as a result of early colonial policy, but also to improve our understanding of precolonial practice.

Indian contributions to Orientalist scholarship are an important aspect of Tom Trautmann's studies of the Madras School of Orientalism. Along the same lines, I (Cynthia Talbot) look at the role played by one Indian scholar in the production of modern knowledge in "Contesting Knowledges in Colonial India: The Question of *Prithviraj Raso*'s Historicity." Because the main focus of the essay, Kaviraj Syamaldas, was active in late nineteenth-century north India, the milieu—and the state of colonial knowledge—is quite different from that in the early nineteenth-century south Indian case examined by Trautmann. A conjuncture of knowledge can also be said to have occurred earlier in the colonial era in respect to Rajput history, just as it had in reference to language analysis in Madras, but by the 1880s the outcome of this conjuncture—the romantic vision of Colonel James Tod's Rajasthan—was also being challenged, and not indigenous knowledge alone.

Kaviraj Syamaldas provides a fascinating counter-example to the stereotype of the westernizing "Babu" who participated in the prestigious sphere of English-language scholarship on India. From a hereditary bardic community and employed in the service of the Mewar king, Syamaldas nonetheless was the first to apply modern historiographic practices to the study of *Prithviraj Raso*, the vernacular epic about the life of Prithviraj Cauhan. He concluded that it was not an eyewitness account of the king's late twelfth-century lifetime, but in actuality a work that dated about four centuries later. His findings were translated into English by someone else and published in the *Journal of the Asiatic Society of Bengal*; a Hindi version of the article appeared elsewhere. A rebuttal of Syamaldas's position, or rather a "defense" of *Prithviraj Raso,* was quickly issued in both English and Hindi by Pandit Mohanlal Vishnulal Pandya. Like Syamaldas, Pandya was in service at the Mewar court, but his roots were in British India and he had strong ties with the Benares intellectual scene. In arguing in favor of *Prithviraj Raso*'s authenticity as a literary work from Prithviraj Cauhan's time, Pandya was representing the interests of certain segments of Mewar society and simultaneously the new Hindu nationalist consciousness coming out of Benares. For Pandya and others committed to promoting Hindi as the language of Hindus, *Prithviraj Raso*'s status as the earliest text composed in the language made it unassailable.

Thus, at the same time that we see rigorous historiographic practices being adopted by a bard at a modernizing princely court, we witness the emergence of a more popular, and romantic, form of historiography that relied heavily on James Tod and often circulated in the vernacular press. By the late nineteenth century, there were multiple networks of information within the subcontinent resulting in competing knowledges of India. This essay provides a glimpse into the intellectual environment of Indian scholars in the late nineteenth century, complementing Trautmann's writing on race science and other late nineteenth-century developments in Europe.

Parna Sengupta considers the complex and problematic relationship between past and present that has been at the heart of much of Tom Trautmann's research, in "Astral Time: Almanacs and Colonial Modernity in Bengal." She does so through analysis of a particular kind of object—the *panjika* almanac—that purports to be a tool for the comprehension and control of time, another of Trautmann's interests. The immediate impetus for her essay, Sengupta tells us, was a talk by Trautmann titled "Finding India's Deep History" that focused attention on the prevalent belief in a sharp rupture between the precolonial past and the colonial modern.[2] This is the backdrop for the claim made by the Gupta Press that their almanac is an embodiment of authentic tradition, serving as a bulwark against the ravages of modernity and pragmatism.

Sengupta argues instead that the Bengali almanac, a genre of printed text that became highly popular once vernacular publishing expanded in the second half of the nineteenth century, was no precolonial relic but rather something that partook from the past while adapting itself to the present. The Indian science of astrology did indeed have ancient roots, but its adoption of numerous elements of Greek astronomy in the early first millennium AD demonstrates its long-standing capacity to assimilate and change over time. The shift to print in the production of almanacs had profound effects in making astrology much more accessible, to both consumer-customers and practitioners. It also led to the introduction of a number of innovations borrowed from European conventions, such as lists of festivals, and also of advertisements and visual images. But the appeal of almanacs continued to be their alleged ability to read cosmological configurations and thereby forecast the future. The *panjika* was thus, in Sengupta's apt words, "very much a text created to navigate colonial modernity," that nonetheless derived authority from its relationship to the ancient science of astrology.

Anne Hardgrove envisions the site of Khajuraho as a kind of historiographical palimpsest in her essay "Sex and the City: Debates over the Medieval Pasts of Khajuraho." It is as if Khajuraho were a shining surface upon which successive generations have inscribed their perceptions of it, perceptions that might be largely imagined or perhaps even reflections of the self cast back by the mirror-like object of study. While Hardgrove surveys a long expanse of time in this essay, she sees the early colonial encounter with the site as key to the significance it has for us today. That is, just as Tom Trautmann has been wont to do, Hardgrove finds that the present-day meaning of the Indian past, as instantiated at Khajuraho, was largely determined by nineteenth-century colonial understandings.

Since Capt. T.S. Burt of the Bengal Engineers first published an article on Khajuraho in 1839, its claim to fame has been the erotic sculptures that adorn the walls of several temples there. Burt was repelled by the frank sexuality of the sculptures, describing them as "extremely indecent and offensive," yet, as Hardgrove points out, he was simultaneously titillated by them. The archaeologist Alexander Cunningham's stance on Khajuraho has been the mainstream position ever since the middle of the nineteenth century: the sophisticated sculptural techniques and elaborate architecture of Khajuraho's temples are appreciated as a signpost to India's greatness (displaced to the ancient past), while the eyes are metaphorically averted from close scrutiny of what is depicted on the walls. Discomfort with the implications of Khajuraho's sculpture was shared by Indian nationalists, even into the period of independence, although in recent years its commodification appears to have proceeded at full speed.

In her brief discussion of the reactions of medieval Muslim visitors to the site, Hardgrove highlights the culture- and time-specific character of the dominant understandings of it. Al Biruni and Ibn Battuta both mention Khajuraho, but note only the fact of its idolatry and not the erotic nature of the imagery. It is not clear if the dilapidated condition of the temples in the early nineteenth century was due to natural causes or hastened by deliberate action. Nonetheless, as Hardgrove observes, modern discourse on Khajuraho has repeatedly pointed a finger of blame at Muslims for their alleged desecration of the site.

Like Tom Trautmann, who was his fellow graduate student at SOAS, David N. Lorenzen has recently interrogated the relation between premodern and modern understandings of Indian society and culture. More specifically, Lorenzen has studied several early European missionaries and Orientalists whose conceptualizations of Indian religions owed much to existing Indian notions. In "Hindu Sects and Hindu Religion: Precolonial and Colonial Concepts," Lorenzen surveys a broad sweep of time in order to explore the ways in which the diverse religious strands within Indian religion have been classified. Not content to look backward from a point of time in the colonial present, Lorenzen begins in the precolonial period and assesses the degree of continuity in the modes of classifying religions from the medieval to the modern era.

Lorenzen starts his discussion with a consideration of Asokan inscriptions, in which Brahmans were already differentiated from the Sramana ascetics of Buddhism and Jainism. Having made his point that a sense of religious difference is apparent even in these early records, Lorenzen looks next at two sets of medieval materials. First are the Sanskrit *Sarvadarsanasamgraha* and *Samkaravijaya*, which can be loosely characterized as catalogs of religious schools (both real and imagined), composed from the Advaita Vedanta perspective. *Sarvadarsanasamgraha* distinguished the systems that accepted Vedic authority from those that did not, while *Samkaravijaya* grouped together sects that were dedicated to Vishnu, or to Siva, or to the goddess—thus creating subdivisions within the larger sectarian world. Very different in orientation are the roughly contemporary vernacular hagiographies, such as Nabhadas's late sixteenth-century *Bhaktamal*, which often encompass saints of more than one sectarian bent and acquaint us with a popular world of diverse sectarian groups.

These medieval texts must have had a wide circulation, for their influence is visible in later times. Roberto de Nobili, the Italian Jesuit missionary, may well have followed a classificatory scheme derived from the *Sarvadarsanasamgraha* and *Samkaravijaya*. He distinguished smaller categories among the "idolaters" or Hindus in a manner that was consonant with the viewpoint of a south Indian Brahman of Advaita Vedanta leanings. In the case of H.H. Wilson, the first Orientalist to write a lengthy exposition on Hindu sects (in the period 1828–32), the evidence is even stronger since Wilson cites all three texts described above. Thus the classificatory schema utilized by Wilson and subsequent scholars such as R.G. Bhandarkar and J.N. Farquhar, also discussed by Lorenzen, owed a debt to medieval categorizations of religion. On the other hand, colonial and modern scholars described the various sects in a radically different style, concentrating on the evolution of sectarian communities and their practices. As Lorenzen notes perceptively, it is in the application of historical frameworks that colonial/modern thinking about religion deviated most from what had preceded it, but the basic classifications of religions and sects had their roots in a more distant time.

Taking the Long Perspective: The Precolonial Past

The essays in the last set all interrogate aspects of India's past before colonial rule. We begin with Romila Thapar, who in asking "Was There Historical Writing in Early India?" poses a question that applies to the entire span of India's ancient and medieval history. Trained under the same teacher and at the same institution, Thapar and Tom Trautmann have in common a primary identity as historians of ancient India. Although the bulk of Thapar's writings have concentrated on the period before AD 1200, she has long shared Trautmann's concern with the nineteenth-century roots of our knowledge of the ancient past. Thapar thus begins her essay by considering the accusation that India lacked a sense of history, widely articulated in the colonial era although found also in earlier Muslim sources. This allegation was partly a consequence of Orientalist preoccupation with the early texts of the Brahmanical tradition, which led them to overlook the more pronounced historical sensibilities in Buddhist, Jain, and Puranic literature. The European preconception that India was a static society subject to Oriental despotism also negated the possibility of an Indian historiography: if India had experienced little actual change, how could a consciousness of the passage of time ever develop, much less historical writing?

In recent years, we have become more aware of the existence of multiple varieties of historical writing, even within the Western and Islamic worlds. The Judeo-Christian sense of historiography as the linear record of the unfolding of God's will was in distinct contrast to the Greco-Roman conception of historiography as a useful, but hardly essential, narrative of secular events. In a similar vein, we have become more sophisticated in our recognition of the components of history writing: the mere laying out of a sequence of events is not sufficient to constitute history, which also requires an effort to account for the sequentiality. This changed understanding of historiography has enabled us, Thapar explains, to better appreciate how the Indian past was perceived and recorded.

Here Thapar breaks new ground in advancing a thesis of historiographic progression, from an early stage where historical consciousness was embedded in other kinds of texts to a later stage when genres of writing emerged that directly embody a consciousness of history. An example of the former is the *dana-stuti* hymn of the *Rigveda*, in which a chief is praised for generosity to a poet who proclaimed his military success; the classical epics are likewise occasions for embedded history. From the Gupta period onward, historical traditions surface in more overt ways, eventually giving rise to entirely new genres: the *carita* biography, the *vamsavali* chronicle, and the *prasasti* of royal inscriptions. These literary forms in which historical consciousness is fully embodied correspond with the increasing complexity of state systems. Together with the historical perspectives of Jain and Buddhist authors, they comprise a wealth of information on how the past was viewed in earlier times. Thapar ends with a call for further study of these perceptions of the past, which she suggests could illuminate other aspects of the societies that produced them, such as their changing identities, social hierarchies, and ritual claims.

Carla M. Sinopoli departs from the text-based research that dominates this volume to consider archaeological remains instead, in "Local Histories and Historical Narratives in the Central Tungabhadra Region of South India." The object of her study is not a person, text, or idea but rather one small region in Karnataka along the Tungabhadra river, covering about 200 sq km from the modern city of Bellary westward to the site of the Vijayanagara imperial capital. Sinopoli examines the almost 5000-year-long material record of this region, from the time of the Neolithic communities who left evidence of their activities in the form of ashmounds up to the demise of the Vijayanagara capital at Hampi. This excursion into "archaeological time" is a response to Tom Trautmann's repeated engagement with the topic of time and its constructions. An archaeological perspective, scrutinizing a small space for a long period of time, presents a marked contrast to the master narratives of history which, in Sinopoli's words, "are almost inevitably discontinuous in space, favoring temporal continuities over geographic ones." Because they shine a spotlight on certain favored localities only at the moments of their greatest power or influence, standard accounts of Indian history obscure the actual trajectories of development and cast into shadow the majority of times and places.

What we learn from Sinopoli's investigation of the deep history of the central Tungabhadra is that the importance of a specific region may vary over time. Sinopoli begins, in concert with Trautmann's inclinations, with a survey of the nineteenth- and twentieth-century scholarship on the region, which focused especially on the monumental remains of the Vijayanagara capital and the Asokan inscriptions found at Nittur, Maski, and elsewhere. Less well-known to the public is the research on the Neolithic era initiated by Robert Bruce Foote, who argued in favor of an extended timeline for south India's prehistory. The central Tungabhadra, and the inland Karnataka plateau in general, was a relatively densely populated region during the southern Neolithic period, from ca. 3000–1400 BC. The more than 200 ashmounds that have been discovered—most likely the residues of ritual activity—establish the central Tungabhadra as a core area of settlement and innovation in this era; in the subsequent Late Prehistoric age (ca. 1200–0 BC), the region's continuing population density is attested by numerous megaliths and other remains. For over a millennium afterwards, however, the central Tungabhadra becomes a peripheral player in the human landscape of the peninsula, and only with the founding of the Vijayanagara state in the fourteenth century AD does it regain a prominent position.

In a joint article published several years ago, Trautmann and Sinopoli called for increased collaboration between archaeologists and historians (Trautmann & Sinopoli 2002: 518); Sinopoli's essay here calls welcome attention to the ample benefits for historians of adopting the differing dimensions of archaeological time and also to archaeology's unique ability to access the material culture of everyday life in the past.

Kenneth Hall investigates a single space over a substantial period of time in "Secondary Cities and Urban Networking in Cola-era South India," much like Sinopoli in her contribution to this book. The geographical scope of Hall's study is more restricted than Sinopoli's, consisting of the single urban center of Tiruvorriyur in the northern Tamil region of Tondaimandalam, as are his chronological parameters, which range from approximately the ninth through the thirteenth century AD. This essay represents an extension of Hall's PhD research conducted under Tom Trautmann's supervision, which similarly utilized inscriptions in order to examine hierarchical networks. While Hall's dissertation focused primarily on commercial centers and marketing networks, here he adopts the interdisciplinary perspective of urban studies and poses questions about the role of the intermediate city. The central issue is the extent to which the secondary city acted as an agent for the interests and institutions of larger urban centers or whether its activities aligned more with local interests.

Tiruvorriyur—a representative secondary urban center, with economic and social links to the larger city of Kancipuram to its southwest—serves as Hall's case study. It gained a name for itself early on as a sacred religious site and several inscriptions record endowments made to its Brahman villages prior to Cola conquest of the region in the early tenth century. The built environment of Tiruvorriyur expanded greatly under the Colas, due to the patronage of the kings and their subordinates. Tiruvorriyur, named after the father of the founder of the imperial dynasty, had a special significance for the Colas as a source of ritual legitimacy. Royal inscriptions highlighted the rulers' interdining with Tiruvorriyur's Brahman leaders, who were drawn not only from affiliated Brahman villages but also from its sectarian community of Pasupata Saivas. As the temple gradually acquired villages and rights over land, Tiruvorriyur increasingly became a site of political and economic, as well as religious, importance, so much so that a distinct commercial quarter and a prosperous marketplace emerged there. The temple forged strong networks with local agricultural and herding communities, and the town became a hub of local mercantile and artisanal activity. Despite its connections to the major commercial center at Kancipuram, Tiruvorriyur never became a provider of trade goods, nor were its merchants affiliated with any supra-regional mercantile organizations—in the long run, it continued to retain "its rural roots and local accountabilities."

A quarter century ago, Trautmann and several associates called for the computer indexing of south Indian inscriptions, so that epigraphy could be put to uses other than the determination of dynastic chronologies (Trautmann et al. 1985). Hall's research on the Cola period, both now and previously, illustrates the rich insights into a locality's development that can result from a thorough study of its inscriptional record over time.

Intellectual disagreements among scholars could be just as virulent during the seventeenth century as in later times, as we see from the case studied by Madhav Deshpande in "Will the Winner Please Stand Up: Conflicting Narratives of a Seventeenth-Century Philosophical Debate from Karnataka." Deshpande examines a slew of Sanskrit texts that were written as critiques of each other, some with titles expressing unrelenting hostility toward the adversary whose ideas were being crushed or demolished and whose faces were being (metaphorically) smacked and slapped. This outpouring of malice was initiated by the Sanskrit grammarian Bhattoji Dikshita and his family, who subscribed to the Advaita Vedanta philosophy, and responding to it were a series of adherents to Madhva's Dvaita Vedanta. The abundance of written material from differing perspectives provides us with an unusually detailed glimpse into scholarly rivalry in an early modern south Indian mode.

The focal point of Deshpande's essay is a debate that took place in the early seventeenth century at the royal court of the small Nayaka kingdom of Ikkeri, between the Advaitin Rangojibhatta and Dvaitin Vidyadhisa. Numerous references to this specific debate exist, including an in-depth account written by the participant Vidyadhisa that was discovered recently by Deshpande in private hands. There are flagrant discrepancies in the various renditions of what took place—with the pro-Advaita Vedanta writers predictably casting Rangojibhatta as the victor, while the Dvaita followers conversely laud the success of Vidyadhisa. The immediate stakes were presumably a remuneration of some sort from the Ikkeri king, but the long-term prestige of the respective schools of thought was also at issue. The relevant texts are so affected by partisan sentiments that Deshpande concludes, in a post-modern moment, that we will never be able to reconstruct the actual event.

Deshpande's endeavor here is not unlike that undertaken by Tom Trautmann in his analysis of the different tales about minister Canakya and his relationship to the king Candragupta Maurya, in his book *Kautilya and the Arthasastra*. Trautmann also meticulously pored over several Sanskrit narratives as well as some from the classical Mediterranean world, searching for the original form of the Canakya legend. Like Deshpande, Trautmann admits the impossibility of ascertaining what really happened; nonetheless, both Deshpande and Trautmann offer us their best estimate, for "scepticism" about the source materials, as Trautmann reminds us, "is a poor substitute for criticism" (1971: 67).

Each of the essays in this volume, whether concerning the

precolonial Indian past or perceptions of this past in more recent eras, can thus be aligned to some aspect of Tom Trautmann's copious and varied body of scholarship. While it cannot fully reflect or represent Tom's extensive impact on the world of knowledge, this collection of essays is a tribute to the many ways in which he has inspired his colleagues and students.

NOTES

1. Tom Trautmann held a joint appointment in the History and Anthropology departments at the University of Michigan as the Marshall D. Sahlins Collegiate Professor of History and Anthropology, and had been involved in Michigan's innovative joint doctoral program in Anthropology and History. He also served as editor of the well-regarded interdisciplinary journal, *Comparative Studies in Society and History*, from 1997 to 2006. (For a discussion of his experience as CSSH editor, see Trautmann 2008.)
2. This talk has now been published in article form, see Trautmann 2009a.

REFERENCES

Cohn, Bernard S. 1987. *An Anthropologist among the Historians and Other Essays*. Delhi: Oxford University Press.

Trautmann, Thomas R. 1971. *Kautilya and the Arthasastra: A Statistical Investigation of the Authorship and Evolution of the Text*. Leiden: E.J. Brill.

———. 1987. *Lewis Henry Morgan and the Invention of Kinship*. Berkeley: University of California Press.

———. 2008. "Being Editor." *Comparative Studies in Society and History* 50.1: 21–25.

———. 2009a. "Finding India's Deep History." In *The Clash of Chronologies: Ancient India in the Modern World*. Delhi: Yoda Press.

———. 2009b. "Riot over Ryotwar." In *The Madras School of Orientalism*, ed. T.R. Trautmann. Delhi: Oxford University Press.

Trautmann, Thomas R., Richard D. Saran, Peter A. Granda, and Armgard Ruckert. 1985. "The Study of South Indian Inscriptions." In *Studies of South India: An Anthology of Recent Research and Scholarship*, ed. Robert E. Frykenberg and Pauline Kolenda, 1–29.

Trautmann, Thomas R. and Carla M. Sinopoli. 2002. "In the Beginning was the Word: Excavating the Relations between History and Archaeology in South Asia." *Journal of the Economic and Social History of the Orient* 45. 4: 492–523.

Musings on (Mosaic) Ethnology, Language, and Kinship

2

Language Fields

Robert Needham Cust's Language Map of South Asia, 1878

JUDITH T. IRVINE

In his book *Languages and Nations: The Dravidian Proof in Colonial Madras*, Thomas Trautmann (2006) discusses several "technologies of location," collective projects that generations of scholars have used to organize their subject matter and its place in the universe. The three such technologies he dwells upon most are: (1) frameworks for locating geographical objects; (2) chronological tables for organizing historical events; and (3) genealogical schemes, especially the Mosaic/Biblical classification of peoples, for placing human communities (the "nations" of his title). The book then takes up the theme of the Biblical classification of peoples, asking how this "technology of location" turned into a classification of languages—a process that depended crucially essay the Orientalist study of languages in India. In the present essay I propose to link this process to another of his "technologies of location": the geographical one. Creating geographical maps of languages, I suggest, was one of the means by which language classifications could become understood as the pedigrees of nations, as the Biblical model faded from scholarly view.

My discussion focuses on the life and works of Robert Needham Cust, an Orientalist scholar who spent about 25 years as a civil servant in British India. I first encountered Cust through his 1883 book, *The Modern Languages of Africa*, a two-volume inventory and discussion accompanying a language map of the African continent. A few years earlier, in 1878, he had published a similar map and book, *A Sketch of the Modern Languages of the East Indies,* mainly concentrating on British India and bordering regions. (Later, he continued the project into other parts of the world, producing language maps and inventories for Oceania, the Caucasus, and more.)

Language mapping was beginning to be "in the air," so to speak, in the 1870s when Cust began to prepare his India map and book. In India, the Great Trigonometrical Survey, though still ongoing, had by this time produced detailed maps of much of the subcontinent, maps on which other kinds of survey activities could be based.[1] And although India was more thoroughly mapped by the 1870s than many other parts of the world, the mid- to late-nineteenth century was a time of widespread enthusiasm for cartography in general. It was also a time of rapidly accelerating scholarship in linguistics, both theoretical and empirical. Combining these threads, research in linguistic geography enjoyed a rapid expansion after about 1870. Dialect geography based on surveys and maps became a major line of work, increasingly institutionalized via regional dialect societies and, before long, state-sponsored projects. (In 1877, notably, Georg Wenker published his now famous study mapping linguistic variation in the Rhineland; so positive was the immediate reception that the Kaiser's government sponsored a project for a linguistic atlas of Germany, just as research also got underway for the linguistic atlas of France.) Meanwhile, linguistic research into the historical relationships among languages and language families was making new strides and gaining in scholarly prestige.

Cust kept in touch with all these developments. Although languages had certainly been surveyed and mapped before, and some (such as Wenker's map) presented a close-in and much more detailed view, Cust's maps of India and Africa were innovative at the time when he published them. Their large scale, their level of detail—considerable for a large-scale map—and their explicit link with language-family classifications of the most up-to-date linguistic science, were unusual. They won him a substantial international reputation among linguists and geographers of the day.

The work on languages in South Asia was both the first of Cust's linguistic survey projects and the closest to his own experience and language competence. He had studied Sanskrit, Hindustani, and Persian at Haileybury College (training ground for the India service), and Bengali at the College of Fort William in Calcutta; he had spent some of his furlough time in Europe studying with Orientalist scholars in Paris and London; and he had also acquired Punjabi, and perhaps some other Indian linguistic varieties, independently, while in India.[2] His involvement with Indian linguistics and colonial politics continued throughout his life, long after he had left the subcontinent. Of Africa, in contrast, he had no first-hand knowledge of any language, place, or people, south of the Mediterranean littoral (which he visited for a few weeks in 1882) and the Red Sea route to India. Like other Victorian scholar-systematizers, however, Cust was so confident of the logic and merits of his method of organizing his materials that his personal degree of experience—almost zero, for Africa—was not a major concern. Instead, systematicity was key, as he explained at the beginning of his Africa book:

> What can I say in justification of a volume upon the "Modern Languages of Africa," concerning which I know absolutely nothing? In all humility I attempt now, as I did then, to fill a vacuum, which had forced itself upon my notice... Why did I do it? Because there was a work, which somebody ought to do who had leisure, money, industry, and intelligence. Nor was I deterred by the fact, that in the long list of Languages which I have collected, I have not the slightest knowledge of any one, except of Arabic. A librarian is said to be lost, if he opens one book of his library, as he

has to do with the outsides, and not the insides: so was it with me. (Cust 1883: 1 and 7).

Regardless of the compiler's knowledge or lack of knowledge of a particular world region, therefore, its linguistic information needed to be compiled and organized. The organizational skills necessary for this task were exactly those, Cust asserted, that he had acquired in his work in the India service:

With such a wealth of Materials pouring in upon me from every quarter, and a deepening conviction of the importance of the task, as well as the difficulty, I could only go on, and...lay down clear and distinct principles upon which this work should be constructed. Possessed of a trained capacity for order and method, a strong will and love for steady work, which is the characteristic of old Indians, I had to grapple with this entangled subject, just as twenty-five years ago I should have grappled with the affairs of a District in India which had got into disorder, or with the Accounts of a Treasury which had fallen into arrear (Cust 1883: 6–7).

As the first of his efforts at producing a comprehensive linguistic survey, Cust's India book had—in his own view—some shortcomings that needed to be corrected, if not in the second edition that never came about, then in his next such endeavor.[3] Accordingly, the Africa book is larger (two volumes) and its map represents putative linguistic relationships more systematically. The two publications have a similar shape, however. They compile and organize information provided by scholars, missionaries, census-takers, civil servants, military men, travelers, and anyone else who offered comments on languages spoken in some particular region. The chapters organize the material by language-family, with headings and subheadings for branches and particular languages. Each branch and each language entry is briefly described, with notes on linguistic structure, geographical area, population, writing system if any, and sources of information, with comments on their relative reliability. An appendix, or "Schedule," summarizes the language classification in outline form, while a large fold-out language map

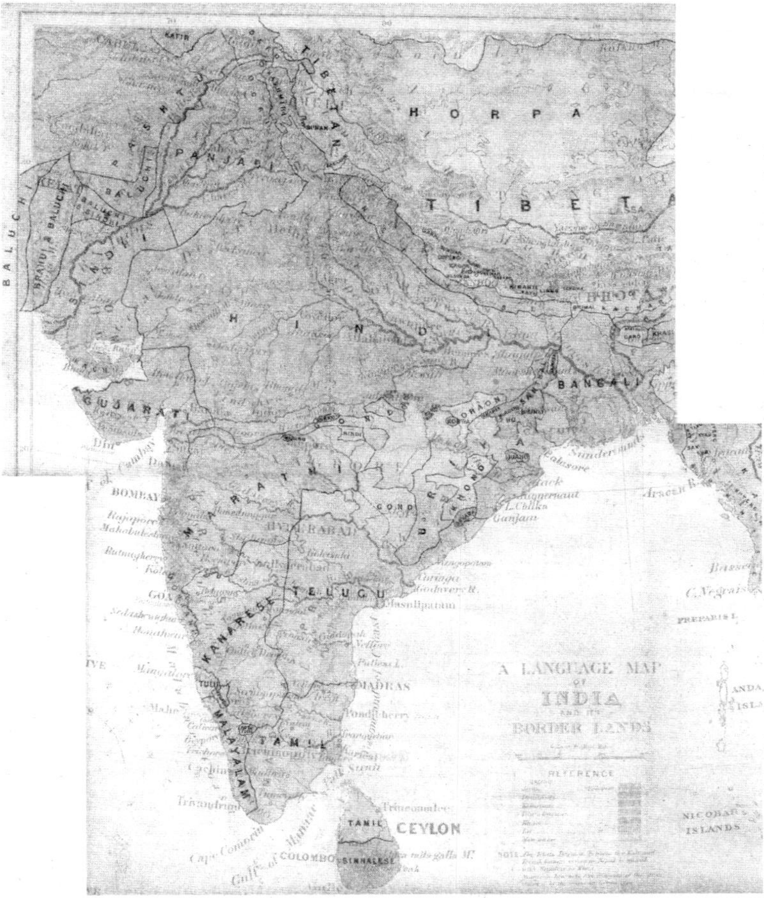

Figure 2.1 Language map of South Asia

depicts the families, subfamilies, and major languages; in the Africa map their names are printed in different typefaces according to their place in the hierarchy of classification. In both maps the major language families, as Cust envisioned them, are shown in different colors. Figure 2.1 reproduces the India map, while Figure 2.2 shows a section of the Africa map.[4] For the Africa map, I have supplied hatchings and other markings to represent the different colors.

Figure 2.2 Language map of Africa, section showing West Africa

Notice that the maps provide boundary lines between languages and families, even when the descriptive text for a particular language says that its exact boundaries are hard to define, or that it has speakers in another language's territory. On Telugu, for example, the text comments that "a large portion of Telugu-speakers have intruded themselves within the Tamil Language-Field, and there are some in the independent territory of Mysore" (Cust 1878: 68). It is as if the language map is imagined in the same visual terms as the territorial nation-state, which in Europe had a standard national language and laws that were supposed to apply just as firmly to areas near the border as to those in the center. In fact, the boundaries and colors on these language maps remind me of the political maps that used to hang in classrooms in my high school (and can still be found in classroom settings, although the political units have usually been brought more up to date). In the maps I remember, Europe looked like a jigsaw puzzle, with the countries as distinct colored pieces, while the same colors reappeared—in that era when colonial empires had not yet completely broken apart—to mark that country's possessions in the rest of the world. Thus Britain and its colonies were all pink—or so I recall them; France and its possessions were green, Portugal purple, and so on. (Meanwhile, the Soviet Union and its satellite states in Eastern Europe were colored a gloomy black.)

Cust's self-imposed task of systematizing the linguistic information for a large region was difficult, as he did not hesitate to acknowledge. So much material, and so much of it inconsistent and unreliable! And "a lax phraseology had complicated the subject"(1878: 5)! His recourse was to rely heavily on geography for assessing the evidence at his disposal. "No other method but the geographical can secure accuracy," he commented in the India book (1878: 16; see also pp. 8–9). For the African linguistic material, he supplied more detail, describing his method as follows:

> I place one foot firmly down upon Geographical facts, and the other upon such a statement of Linguistic facts as seem to my judgment sufficient.

> I do not admit the existence of a Language to be an established fact, unless I can indicate on the Map from actual knowledge, or reasonable presumption, the place where it is spoken. We have got beyond the period of vague Geographical uncertainty. Under my directions a Language-map has been prepared by the most able Cartographer, Ravenstein (specially employed by the Royal Geographical Society to construct the large Map of Equatorial Africa), and, unless he can find a place in his Map for the tribe, the Language can find no place in my Schedule (Cust 1883: 7–8).

In other words, if a language could not be pinned down to some particular geographical location, it could not be supposed to exist. It was an error, a fantasy, or an outright lie—a "forgery" (Cust 1883: 22).

From today's perspective, this kind of language map is problematic in several respects. It is not only a question of whether recent linguistics has confirmed the particular classifications of the languages. On that score, Cust did pretty well for India. In fact, a century later, a linguist pointed to the achievements of this "forgotten predecessor" for his comments on the Munda languages (then called Kolarian), initiating comparative Munda studies (Zide 1981). For Africa, he did less well, relying on a classification scheme proposed by the Viennese scholar Friedrich Mūller—a scheme that based language families explicitly on race, defined by the form of the speakers' hair.[5] Thus Mūller's (1876–1888) work divides the languages of the world into those spoken by the woolly-haired (subdivided into the tufted and the fleecy) and the smooth-haired (subdivided into the stiff and the curly). The more important problem, however, is that this kind of language map erases multilingualism, constructs linguistic differences as absolute, and pins mobile populations down to dubious "homelands," which are identified with a single standard variety. The map not only places languages on territories; it also treats language as if it *were* territory—the territory of a nation or a subnational province.

How did this come about? As I have mentioned, Cust took his experiences in the Indian civil service as his guide and his qualification for undertaking the work. What, then, did his service in India actually entail? A protīgī (more or less) of John Lawrence, Cust served most of his career in the Northwest Provinces and the Punjab. Holding various administrative positions from his arrival in India in 1843 to his final departure in December 1867, he eventually rose from District Officer and Collector of Land Revenue to Commissioner, and important judicial and revenue offices in North India.[6] During the period of his India service he contributed many papers to the *Calcutta Review* and other journals, in addition to writing administrative reports, draft bills such as a bill of a code regulating rights in land and land revenue procedure in northern India (1870), and a Manual for the Guidance of Revenue Officers in the Punjab (1866). He left India abruptly in 1867, "under domestic affliction" as he later put it.[7] The deaths of his second wife and his mother at nearly the same time had sent him into an emotional crisis.

Much of Cust's work in India was concerned, in one way or another, with collecting tax revenue and adjudicating land tenure issues on which the revenue was largely based. The Collector served in many other capacities as well: as Magistrate, frequently judging disputes between landlords and tenants; as Registrar of landed property in the district; and as the district's Treasurer and Accountant. In "The Collector of Land-revenue in India," written in the 1850s, Cust described his duties and daily life. For the execution of those duties, his collection of field maps and the documents indexed to them were especially important:

> Enter the record room of the Collector, and you will find a map of every one of the thousand villages, showing distinctly the size and position of every field, with a number, which facilitates reference to the accompanying deed, by which the name of the owner, of the cultivator, of the area and the crop, is at once ascertained. And, moreover, to correct the errors and changes, which may creep in by lapse of time, annual papers are prepared in each village, showing with reference to the record prepared at the time of Settlement what changes have taken place. Although these returns

> are not always trustworthy, and a bad superintendence...has allowed the truthfulness of those papers in many districts to become much questioned, still the machinery is always at hand, by which a few months' labour would restore the correctness which time may have impaired.... The superintendence of the constant alteration is a labour of no slight importance (Cust [1854] 1880: 184).

Evidently the Collector, Cust wrote, often had to go out and inspect the fields on site to correct the field map, and he often had to adjudicate disputes about ownership and use rights to the land, some of the disputes involving contested boundaries. Writing home in 1846 to his sister Georgiana about the duties of his first administrative assignment at Hoshiarpur, in the Punjab, Cust remarked that he had "a hundred irons in the fire [maintenance and construction of jails and police stations], not the least is settling the boundaries of 2,000 villages, who have been quarrelling."[8] When he reported on his assignment the following year, he claimed that "the boundaries of every village have been permanently demarcated, and all cause for future contention on that head removed" (Cust [1847] 1887: 102). Assembling the appropriate information on which dispute settlement could be based was particularly challenging in newly-conquered regions: "When once the machinery is set a-going, it requires but system, judgment, and regularity to carry on the details of Civil Government, but in a newly-ceded Province, we had to create where nothing previously existed, to collect together the heterogeneous components, to meet the thousand and one calls upon time and resources" (Cust [1847] 1887). With only a few differences of wording Cust might have been writing about his linguistic projects: collecting heterogeneous information, assessing the reliability of sources, settling contradictions and establishing territorial boundaries, and systematizing the whole.

It was in the administration of justice in India that language problems had their most direct connection with civil service work. In an essay on "Civil Justice in the Panjáb" (1859), Cust argued that the Collector or Commissioner's role as district magistrate judging cases about lands and other matters obliged him to command some local vernacular language, and at least to be informed as to what other languages were spoken in his district (Cust [1859] 1880). The complaints to be judged came in many languages; a judge could not possibly deliver justice in court if he did not even know enough about the languages of his district to decide which ones might require hiring court interpreters (Cust [1882] 1895). In this opinion Cust was not alone. Many other British colonial officers and policy-makers made similar arguments about language policy in the courts, although Cust was certainly prominent among the position's proponents. In 1862 he addressed a petition to the Punjab government on the question of language in judicial administration, a petition that was much discussed and became known as "Cust's Rule" (although it was eventually denied; for more detail and context see Mir [2006: 416] and later pages of the present essay). The issues at stake in these discussions of language policy in the courts included the question of the judicial officer's personal command of a vernacular language, as well as the question of whether to use a local vernacular such as Punjabi instead of Urdu, as the official language of the court. Cust went further, however. In addition to these questions, he argued, the administration of justice required a survey of the languages spoken within each judicial catchment area, a survey best accomplished via detailed language maps. As he wrote in a letter to the Viceroy of British India:

> What is required is a Language-Map on a fixed scale of each province, coloured to show the fields, where particular languages are spoken by the bulk of the lower classes, and where two or more languages are spoken in the same field, or where a compound of two adjoining languages is spoken on the debateable frontier. With such information the Governor could appreciate the linguistic requirements of his province (Cust [1880] 1891: 329).

For purposes of court administration, then, linguistics became a subdivision of geography. And Cust often thought of language as a geographical phenomenon anyway. For example, these are precisely the terms in which he presented a discussion of African linguistics (philology, as it was often then called) in 1893, when he was invited to give a paper updating the progress of African philology in the 10 years since the publication of his two-volume book. "Philology in the mode, in which I propose to treat it, is a part of Geography," he wrote (Cust [1893] 1895: 33).

There seems to have been a long line of British officials in the India Service who involved themselves in linguistic work as an outgrowth or adjunct to their role as magistrates. For some, the study of Indian legal and religious texts was the spur; for others, like Cust, the language of court proceedings seems to have been more relevant. Moreover, Cust was not the only one to construct a language map. A missionary language map of India was produced as early as 1822, and there were a few others, such as Sir Erskine Perry's map, on which I shall comment later.[9] Still, it is tempting to draw a connection between Cust's ideas about language-mapping and the particular forms of land tenure he was dealing with in the Northwest Provinces and the Punjab. In his essay on the Collector of land-revenue, he described a certain process of transferring rights in land as "peculiar to those village communities, aptly called village republics, which are the distinguishing feature of the North-West Provinces and the Panjáb, and, we may add, their glory; for they are the best proof, that an absolute Government has not destroyed the existing rights of property" (Cust [1854] 1880: 181). There, he continued, land was held as in a "joint-stock community," in some respect a collective possession.[10] Land itself "is in all countries, and has been in all ages, the most prized possession of man.... When inherited from a long line of ancestors, it suggests feelings second only in intensity to the love of blood relations. There is an attachment to the soil which has maintained an ancient lineage, and a reverence for the magnificent trees which were planted by his forefathers, and are a link to connect him and his children in a remote generation" (Cust [1854] 1880:174–75). For Cust, in short, land tenure was the possession of a community of blood relatives linked in emotional attachment to their soil and its products—and speaking a particular language.

(Notice, incidentally, that this view—linking language with a familial attachment to the soil—assumes that the people practise intensive cultivation, as opposed to shifting cultivation. Intensive cultivation is the traditional agricultural practice in Europe and in India, but not, for the most part, in sub-Saharan Africa. Most African agriculture until very recently was shifting cultivation, with a sparser population and much greater mobility.)

For Cust and those who shared his image of land, people, and language, the expression "language-field"—which Cust often used—had a quite literal sense. And when we recall his reliance on detailed field-maps as the rational (or at least, rationalizable) basis of administration in India, as well as his strict reliance on his "geographical method" for identifying languages, perhaps we can grasp the importance the cartographical technology had for him. It appeared to him to be the solid foundation on which linguistic facts could be secured, and on which important yet much more tentative inferences about language families—the "pedigrees of nations"—could be, literally, grounded.

A seeming paradox remains, however, for if you examine his books on language, you will find that Cust's descriptive text recognizes many complexities and subtleties that are ignored in the Schedule and the Map. For India as well as Africa, Cust's text acknowledges the existence, in Africa even the pervasiveness, of multilingualism. Also acknowledged are the fuzziness of language boundaries and, in India, the existence of special registers and literary languages whose distributions may differ from those of the vernaculars. In the text, then, various problems are recognized that would make the language map, with its sharp border-lines and solid colors, at best an inexact representation of any sociolinguistic facts. These ambiguities vanish from the Schedule and the Map. Why are Cust's two representations of linguistic distributions—in the discursive text and in the Map (and Schedule)—different?

The answer lies, again, in Cust's ideas about agricultural labor and the difference between people who work the land and people who do not. Language mapping was to focus on the "agricultural classes"; other languages, such as trade-jargons, argots, and the languages known only by educated people, should be cleared away (Cust [1886] 1887: 71–74).[11] These ideas are consistent with Cust's "reformist" political position in his earlier years in the India service. As a follower of John Lawrence, his administrative work favored the interests of village farmers over the interests of any Indian elites ("feudal" rulers, religious authorities, or bureaucrats). In his first posting in Hoshiarpur, he described the administrative principles for governing this region newly-ceded to British rule, and concluded,

> Such are the leading provisions, which have been made for the welfare of the people who have been transferred to British rule, meaning by the people the agricultural and commercial population, the sinews of the strength of a nation, and who ought to be the first care of an enlightened Government.... We care not for, we seek not the approbation of, the aristocratical spawn, the sons of the freebooters, who have been sent back to their hereditary duties of the plough by the operation of the new system...or the seditious Priest, who has been compelled to disgorge the Revenues of the State, which he had misappropriated (Cust [1847] 1880: 104).

Where language was concerned, Cust's focus on the speech of agricultural communities was consistent with ideas current in Europe at the time. Spoken language, in this view often associated with Johann Gottfried Herder and Jakob Grimm (among others), was the expression of the special "spirit of a people" (*Volksgeist*)—a spirit most authentically located among rural and working-class people, whose folk practices had not been distorted by the influence of multilingual, cosmopolitan elites.[12] These were also the ideas underlying the studies of dialectology and dialect-mapping, which burgeoned in the late nineteenth century and similarly focused on the agricultural peasantry of Europe.

This cluster of ideologized notions concerning land, agriculture, and language can perhaps shed some additional light on "Cust's Rule" and his representations of Punjabi. As Mir (2006) explains, British colonial language policy in the Punjab was caught in a tension between rationalized principles of rule and local circumstances. On the one hand, the courts (as Cust argued) ought to use the same language as the people who brought complaints to them; on the other hand, the British associated Punjabi language with the Sikh regime they had just conquered and whose political aspirations they feared, in the decades after the Sikh Wars, were still alive. To legitimate Punjabi in court usage and court documents might lend legitimacy to a Sikh polity. The compromise, if one can call it that, was to promote Urdu ("Hindustani" in Cust's terminology), a language closely connected with the vernacular Hindi spoken in the neighboring regions of North India.[13] Since Punjabi was obviously related to Hindi, and since there were clerks and Indian bureaucrats available who controlled Urdu, the British officials who set policy for the Punjab stuck to Hindi/Urdu for court business. Cust was too much the philologist and reformer, and too close to the day-to-day work of the courts, to accede to any notion that ordinary Punjabis could understand Urdu; thus "Cust's Rule," advocating the use of Punjabi in court. (As I have noted earlier, the "Rule" was rejected by the British higher authorities.) Still, Cust did recognize Punjabi's close linguistic relationship to Hindi. In his text he called Punjabi "the Western branch of the Hindi Language" and suggested that "it would be the merest pedantry on the part of any one to enumerate the Panjábi Language, as one of his acquirements, in addition to that of Hindi" (1878: 38). Nevertheless, "no portion of the population of any one of the Districts within the Language-Field of the Panjábi, as above defined, can be said to have Hindustáni[i.e., Urdu] for their

Vernacular" (Cust 1878: 39). It was not the native language of the agricultural and working classes. Consequently, while Cust's text admits the complexity of these sociolinguistic relationships, his Schedule and Map—representations of vernaculars spoken by rural populations—come down firmly on the side of Punjabi's distinctiveness. Cust reprinted his map, with **PANJABI** in boldface, in a (slightly) revised version prepared for the British and Foreign Bible Society and appended to his comments on the Census of 1881—comments where he again strongly advocated language maps as instruments of good government (Cust [1886] 1887).

As we have seen in Cust's work, the map and the language schedule linked to it became linked locational technologies by which people and their relationships could be understood. But there is another step, I suggest, common to Cust and others of his day, in which the map virtually took over as a representation, in effect replacing the people whose speech it supposedly depicted. In a sense, the people who spoke these languages and occupied the land were erased; at least, they did not need to be represented directly, since they were already accounted for in the cartography. For a relevant example, consider a curious statement in a work on language in India written by another colonial jurist, Sir Erskine Perry—someone Cust mentioned as a notable predecessor. Writing in 1853, Perry explained why it was so difficult to construct "an accurate language-map of India": "for, first of all, the limits of two neighbouring languages often occur in wild, unexplored, or unpeopled, tracts of country, so as to prevent the tracing of a precise boundary line" (Perry 1853: 289).[14] If language boundaries occur in unpeopled tracts, languages don't seem to need speakers at all.

Maybe Erskine Perry's statement was just an unfortunate gaffe, a bit of careless writing that was not very consequential. Still, it was consistent with other practices which, in linking language with territory, elided any other representation of a language's speakers. What may be more important, therefore, than Perry's particular wording, is that Cust's language maps—and other maps in this style—either downplay (in the case of India) or omit (in the case of Africa) any representation of political units as distinct from the languages and the populations they might be taken to imply. While all maps are selective, this strategy for selective representation differs from that of a mapmaker who outlines the territory of a state and places languages or populations within it. Instead, the Cust-style language map fits well with a belief that political community derives from, or should derive from, linguistic and ethnic community (one would have to assume those are the same thing, by the way), and that language is somehow more essential, and prior to, any particular kind of social formation, for which it can then serve as warrant. In India, Cust wanted political administration to adjust to local linguistic conditions. In Europe at exactly the same time, the German Kaiser looked favorably on Wenker's language map of the Rhineland, which could be seen as determining the legitimate boundary of Germany as opposed to anything French. In Africa, Cust's language map was published just prior to the Berlin Conference of 1884 and the "Scramble for Africa" in which the European powers divided up the continent. There are no African states on Cust's map.

Let us now turn briefly to the implications of the "language families" and "language groups" represented in Cust's maps and inventories. What kinds of families and groupings were they? The obvious possibility, given the ideas cited earlier about "blood relations" among the generations who work the land—and given Cust's reliance on Friedrich Müller's racial grouping of language families—was race. The connection of language with race was not quite automatic at this time, however. As Trautmann (2006) points out, in the mid-nineteenth century when British and other European discourses about languages and peoples began to introduce ideas about race, some writers asserted that race and language might not necessarily coincide. If they did not coincide, then the British did not need to see themselves as sharing a primordial essence with the inhabitants of India just because English belonged to an Indo-Aryan language family. As the nineteenth century approached its close, "race science" grew more influential, and it trumped language more often than not.

But even if language family did not have to mean racial homogeneity, the reasons why it did not could often still be interpreted in racial terms, via a geographical and historical narrative of migration and conquest.[15] In India that narrative brought conquering Aryans from the north into contact with darker Dravidians. In Europe, the known history of conquests (such as the expansion of the Roman Empire) could be interpreted with a racial twist, according to which the conquerors established linguistic domination over separate, conquered races. As for Africa, it was supposed that its population had no history. Africa, in that view, had only races, the chronology of whose relations could be deduced through geography and linguistics. "We know that Swiss, French, and Belgians speak French, but History tells us that they have a different origin: in Africa History is silent," Cust remarked (1883: 52).[16]

What of the aftermath of Cust's language-mapping enterprises in India and in Africa? Cust lived until 1909, and he continued until almost the last months of his life to follow developments in geography, linguistics, politics, and missionary work—and write copiously about all of them. Although he never returned to India after 1867, he was very much involved in imperial policy and in promoting census and survey work, especially focused on language. He pushed hard for linguistic data to be included in the census of 1881, for example. In 1898, in the *Journal of the Royal Asiatic Society*, he described a collaborative project with George Grierson that proposed a much more detailed survey of the languages of British India, correlated with land-revenue settlement reports.[17] A few years later he handed over to Grierson all his linguistic material on India. Grierson's *Linguistic Survey of India* (1903–27) has been widely cited ever since, as a baseline source of linguistic and demographic information for colonial India. Cust considered Grierson his successor; whether Grierson saw himself in that light is less clear.

In Africa there was no successor work of the same kind until much later. Perhaps the lack of an obvious replacement gave Cust's work greater longevity. Although some reviews of his book criticized its use of Friedrich Mūller's language classification, other aspects of the work—the inventory, discussion, and especially the map—came in for considerable praise, for example in the review in *Science* (1884) by "H.H." (presumably Horatio Hale). Cust distributed his book to linguists all over the world, and to missionary organizations concerned with African languages for purposes of Bible translation. His work was still cited as a useful reference in many volumes of the Ethnographic Survey of Africa, a series of studies of peoples published by the International African Institute, London, mostly in the 1940s and 1950s. Evidently, the inventory and map long outlived Mūller's classification scheme. What eventually replaced them was work by American academics who had no particular personal or scholarly connection to Cust. Joseph Greenberg's (1955: 1963) classification and George Peter Murdock's (1959) map of African ethnic groups as identified by language displaced Cust's survey so thoroughly that Africanists now scarcely remember his name. Still, although Murdock did not cite Cust, his map is constructed on some similar principles; and language maps of the type Cust constructed, including some that erase any political boundaries, are still to be found among those produced today.

Cust was a compiler and systematizer, not a particularly original thinker. The linguistic and bibliographic projects he launched into so zealously were neither the first nor the last of their kind, although at the time they were the most elaborate and their influence was considerable. But perhaps it is exactly the mechanical aspect of his projects, with their reliance on system and rationalized order, that brings out the importance of the "technology of location."

Cartography became, in this work, the technology for locating languages, and for locating people through languages, in the classificatory schedules that replaced the Mosaic genealogy.

NOTES

Abbreviations. Cust collected many of his shorter works in a series of seven volumes, entitled *Linguistic and Oriental Essays*, between 1880 (series I) and 1904 (series VII). These titles are abbreviated as *LOE* I, etc.

1. See Edney's discussion of the role of cartography as an instrument of rule in British India, unifying and homogenizing knowledge of the subcontinent within a cartographic "house of certainty" (Edney 1997: 25). In 1878, the same year as Cust's publication of his language map and inventory, the Survey of India was formed to unify and coordinate all kinds of survey information alongside the geographic archive.
2. See Penner's 1987 biography of Cust for more detail. In his *Memoir*, Cust (1899) wrote that he had acquired knowledge of many languages and their literatures before even setting foot in India: Latin, Greek, Sanskrit, Hebrew, French, German, Italian, Urdu, Persian, and Arabic (cited in Penner 1987: 47).
3. See Cust 1883: 6 and 11.
4. The map of African languages was so large that it was printed in two sections. I have reproduced only part of the upper (northern) section; I am grateful to Daphne Gallagher for assistance in preparing the black-and-white version. The whole map, in color, can be viewed online through the US Library of Congress Geography and Map Division, at: http://hdl.loc.gov/loc.gmd/g8201e.ct001441.
5. Note that Friedrich Müller is not the same person as Friedrich Max Müller, an Orientalist and linguist of approximately the same generation, of German origin but working in England. F. Max Müller is the better-remembered of the two today.
6. He also served on the Calcutta Legislative Council, where he acted as Home Secretary for a few months, and on the Sadr Board of Revenue at Allahabad. For more detail see Penner 1987.
7. The comment comes from Cust's afterword on his paper, "A Newly-Conquered District in the Panjab," when he re-published it in a

collection of his shorter works (*LOE*, Series II, 1887: 105). This paper was originally published in the *Calcutta Review* in 1847.

8. Robert Cust to Georgiana Cust Taylor, 13 October 1846; cited in Penner 1987: 114.
9. The 1822 map, constructed by Baptist missionaries at Serampore, is reproduced in Mir 2006: 409. Cust does not mention this map when citing precedents; instead, he attributes "the first idea of a Language-Map" to Erskine Perry (Cust 1878: 2). The Serampore missionaries are mentioned only as having produced some "translations of the Bible in several Dialects, alleged to be of Rajpootana…and never tested by use" (Cust 1878: 48).
10. Later, Cust distinguished between the North-Western Provinces and the Punjab, where land tenure was more free of "superior land-owners" and "the evils of the Sale Law" (from Cust's introduction to his *Manual for the Guidance of Revenue Officers in the Panjab*, 1866).
11. These arguments come from Cust's critique of the 1881 census of British India.
12. For extended discussion see Bauman and Briggs (2003).
13. Cust calls Urdu, or "Hindustani," a "lingua franca" that he considers essentially a dialect of Hindi but one that is not associated with a particular territory (1878: 47).
14. See also Perry 1855: 241.
15. As Cust (1883: 79) argued, "instances occur of a conquering Race and Language having carried all before it, and then falling from its political power, but still leaving the influence of its Language in the Territory, where it once ruled supreme."
16. Cust's views on race were more complex than this quote might suggest. The passage goes on to argue that because we know people can change their language, as for example when the Zulu conquered their neighbors, one cannot simply assume that race and language exactly coincide. He claims that he adopted Müller's classification because of the Viennese scholar's extensive linguistic documentation of the languages so grouped. Moreover, Cust staunchly defended the rights of mission-educated Africans when British authorities tried to oust Africans from leadership positions in Christian churches. Nevertheless, other strands of Cust's work support racial

interpretations as a default—operative unless and until one had specific information to the contrary.

17. Cust 1898. The "certain portions" mentioned in the title of this article,"Detailed Survey of the Languages and Dialects spoken in Certain Portions of British India," in fact included all of British India except Madras and Burma.

REFERENCES

Bauman, Richard, and Charles Briggs. 2003. *Voices of Modernity: Language Ideologies and the Politics of Inequality*. Cambridge: Cambridge University Press.

Cust, Robert Needham. 1866. *Manual for the Guidance of Revenue Officers in the Panjáb*. Lahore: Kohinoor Press, for Sookhun Lall.

———. 1870. *Draft Bill of a Code Regulating Rights in Land and Land Revenue Procedure in Northern India*. London: William Allen.

———. 1878. *A Sketch of the Modern Languages of the East Indies, Accompanied by Two Language-Maps*. London: Trubner & Co.

———. [1854] 1880. "The Collector of Land-Revenue in India." In *Linguistic and Oriental Essays* [henceforth *LOE*] I, 172–97. London: Trūbner. Originally written 1854.

———. [1859] 1880. "Civil Justice in the Panjáb." In *LOE* I, 198–223. London: Trubner & Co. Originally published 1859, Amritsar.

———. 1883. *A Sketch of the Modern Languages of Africa, Accompanied by a Language-Map*. London: Trubner & Co.

———. [1847] 1887. "A Newly-Conquered District in the Panjáb." In *LOE* II, 86–109. London: Trubner & Co. Originally published in the *Calcutta Review*, 1847.

———. [1886] 1887. "The Races, Religions, and Languages of India as Disclosed by the Census of 1881." In *LOE* II, 52–85. London: Trubner & Co. Originally published 1886.

———. [1880] 1891. "'The Census of British India,' Letter to the Viceroy of British India." In *LOE* III, 327–30. London: Kegan Paul, Trench, and Truebner. Originally published 1880.

———. [1882] 1895. "Letter to Sir W.W. Hunter, President of the Education-Commission of British India, 1882, on the Subject of the Vernacular Languages of India." In *LOE* IV, 97–101. London: Luzac. Originally published 1893.

Cust, Robert Needham. [1893] 1895. "On the Progress of African Philology up to the Year 1893." In *LOE* IV, 28–52. London: Luzac. Originally published 1893.

———. 1898. "Detailed Survey of the Languages and Dialects Spoken in Certain Portions of British India."*Journal of the Royal Asiatic Society*, 35–42.

———. 1899. *Memoir of Past Years of a Septuagenarian*. London: Privately printed.

Edney, Matthew H. 1997. *Mapping an Empire: The Geographical Construction of British India, 1765–1843*. Chicago: University of Chicago Press.

Greenberg, Joseph H. 1955. *Studies in African Linguistic Classification. Reprinted from the Southwestern Journal of Anthropology for Language and Communication*. Bradford, CT: Compass Publishing Co. for the Research Center, Columbia University and the Program of African Studies, Northwestern University. Originally published in the *Southwestern Journal of Anthropology* 5 (1949): 79–100. 190–98, 309–17; 6 (1950): 47–63, 143–60, 223–37, 388–98; 10 (1954): 405–15.

Greenberg, Joseph H. 1963. "The Languages of Africa."*International Journal of American Lingusitics*, 29, No. 1, pt. II. Revised version of Greenberg 1955.

Grierson, George A. 1903–1927. *Linguistic Survey of India*. Calcutta: Office of the Superintendent of Government Printing, India.

Hale, Horatio (?). 1884. "The Languages of Africa" (review of Cust, *A Sketch of the Modern Languages of Africa*). *Science* 4, no. 86: 310–11.

Mir, Farina. 2006. "Imperial Policy, Provincial Practices: Colonial Language Policy in Nineteenth-century India." *Indian Economic and Social History Review* 43, no. 4: 395–427.

Müller, Friedrich. 1876–1888. *Grundriss der Sprachwissenschaft*, 6 vols. Vienna: Hṭlder.

Murdock, George Peter. 1959. *Africa: Its Peoples and their Culture History*. New York: McGraw-Hill.

Penner, Peter. 1987. *Robert Needham Cust 1821–1909: A Personal Biography*. Lewiston ME and Queenston ON: Edwin Mellen Press.

Perry, Sir Thomas Erskine. 1853. "On the Geographical Distribution of the Languages of India." *Journal of the Bombay Branch of the Royal Asiatic Society* 4: 289–318.

———. 1855. *A Bird's Eye View of India*. London: Murray.

Trautmann, Thomas. 2006. *Languages and Nations: The Dravidian Proof in Colonial Madras*. Berkeley and Los Angeles: University of California Press.

Wenker, Georg. 1887. *Das Rheinische Platt*. Düsseldorf: Selbstverlag.

Zide, Norman H. 1981. "Robert Needham Cust and the Beginnings of Comparative Kolarian (Munda) Studies." In *Suniti Kumar Chatterji Commemoration Volume*, ed. Bhakti P. Mallik, 298–320. University of Burdwan.

3

Thomas Maurice and Domestic Orientalism, *c.* 1790–1820

MICHAEL S. DODSON

> I cursorily mentioned Mr Volney's impious attempt to mythologize away the whole of the Christian system, by insisting that the history and miracles of Christ were borrowed from those of the Indian Creeshna.... Thus is the truth of history insulted, and the corroborating testimony of ages set aside, for the...purpose of plundering Christian Europe into all the horrors of atheistical France.
>
> —Thomas Maurice, *The History of Hindostan* (1798)

> We cannot but own, that in the details of history, truth and fiction are so blended as to be scarce distinguishable.
>
> —William Jones, "Tenth Anniversary Discourse" (1793)

Of the numerous characters of British orientalism introduced to a reader of Thomas R. Trautmann's far-reaching and important 1997 book *Aryans and British India*, it is perhaps Revd Thomas Maurice (1754–1824) who could be said to have most intrigued (and mystified) me as I first encountered Tom's book as a PhD candidate at Cambridge. Maurice was a prolific author of Asian history and mythography, a noted poet, and from 1799 the assistant keeper of manuscripts in the British Library, as well as being an ordained minister (Leask 2004). Most relevant to me (and also daunting, I must admit) as I pursued my own enquiries into British orientalist research were Maurice's numerous works of Indian, and more broadly Asian, history, including his seven-volume opus *Indian Antiquities* (1794–1800), *The History of Hindustan* in two volumes (1795–98, 2nd edition in 1820), *The Modern History of Hindostan* in two volumes (1802–10), *Brahmanical Fraud Detected* (1812), *Observations on the Ruins of Babylon* (1816), and *Observations on the Remains of Ancient Egyptian Grandeur and Superstition* (1818), all of which were self-published and financially supported through subscription. While I have considered Maurice's historical-mythographical work in a limited way previously,[1] it is a pleasure to have the opportunity to revisit the question of Maurice's historiographical importance at greater length within this forum, as a testament to the importance of Tom's *Aryans and British India* for my own thinking about British orientalism.

Thomas Maurice was, in essence, what I would describe as a "domestic orientalist," and with the use of this terminology I mean to highlight two important points. The first is that Maurice was something of an "armchair orientalist"; he never traveled to Asia and much of his knowledge of Asian history and religion was gained through classical literary and historical sources as well as the published accounts of those orientalists resident in India in the Company's service, including, importantly, contributors to *Asiatick Researches* such as William Jones in Calcutta and Francis Wilford in Benares. Moreover, Maurice had no significant knowledge of Asian languages (even though he once claimed to be learning Persian at the behest of William Jones; Maurice 1794:1.62). Beyond this, the second point to note is that Maurice's historical work was wholly meant to answer a set of questions related to an essentially domestic British agenda. Maurice was concerned, above all, with utilizing Asian historical and mythological information, considered then to be amongst the oldest extant human records, to uphold Biblical narrative, specifically the Mosaic chronology of early human civilization, against deist critiques and atheistic (and principally French) skepticism, as well as with promoting an understanding of the evolution of European civilizational superiority from common human origins.

In *Aryans and British India*, Maurice's historical and mythographical *oeuvre* is characterized by Trautmann as a sort of subspecies of what he identified as "Indomania," namely, a "Christian Indomania." "Indomania," of course, was a term Trautmann used to distinguish orientalist scholarship marked by its British author's enthusiasm for South Asian culture and history (1997: 62–64). This enthusiasm can be said to have derived not simply from a fascination with the new and unusual, but with the realization that the European encounter with the textual records of India afforded by colonial rule appeared to provide an independent (that is, non-European) testimony to humanity's earliest history. It was, then, principally an antiquarian enthusiasm. For a Christian minister such as Maurice (even more so than for the pious William Jones), this "Indomania" was rendered into an enthusiasm for Asia specifically so far as it stood as confirmatory to the truth of the Bible. Yet Trautmann took care in his book to distinguish the notion of early Indo-maniacal "enthusiasm" for South Asia from any potential apologia for a specifically colonial scholarship. (This is a conflation that Garland Cannon, for example, has attempted to popularize as a critique of Edward Said's *Orientalism* thesis and as a defense of the scholarly "reputation" of William Jones).[2] In this sense, one of Trautmann's important contributions in his study of orientalist research was his renewed emphasis upon the argument that late eighteenth- and early nineteenth-century scholarly enthusiasm (and even sympathy) for Indian history and civilization should not be understood as mutually exclusive from the politics of establishing and perpetuating empire, but rather, as integral to it.

Equally, though, the historical processes which contributed to the demise of "Indomania" and the rise of "Indophobia" in the nineteenth century (specifically the 1810s and 1820s) have been difficult to delineate with any sense of confidence. This is the transition, as characterized by Trautmann, to nineteenth-century historical works, such as James Mill's *History of British India* (1817) or John Bentley's *A Historical View of the Hindu Astronomy* (1823), which emphasized not only European civilizational superiority, but also did so with concomitant characterizations of Indian cultural and intellectual abasement, and an emphatic denial of Indian claims to a high civilizational antiquity. The enthusiasm for all-things Indian was drained from British historical scholarship, in other words, (dismissed by Mill as simply a symptom of the subject's novelty) and replaced by a much more overt linking of British understandings of Indian history and culture to their own empire's "civilizing mission." This linking was conducted principally through the detailed elaboration of abstracted structures of national hierarchies and respective national progress, as in Mill's multi-volume character assassination of Indian (Hindu and Muslim) civilization (see Majeed 1992). To be certain, there were some elements of continuity between early orientalist and later liberal thought, including the propensity to understand Indian civilization solely on the basis of its textual production (Trautmann 1997: 128–29). Maurice's work did, for example, also anticipate elements of later liberal-utilitarian research, including his own invocation of historiographical authority on the basis not of first-hand knowledge, but rather a rational distillation of secondary scholarship (Maurice 1794: 1.60–61). Yet the shift away from earlier strategies of utilizing Indian textual material and attributions of Indian antiquity in support of the Mosaic chronology is perhaps best glimpsed in John Bentley's 1823 discussion of Indian astronomical knowledge, in which he argues specifically that any attribution of an antiquity to Indian cultural forms not only helped, through the authority of that antiquity, to support a range of "horrid abuses and impositions," including "the burning of widows, the destroying of infants, and even the immolation of men," but also, and more importantly, it served to "overturn the Mosaic account, and sap the very foundation of our religion." For Bentley, any claims Indians made to scientific knowledge were to be understood as relatively recent in origin, and likely borrowed from Europe (1823: xxi). The potential threat contained within Asian historical records required a neutralization, and thus the transition to Indophobia, in essence, can be read as representing a shift to a revised British conception which held that Indian textual records had little, if anything, to say about Britain's own civilization and its genealogy, but much to say about Britain's new "stewardship" role in the world.

How, then, might we understand this transition, and the place of Thomas Maurice's own domestic orientalism within the ebb and flow of British historiography of Asia? The rise of distinctive intellectual movements in Britain such as evangelicalism and utilitarianism can partly account for the transformation just outlined, as can the rise in British cultural self-confidence engendered by the abolition of the slave trade in 1807, the East India Company's defeat of Mysore and the Maratha confederacy in India, as well as British victory over Napoleonic France by 1815. I will argue in this essay, however, that in addition to these factors there were also important characteristics internal to the historical methodology of "Christian Indomania," as typified in the works of Thomas Maurice, which contributed to its own obsolescence in the more mature imperial era of the 1820s and onward. Partly this was due to elements of Maurice's "domesticity", and in particular his utilization of all evidence from Asian sources, regardless of its nature, to support a single Mosaic narrative. More pertinent, I think, to Maurice's self-ushered demise was the perception of his virtual embodiment of all that was deemed threatening about Asia, in terms of both his methodology and his personal authorial style. Maurice's historical domesticity was, in other words, permeated by Asia, rendering it useless in the demarcation of the distinctive "truths" of British civilizational norms.

MYTHOGRAPHICAL HISTORIES OF ASIA AND EUROPE

Imperialism and the writing of history were mutually self-supporting in a number of ways, not the least of which was the role played by historical research in confirming European understandings of their own civilization's historical evolution (Said 1979). Thus, the stakes for European self-conceptions of their place in history and in the world were exceedingly high in the publication of research on Indian history and mythology in the decades surrounding the turn of the nineteenth century (Dodson 2009). The threat posed by "knowing Asia" was potentially a grave one for Britons by virtue of the potential for disruption of established historical-civilizational narrative. This phenomenon is evident in the uproar caused by the publication of Nathaniel Brassey Halhed's 1776 *A Code of Gentoo Laws*, which was amongst the very first widely available and "authoritative" accounts of Indian civilization to circulate in Britain.[3] In the preface to that work, Halhed suggested on the basis of claims made within a number of Sanskrit texts that Indian civilization might possess an antiquity greater than that conventionally allowed by the Bible—"an antiquity infinitely more remote than is authorized by the belief of the rest of mankind"—and that these claims should be viewed as potentially authoritative by virtue of their plausibility, and because Hindus themselves possessed confidence in them (1776: xxxvii). One important element of that plausibility for Halhed was the near correspondence of elements of Hindu doctrine with that contained in the Old Testament, including ideas of the extraordinary longevity of both the Patriarchs and the ancient Brahmans, as well as the similarity apparent in elements of Hindu and Christian chronology, especially towards the era of the deluge (1776:xxxvii–xxxix). Beyond the resemblance of later Hindu chronology with the Mosaic, however, Halhed also noted the "wonderful correspondence" of the laws of Manu with those of

Moses. The question for Halhed, which would later come to absorb Thomas Maurice as well, was the nature of that apparent inter-relationship. Halhed saw no reason to believe that Indians had borrowed elements of their ancient religion from the West, but did entertain the open question of whether India might be the ultimate source of elements of the Pentateuch through its influence upon Egypt (1776:xliii–xliv).

For his scholarly efforts, Halhed received a strenuous and point-by-point rebuke in a 1778 pamphlet authored by Revd George Costard, who characterized Halhed's conclusions as "too hastily advanced," and his work as a whole as marred by "assertions totally void of truth" (Costard 1778: 47). At the most basic level, Costard could see little correspondence between Manu and Moses by virtue of his understanding that ancient law, on the model of the 10 commandments, was "delivered in short definitive sentences." Drawing on an evolutionary model of civilization which ranged from simplicity to complexity, Costard similarly understood "knavery" and "commerce" to have combined in later years to necessitate an expansion and complication of law (itself also a symptom of societal corruption!), leading him to conclude that the Hindu law contained within the *Code* was clearly relatively recent in origin, thereby throwing Halhed's attribution of civilizational antiquity to India into grave doubt (1778: 3).

Such debates over not just the possibility of an extraordinary Indian antiquity, but also the nature of such antiquity's relation to Europeans, were, in essence, between those who identified themselves as church Christians and those who were deists, including not only Halhed, but also other early orientalists such as Alexander Dow and J. Z. Holwell. Siraj Dean Ahmed has perceptively argued that the main point of contention between these two groups was the understanding of Judeo-Christian tradition as central to the evolution of civilization, on the part of mainstream Christians, as opposed to such tradition being viewed as a corruption of the original "natural religion" of which Hinduism was deemed to be a representative. Orientalist research, in other words, could in the hands of a deist like Halhed become a radical critique of European history and tradition by arguing that it was present-day Christian practice which was the degenerated and corrupted practice (as opposed to the Hindu), and that European religion could only be regenerated by returning to the religious "fountainhead," which, in several important respects, Hinduism represented (Ahmed 2009: 176–77). In the last two decades of the eighteenth century, however, and into the early nineteenth as well, the nature of the potential threat which scholarship on Asian history and civilization posed to specifically British self-understandings was augmented beyond the deist critique by the ideological challenge posed by the French revolution, and the enthusiasm with which French intellectuals such as Voltaire and Jean-Sylvain Bailly picked up on early orientalist findings to advance essentially atheistic arguments.

It is in this specific context, in the utilization of orientalist research to undermine British-Christian historical identity on two fronts, the deist and the atheist, that Thomas Maurice wrote his mythographical histories of India in the 1790s and early 1800s as a defence of church doctrine, the truth of the Bible, and European historical-civilizational norms. French skepticism, especially, seemed to challenge Maurice's notions of appropriate scholarship, and the suggestion alone of French challenges to Christianity based in orientalist research were characterized by Maurice as part and parcel of the "momentous crisis" spurred by "infidelity," and which, moreover, imperiled Britain's "national faith" (1798a: 7; 1795a: 1.xxi). Maurice was amongst the most visible, to be certain, of Christian scholars in Britain who took up such challenges to seemingly "acceptable" interpretations of the historical link between Indian mythology and Christianity. But importantly, unlike many of his peers working within the Christian tradition (such as George Costard), Maurice did not view the recent orientalist discoveries of Indian history and theology as representing a potential imperilment of Christian doctrine, thus requiring arguments which denied the "particular genius" of Asia. Indeed, Maurice noted that he would work to "substantiate every just and well-founded claim the Hindoos can urge to superiority." This was not to say that Maurice accepted Indian claims to an extreme antiquity, though; he rejected that idea most forcefully as undermining the Mosaic chronology (1794: 1.45–46). Instead, and like William Jones, Maurice viewed recent discoveries of Asian history and religious thought as opportunities to provide a further confirmation of Christianity. His mission in his books was thus two-fold: to defend Hindu religious belief, especially, from well-meaning, but essentially unwarranted, attacks from British Christians; and to reclaim orientalist research into Hinduism and other Asian religions for the support, rather than the undermining, of the Mosaic chronology.

Maurice's principal arguments were representative of a Christian conceptualization of the ancient world as possessing a more perfect knowledge of the nature of God; knowledge in the ancient world was, in other words, Providential knowledge. In this ancient world, humankind lived in what Maurice called the "pure primeval condition," which he understood as providing ancient peoples with faculties "better calculated" (than in the "fallen" present era) to contemplate "divine perfections" and to ascertain the "great celestial truths" (1800a: 20). As such, the most ancient records of humankind were to be considered as containing the most authoritative of human religious knowledge. Yet these records were inherently problematic. First, through a process of gradual corruption, in which "the unity of the divine essence" was increasingly understood through attributions of plurality, ancient knowledge had to be interpreted from within expressions of Pagan polytheism. Second, the most ancient knowledge of humankind was expressed very often through what Maurice understood as "astronomical mythology," such that astronomical figures were thought to record the most important ancient historical events. The "Sabian superstition," or the "worship of the stars and planets," was a practice in which an ancient knowledge of "the attributes of God, and even the virtues of men, personified, came to be exalted into divinities." This knowledge was then literally recorded, through a process of mythologization, as astronomical phenomena (1800a: 20–21; 1794: 2.110ff.). In this respect, Maurice referred to the "ample and recording tablet of the skies," which were to provide for the historian-mythographer "the real history of the first grand family of the post-diluvian world" (1795a: 1.vi; 1794: 1.36).The history of the earliest human civilizations, then, was thought to only be recoverable through a process of mythographical interpretation which involved a reconstruction and comparison of respective Asian and European astronomical mythological forms: a "dark and intricate labyrinth" through which "historic truth in those distant æras is to be explored" (1795a: 1.i).

Consistent with his assumption of the truth of the Mosaic narrative, Maurice set out to argue that Chaldea was the origin of humankind, and that the similarities between the mythologies, languages, and other cultural remnants of ancient Egypt, India, Iran, and Greece, principally, were all evidence of that common origin. The ancient world's major civilizations, in other words, could all be traced back to Chaldea through an examination of their common inheritances. Maurice's argumentation ranged over a number of different, but all inter-connected, examples. For instance, Maurice made use of emerging research on Asian orthography and vocabulary to establish connections between the "primitive languages" of India and Chaldea. He quoted William Jones at length, utilizing elements of his third anniversary discourse to the Asiatic Society in Calcutta (delivered in 1786) to posit that the similar shape of ancient written characters (though sometimes with the "change of straight lines to curves") pointed to a common origin for Sanskrit's *devanagari* script and the Chaldaic script of ancient Hebrew (Jones 1788; Maurice 1800a: 32). More often, though, Maurice drew a number of etymological comparisons as evidence, often of a wildly speculative kind, and thus appeared to abandon Jones' own call for the grounding of historical enquiry in "extrinsick" evidence in favor of the mode of analysis utilized by Jacob Bryant in his *A New System*.[4] Maurice thus asserted, for example, that the Hindu god Brahma, the "creator" was likely related to the Hebrew *bra*, or *bara*, "created" (1800a: 34), while the name Adam was related to the Sanskrit root *Adim*, "the first."[5] Similarly, the Hindu law-giver "Menu" was to be identified with "Nuh" or "Noah"; the Hindu mythological figure Bali was no other than Belus (1795a: 1.iii; 1794: 1.31); and even the river Nile drew its name from the Sanskrit word *nila*, meaning "blue" (1794: 3.63).

Maurice also grounded his argument in examples from temple architecture, and especially from the details of pyramidal structures which he considered to be the most ancient, ranging from the Egyptian pyramids to the "pagoda" of Tanjore.[6] Indeed, drawing inspiration from the work of antiquary Richard Gough,[7] Maurice was particularly interested in showing through similarities in temple architecture that India and Egypt especially had enjoyed a "very familiar intercourse" in the distant past, and argued that all such pyramidal monuments were, amongst other things, used as ancient observatories (1794: 3.86). Although Maurice's actual analysis in his first and most prolonged attempt at comparative architectural history in the third volume of *Indian Antiquities* was, in fact, rather short on detailed content (and indeed, on comparative elements), he did argue, for example, that temples in both India and Egypt contained indications of a common theology, including images of serpents and the phallus, or *linga*, and that the worship of the sun, common to all early religious traditions,[8] was in all likelihood to be more readily conducted atop such large structures. Indian and Egyptian temples were also deemed similar in their use of a "quadrangular" shape, as an allusion to the "veneration of the four elements" and "the four cardinal points of the universe" (1794: 3.129–31). Importantly, Maurice also asserted that large pyramidal structures were clearly modeled upon the first such monumental observatory, the tower

Figure 3.1 The Great Pagoda of Tanjore: evidently formed after the model of the Tower of Babel

of Babel, located as it was in the "extensive and beautiful plains of Chaldea" (1794: 3.133) where astronomical science was born (Figure 3.1), and that it was from Egypt's architectural example that the more sophisticated achievements of Greece were evidently drawn (1794: 3.139–41).

Consistent with his notion that the mythologies of the ancient world were all based upon a basic shared ancient astronomy with its origins in Chaldea, Maurice also drew correspondences in a number of his publications from evidence specifically based in the zodiac. For example, the southern constellation of *Argo Navis*, recognized by the ancient Greeks, Egyptians, Persians, and Indians as a ship, and around which distinct mythologies were constructed, represented for Maurice a shared remembrance of the ark of Noah. (The Egyptians saw the constellation as the ship which carried Isis and Osiris during a world-wide flood, while the Greeks saw the ship "Argo," which Jason and the Argonauts sailed in search of the golden fleece.) Similarly, the "aquatic objects or animals" of the southern hemisphere (including, one would assume, that of "Hydra") all pointed to a remembrance of the deluge. The Indian, Greek, and Egyptian zodiacs bore striking resemblances to one another in their use of 12 signs (1794: 1.32), and within the Indian zodiac, as well, figures such as Virgo, "drawn standing on a boat in water," provided independent confirmation of that event, especially when Maurice considered this alongside the fact that the first three *avatar*s of Vishnu, Matsya (the fish), Kurma (the tortoise), and Varaha (the boar), all had important mythological connections to water.[9] Varaha, for example, was depicted as having carried the earth on his tusks from out of the cosmic ocean where it had been taken by the demon Hiranyaksha.

But perhaps Maurice's most important intervention into mythographical history was his set of observations surrounding the doctrine of the Trinity. So important to his overall argument was the seemingly ubiquitous nature of the "divine triad" across world mythologies that Maurice extracted elements of several volumes of *Indian Antiquities* into a separate stand-alone book (of which he printed 250 copies) dedicated to this topic specifically. Maurice's thesis was that across the Asian world there had arisen a notion of the plurality of the "divine essence," and that this plurality most often took the form of a triad, characterized as the multi-faceted "supreme Governor of the world" (1800a: 295). Maurice described, for example, the Indian triad of Brahma, Vishnu, and

Shiva as the creator, preserver, and "regenerator" of humankind, respectively, noting that despite their apparent diversity they were but expressions of a divine unity. In this respect, Maurice speculated that India's trinity was not a trinity of divine attributes, but three aspects of the same single god, given that any god with the power to create, namely Brahma, must also have the power to preserve and to recreate.[10] Other Hindu religious practices and symbols also pointed to the ubiquity of a divine triad ("that mystic number") in India, Maurice argued, including the habit of praying three times per day; the wearing of a sacred cord by *Brahmans* composed of three threads; the existence of three original *Vedas* (the *Rig*, *Yajur*, and *Sama*); Shiva's "three-forked sceptre" or trident; and even the tri-literal nature of the sacred syllable "*aum*" (1800a: 374–78, 384).[11] India's trinity, moreover, dated to a particularly ancient era by virtue of the fact that there appeared a single-bodied, three-headed sculpture of Brahma, Vishnu, and Shiva in the cave temple of Elephanta, which Maurice described as being "the most ancient and venerable temple of the world," dating in all likelihood "as near the deluge as the progress of science will allow us with propriety to fix it" (1800a: 372–73).[12] In Persian mythology as well, Maurice described the Zoroastrian trinity of Oromasdes, Mithra, and Ahriman, noting especially the qualities of Mithra, who was conceived as a mediator between God and man (1800a: 345–69). Similarly, in Egyptian religion, the triad was composed of Osiris, the sun and primordial source of divinity; Cneph, the spirit that "pervaded and animated" the world; and Ptha (Ptah), the "fire that issued from the solar orb" (1800a: 304). The triad of Egyptian deities was also linked by Maurice to similar Hindu gods. Cneph, he argued, the winged spirit, was none other than the Hindu deity Narayan, "a spirit of a blue colour." More remarkable (certainly in terms of Maurice's reasoning) was that Cneph was thought to have given rise to Ptah from his own essence, just as Brahma (whom Maurice identified with Narayan) produced Vishnu. Ptah's character, moreover, being the fire issuing from the sun (or, the "son of the sun"!) was evidence of a remnant of the Chaldaic doctrine of the "all-pervading Fire."[13]

The point to Maurice's argumentation, in essence, was that the parallels which he observed between the various "divine triads" within Hindu, Egyptian, Persian, and Christian theology confirmed not only God's "sublime mysterious truth," but also his genealogy of religious knowledge, in which the singularity of God was made plural by humankind through the dispersal from Chaldea (1800a: 34–36). These points are worth elaborating. On the one hand, Maurice's understanding that the "divine triad" existed in multiple religious traditions convinced him that the doctrine bore "striking internal marks of a divine origin," making it "very unlikely to have been the invention of mere human reason." The trinity, in other words, was not a human invention, but a truth revealed by God. On the other hand, the relative ubiquity of the "divine triad" could be read only as evidence, in Maurice's thought, of its propagation from a single point of origin. This was, then, understood to be a truth made known to the ancient patriarchs of the lineage of Shem, who in turn spread it throughout the ancient world (1800a: 36). Quite apart from the logical problems inherent in such a form of argumentation, Maurice's principal complication in advancing this line of reasoning to his peers was the apparent lack of a trinity in the most ancient Hebrew scripture. It falls outside the realm of this essay to consider this point in any detail, but it will suffice to say here that Maurice claimed also to have discovered evidence that, in its ancient form, Judaism did indeed subscribe to the notion of a "plurality in the divine nature" and a "Trinity in Unity." This finding simultaneously neutralized potential opposition to his genealogy of religion and placed the Jews firmly into a narrative of Asian religious history.[14]

Importantly, Maurice seems to have understood that the attribution of elements of commonality between different Asian mythologies and astronomical sciences did not necessarily point to a specific historical trajectory, or rather, an inherent explanation for such commonality. He thus argued, taking the example of the genesis of the zodiac, that it was a well-accepted fact that the Greeks had borrowed the principles of astronomy from the Egyptians, and adapted it to their own mythological needs, but that despite the striking resemblances between zodiacal figures and Egyptian hieroglyphics, Egypt was not to be considered the original home of the zodiac. This he set out to prove by noting that the order of the seasons depicted in the zodiac was inappropriate for the Egyptian climate. Virgo, for example, the symbol of the harvest (a young female with an ear of corn, Maurice noted) came in September, but in Egypt, dependent as it was on the flooding of the river Nile, the harvest came in March. Likewise, Aquarius, a figure depicting the "chilling rains of the bleak winter-season" in January was rendered nonsensical in a hot desert region such as Egypt where January was to be considered "the finest season." The origin of the zodiac must lie elsewhere, Maurice reasoned, and he looked instead to Chaldea (1794: 1.33–35). Indeed, Maurice used a similar method of reasoning in arguing that the knowledge of physics, spherical trigonometry, and the true nature of the solar system common to both Pythagoras and Yavanacharya originated in India, not Greece, because Brahmans, if they were to actually travel outside the subcontinent would have "violated a leading precept of the religion and policy of Brahma" (1794: 1.46–47). Through such logic, Maurice constructed throughout his work a trajectory of knowledge formation and mythological adaptation which consistently worked backwards from Greece to India and Egypt, and thence to the primeval land of Chaldea.

MAURICE'S MYTHOGRAPHY AND THE HISTORIOGRAPHICAL THREAT OF ASIA

Thomas Maurice's large body of historical-mythographical work anticipated, as I noted earlier, many aspects of the turn in early nineteenth-century orientalist scholarship on India typified by James Mill, including the emphasis upon "armchair authority," while also maintaining elements of the enthusiasm for Asian civilization which marked the earlier work of William Jones. In an important sense, Maurice's scholarship literally spanned the divide marked by the turn of the nineteenth century, and the transition from elements of "world history" narrative to imperial history (see Dodson 2009). But we should make no mistake that however much he claimed an appreciation for India, Maurice also believed emphatically that Christian history, and more broadly European history, were the only basis upon which to construct an authoritative history of Asia. In all respects, then, for Maurice, as for Mill (and indeed Jones), Asian religion, culture, and history were to be employed in the service of British identity processes. But the interesting question here is, if, as I've suggested, there was so much at stake for British self-understandings in the production of orientalist scholarship on Asia, and if Maurice was a vocal and visible critic of apparent normative transgression by deists and atheists, why then is Maurice and his work not taken particularly seriously by historians, and indeed, why is he so often rendered into a figure of "fun" and derision? In this respect, it should be borne in mind that Maurice apparently enjoyed some degree of popularity amongst the British reading public, as a number of his books went through several reprints and subsequent editions, and the list of subscribers for the first volume of his *Indian Antiquities* includes a number of very prestigious individuals, as well as the East India Company itself (Maurice 1794: 1.26–27). Trautmann, for example, has characterized Maurice as a derivative scholar who lacked the singular genius of someone like William Jones, noting that his body of scholarship was "impressive in extent if not in quality." Here Maurice's "domestic" qualities were to be contrasted with the linguistic and geographical pedigrees of William Jones. In what is, admittedly, a humorous juxtaposition, Maurice's scholarship is also represented as the latter portion of Trautmann's characterization of early orientalism as a "mixture of pearls and dung" (1997: 75, 97). Brian Young, as well, in an otherwise very serious attempt at placing Maurice's scholarship into its British intellectual context, notes him to be "eccentric," occasionally hysterical, and long-winded (2000: 92, 96–97).

It is true, quite simply, that it is easy to portray Maurice as a figure of ridicule. He *was* incredibly long-winded, tended to veer off topic for multiple pages at a time, often argued in a highly circular fashion, and Maurice certainly didn't help himself when, for example, he complained (as he often did) in the prefaces to his work that unenlightened critics were proving "extremely injurious" to his book sales.[15] Moreover, Maurice's scholarly reputation was injured by the scandal surrounding the 1805 revelation that Francis Wilford, upon whose writings Maurice drew heavily, had been defrauded by his chief *pandit* in Benares through the forging of a substantial number of spurious *Puranas* (Wilford 1805: 245–65; Trautmann 1997; Dodson 2007: 57–59). Maurice, like Wilford himself, dismissed the lasting importance of such impositions, as well as characterizing them as further evidence that Brahmans were likely to have "borrowed" or copied elements of the Mosaic doctrine from Chaldea (Maurice 1812: 3ff.). Despite such apparent setbacks, one certainly does get the sense in reading Maurice that he felt that his intellect was consistently under-appreciated during his own lifetime, and that his personal ambitions were never fulfilled, even within his chosen profession of the clergy.

But perhaps most damaging to Maurice were the regular attempts made to exploit the substantial logical flaw in arguments which turned on the attribution of common religious doctrine together with specific historical trajectories, not to mention Maurice's own seeming desire to police all statements on the relation of Christianity to Asian religious traditions. Thus Maurice was compelled to explain, for example, why, despite the apparent etymological similarity, it was simply impossible that "the history and miracles of Christ were borrowed from those of the Indian Creeshna," as had been suggested by Constantin Franśois de Volney (Maurice 1798b: vi; Volney 1791).[16] Moreover, when the fifth volume of *Asiatick Researches* was reprinted in a British edition in 1799, it contained an additional unauthorized "advertisement" which noted the similarity of Hebrew and Hindu scripture, as well as the "very high antiquity" of the latter. Whether "the Hindu Brahmens borrowed from Moses, or Moses from the Hindu Brahmens," the anonymous editor stated, was a matter for further investigation (Anonymous 1799: iii–xi). Maurice railed against such suggestions, arguing yet again that Noah was likely the same historical personage as "Menu," and that, as such, the legal code of "Menu" and the Mosaic Pentateuch closely corresponded, though it still by no means followed for Maurice that Moses borrowed from Hindu scripture. Rather, Maurice argued, Moses was divinely inspired, and the Hindu law codes of "Menu" dated to some 200 years after Moses' departure from Egypt (1800b; 1812: 13–20). Maurice's last sustained attempt to defeat his critics, one and all, was published as a series of letters to the Episcopal Bench in 1812. Published as *Brahmanical Fraud Detected*, Maurice's argumentation consistently and literally turned in upon itself, as he argued that Indian scholars perpetrated wholesale scriptural fraud and charlatanism in both contemporary and ancient contexts, yet that where Indian mythology coincided with Christian doctrine, it was ultimately supportive of the originality of the latter (but not that Christian doctrine required it, of course). That the figures of Krishna and Christ might have common origins, Maurice admitted the possibility, but that Krishna was an absurdist degeneration of the Saviour, Maurice insisted upon it. This was, in its essence, the "truth" of Maurice's historiography, and for him, at least, it was consistently unambiguous.

Interestingly, a similar attitude of disdain (or perhaps simply dismissal) has been taken by historians with respect to Maurice's similarly large body of poetic work. Without question, as Trautmann also notes (1997: 75), few people now appreciate such gems as this, from Maurice's 1795 elegy for William Jones:

Dear as to dungeon slaves the solar gleam,
Or wretches doom'd to dig the buried ore,
On raptured Casi dawns the gladsome beam,
Which British freedom, British science pour.

To chase the tenfold gloom, my Jones, was thine,
To cheer the Brahmin, and to burst his chains;
To search for latent gems the Sanscreet mine,
And wake the fervour of her ancient strains.

(Maurice 1795b: 36)

Certainly not every contemporary of Maurice appreciated his poetry either. Lord Byron immortalized his feelings for Maurice's poetry, and his pastoral *Richmond Hill* (1807) in particular, in this way:

As Sisyphus against the infernal steep
Rolls the huge rock whose motions ne'er may sleep,
So up thy hill, ambrosial Richmond! heaves
Dull Maurice all his granite weight of leaves:
Smooth, solid monuments of mental pain!
The petrifactions of a plodding brain,
That, ere they reach the top, fall lumbering back again.

(Byron 1873: 427)

Yet Maurice's poetry was, in his time, generally acknowledged to have been very good, Byron's lampooning notwithstanding. In a review of Maurice's elegy for William Jones published in *The Monthly Review* in 1795, Revd. Alexander Geddes noted that Maurice's "diction is pure, the phraseology is unembarrassed, the epithets are well chosen, and the transitions though bold are seldom unnatural." Geddes further characterized Maurice's verses as being animated by a fancy risen "on no weak nor vulgar wing"; indeed, the elegy appeared to be "near perfection," convincing Geddes that Maurice's "talents for poetry are superior even to his abilities as an historian" (Geddes 1795;with that point many would undoubtedly agree). Another reviewer in the same publication compared Maurice's elegy favorably with that produced the same year by William Hayley (1795), a would-be poet-laureate,[17] noting that Hayley's poem lacked the "sublimity" of Maurice's (Anonymous 1795).

I want to suggest here that these contemporary characterizations of Maurice's poetry in fact hold an important key for understanding the reason why his historical and mythographical work did not receive wide sanction in the nineteenth century. Indeed, it could be said that as historians ourselves, the frustration we often feel while attempting to interpret Maurice's *oeuvre* is itself an indicator that mythographical history of that sort has been, and always will be, at odds with our own historiographical inheritance; an inheritance which lies not in emotive defences of the Mosaic doctrine, but in the rational practices of imperial history. In short, it seems to me that Maurice's historical work was abandoned in his own lifetime by virtue of the fact that it channeled, or rather embodied, the historiographical threat posed by Asia, specifically in terms of his hyperbolic style and his haphazard historical methodology which (unwittingly) incorporated deep logical flaws in causality. This embodiment, moreover, led to an embracing on Maurice's part of the ambiguity inherent in the relationship between Asia and Europe.

What exactly, then, could Maurice's "muse" tell us about the way in which his history was viewed in the newly ascendant imperial age? The comparison made within *The Monthly Review* of Maurice's and Hayley's respective "muses," as displayed in their elegies to William Jones, pointed to a relatively inflated artistic passion on the part of Maurice, and nicely anticipates, I think, an important point of critique which, by the early nineteenth century, had already naturalized William Jones' own formulations of Asian poetic, artistic passion. *The Monthly Review* article noted that:

> the muse of Mr Hayley is a pleasant, well-bred gentlewoman, who moves along with a graceful air: her march is uniform, and all her steps, though still easy and elegant, are measured: for she never, or seldom, deviates from the flowery path in which she delights to tread. The muse of Mr

> Maurice is an impetuous Amazon, who stalks with majestic strides, surmounting fences with the unceremonious bounds of genius, and ascending the top of Parnassus by the shortest way. Mr H. has all the sweetness and verbosity of Ovid; Mr M. possesses a great share of the strength and laconism of Pindar; the former has more method and art, the latter more fire and energy.
>
> (Anonymous 1795: 293)

This characterization of Maurice's muse, raging wild and out of bounds like an Amazon, can be understood as an attribution of Maurice's embrace of a specific Asian poetic sensibility, of its passion and sensuality, if one reads this in conjunction with Jones' own musings on the differences between Europeans and Asians in the realm of poetry. In his "Essay on the Poetry of the Eastern Nations," Jones noted that Asians (and Arabs particularly) possessed a poetic sensibility more highly developed than the European by virtue of the leisure, the life of "indolence," they enjoyed in warm climates. While the appreciation of Arabic and Persian poetry might serve to reinvigorate European poetry, grown stale through generations of repetition, for Jones that artistic passion also clearly served as a line of demarcation to the rational sensibility of the European. Such artistic reinvigoration was, in other words, to be controlled through the application of orientalist historiography (Jones 1799).

The critique which, more than any other, revealed Maurice's mythographical history as a failure in the new imperial age appeared in an 1805 number of the *Edinburgh Review*. Alexander Murray, an accomplished linguist and future author of *Outlines of Oriental Philology* (1812), began this review by decrying the difficulty of providing a full and accurate history of Asia, including the difficulty of acquiring Asian languages (particularly Sanskrit) and the relative paucity of reliable source material available in Britain. Thus the failure he perceived in Maurice's work was at least partly a reflection of Britain's own failure to adequately secure access to substantial stores of historical source material, and also in adequately preparing its young men for service overseas with the requisite knowledge of Indian languages. Thus, Murray argued, that while Britain might rule India, it had as of yet still failed to know India (1805: 289–91). But Maurice, in particular, was perceived by Murray to be inadequate to the task of writing India's history not just because he lacked linguistic expertise or because he used "common sources," but because he had in essence abandoned the classical European model of history writing, and seemed to have become nearly infected with an Asian mode of enquiry. The classical model which Murray advocated valued "a relation of important actions and events delivered in language suitable to the subject, and interspersed with statements of the causes, as far as they are known, from which they arose" together with an "accuracy and depth in the occasional reflections and observations," on the model of not only Herodotus, but also David Hume, William Robertson, and yes, even the skeptical Voltaire (Murray 1805: 291). Maurice, however, in contravention of this model had provided "no satisfactory evidence" of the nature of the relationship he advocated between ancient India and Egypt, and often relied upon false etymologies, half understood, and interpreted through the lens of John Hutchinson's controversial attempts to recreate a pristine, unadulterated Hebrew (Murray 1805: 292–93; see Hutchinson, 1724). Maurice's argument that Indian civilization had remained largely stagnant and unchanging was similarly provided without evidence, Murray noted, and was a notion unsupported by the well-known fact that "ignorant nations" were infinitely mutable (1805: 293).

The fundamental flaw in Maurice's work for Murray was that, while he might be amenable to Maurice's defense of the Mosaic chronology and European historical narrative, his method for doing so in fact undermined their authoritativeness, and the exclusivity of European rational enquiry. Maurice had pursued a "vague and illogical plan of reasoning," and seemed to consider "a minute dissertation on any obscure topic relating to the country, *balancing* of authorities, long verbal quotations, and lumping together of opinions, as good history writing" (Murray 1805: 294–95).[18] Maurice's historical style, in other words, could be seen to vie "with the Mahomedan," presented "in all the pomp of Asian diction" (Murray 1805: 295, 297). His "epithet and ornament," in other words, could not conceal "the great scarcity of facts under which the narrative labours" (Murray 1805: 297). Such a characterization of Maurice's historical work, as embodying the "Asian" and "Mahomedan" in its character, was in Murray's review made all the more remarkable for what he acknowledged such a thing revealed about Britain and her particular vulnerabilities. Maurice had laid bare in his historiography, Murray felt, "the weakness of European knowledge concerning India…in the most humiliating form" (1805: 297).

Maurice, in his inimitable style, replied to Murray's short review with an 88-page pamphlet, itself duly and approvingly reviewed in the conservative, pro-church *British Critic* (1805).[19] Moreover, he continued to self-publish his mythography, drawing on current archaeological and orientalist discoveries, such as Claudius James Rich's surveying of the reputed site of Babylon, until his death at the age of 70 in 1824. But Maurice's era had clearly passed, to be replaced with, on the one hand, vicious missionary attacks upon Hindu culture, such as William Ward's *A View of the History, Literature, and Mythology of the Hindoos* (1823), and on the other hand, liberal-utilitarian histories of respective national progress such as that of James Mill. Maurice's mythography had, in its enthusiasm and relative effulgence, in its embodiment of Asian sensibility, and in its acceptance that Asia in general, and India in particular, might possess something to teach Europe, crossed a line which separated Europe from Asia; a line being drawn ever more emphatically with the consolidation of the imperial age. If the truths of European civilization, and the truth of Christianity, were to be elaborated in the nineteenth century, this was now to be a process conducted emphatically not on the terms of Asian civilization and its past, but on the intellectual, cultural, and civilizational terms of Britain's imperial present.

NOTES

1. There is very little scholarly work published on Maurice's history writing. Apart from Trautmann 1997, perhaps the best discussion to date of Maurice is Young 2000. There are also more limited discussions in Dodson 2007 and Leask 1992, but not much else, to the best of my knowledge.
2. See Cannon 1990, especially xiv–xvi; also many of the contributions in Cannon and Brine 1995. More recently, the idealist position of early orientalism is reiterated in the context of Arabic and Islamic studies in Irwin 2007.
3. Authoritative because, I argue, it was based on the translation of Sanskrit texts by *pandits*, rather than upon hearsay. See Dodson 2007: 23–24.
4. On this point see Dodson 2007: 26–27. This characterization of Maurice, though, might be unfair, for Maurice almost always used etymological comparison in conjunction with other forms of supporting evidence. In that sense, one can charitably read Maurice as attempting to improve upon Bryant's work through the incorporation of more diverse types of source material. See also Young 2000: 98.
5. Maurice is probably referring here to the Sanskrit word *adi*, which can be used in a number of ways, including as a noun, meaning "the beginning"; at the end of a *bahuvrihi* compound, meaning "beginning with" or "etcetera"; and in an adjectival form, *adima*, meaning "first." This is not, however, a verbal root within Sanskrit as Maurice seems to suggest.
6. Ancient by virtue of the ease with which monumentality could be constructed. On this point, the temple of "Jaggernaut," despite often being considered as ancient, was dismissed by Maurice as of relatively recent origin (perhaps from the eleventh century) because it is "circular." See Maurice 1794: 3.26–29.
7. See Gough 1785. Gough, like Maurice, felt that Britons had, to their peril, not conducted a thorough enough study of India's history and civilization.

8. Apart from vol. 3 on architecture, sun worship is also discussed in Maurice 1794: 2.83–130, and elsewhere.
9. Maurice describes these connections in numerous places throughout his body of texts (he was not one afraid of repeating himself, or of quoting himself at length). As an entry point, see 1794: 1.36–44.
10. The Indian trinity is described in Maurice 1800a: 371–91.
11. Maurice seems not to have worried that in the *devanagari* script "aum" is composed either of a single special symbol, or the character "au" + *anusvara.*
12. Maurice ascribes Elephanta such an ancient status based on its use of a flat roof and the lack of structural arches. In fact, the rock-cut temples there date to between approximately the eighth to the ninth century AD at the earliest.
13. Maurice discusses the Egyptian trinity in 1800a: 293–326.
14. This discussion is found in Maurice 1800a: 59–241.
15. See, for example, Maurice's own account of the difficulty of the task he was undertaking, and the lack of appreciation for it by British subscribers, in 1794: 1.32, 50–55, 75ff.
16. Volney's skeptical work appeared in English translation from 1795.
17. Hayley had been offered the position of poet laureate in 1790, but turned it down.
18. Italics in original.
19. Reviewed in *The British Critic* 26 (July–December 1805): 96–97.

REFERENCES

Ahmed, Siraj Dean. 2009. "Orientalism and the Permanent Fix of War." In *Postcolonial Enlightenment: Eighteenth-Century Colonialism and Postcolonial Theory*, ed. Daniel Carey and Lynn Festa, 167–203. New York: Oxford University Press.

Anonymous. 1795. [review of] *An Elegy on the Death of the Honorable Sir William Jones* [by William Hayley]. *The Monthly Review*; or, *Literary Journal, enlarged*, n.s. 18 (September-December): 292–94.

Anonymous. 1799. Advertisement to *Asiatic Researches*; or, *Transactions of the Society Instituted in Bengal, for inquiring into the History and Antiquities, the Arts, Sciences, and Literature, of Asia* 5(London edition).

Bentley, John. 1823. *A Historical View of the Hindu Astronomy, from the earliest dawn of that science in India, down to the present time*. Calcutta: Baptist Mission Press.

Byron, George Gordon. 1873. "English Bards and Scotch Reviewers: A Satire."In *The Poetical Works of Lord Byron*, 421–37. London: James R. Osgood and Co.

Cannon, Garland. 1990. *The Life and Mind of Oriental Jones: Sir William Jones, the Father of Modern Linguistics*. Cambridge: Cambridge University Press.

Cannon, Garland and Kevin R. Brine. 1995.*Objects of Enquiry: The Life, Contributions, and Influences of Sir William Jones, 1746–1794*. New York: New York University Press.

Costard, George. 1778. *A Letter to Nathaniel Brassey Halhead, esquire, containing Some Remarks on his Preface to the Code of Gentoo Laws lately published*. Oxford: Clarendon Press.

Dodson, Michael S. 2007. *Orientalism, Empire, and National Culture: India 1770–1880*. Basingstoke; New York: Palgrave Macmillan.

———. 2009. "On Sources and Authenticity: British Imperial Expansion and the Writing of Asian Histories, c. 1760–1830."*Historical Studies: Proceedings of the Irish Conference of Historians*23.

Geddes, Alexander [anonymously]. 1795. [review of] *An Elegiac and Historical Poem* [by Thomas Maurice]. *The Monthly Review*; or, *Literary Journal, enlarged*, n.s. 17 (May-August): 194–95.

Gough, Richard. 1785. *A Comparative View of the Antient Monuments of India, Particularly those in the Island of Salset near Bombay*. London: J. Nichols.

Halhed, Nathaniel Brassey. 1776. *A Code of Gentoo Laws, or, Ordinations of the Pundits, from a Persian Translation, made from the Original, written in the Shanscrit Language*. London.

Hayley, William. 1795. *An Elegy on the Death of the Honorable Sir William Jones*. London: T. Cadell & W. Davies.

Hutchinson, John. 1724. *Moses's Principia. Of the invisible parts of matter; of motion: of visible forms; and of their dissolution, and reformation*. London.

Irwin, Robert. 2007. *For Lust of Knowing: The Orientalists and Their Enemies*. London: Penguin.

Jones, William. 1788. "The Third Anniversary Discourse, delivered 2 February, 1786."*Asiatick Researches* 1 (Calcutta edition): 415–31.

———. 1795. "The Tenth Anniversary Discourse, delivered 28 February 1793."*Asiatick Researches* 4 (Calcutta edition): 1–17.

———. 1799. "An Essay on the Poetry of the Eastern Nations." In *The Works of Sir William Jones*, vol. 4, 527–48. London.

Leask, Nigel. 1992. *British Romantic Writers and the East: Anxieties of Empire*. Cambridge: Cambridge University Press.

———. 2004. "Maurice, Thomas (1754–1824)."*Oxford Dictionary of National Biography*. http://www.oxforddnb.com/view/article/18387.

Majeed, Javed. 1992. *Ungoverned Imaginings: James Mill's* The History of British India *and Orientalism*. Oxford: Clarendon Press.

Maurice, Thomas. 1794. *Indian Antiquities: or, dissertations, relative to … Hindostan*, 5 volumes. London. [vol. 6 published in 1796, vol. 7 in 1800]

———. 1795a. *The History of Hindostan, its arts and its sciences, as connected with the history of the other great empires of Asia, during the most ancient periods of the world*, volume 1. 1st ed. London.

Maurice, Thomas. 1795b. *An Elegiac and Historical Poem, sacred to the memory and virtues of the Honourable Sir William Jones*. London.

———. 1798a. *Sanscreet Fragments, or Interesting Extracts from the Sacred Books of the Brahmins, on subjects important to the British Isles*. London.

———. 1798b. *The History of Hindostan; and its arts, and its sciences, as connected with the History of the Other Great Empires of Asia, during the most ancient periods of the world*, volume 2. 1st ed. London.

———. 1800a. *A Dissertation on the Oriental Trinities: extract from the fourth and fifth volumes of Indian Antiquities*. London

———. 1800b. [review of] *Asiatic Researches; or Transactions of the Society… Volume the Fifth. Printed, verbatim, from the Calcutta edition. The British Critic*16 (August): 147–60.

———. 1805. *A Vindication of the Modern History of Hindostan, from the gross misrepresentations, and illiberal strictures, of the Edinburgh Reviewers*. London.

———. 1812. *Brahmanical Fraud Detected: or the attempts of the sacerdotal tribe of India to invest their fabulous deities and heroes with the honours and attributes of the Christian Messiah, Examined, Exposed, and*

Defeated, in a series of letters to the Right Reverend the Episcopal Bench. London.

Mill, James. 1817. *The History of British India*, 3 vols. London: Baldwin, Cradock, and Joy.

Murray, Alexander [anonymously]. 1805. [review of] *The Modern History of Hindostan* [by Thomas Maurice]. *Edinburgh Review* 5, no. 10 (Jan): 288–301.

Said, Edward. 1979. *Orientalism*. New York: Vintage Books.

Trautmann, Thomas R. 1997. *Aryans and British India*. Berkeley: University of California Press.

Volney, Constantin-Fransois. 1791. *Les Ruins, ou Mīditation sur les Rīvolutions des Empires*. Paris.

Ward, William. 1822. *A View of the History, Literature, and Mythology of the Hindoos*, 3 vols. London: Kingsbury, Parbury, and Allen.

Wilford, Francis. 1805. "Essay on the Sacred Isles in the West, and other essays connected with that work."*Asiatick Researches* 8 (Calcutta edition): 245–367.

Young, Brian. 2000. "'The Lust of Empire and Religious Hate': Christianity, History, and India, 1790–1820." In *History, Religion, and Culture: British Intellectual History, 1750–1950*, ed. S. Collini, R. Whatmore, and B. Young, 91–111. Cambridge: Cambridge University Press.

4

Henry George Raverty and the Colonial Marketing of Pashto

SHAH MAHMOUD HANIFI

Henry George Raverty (1825–1906) can be safely referred to as the foremost colonial authority on the Pashto language.[1] The volume and merits of Raverty's Pashto *oeuvre* distinguish him from the thousands of officials who engaged the language and its speakers during the colonial period between Mountstuart Elpinstone's first official appearance on the North-West Frontier of British India in 1809 and Sir Olaf Caroe's final presence in 1947 as the Empire was being dismantled.[2] As more than one commentator has indicated, Raverty was not a trained scholar and his writings about Pashto are not without their contradictions and deficiencies. A full treatment of Raverty's career would need to engage the entire corpus of his textual production and delve into his professional history and personal relationships in considerable detail, which is not possible in this context although such a comprehensive investigation would be most worthy and welcome. The three circumscribed goals of this paper are to briefly: a) situate the Pashto language and its speakers in the context of Sir William Jones' Indo-European theory, b) compare the views of Raverty to two other canonical colonial authorities who also "tested" Jones' theorizing of Pashto, and c) consider Raverty's career in the context of the colonial market for vernacular language materials.

SIR WILLIAM JONES AND THE PROMISE OF PASHTO

In the now famous Third Discourse on the Hindus delivered as a lecture in 1786 and published in 1788, Sir William Jones (1746–1794) argued that distinct languages such as Greek, Latin, Sanskrit, and Persian share the same origins in a hypothetical proto-Indo-European language. Jones' language family tree model provided a master genealogy that revolutionized thinking about possible common ancestries of widely distinct contemporary civilizations. Thomas R. Trautmann (1998) argues that Jones' project of cultivating knowledge of Sanskrit and other Indian languages generated an "Indomania," or a new India-focused Orientalism on the Far Eastern world of Hinduism. This new Orientalism departed from the older terrain of Orientalism grounded in the Near Eastern world where Islam as articulated by the Arabic and Persian languages preponderated.[3] Trautmann sees Jones' knowledge of Sanskrit as allowing for a reconciliation of sorts between the integrated cycles of time characterizing Hinduism on the one hand and the unilinear chronology of Biblical time as then framed by Anglican church ideology on the other. Trautmann finds Jones' approach to universal history to be a "Mosaic ethnology" with the power to provide historical and linguistic connections between disparate civilizations, thus making India "safe (and) good to think" for Europeans.[4]

The institutional context for the historical philology of the new Orientalists was the Asiatic Society of Bengal that Jones formed in 1784 with the support of the increasingly influential Governor General of India Warren Hastings. In like manner as Jones, Hastings was familiar with Persian, keen to learn Sanskrit, and an avid collector of manuscripts for which there was a thriving market.[5] Through donations and purchases in its inaugural year the Society acquired handwritten manuscripts and printed texts in multiple languages, as well as written and printed translations and recensions of and commentaries about original manuscripts and texts. Some of these writings the British East India Company had accumulated in various ways during the preceding decades through the work of its agents, factors, officials, and clients. The intellectual vehicle Jones and his colleagues and clients used to present these documents and their ideas about them was the *Asiatick Researches* publication, the first four volumes of which appeared in 1788.

Among these foundational documents for the Society to consider was a set generated by a high-ranking Company Officer named Henry Vansittart who served for a short time as the Governor General of India and in that capacity communicated with the founder of the Afghan kingdom Ahmad Shah Durrani, whose capital city was Qandahar, the city where he alone among the rulers of Afghanistan is interred.[6] It is unclear whether the documents of interest here were presented directly by Vansittart or if they were presented on his behalf to the Society, perhaps through the agency of Warren Hastings. The documents included an English translation of a Persian abridgement of a Pashto text that attracted attention for conveying a "very wild description" of Afghans as being among the Lost Israeli Tribes, and thus descended from the Jewish people. Details of the Lost Tribes and the events surrounding the Great Flood or Deluge were among the most important geographic and chronological markers used to interrogate and interrelate languages and cultures within the global connections and philological theories Jones was fashioning around the Indo-European idea. The second document presented to the Society through Vansittart's agency was a specimen of the Pashto language. It is unclear who is responsible for the translation that accompanies this brief linguistic sampling, but the passages offer a clear critique of both Brahmans and Sayyids as Hindu and Islamic clerical elites, respectively, while also associating the city of Peshawar with fire and the grave (Vansittart and Jones[1790] 1979: 60).

Jones published Vansittart's translation and commentary on the synopsis of the Afghan descent from the Jews that was written in Persian, the Pashto text sample and translation, and his own opinion on the significance of this material in the second volume of *Asiatick Researches*, which appeared in 1790. By then Jones had been studying the languages of India for over six years, and his weighty conclusions reflected familiarity with a Pashto dictionary and involved a postulate about the terminological correspondence between the geographical designate Hazaret in the vicinity of Peshawar and"the word used by Esdras" (Esdras is a book found within the Septuagint, or the Greek translation of the Hebrew Bible).[7] The key for Jones in his theorizing about the Afghans as a Lost Israeli tribe was the "manifest resemblance" he detected between the Pashto and Chaldaic languages.

Jones concluded his remarks on behalf of the prestigious new Asiatic Society, and through it the Bengal and English governments, however indirectly, with the statement that "the account of the Afghans may lead to a very interesting discovery...and I strongly recommend an inquiry into the literature and history of the Afghans."[8] There could be no more consequential intellectual and political endorsement for the study of the Pashto language. Pashto was then coming to be institutionally comprehended through the work of Jones and Vansittart as a language spoken by Afghans, who formed a community equated with Pathans, who hailed from the Peshawar province of Kabul otherwise known as Roh, and who wrote in Persian. The category Pathan arose in late-Mughal historiography and the arrival of Jones and the British signaled an increasingly common but inconsistent use of the term in English language writings to refer to contemporary and historic communities of Persian- and Pashto-speaking Afghans residing in and moving through India. The complex and changing relations between written and spoken Persian and Pashto among Afghan communities *in situ* and in diaspora aside, it is clear that via the Chaldaic connection Pashto, Afghans, and Pathans became important links in a new

Orientalist chain connecting Asian and European peoples, and by extension the geographies and histories of Judaism, Christianity, Islam, and Hinduism. No matter whether Jones was hoping to bring the Lost Tribes back into World Time or give World Time back to the Lost Tribes, these were indeed heady conceptual burdens for Afghans *cum* Pathans and their Pashto to bear!

RAVERTY AND OTHER COLONIAL EXAMINERS OF THE JONES HYPOTHESIS

The high profile and magnitude of Jones' claims about Pashto and Afghans prompted hundreds if not thousands of colonial officials and researchers across approximately five generations to consider the Lost Tribe hypothesis. The mission dispatched in 1808 to the Durrani monarch Shah Shuja led by Mountstuart Elphinstone (1779–1859) marks the first fully credentialed point of diplomatic contact between the British and the rulers of what subsequently became recognized as Afghanistan.9 Despite the significance of this mission Elphinstone's fame as an administrator and scholar accrued primarily through his tenures as the Resident at Poona and Governor of Bombay, between 1811–17 and 1819–27 respectively, and through the 1841 publication of his *A History of India in the Hindu and Mohametan Periods*. Sir Olaf Caroe (1892–1981) represents the culmination of formal British colonization of Pashto speakers in South Asia. Between 1923 and 1934 Caroe's responsibilities as a colonial administrator included the localities of Peshawar, Mardan, and Kohat and the entire North-West Frontier Province, and as a Foreign Secretary between 1939 and 1946 he was in charge of the External Affairs Department in which capacity he organized the Viceroy's Study Group in 1942. In 1946 Caroe was appointed Governor of the North-West Frontier Province of British India where his few months of service were marked by a number of difficult circumstances and decisions leading up to Partition. Together Elphinstone and Caroe stand as chronological bookends that frame Raverty's writings on the Pashto language, and all three of these authors responded directly to Jones' claims about the Jewish descent of the Afghans.[10]

Elphinstone advanced no farther than Peshawar into territories where Pashto is commonly, let alone primarily, spoken. During his stay in the city between lateFebruary and midJune 1809, and after the mission itself, Elphinstone tested the Chaldean connection theory. The primary results of Elphinstone's examination of Jones' theory were issued in the first edition of *An Account of the the Kingdom of Caubul* that was published in 1815, and these conclusions were expanded upon in the second edition of the work that appeared in 1839.[11] Elphinstone discounted due to internal contradictions the narratives of Afghans as descendants of a lost Jewish tribe he was exposed to during his mission, and debunked each of the four arguments advanced by Jones in support of that position. Elphinstone sealed his rejection of Jones' position with reference to a comparison of Pashto words with words meaning the same thing in an array of other languages, from which he concluded "(n)ot one word of the two hundred and eighteen has the smallest appearance of being deducible from the Hebrew or Chaldaic."[12] Elphinstone punctuated his critique of the Jones hypothesis with reference to the esteemed Russian scholar Bernhard Dorn who translated and provided commentary on a key primary text dealing with these issues, the *Makhzan-i Afghani*.

As with Elphinstone and Jones before him, Dorn could claim only rudimentary familiarity with Pashto. But the master language of the discussions of Pashto was Persian; specifically it was an expansive and therefore synthetic form of Indo-Persian historiography that spawned layers of copying, translations, recensions, anonymous reference, summarization, embedded and separated commentaries, and of course in all of this, manipulation. Dorn was familiar with at least 30 manuscripts that fed into his translation of and commentary upon the *Makhzan-i Afghani*, which is arguably the key primary Persian language text in the discussion of the linguistic and cultural origins of Pashto speakers and Afghans.[13]

In the mid-twentieth century Caroe had at his disposal a great deal more information than Elphinstone or Dorn were privy to bearing on the subject of Judeao-Afghan connections as Jones first conceived of them through alleged similarities between the Pashto and Chaldaic languages. The mass printing of manuscripts led to a proliferation of new editions, translations, and commentaries of the texts engaged by nineteenth-century colonial officers such as Elphinstone and Raverty. Caroe quickly distanced himself from Jones' Jewish descent theory for the Afghans by arguing that proponents of those connections did not account for two separate ancient Jewish captivities. He concluded his rejection of the Jewish descent theory by stating that any such associations were mythical and "smell of the Delhi lamp."[14] In the course of his critique Caroe usefully reminded readers of the importance of oral narratives existing in relation to written texts. Caroe also reiterated the emphasis placed by colonial authorities dating back to Vansittart on the critical roles played by the Persian language and the enigmatic Pathan social category, in mediating the discourse on the Pashto language and Afghans.[15]

Elphinstone and Caroe were the first and last colonial authorities, respectively, to offer substantive published commentary on Pashto-speaking communities. Pashto speakers and their descendents *in situ* and in diasporic conditions became commonly associated during the life-course of British Indian colonialism with both Afghans and Pathans. The categories Afghans, Pashtuns, and Pathans generally became increasingly metonymically linked during the period of formal British colonialism, and they have been further trilaterally imbricated in the post-colonial period. Raverty closely associated these three terms, and indeed the word Rohilla, and as such helped to forge the cultural, historical, and philological linkages between the communities so identified. Chronologically Raverty's writings fall between those of Elphinstone and Caroe, but the volume and content of Raverty's *oeuvre* reads in glaring contrast to the works of his more famous and widely read colleagues.

Raverty can be distinguished from Elphinstone and Caroe by the depth of his knowledge of Pashto, and in particular by his concurrence with Jones' Jewish descent theory for the Afghans.[16] The process by which Raverty reached his conclusion that "the Afghans are a lost tribe of Israel" involved disagreements with Jones, such as over the Greek term Paropamisadae and its connection to historic and contemporary Pashto speakers(Raverty [1855] 1987: 15). Beyond the separation from Elphinstone and Caroe on this important point, Raverty stands apart from all other colonial writers due to the nature and extent of his engagement of the Pashto language and its speakers. The prefatory and introductory remarks to his Pashto grammar and Pashto dictionary that were originally published in 1855 and 1860, respectively, contain extensive commentary on the Jewish descent theory. These passages alone draw attention to the great ranges of Raverty's linguistic, historic, and geographic erudition that are conveyed much more fully and sometimes in extremely complicated and opaque ways in his grammar, dictionary, and wider body of writings.

Length and density are primary distinguishing features of Raverty's writings, and as a rule those qualities carry inherent shortcomings. In his identification and explanation of issues that differ from other authorities, Raverty writes with those traits, and at times appears somewhat caustic if not hostile in expressing his views.[17] This is certainly the case when Raverty addresses the opinions of others on Jones' theory, as for example in the words he dedicates to Wolff and Barnes (Raverty [1860a] 1982: 28–29). Among the nineteenth-century authorities and even when considering the entire collection of frontier officials active in the colonial era, Raverty appears most appreciative and in command of written and spoken Pashto, as well as numerous other languages surrounding and relating to it in the past and present, most especially and importantly Persian.[18]

Raverty's greatest contribution to the philological debates inaugurated by Sir William Jones is methodological. In the introduction to his grammar Raverty comments on Jones' position by discussing how traces of "original languages" can never be extinguished and that the most relevant migrations for the philological analysis of the Pashto language have generally come from the west, all of which serves to buttress the Jewish descent theory (Raverty[1855] 1987: 1–35).[19] The geographic and historic template from which Raverty proceeds to discuss language is decidedly *annaliste*, if reprieve can be granted for anachronistic invocation of the term.[20] Perhaps most significantly Raverty argues that full knowledge of surrounding languages is required before a sound comparison of any aspect of one single language can be made to that language's relatives.This is indeed a high-bar position, and Raverty was not shy but arguably arrogant in positioning his contributions in the uppermost echelon in relation to the previous work of all others. Raverty clearly understood a now commonplace rule that studying similarities and variances between mere items of vocabulary is a different enterprise than identifying and analyzing grammatical homologies (Raverty [1855] 1987: 21, 17–24). Raverty continued to combine big ideas and small details in pursuit of Pashto philology after the publication of his grammar. In the introduction to his dictionary Raverty addresses conceptual distinctions between languages, idioms, and dialects as those categories apply to contemporary and historic communities of Pashto speakers, as well as the details of casing, gender, pluralization, pronouns, tenses, and voweling in Pashto (Raverty [1860a] 1982: viii–xi).

In his published work Raverty addressed the practical side of the methodology coin as well as the intellectual. Throughout the introductions and prefaces to his grammar and dictionary Raverty provides unique and important information on, for example, the practices of local women scribes who pen Pashto texts in their fathers' name ([1855] 1987: 27), the background and credentials of his tutors and translators or *munshis* ([1855] 1987: vii–viii; [1860a] 1982: xv–xvi), the special fabrication of Pashto type for printing his work via "Gutenberg's blessing,"and the attempt to use special indicators such as capitalization, underlining, and red ink to enhance the meaning value for certain words ([1855] 1987: x; [1860a] 1982: xviii).

In these pages Raverty mentions the 17 years he spent studying nine Oriental languages, and provides concrete information about the financial incentives and rewards he received for his language studies ([1855] 1987: vii), while also lamenting that the debt he incurred in doing so "never brought advantage or advancement ([1860a] 1982: vii)." Raverty also comments on the ignorance of Pashto language examiners, offers only slightly veiled references to a competitor who beat him to the punch of receiving official endorsement for work on the Pashto language without having to undergo scrutiny by under-competent judges, and refers to the practice of subscription-based intellectual exercise on the Pashto language ([1855] 1987: viii–ix.).

ARCHIVAL GLEANINGS INTO THE MARKET FOR PASHTO LANGUAGE MATERIAL

The competency, density, and volume of Raverty's publications on Pashto distinguish him from other English-language interlocutors of the language, its speakers, and their environment.Unpublished archival sources reveal that Raverty's career involved a suspension without pay from his official duties on charges of bribery and corruption, and a series of petitions and appeals about the dismissal that appear to have culminated in his reinstatement to official colonial service in British India.[21] It is striking that Raverty experienced this tumult during the approximate five years between the publication of his monumental grammar and his dictionary of the Pashto language.These difficult experiences Raverty endured draw attention to a number of issues related to the marketing of Pashto and other vernacular language material in colonial India.[22]

The large-scale printing of Pashto language texts for market consumption began with William Carey and the Baptist

Missionary Press of Serampore, which issued a Pashto language Bible in 1818.[23] For both ideological and practical reasons a close working relationship developed between Jones' Asiatic Society and the Baptist Missionary Press that were and remain in very close proximity (the sites are a few blocks apart). However, it is clear from various published versions of the first volumes of *Asiatic Researches* that the printing of Pashto began earlier than 1818 and that Pashto printing was not fully monopolized by the Serampore Baptists. Raverty's comments about new Pashto types being specially cut for printing and publishing his grammar and dictionary speak to an evolving set of production technologies. His published comments also address the expense and debt generated during the production of his Pashto language materials and the trials and tribulations of marketing his work.

All of that published information is confirmed and elaborated upon in archival sources that reveal the considerable expense and intense competition surrounding the printing and marketing of Pashto language materials, both at the provincial and all-India level. Raverty's work incorporates 40 separate Pashto characters, each of which is identified in relation to multiple other characters and sounds in multiple other languages such as the perhaps obvious Chaldaic, Hebrew, Aramaic, Sumerian, Armenian, and Georgian, but also apparently less clearly relevant languages such as Phoenician, Manchu, Tibetan, and Albanian. In other words, Raverty's extreme commitment to Jones' philology made his work intellectually unique and valuable, but also very challenging and expensive to produce. In the end, Raverty's detailed consideration and treatment of the Pashto language in its own right and in relation to other languages was not easily or very well marketed, which gave rise to a series of incidents and communications that structure the archival narrative of his fiscal complaints and legal troubles.[24]

On the consumption side of his writings, Raverty's work on the Pashto language was certainly partially geared to academics and "Orientalists," but the major audience for his Pashto material was military and indeed Raverty explicitly marketed his writing to the military establishment. And it was the colonial military establishment that drew Raverty's wrath for its lack of appreciation and incorporation of his Pashto language work. The language exam system for colonial officers evolved considerably in the nineteenth century, as did the place of the Pashto language in that growing exam bureaucracy. Raverty's experiences indicate that competition was fierce for the considerable sums to be made for Pashto language materials that were successfully marketed within the context of official examinations. Raverty's work does not appear to have ever been featured in the official exam system. Instead, works authored by Vaughn (1854) before him, and subsequently Hughes and Plowden (1874), and later Roos-Keepel and Khan (1901), at least, were officially adopted or informally sanctioned as proper study and teaching aids for the colonial handling of Pashto.

Henry Walter Bellew was a contemporary of Raverty who was also vying to create space within the military exam bureaucracy for his version of the Pashto language and instructional materials for it. Bellew indicates the exams in colloquial Pashto were first held in January 1863 and carried a Rs. 500 reward if successfully completed ([1867] 1986: vii–viii). In 1865 that exam was "assimilated mutandis mutadis to the second standard Hindustani," and Bellew's grammar was explicitly structured with that exam format in mind ([1867] 1986:viii). Bellew demonstrates nowhere near the level of detailed command of Pashto or other languages as Raverty did, and also, unlike Raverty, Bellew viewed Pashto as a dialect of Sanskrit. Bellew wrote his Pashto grammar "somewhat on the model of Forbes' Hindustani Grammar" and based it upon the assumption that its user would already be familiar with Hindustani ([1867] 1986: ix). The Hindustani modeling made Bellew's Pashto grammar much more familiar and intelligible to colonial officialdom than Raverty's occasionally eccentric writings, and Bellew's use of only 20 characters for the Pashto language gave his work a substantially more simplified and manageable feel than that of Raverty.[25] Bellew and Raverty were contemporaries in the colonial engagement of Pashto, but in terms of intellectual depth as it relates to successful marketing of ideas they were worlds apart.

Raverty's work on the Pashto language and its speakers remains unsurpassed in terms of volume and a number of other positive academic qualities. The very characteristics that make his work so intellectually appealing made it very difficult to market in the context of colonial India and the physical and textual places being constructed therein for Afghans and Pashto. The foregoing has offered limited consideration of Raverty's Pashto language work within the narrowed contexts of Jones' philology, vernacular language printing, and colonial military examinations in nineteenth-century British India. There is clearly much more to learn from Raverty's life and work and many more ways and areas to do so, both inside and outside of India and the colonial context. Raverty's lessons most certainly apply to twentieth-century Afghanistan where government printing and engagement of the Pashto language structured a form of nationalism historically organized and marketed around the idea of Aryanism.[26] With that arena in mind, it is very good to think of the work of Thomas R. Trautmann and Sir William Jones as influencing future studies of Pashto, Aryanism, and pre-Islamic, non-Islamic, and Islamic Afghanistan, whether or not those prospective studies are conducted to further an explicit or implicit nationalist inquiry, and no matter how any single nation in Afghanistan is philologically situated in relation to other language/s and nation/s inside or outside of the country.

NOTES

1. Today speakers of Pashto (alternate spellings and transliterations of this word and language include but are not limited to Pashtu, Pakhto, Pakhtu, Pushto, Pushtu, Pukhto, Pukhtu, Paxto, Paxtu, Pashtoo, Pushtoo) are generally concentrated along the borderlands or frontier zone between contemporary Afghanistan and Pakistan,

but historically the language, particularly in printed form, has been situated in and relevant to the wider areas of north India or Hindustan. See Green 2008 for a useful discussion of Pashto in the Mughal period and during the transition to British rule. Green provides a tantalizing reference to the "emergence of a Pashto ecumene from the printing presses of Delhi and the Punjab in the nineteenth century" period that is the temporal context of this essay (2008: 205).

2. A selection of the most relevant works for the purposes of this essay include Raverty 1850, 1854, [1855] 1987, [1860a] 1982, 1860b, 1871, [1878] 1976, [1880b is there no 1880a?] 1978, 1881 (with Juzjani), 1894, and 1995. For additional pertinent Raverty writings see Edwards 2004 and Jan 2002.

3. While in Europe before coming to India in 1783 Jones gained competency in Persian, Arabic, Hebrew, Turkish, Greek, Latin, French, and German, at least (Trautmann 1998: 94–95). Jones was in fact commissioned by the King of Denmark to produce a French translation of Muhammad Mehdi Khan Astarabadi's Persian language history (see Astarabadi and Lockhart 1765–66) of Nadir Shah Afshar (ruled ca. 1729–47) that appeared in 1770. Once stationed in Bengal, but prior to turning their focus to Sanskrit and other Indian languages, Jones and the "new Orientalists" approached India through Persian (Trautmann 1998: 97) due to the prevalence of that language within the Mughal state structure, north Indian society, and the wider Indo-Persian world (including contemporary Afghanistan, Iran and large parts of Central Asia, at least) for at least the preceding five centuries. See Franklin 2004 for more on Jones.

4. For "Mosaic ethnology" see Trautmann 1998: 107 and *passim*. For India being made "safe to think" see Trautmann 1998: 99, 110. For India as "good to think" see Trautmann 1997: 61 (via Levi-Strauss 1963: 89).

5. Jasanoff 2005: 65–68, more broadly 63–71, and *passim*. As the Governor General, Hastings also commanded the Company archives and records at Fort William.

6. Ganda Singh addresses Ahmad Shah's communication with Vansittart ([1959] 1981: 374–76). See Singh 1959 for more on Ahmad Shah Durrani, Embree 2004 for Vansittart.

7. Vansittart and Jones [1790] 1979: 61. The Septuagint is in more specific terms the Koine Greek translation of the Old Testament that

was performed in Alexandria between the third and first centuries BC. Esdras is considered canonical by some Orthodox Christian communities, while most Jews, Catholics, and Protestants consider it to be apocryphal (see "Septuagint," in *Wikipedia, The Free Encyclopedia*, http://en.wikipedia.org/w/index.php?title=Septuagint&oldid=274534441 [accessed 4 March 2009]).

8. Vansittart and Jones [1790] 1979: 60. Jones' full statement on Vansittart's submission reads as follows: "This account of the *Afghans* may lead to a very interesting discovery. We learn from ESDRAS, that the ten tribes, after a wandering journey, came to a country called *Arsareth*; where, we may suppose, they settled: now the *Afghans* are said by the best *Persian* historians to be descended from the *Jews*; they have traditions among themselves of such as descent; and it is even asserted, that their families are distinguished by the names of *Jewish* tribes, although, since their conversion to *Islam*, they studiously conceal their origin; the *Pushto* language, of which I have seen a dictionary, has a manifest resemblance to the *Chaldaic*; and a considerable district under their dominion is called *Hazareh* or *Hazaret*, which might have easily been changed into the word used by ESDRAS. I strongly recommend an inquiry into the literature and history of the *Afghans*" (italicization and capitalization in the original).
9. See Hanifi 2008 for more on the economic and epistemological impact of British Indian colonialism of Afghanistan in the nineteenth century.
10. For Elphinstone, see Bayly 2004 and Elphinstone 1815; for Caroe, see Prior 2004 and Caroe 1957.
11. Elphinstone [1815] 1972: 2.251–52 and 2.205–8. A third edition of *An Account of the Kingdom of Caubul* was published in 1842.
12. The languages against which Elphinstone and his team compared Pashto words were "Persian, Zend, Pehlevee, Shanscrit, Hindostauneee, Arabic, Armenian, Georgian, Hebrew, and Chaldaic" (Elphinstone [1815] 1972: 2.251–52).
13. See Dorn and Allah 1829: xi–xv. Dorn appears comfortable with and critical of this challenging material and his extensive research led him to conclude "Oriental authors are mostly mere copyists of their sources," an unflattering but frank evaluation of the historical methodology giving rise to the texts he used (Dorn and Allah 1829:

x). Dorn identified inconsistencies in and between these manuscripts in question and noted 11 different referents in these texts for Afghans (Annotations to First Part of the *Makhzan-i Afghani*, Dorn and Allah 1829: 62–64). Beyond Afghan, Pashtun, and Pathan, these include Bani Israel, Rohilla, Sulaimani, al-Afghaniyatu, Bani Asif, Awghan, Aghwan, Aghban, and Bani Afghana (Dorn and Allah 1829: 62–64). Dorn also recognized that during hand copying of manuscripts writers could and did make mistakes as well as conscious alterations, whether for one or a combination of personal reasons, political patronage, or audience reception considerations. In the last instance Dorn determines that "we cannot with success maintain that the Afghans are descended from either the old Persians or the Indians" and that "Afghans are aborigines to their country" (Dorn and Allah 1829: 72). See also Raverty's comments on Dorn's *Chrestomathy* (Raverty [1855] 1987: 17 fn.).

14. Caroe [1957] 1983: 5–9; see page 8 for the Delhi lamp reference. See also Prior 2004 and Rittenberg 1988, chapters 8 and 9, for some details relating to Caroe's activities leading up to Partition and the creation of Pakistan in 1947.
15. Caroe [1957] 1983: 8–9. See chapter 1, pages 3–24, for more of Caroe's commentary on the written genealogies of Pashto language speakers that includes consideration of works authored and ideas proffered on the Jewish descent theory by Dorn, Elphinstone, and Raverty.
16. See Raverty [1860a] 1982: vi–xvi, with page vi having notice of the 'Bani Israel' phrase as a self-referent and page xii containing a concluding position statement. See also "Introduction" in Raverty [1855] 1987, especially pages 6–26, for the wealth of details mustered in support of this claim as well as a good panoramic scope of the large number of terms of indigenous textual sources and contemporary authorities then involved in this complex debate. Raverty uses a quote from Sir William Jones to introduce his own Introductory Remarks on his dictionary: "The gross errors of European writers on Asiatic literature have long since convinced me that no satisfactory account can be given of any nation with whose language we are not perfectly acquainted." This quote is not cited and as such reflects one of the primary systemic shortcomings in Raverty's copious footnotes that form a distinct parallel narrative with his main text when they appear.

17. See Edwards 2004 where it is noted about Raverty that "his frankness in controversy cost him many friends." To help balance the analytical scales it should be noted that in his dispensation of praise Raverty is also lavish, as in the wording used to convey adoption of Sir William Jones' orthographic (and transliteration) scheme. See Raverty [1860a] 1982: xvii.
18. Beyond Dorn and Elphinstone nineteenth-century authorities on Pashto include Leech (1838), Leach (1839), Vaughn (1854), Bellew (1867), Trumpp (1873), Hughes and Plowden (1874), Ahmad and Hughes (1882), and Darmester (1888). In addition to Caroe, Roos-Keppel and Khan (1901) is a noteworthy twentieth-century colonial authority on Pashto. Without providing full citations it is useful for readers to be aware of additional English language scholarship relating to the Pashto Language. Such material published in the US includes a substantial body of writings authored by Elena Bashir, Oscar Louis Chavarria-Aguilar, Wilma Heston, Herbert Paper (and D.A. Safeev), Herbert Penzl, Benedicte Grima Santry, Habibullah Tegey and Barbara Robson. Additional English-language writings on Pashto produced outside of the US include texts produced by V.V. Kushev, Q.A. Khaliq, D.N. MacKenzie, Georg Morgenstierne, Guljan Wror Wardak, and Christopher Shackle.
19. This introduction to Raverty's grammar was also published as "Some Remarks on the Origin of the Afghan People and Dialect and on the Connexion of the Pushto Language with the Zend and Pehlavi and the Hebrew" in the journal Jones established that was then titled the *Journal of the Asiatic Society of Bengal* (Raverty 1854).
20. See, for example, Raverty [1855] 1987: 1–2. *Annalistes* are practicioners of what is broadly termed the *annales* school of historiography personified by Fernand Braudel among others, including Lucien Febvre and Marc Bloch. Geography and geographical considerations are important components of Braudel's and the annalistes' work.
21. Archival files consulted in 1996 indicate Raverty's legal troubles began around the time his grammar was published in 1855 and ended near the 1860 date of his dictionary's publication. The files in question are entered under "Raverty, Lieut. H.G." in the Foreign Department Indices for the decades 1850–59 and 1860–69 at the National Archives of India, New Delhi. Consultation of these files was made possible by

funding provided by the Joint Committee on South Asia of the Social Science Research Council and the American Council of Learned Societies with funds provided by the Near and Middle East Research and Training Act, and the Council of American Overseas Research Centers in conjunction with the American Institute of Indian Studies and the American Institute of Pakistan Studies.

22. See Mantena 2005 and Mir 2006 who discuss the institutionalization of vernacular languages in Tamil Nadu and the Punjab, respectively. Mantena considers how Sir William Jones' philology imposed new progressive modernizing histories on Indian languages through a case study of the work of C.P. Brown on the Telugu language. See Mantena 2005: 523–28 for attention to the important role for dictionaries and grammars in that project. Mir considers the imposition of official language policy in the Punjab where the most apparent vernacular language of Punjabi was "displaced" by Urdu. See Mir 2006: 411–23 for consideration of the administrative rationales for using Urdu and a discussion of local printing, publishing, and information circulation in the Punjab. Mantena's work on Brown and the philology of Telugu and Mir's on colonial language policy in the Punjab combine to provide a number of useful points of comparison for more fully understanding Raverty's Pashto language-centered intellectual and professional biography.
23. See Carey 1818. See Priolkar and Rivara 1958: 356 for a plate containing a sample page from the Pashto New Testament published in Serampore in 1821. For additional information on Carey, the Baptist Missionary Press, and the printing of Bibles in many other Indian languages, see the website of the Center for the Study of the Life and Work of William Carey, and especially the sections "Works/ Bible Translations" (2008b) from the bibliography and on the Baptist Missionary Society (2008a).
24. There are at least two parallels between the material and social factors that contextualize the printing and marketing of books in early modern Europe and the production and consumption of vernacular language materials in colonial India. In both settings new printing technologies long co-existed with a lingering handwritten manuscript tradition, thus forming an incunabula era. See Eisenstein 1993: 3–41 for an analysis of the emergence of printing in Europe and incunabulum.

The high cost of book production in early modern Europe where paper constituted the largest expense within the printing process can be compared to the nineteenth-century Indian printing theatre where costs appear concentrated around the fonts and types used to print a wide variety of languages in indigenous scripts. See Febrve and Martin 1976: 29–43 and 109–15 for the introduction of paper to Europe and how it impacted the cost of book productions, respectively.

25. Compare Bellew's 20 Pashto characters (Bellew [1867] 1986: 3) to Ravety's 40 (Raverty [1855] 1987: 2–3). See Power 2004 for more on Bellew.
26. See Schinasi 1979: 143–44 for a brief history of the printing press in Afghanistan from roughly the 1870s till the second decade of the twentieth century. Schinasi offers the only existing monograph-length consideration of nationalism in Afghanistan, but James Caron at the University of Pennsylvania will soon complete a Ph.D. dissertation on the subject. See Gregorian's consideration of nationalism in Afghanistan in 1969: 206–26, and Tom Trautmann 1997 and 2005 for considerations of the Aryan idea.

REFERENCES

Ahmad, Mawlawi and Thomas Patrick Hughes. [1882] 1893. *Ganj-i-Pukhto, or, Pukhto Treasury: Being the Government Text-book for the Lower Standard of Examination in Pukhto, the Language of the Afghans*. London: S.H. Allen. Originally published in 1882.

Astarabadi, Muhammad Mehdi Khan. [1765–66] 1875. *Tarkikh-i Jahangusha-ye Nadari*. Bombay: Matb'a-I Haidari. Originally published in 1765–66.

Bayly, C.A. 2004. "Elphinstone, Mountstuart." *Oxford Dictionary of National Biography* 18: 323–26. Oxford: Oxford University Press.

Bellew, H.W. [1867] 1986. *Pushto Instructor: A Grammar of the Pukkhto of Pukshto Language, on a New and Improved System, Combining Brevity with Practical Utility, and Including Exercises and Dialogues, Intended to Facilitate the Acquisition of the Colloquial*. Peshawar: Saeed Book Bank & Subscription Agency. Originally published in 1867.

Carey, William.1818. *The Holy Bible, Containing the New Testaments. Volume V Containing the Old and New Testaments*. Serampore: Mission Press.

Caroe, Olaf Kirkpatick. [1957] 1983. *The Pathans, 550 BC–AD 1957*. Karachi: Oxford University Press. Originally published in 1957.

Center for Study of the Life and Work of William Carey, D.D. (1761–1834). 2008a. "Baptist Missionary Society."http://www.wmcarey.edu/carey/bms/bms.htm (Created 17 January 2001; updated 21 July 2008; accessed 4 March 2009.).

———. 2008b. "Works/ Bible Translations."http://www.wmcarey.edu/carey/bibles/translation.htm. (Created 20 December 2000; updated 12 November 2008; accessed 4 March 2009.).

Darmester, James. 1888. *Chants Populaires des Afghans*. Paris: Imprimerie Nationale, E. Leroux.

Dorn, Bernhard and Ni'mat Allah. 1829. *History of the Afghans: Translated from the Persian of Neamet Ullah, by Bernhard Dorn*. Oriental Translation Fund, London. Publications, 5.1–5.2. London: Printed for the Oriental Translation Committee, and sold by J. Murray [etc.].

———. [1847] 1982. *A Chrestomathy of the Pushtu of Afghan language: To Which is Subjoined a Glossary of Afghan and English*. Osnabruck: Biblio Verlag. Originally published in 1847.

Edwards, Edward. 2004. "Raverty, Henry George," rev. Schulyer Jones. *Oxford Dictionary of National Biography* 46: 132–33. Oxford: Oxford University Press.

Eisenstein, Elizabeth. 1993. *The Printing Revolution in Modern Europe*. New York: Cambridge University Press.

Elphinstone, Mountstuart. [1815] 1972. *An Account of the Kingdom of Caubul*. 2 vols. Karachi: Oxford University Press. Originally published in 1815.

Embree, Ainslee. 2004. "Vansittart, Henry." *Oxford Dictionary of National Biography* 56: 126–30. Oxford: Oxford University Press.

Febvre, Lucien and Henri-Jean Martin. 1976. *The Coming of the Book: The Impact of Printing 1450–1800*, ed. Geoffrey Nowell-Smith and David Wootton, trans. David Gerard. London: Verso.

Franklin, Michael J. 2004. "Jones, Sir William." *Oxford Dictionary of National Biography* 30: 665–74. Oxford: Oxford University Press.

Green, Nile. 2008. "Tribe, Diaspora, and Sainthood in Afghan History." *Journal of Asian Studies* 67: 171–211.

Gregorian, Vartan. 1969. *The Emergence of Modern Afghanistan*. Palo Alto: Stanford University Press.

Hanifi, Shah Mahmoud. 2008. *Connecting Histories in Afghanistan: Market Relations and State Formation on a Colonial Frontier*. New York: Columbia University Press. http://www.gutenberg-e.org/hanifi/index.html.

Hughes, Thomas Patrick, and T. C. Plowden. [1874] 1983. *Translation of the Kalíd-i-Afghání, The Text Book for the Pakkhto Examination, with Notes, Historical, Geographical, Grammatical, and Explanatory*. Lahore: Munshi Gulab Singh & Sons. Originally published in 1874.

Jan, Ali. 2002. "Ahmad Jan: Founder of Modern Pashto."*Sarhad Conservation Network*. http://www.geocities.com/scn_pk/ahmadjan.html. (accessed 4 March 2009).

Jasanoff, Maya. 2005. *Edge of Empire: Lives, Culture, and Conquest in the East, 1750–1850*. New York: Knopf.

Jones, Sir William. [1788] 1979. "The Third Anniversary Discourse." *Asiatic Researches* 1: 343–55.

Juzjani, Minhaj Siraj and H.G. Raverty. [1881] 1970. *Tabakat-i-Nasiri: A General History of the Muhammadan Dynasties of Asia, Including Hindustan; from A.H. 194 (810 AD) to A.H. 658 (1260 AD) and the Irruption of the Infidel Mughals into Islam*. New Delhi: Oriental Books Reprint Corp. Originally published in 1970.

Leach, R. 1839. "A Grammar of the Pashtoo, or Afghanee Language." *Journal of the Asiatic Society of Bengal* 8: 1–16.

Leech, R. 1838. "A Vocabulary of the Laghmani, Tirahi, Highlands of Deer, Moghal Aimaks Dialect." *Journal of the Asiatic Society of Bengal* 7: 780–87.

Levi-Strauss, Claude. 1963. *Totemism*. Boston: Beacon Press.

Lockhart, L. [1938] 1993. *Nadir Shah: A Critical Study Based Mainly Upon Contemporary Sources*. Jalandhar, India: Asian Publishers. Originally published in 1938.

Mantena, Rama Sundari. 2005. "Vernacular Futures: Colonial Philology and the Idea of History in Nineteenth Century South India." *Indian Economic and Social History Review* 42: 513–34.

Mir, Farina. 2006. "Imperial Policy, Provincial Practices: Colonial Language Policy in Nineteenth Century India."*Indian Economic and Social History Review* 43: 395–427.

The Oxford Dictionary of National Biogaphy. 1901-present. London: Oxford University Press (entries for Henry Walter Bellew, Sir Olaf Kirkpatrick

Caroe, Mountstuart Elphinstone, Sir William Jones, Henry George Raverty, and Henry Vansittart). Originally published in 1901.

Power, D'A. 2004. "Bellew, Henry Walter," rev. James Falkner. *Oxford Dictionary of National Biography* 5: 16–17. Oxford: Oxford University Press.

Priolkar, Anant Kakba, and Joaquim Heliodoro da Cunha Rivara. 1958. *The Printing Press in India, Its Beginnings and Early Development, Being a Quatercentenary Commemoration Study of the Advent of Printing in India in 1556*. Bombay: Marathi Samshodhana Mandala.

Prior, Katherine. 2004. "Caroe, Sir Olaf Kirkpatrick Kruuse." *Oxford Dictionary of National Biography*10: 198–99. Oxford: Oxford University Press.

Raverty, H.G. 1850. "An Account of the City and Province of Peshawur." *Transactions of the Bombay Geographical Society* 10: 1–47.

———. 1854. "Some Remarks on the Origin of the Afghan People and Dialect and on the Connexion of the Pushto Language with Zend and Pehlavi and the Hebrew." *Journal of the Asiatic Society of Bengal*: 550–88.

———. [1855] 1987. *A Grammar of the Puk'hto, Pus'hto, or Language of the Afghans*. New Delhi: UBS Publishers. Originally published in 1855.

———. [1860a] 1982. *A Dictionary of the Pukhto, Pushto, or, Language of the Afghans: With Remarks on the Originality of the Language and Its Affinity to the Semitic and Other Oriental Tongues, Etc. Etc*. Karachi: Indus Publishers. Originally published in 1860.

———. 1860b. *The Gulshan-i-roh: Being Selections, Prose, and Poetical, in the Pushto, or Afghan language*. London: Longman, Green, Longman, and Roberts.

———. [1862] 1981. *Selections from the Poetry of the Afghans: From the Sixteenth to the Nineteenth Century, Literally Translated from the Original Pushto; with Notices of the Different Authors, and Remarks on the Mystic Doctrine and Poetry of the Sufis*. Peshawar: De Chapzai. Originally published in 1862.

———. [1878] 1976. *Notes on Afghanistan and Parts of Baluchistan*. 2 vols. Quetta: Gosha-e-Adab. Originally published in 1878.

———. 1880a. *The Pus'hto Manual: Comprising a Concise Grammar; Exercises and Dialogues; Familiar Phrases, Proverbs, and Vocabulary*. London: W.H. Allen & Co.

———. [1880b] 1978. *Selections from Pushto Poetry*. Lahore: al-Biruni. Originally published in 1880.

Raverty, H.G. 1894. "The Independent Afghan or Patan Tribes." *Asiatic Quarterly Review* 7: 312–26.

———., ed. 1871. *The Fables of Aesop al-Hakim*. London: Williams and Norgate.

Raverty, H.G. and Ahmad Nabi Khan. 1995. *Ghaznin, and Its Environs: Geographical, Ethnographical and Historical: An Account Extracted from the Writings of the Little Known Afghan and Tajik Historians, Geographers and Genealogists*. Lahore: Sang-e-Meel.

Rittenberg, Stephen. 1988. *Ethnicity, Nationalism, and the Pakhtuns: The Independence Movement in India's North-West Frontier Province*. Durham: Carolina Academic Press.

Roos-Keppel, George and Abdul Ghani Khan. 1901. *A Manual of Pushtu*. London: Sampson Low, Marston & Co.

Sarhad Conservation Network. "Ahmad Jan: Founder of Modern Pushto Literature." http://www.geocities.com/scn_pk/ahmadjan.html. Accessed 28 February 2009.

Schinasi, May. 1979. *Afghanistan at the Beginning of the Twentieth Century: Nationalism and Journalism in Afghanistan; A Study of Seraj Ul-Akhbar (1911-1918)*. Naples: Instituto Universitario Orientale.

Singh, Ganda. [1959] 1981. *Ahmad Shah Durrani: Father of Modern Afghanistan*. Lahore: Tariq Publications. Originally published in 1959.

Trautmann, Thomas, R. 1995. "Indian Time, European Time." In *Time: Histories and Ethnologies*, ed. Diane Owen Hughes and Thomas Trautmann, 167–97. Ann Arbor: The University of Michigan Press.

———. 1997. *Aryans and British India*. Berkeley: University of California Press.

———. 1998. "The Lives of Sir William Jones." In *Sir William Jones 1746–1794 A Commemoration*, ed. Alexander Murray, 91–121. Oxford: Oxford University Press.

———, ed. 2005.*The Aryan Debate*. New Delhi: Oxford University Press.

Trumpp, Ernst. [1873] 1969. *Grammar of the Pasto or the Language of the Afghans, Compared with the Iranian and North-Indian Idioms*. London: Messrs. Trubner & Co. Originally published in 1873.

Vansittart, Henry and Sir William Jones. [1790] 1979. "On the Descent of the Afghans from the Jews." *Asiatic Researches Comprising History and Antiquities, the Arts, Sciences, and Literature of Asia* 2: 54–61.

Vaughn, Sir John L. 1854. *A Grammar and Vocabulary of the Pooshtoo Language: As Spoken in the Trans-Indus Territories under British Rule, etc.* Calcutta: Messrs. Thacker, Spink, and Co., and Messrs. R.C. Lepage and Co.

Wikipedia contributors. "Septuagint." In *Wikipedia, The Free Encyclopedia.* http://en.wikipedia.org/w/index.php?title=Septuagint&oldid=274534441 (accessed 4 March 2009).

5

Muslim Kinship in the Dravidian Heartland

Kinship Terminology and Close Kin Marriage among Urdu-speaking Nawayats

SYLVIA VATUK

This essay takes off from some brief remarks on Muslim kinship in South Asia that appear in the third chapter of Thomas Trautmann's 1981 *Dravidian Kinship*, a major contribution to scholarship in the field of the anthropological study of comparative kinship systems, those of South Asia in particular. This theoretically pioneering and impressively comprehensive work aims at "recovering the history of Dravidian kinship" systems in southern India (1981: 5), by tracing them back to a presumed ancestral source, an originary "Proto-Dravidian" system. Trautmann attempts to reconstruct the latter, not only by examining meticulously and comparing with one another the multitude of examples of Dravidian kinship systems described in the ethnographic literature, but also by seeking evidence of past kinship and marriage practices in a wide range of ancient Indian texts and inscriptions.

Trautmann's book deals almost exclusively with the kinship systems of south Indian Hindus. The only Muslims he discusses in any detail are the matrilineal Mappillas of Kerala, who, like others in that region, are speakers of Malayalam, a Dravidian language. Trautmann describes the Mappillas not in order to shed light on Muslim kinship, *per se*, but rather in order to help explain the "seemingly aberrant" system of their Hindu Nayar neighbors (1981: 168–71). The Mappillas and Nayars speak the same language and both trace descent through women. However, they have quite different kinship terminologies, marriage systems and post-marital residence patterns. Especially noteworthy is the fact that, whereas the Mappilla terminology is of the classic Dravidian type, the Nayar terminology lacks some of that system's key features, most notably the kinship category of "cross-cousin/potential spouse" that is so central an element of the Dravidian prescriptive marriage system.[1]

The only other mention of Muslim kinship in Trautmann's book occurs in an earlier chapter, where the author describes and analyzes the main features of the Indo-Aryan kinship system of north India, "explicating [its] interactions...along the overlapping frontiers" with the Dravidian systems, upon which, he maintains, it has exerted considerable "exogenous influence" during the past two millennia and more of South Asian history (1981: 91). Here one paragraph is devoted to comparing the kinship systems of north Indian Hindus with those of their Muslim neighbors (pp. 109–10). Trautmann notes that whereas the kinship terminologies employed by members of the two religious communities are almost identical, their marriage rules and gift-giving practices differ significantly. North Indian Hindus prohibit marriage among close consanguineal kin—whether related through the maternal or the paternal line—and also avoid "sibling exchange"—i.e., the marriage of a brother and sister from one family to a sister and brother from another. This latter avoidance is a corollary of the Hindu conception of marriage as a "gift of a virgin" to a worthy groom (*kanyādān*), according to which the relationship between two families linked by the marriage of their respective children is culturally constructed as an asymmetrical one. Those who have given a daughter in marriage are regarded as owing life-long deference to the family that has deigned to accept her.

One way in which this hierarchical relationship between bride-givers and bride-takers is expressed is through gift-giving and hospitality. Throughout their daughter's life and even after her death, the former are expected to keep up a continuous flow of unreciprocated ceremonial gifts to her, her husband, and her in-laws. The first and most substantial of these gift transfers is the so-called "dowry" (Hindi *dān-dahej*), which is handed over at the time of the wedding and usually consists of a combination of cash, clothing, jewelry, household goods and other items of value (see, for example, Vatuk 1975; Raheja 1988; Tambiah 1989; Roulet 1996). The prescribed gifts at later life-cycle rituals, at annual festival observances, and when individual members of the respective kindred encounter one another more informally are typically more modest in kind and quantity, but flow in the same direction. Even if the bride's kin are unable to be as lavish in their gift-giving as they would like (or may be expected) to be, they must, in order to maintain their self-respect, strictly avoid accepting any reciprocation from their daughter, her husband or her affines. In such a cultural context exchange marriage would clearly be problematic. By making it impossible to sustain a strictly unidirectional flow of gifts, such a marriage would confuse the important conceptual distinction between bride-giver and bride-taker.[2]

Trautmann uses the Hindi terminology employed by Hindus in UP (see Dumont 1962, 1966, 1973; Vatuk 1969, 1975, 1992) to exemplify the Indo-Aryan type. He demonstrates that this terminology and the above-cited north Indian Hindu marriage and ritual gift-giving practices are structurally consistent with one another. Thus, as he points out, Hindi speakers systematically distinguish consanguineal relatives from affines, paternal kin from maternal kin, sons' and brothers' children from daughters' and sisters' children, and so on. The only exception to this pattern occurs in the speaker's own generation, where cousins of all kinds are classified together and referred to with the same terms as siblings—in Hindi, *bhāī* and *bahen*, "brother" and "sister." This reflects the fact that among Hindus, cousins, like siblings, are strictly unmarriageable.

The Urdu kinship terminology used by north Indian Muslims (see Vreede-de Stuers 1963, 1968: 32–38; Ahmad 1977) is—except for a few minor lexical differences—identical to the Hindi terminology used by north Indian Hindus.[3] However, according to Trautmann, Muslim marriage preferences and patterns of gift exchange are very different from those of Hindus. Thus, he says, Muslims[4] display "a positive preference" for marrying cousins[5] and other close consanguineal relatives (cf. Das 1973). Instead of practising descent group exogamy, as Hindus do, they practise kin group endogamy. Furthermore, unlike Hindus, they freely engage in brother-sister exchange. Indeed, some north Indian Muslims display a positive preference for such arrangements.[6]

Trautmann also identifies differences in gift-giving patterns between the two religious communities. Among Muslims marriage gifts do not consistently flow from bride-givers to bride-takers. According to Islamic law (*sharī ʿat*), it is the groom, rather than the bride's parents, who is expected to make the major financial outlay at the time of marriage when he endows his new wife with a generous gift of cash or other valuables, called *mahr*. It is meant to remain her personal property, but Trautmann notes that it is sometimes taken by the bride's parents to help cover their share of the wedding expenses (1981: 109–10). In such cases it becomes transformed into what anthropologists often term "bride price" or "bride wealth," signifying a payment made by a man to his prospective bride's family in exchange for the right to affiliate her future offspring to his kin group and to compensate them for their loss of her company and labor power (cf. Goody and Tambiah 1973; Goody 1990).

There are other respects as well in which a *sharī ʿat*-based description of Islamic gift-giving rules fails to conform very closely to north Indian Muslim ethnographic realities. Islamic law does indeed require that, for a marriage to be valid, the amount to be paid as *mahr* must be noted in the marriage contract (*nikāhnāma).* But, at least in South Asia, the groom is not actually required or even expected to hand over this amount on the wedding day. It is much more usual for the officiating cleric to simply enter the *mahr* amount into the marriage contract with a note indicating that its payment is "deferred" (Arabic *muwajjal*) to some unspecified future date.[7] Again, according to Islamic law, the *mahr*, if not already paid, immediately falls due. However, divorcing husbands in India manage, more often than not, to avoid making good on this obligation. Consequently, relatively few Muslim women actually ever receive the promised amount (see Vatuk 2005).[8]

Despite its Hindu origins, the custom of giving a generous "dowry" (*jahez*) when a daughter marries is also very prevalent among South Asian Muslims. It has indeed become increasingly widespread in recent years, notwithstanding the strenuous efforts of reformist critics, who argue that, as an "un-Islamic" custom, it should be strictly avoided by devout Muslims (see Vatuk 2007). In short, while at the level of religious conceptions and prescriptions South Asian Muslims and Hindus indeed have divergent gift-giving patterns, in *practice* the differences between them are slight.

Trautmann explains the differences he observes between Hindu and Muslim marriage and kinship transactional systems in historical terms: "The Muslim culture of kinship," he says, "is in origin the Arabian kinship system as revised and disseminated by Islam" (1981: 109). While one can certainly find some support for this claim in the marriage preferences and prohibitions of Urdu-speaking Muslims—or at least in those of the upper classes—it is of questionable applicability to their kinship terminology. Urdu kinship terms show very little Arabic influence and, furthermore, the two terminological systems are structurally quite different from one another.

Arabic kinship terminology[9] is of a fairly unusual type, in which each of the primary relatives (father, mother, brother, sister, son, daughter) is accorded a unique term, while second- and higher-order kin are designated by combining two or more of these basic terms into a descriptive phrase, equivalent to the English "father's brother," "mother's sister's son," "brother's son's son," and so forth (see Davies 1949 for a Syrian Arabic example).[10] A man's sisters—with whom marriage or sexual contact of any kind would be highly incestuous—are thus clearly distinguished terminologically from his female cousins, who are considered to be highly suitable potential mates.

A preference for marrying close relatives, especially cousins, along with a tolerance—if not a positive preference—for direct exchange marriages, is characteristic of Muslim societies, not only in the Indian subcontinent (Vreede-de Stuers 1968; Das 1973; Jeffery 1979; Pastner 1979, 1981; Donnan 1988; Alvi 2007), but also throughout much of the Middle East (see, for example, Bourdieu 1977: 30–72; Holy 1989, Gingrich 1995), though neither is explicitly prescribed by the Muslim religion.[11] The various Muslim groups that began coming to the subcontinent as early as the seventh century AD doubtless brought these marriage preferences with them. Once settled in India they continued to adhere to Islamic law, insofar as the prohibited degrees of relationship for purposes of marriage are concerned, and persisted in preferring to marry close relatives outside of those prohibited degrees. But they did not retain the Arabic kinship terminology in the diaspora. This should not surprise us, if we remember that most of the Muslims who came into India via the northern, land route did not even come from Arabia and few were native speakers of Arabic.[12] Some spoke Pashto, some (like the Mughals) spoke Turkish or another Central Asian language, others spoke Farsi (Persian), which early on became the dominant literary and administrative medium of communication in the region (see Alam 1998). The kinship terminologies employed by speakers of these languages differ in structure from those of both Urdu and Arabic, though, like the latter—and unlike Urdu—they all make a linguistic distinction between siblings and cousins (for Turkish see, for example, Casson 1974).

It is not possible to say how long it took for the descendants of the various waves of Muslim immigrants to India to begin using an indigenous north Indian system of classifying relatives. But the transition probably began to occur quite soon after each set of incoming migrants arrived and began to learn and use the local spoken language. Males certainly predominated among the newcomers and before long they would have begun setting up households and raising children with local Indo-Aryan language-speaking women, who in most cases would have passed their own languages and modes of classifying relatives on to the next generation. Over time, the conversion of significant numbers of Hindus to Islam would have further contributed to the formation of a Muslim community within which the dominant spoken languages and the kinship terminologies employed were of the Indo-Aryan type, notwithstanding the fact that they conflicted, at least on a conceptual level, with the incoming male migrants' preference for marrying their children to cousins or other close kin.

The rather striking incompatibility between Indian Muslim kinship terminology and marriage rules raises some intriguing questions. The more general issue of the relationship between terminology and marriage patterns has preoccupied several generations of anthropologists. It was indeed of central concern to Lewis Henry Morgan, one of our most important scholarly ancestors, whose life and accomplishments are the subject of another of Trautmann's notable works of scholarship (1987). Morgan(1871) based his comprehensive and influential theory of the evolution of the family upon the premise that kinship terminologies directly reflect *past* marriage patterns and hence provide concrete evidence of *prior* family forms. This notion is no longer widely accepted by anthropologists, but most would nevertheless agree that, while one cannot state it as an invariable rule, there is a notable tendency for the kinship terminology used by speakers of a given language to be largely compatible with their *present* marriage rules, preferences, practices and family forms (for a classic statement of this principle see Radcliffe-Brown 1941). This is clearly one of the underlying assumptions of Trautmann's *Dravidian Kinship* project, just as it was for those who preceded and those who followed him in trying to comprehend how south Indian kinship systems operate. The Dravidian case presents one of the clearest demonstrations of the theory's validity,[13] the north Indian Muslim kinship system, on the other hand, is an obvious exception to it.

In his own discussion of Indo-Aryan kinship terminology and north Indian Muslims, Trautmann does not comment on this anomaly nor, beyond asserting the Arab origins of north Indian Muslim marriage patterns, does he try to reconstruct the historical processes that underlay the formation of their present terminological and kinship structures. Though I do not feel competent to take on either of these tasks myself, my musings on the matter may nevertheless be of some interest to Trautmann, if I am correct in assuming that despite moving on over the past 25 or so years to more weighty historical matters, he has not totally renounced his earlier incarnation as one of our leading scholars of South Asian kinship!

I will offer here some ethnographic observations on this matter of Muslim marriage preferences and kinship terminology, based on many years of research among a Muslim community (*qaum*) that has long resided in one of Trautmann's old stamping grounds, the town of Madras, now Chennai, in Tamil Nadu. The Nawayats are Sunni Muslims who follow the Shafi'i school of Islamic law, rather than the Hanafi school to which most other South Asian Muslims adhere. They trace their descent from Arabs who came across the Indian Ocean by sea, perhaps as early as the eighth century AD, in order, as they say, "to trade and spread the word of Islam." Their ancestors first settled on the southwest coast of India, near Goa, but in subsequent generations many moved on to other parts of south India. Nawayats were prominent—at least from the fifteenth century onward—in the service of various Muslim rulers of the Deccan. It is one consequence of that association that they long ago—we know not when—adopted the south Indian (Deccani) dialect of Urdu as their mother tongue.

Several generations of ancestors of the extended family (*khāndān*) with which I am concerned here had been employed in various civil and religious capacities in the Bijapur court. Some later moved to Arcot (in present-day Tamil Nadu), to serve under Muhammad Ali Walajah, Nawab of the Carnatic.[14] The *khāndān's* founding ancestor, a man whom I will call Ghulam Mahmud, was born there in the mid-eighteenth century. He excelled in his studies and eventually secured an appointment as tutor to one of the Nawab's grandsons. In 1801 the British found reason to annex the Carnatic territory and, when the rightful heir rejected their conditions, installed Ghulam Mahmud's pupil, his paternal first cousin, on the *masnad* (throne). The new Nawab asked Ghulam Mahmud to come to Madras as his Diwan (prime minister). He served in this position for several years and when he died his sons and sons-in-law also received court appointments. Several of his elder grandsons found employment under successive Nawabs.

But when in 1855 the British refused to recognize an heir to the most recently deceased occupant of the *masnad*, the men of Ghulam Mahmud's *khāndān* were forced to find other sources of income. Several moved to Hyderabad to work in the Nizam's administration, establishing a new branch of the *khāndān* in that city. When India became independent from Britain in 1947, a number of men and later a few entire families migrated to Pakistan. More recently others have found jobs in Saudi Arabia and the Persian Gulf or have emigrated to Britain or North America. Today Ghulam Mahmud's descendants, now probably numbering over 2000 persons, are to be found, not only in their home cities of Chennai and Hyderabad, but in many other places around the world as well.

The kinship terminology used by these Nawayats is almost identical to that used by Urdu-speaking Muslims in north India.[15] As among most South Asian Muslims who are not of recent convert origin, eligibility for marriage is determined strictly in accordance with Islamic law, based on a two-fold classification of members of the opposite sex into the categories *mahram* and *nāmahram* (from the Arabic root *h-r-m*, meaning "sacred" or "forbidden"). The significance of these kinship categories lies in customary patterns of the gendered allocation of space. *Mahram* are the only men with whom a respectable, religiously observant Muslim woman may freely associate, the only men who may enter her private and sacred female living quarters or before whom she may appear unveiled. They are allowed these privileges because their relationship to her is such that they could under no circumstances marry (or have sexual relations with) her.[16]

The chief members of the *mahram* category—from a woman's point of view—are her father, her grandfathers (and their male ascendants), her brothers, sons, grandsons (and their male descendants), her parents' brothers and her siblings' sons (and their male descendants). Once a woman marries, her husband and his male relatives of the corresponding categories become *mahram* to her as well.[17] Also counted among her *mahram* are the male relatives of any woman (whether relative or hired wet-nurse) who breast fed her when she was an infant, as well as any other man who was ever nursed by that woman.[18]

The *nāmahram* category is the much larger, residual one, encompassing all other persons of the opposite sex, strangers as well as relatives. It is from among some small, carefully delimited segment of her *nāmahram* that a husband will be sought for her. Her father's brother's son or some other first cousin is often regarded as the ideal choice, but she may instead marry some other close *nāmahram* relative or even a non-relative from a family known to be of a social status equivalent to or higher than her own.

Scholars who have discussed social stratification among South Asian Muslims have often drawn attention to Islam's "egalitarian" ideology, while failing to note the importance that Islamic law places on ensuring that husband and wife are of equal social rank. In Arabic this principle of status equality is known as *al kafā'afī zowāj* (literally, the "equality/similarity of the couple"): i.e., a woman may be married only to a man whose social status is equal or superior to her own. According to Shafi'i law, the principal criteria of *kafā'a* are descent, freedom (i.e., a free woman should not be married to a slave), and religion (a Muslim woman should not be married to a non-Muslim or to one whose ancestors converted to Islam more recently than hers). The occupations of the groom and the bride's father may also be considered in judging whether the prospective spouses are "similar" or not. This is not simply a matter of social preference. According to *sharī'at* (Islamic law), if two persons marry and are later found to be of unequal status, their union can be invalidated (see Ziadeh 1957).

Although today it is no longer unheard of for a young woman or man of this *khāndān* to marry a non-relative, in the past, exclusivity in marriage played a key role in maintaining the family's sense of group-belonging and -boundedness. True similarity of the Muslim couple can be fully assured only if the marriage has joined two people who are either consanguineal relatives or belong to families that have had previous marital connections in the past. In written documents from this family's archives, the expressions *ham kaf*, "of the same *kaf*," and *g͟hair kaf*, "of outside *kaf*," are often used when discussing marital alliances, whether contemplated or already contracted. But in ordinary speech, rather than employ the somewhat literary Arabic-derived word, family members are more likely to describe such marriages as having taken place "within the family" (*khāndānmẽ*), "within our own family" (*apne khāndān mẽ*, *apnī'ashira mẽ*) or "among ourselves" (*āpas mẽ*). Or they may use the adjective *zātī*, which means "one's own," as in the phrase *zātī laṛkā*, "one of our own boys," to indicate a young man of their own *khāndān*.

As these expressions suggest, notwithstanding the presence of a patrilineal ideology that manifests itself in certain contexts—for example, in the way in which family historians present their ancestral genealogies—the kinship universe for these people is ordered conceptually in terms of degrees of closeness, with no clear distinction being made, in most situations, between kinship links traced through women and those traced through men. Such a structure is typical of bilateral kinship systems and corresponds closely to what has been described by ethnographers of a number of Muslim societies in the Middle East, North Africa, Afghanistan and Pakistan (e.g., Pastner 1979, 1981).

When discussing their marriage preferences the Nawayats never say—if speaking in Urdu—that they marry their cousins. This is not surprising, since they have no word for cousin that is separate from their words for brother and sister.[19] And, given the unbreachable barrier to sexual relations between siblings, they could obviously not describe themselves as marrying their brothers and sisters! But, all other things being equal, the closer the relationship the more suitable the match is considered to be and no relative is closer than the first cousin. In the literature on kin marriage among Arabs, and Muslims more generally, there tends to be a preoccupation with the notion that in these societies the most desirable match is between a man and his father's brother's daughter—the patrilateral parallel cousin Much anthropological ink has been spilled in efforts to understand the reasons for this preference and to determine whether and to what extent it is actualized in practice (see, for example, Holy 1989; Bourdieu 1977). Among Nawayats I have heard it said that it is reasonable for a man seeking a wife for his son to first consider his own brother's daughter. Another way of phrasing this is that brothers have a special obligation to one another with regard to the marriages of their respective offspring. It is not at all clear, however, that this is conceived of in terms of the "right" of a young man to be given his *cacāzād bahen* (father's brother's daughter) in marriage, as has been reported by ethnographers working in various Middle Eastern societies. If anything, among Nawayats the notion of "duty" goes the other way. That is, there seems to be some feeling that a young man ought to marry his father's brother's daughter—especially if she does not have other suitors—in order to avoid the possibility that she will remain unmarried or that her marriage will be unduly delayed. The notion that it is incumbent upon the parents of sons to see that the daughters of their close kin are suitably married before seeking elsewhere for a daughter-in-law is even generalized beyond the set of brothers. In the 1980s and 1990s I heard this argument made explicitly in connection with discussions about the pros and cons of what was perceived as a growing tendency for young men of the *khāndān* to express a preference for "outsider" (*ghair khāndān*) women over cousins or other close kinswomen, when brides were being sought for them.

Family members often employ the related concepts of blood purity and purity of pedigree to justify their endogamous preferences and practices. "Marrying among ourselves" is sometimes said to be desirable specifically because it enables the family to "maintain the blood" (*khūn bāqī rakhnā, khūn qāim rakhnā*) or "preserve the pedigree" (*nasab ko mahfūz rakhnā*). The word *khālis* ("pure, unmixed") is sometimes used to characterize the lineage of a person whose ancestors have always observed strict endogamy. With the blood are said to be transmitted "qualities" (*khassiat, khisāl*) that can be lost or diluted through admixture with the blood of outsiders. Among the many good qualities believed to be possessed by their own lineage are moral ones (such as honesty, simplicity, religiosity, and self-respect), abilities (such as intellectual prowess), and physical traits (such as fair skin and tall, thin stature).

Genealogical data from the *khāndān* are consistent with more recent ethnographic and biographical evidence suggesting that in the past marital alliances often reflected arrangements between siblings or first cousins to join their respective children in marriage or, depending upon their relative ages, marry the child of one to the grandchild of the other. These agreements were often made when the two (or at least the female of the pair) were infants or very young children. This practice of child engagement was referred to by the term *bol denā*, "to speak [for]" a girl as a future bride for one's son. The agreement might be very informal, but it was sometimes marked by a brief engagement ritual. The wedding itself did not take place until the bride had at least reached puberty and was often delayed for a few years beyond this. However, already by the 1950s child engagement had become unusual. Nowadays matches are typically finalized only a year or so before, or even closer to, the wedding. Girls rarely marry before the age of 18. As in the past, their grooms are almost invariably even older, sometimes by as much as 10 or more years. There are a number of reasons for these changes in age at marriage that I do not have space to go into here.

URDU KINSHIP TERMINOLOGY AND MARRIAGE RULES

Now I will briefly raise two questions related to the apparent incompatibility between Nawayat kinship terminology and marriage rules and preferences: these would apply equally to upper-class Urdu-speaking Muslims in north India. The first question is an historical one: how did this situation come about and when? Unfortunately, in the absence of the kind of historical and linguistic research that might provide a definitive answer, one can only speculate. There is good historical evidence for the Nawayats' claim to Arab ancestry, something that distinguishes them from most north Indian Muslims. It also distinguishes them from other Urdu-speaking Muslims of southern India, locally referred to as Deccani Muslims or Pattani, who trace their origins to migrants who came into the region more recently from the north. The Nawayats have clearly retained Islamic kinship concepts, rules and preferences concerning mate selection ever since their ancestors' arrival by sea on the southwestern coast of India. It is not known when they ceased speaking Arabic at home and adopted the local languages of the areas in which they settled. Most other south Indian Muslims who claim Arab ancestry—the Mapillas, Labbais, Marrakaiyar and so on—now speak Dravidian languages,[20] but, as far as one can determine from the limited information that is available, the mother tongue of most, if not all, Nawayats is one or another Indo-Aryan language: Urdu in the case of some, Konkani or Marathi in the case of others. The shift in mother tongue was evidently accompanied by the abandonment of the Arabic-type kinship terminology and its replacement with an Indo-Aryan one, even though the new terminology was poorly suited to properly reflect their longstanding marriage patterns and preferences.

Victor D'Souza has carried out ethnographic research and has written at some length about the Nawayats of the Dharwar region in the Kanara district of Karnataka, a group that he distinguishes from those he calls "Nawayats of the Deccan," whom I have been discussing here. The Dharwar Nawayats speak the Konkani language and their kinship terminology is almost identical in structure—though not in vocabulary—to the Urdu one (D'Souza 1953:97–107, 212–15; cf. Karve 1939–41). Consistent with what I have hypothesized above, D'Souza says that the Arab seafarers from whom the Nawayats are descended brought few if any women with them to India and therefore took local women as wives or concubines. Even after settling in the subcontinent, in their occupation as traveling merchants they spent much time away from home, leaving their wives behind to raise the children. The local language and kinship terminology were therefore transmitted from mother to child, while the fathers—who presumably controlled the arrangement of marriages for their offspring—continued to adhere to the close kin marriage preferences they had brought with them from the Middle East (1953:31, 58–59). Such an explanation sounds reasonable, though we cannot document it. D'Souza's theory, incidentally, would probably be hotly rejected by many of Ghulam Mahmud's descendants, as well as by other Nawayats of the Deccanwho, by and large, reject the notion that their male ancestors intermarried with the indigenous population after arriving in India. They contend that their forebears were accompanied on their migration by their wives and families and have reproduced themselves in the intervening centuries by adhering strictly to endogamous marriage practices (see, for example, Wila 1976).

The second question to be raised is: what conceptual and practical issues, if any, arise as a result of the apparent incompatibility between Urdu kinship terminology and a Muslim preference for close kin marriage? And if there are any such issues, how are they dealt with?[21] One area in which one might expect this incompatibility to present itself is when cousins or close relatives who are married to one another refer to or address the spouse or one of his or her family members. I have observed that a woman who has married her cousin—someone whom she previously addressed as *bhāī sahib, bhayyā* or *bhāījān* ("elder brother")—or by his given name with the appropriate kinship affix (e.g., "Ahmad-*bhāī*"),[22] now ceases to use those terms for him. Instead, she begins referring to and addressing him by teknonymy, that is, either according to his relationship to the person to whom she is speaking—thus "your brother" (*tumhāre bhāī*), "your father," "your father's brother" and so on—or according to his relationship to some other person, most commonly (once she has become a mother) one of their children—thus "Hamid's father" (*hāmid ke abbā, hāmid ke vālid*). If the context is clear, she may simply use a third person pronoun, *vo* ("he"), or the more polite third person plural *āp* ("he" or, in address, "you"). But this kind of circumlocution is in any case usual for a married woman, whether she is married to a cousin or not. As a matter of deference, a wife does not customarily speak her husband's name aloud, either in reference or address. Only when speaking about him to someone who is not related to or intimate with the family, might she say "my husband" (*mere shohar*).

While the Urdu terminology has more than one word for "wife" (*bībī* or the more respectful *ahlīya*, for example) men usually avoid using such terms to refer to their *own* wives, especially when speaking to outsiders. They usually prefer instead an expression like *ghar mẽ*, literally "[the one] in the house." In address they may use their wives' names but often use teknonymy instead, just as their wives do when addressing them. Men of the younger generation may use their wife's given name in address and sometimes even in reference. As for relatives by marriage, both spouses generally continue to use the same terms that they used before the marriage, rather than using the affinal terms that are available in the terminology, unless they are speaking to outsiders. So, for example, if a woman has married her father's sister's son, she will continue to refer to and address her husband's mother as *phūphī* ("father"s sister"), rather than calling her *khushdāman* ("mother-in-law"). She will call her husband's elder sisters *āpā* ("elder sister") rather than *nanand* ("husband's sister").[23] Likewise, her husband will continue to refer to and address *her* mother as *mumānī* ("mother's brother's wife"), just as he did before the marriage. In short, following the marriage of cousins or other close relatives, there is usually no rearrangement of the kinship terms used, except between the married couple themselves.

Another aspect of this question relates to the emotional aspect of the marriage preference itself. When young people are brought up in close proximity to their cousins and are taught not only to call them by "brother" and "sister" terms but to treat them in most respects as they do their "real" or "true" siblings, how do they readjust their way of relating to one another once they become aware that they may eventually become husband and wife? There is an entire anthropological literature that is relevant here, which centers on the question of the origin of the incest taboo. The dominant thrust of the received wisdom on this question is often summed up in the phrase "familiarity breeds contempt," credited to the nineteenth-century Swedish sociologist, Edvard Westermarck. His thesis was that if young people are raised in close proximity, as siblings are, they will not feel sexually attracted to one another when they grow up. A number of anthropologists have tried to test this hypothesis—for example, in relation to living arrangements in the old-style Israeli kibbutz and in some parts of China, where it was a longstanding custom to buy or adopt a baby girl and raise her alongside one's son until the two were old enough to be married. They have found that in these situations the young people involved commonly develop an aversion to the idea of engaging in sexual relations with one another and, if compelled to marry, generally fail to have a happy and sexually fulfilling marital life (see Wolf 1995: 1–19 for a summary review of the relevant literature).

The situation in the Muslim family I am discussing here is not precisely analogous comparable to that in cultures described by the ethnographers who have used their observations to lend support to Westermarck's thesis. While cousins of the opposite sex are indeed referred to and, if older, are addressed by sibling terms, they are made very aware from an early age that their relationship is different from that of "real" (*sage*) siblings and that they may one day become husband and wife. If they are living in the same household, older family members are careful to ensure that, beginning at least from the time the girl is approaching adolescence, the two are given no opportunity to become intimate with one another. Even in small homes there is a recognized gendered division of space. The *mardāna*, or men's area, may be just a single room, situated near the front entrance to the house, which also serves as a place to receive and entertain guests. Women may use this room when no outsiders are present, but most of the time they and their children occupy the *zanāna*, typically an open courtyard with one or more rooms on the side or at the rear and usually with a separate entrance. At least by their early teens, boys begin spending most of their time away from the house—just as their fathers and older brothers do. When they are at home or at a relative's home where female cousins are living or visiting, they will normally be expected to stay out of the so-called "ladies"[24] portion of the house, at least until any young unmarried women who are present have been given the opportunity to retreat into an inner room. Marriageable young people living in the same household cannot of course entirely avoid encountering one another on a daily basis. But they are expected to keep one another at a respectful distance and certainly to avoid conversing privately or spending time alone together.

The ostensible reason for these customary avoidances is to prevent the possibility that marriageable relatives of the opposite sex might become attracted to or even romantically involved with one another before the parents have had the opportunity to choose someone whom they may regard as a more suitable partner. But harking back to the literature referred to above, it may be hypothesized that this separation of opposite sex cousins serves another—though perhaps unintended—purpose, namely to guard against the possibility that potentially marriageable relatives may become as familiar with one another as real siblings, in a non-sexual way. Then, if the time should come for them to be married, one or both might be unwilling or unable to switch over from the sibling to the spousal role and the marriage would not be a successful one. Unfortunately, I do not have the kind of intimate data that would allow me to take a position either one way or the other on this matter.

In any event, despite parental efforts to minimize the opportunities for their marriageable offspring to meet and interact, attractions between cousins do sometimes develop. In some cases, once the parents are made aware of the situation, they allow the two to marry. But in family lore there are several instances of young people who would have liked to marry but could not, because, for whatever reasons, one or both sets of parents insisted on marrying their child to someone else.

I have only been able to touch on a few of the issues raised by Trautmann's brief remarks about Muslim kinship in the Indo-Aryan belt and to raise some questions about the relationship between kinship terminology and marriage patterns in a Muslim community in southern India whose kinship system closely resembles that of their north Indian co-religionists. Clearly more ethnographic research is needed in order to answer these questions definitively. When Trautmann was working on his study of Dravidian kinship systems and chose to take a small detour into those of the Indo-Aryan north, published ethnographic accounts of marriage and kinship organization among Indian Muslims were scarce. And regrettably, in the almost 30 years that have passed since then, only a few more studies of this kind have become available.[25] Hopefully this ethnographic lacuna will one day be filled, so that another scholar, following in Trautmann's footsteps, will be able to examine Indian Muslim kinship systems in the same breadth and depth which Trautmann has devoted to the Dravidian ones. Such a project would be a most valuable tribute to his legacy.

NOTES

1. Trautmann shows that the Nayar terminology does not have any terms for relatives of the father and indeed "recognize[s] very few relationships outside the matrilineage and its spouses." He accounts for this in terms of "the transitory character of Nayar [*sambandham*] marriage" (1981:171) and concludes that, for this reason, the Nayar system "cannot be put into a Dravidian paradigm without seriously misrepresenting its character" (1981: 170, 208–14).
2. One way to avail oneself of the money-saving attractions of exchange marriage, without disturbing the bride-giver/bride-taker distinction, is by means of an indirect, three-way, exchange. In this arrangement, family A gives a bride to family B, which gives a bride to family C, which in turn gives a bride to family A. Affinal gifts still flow in the prescribed direction but the givers can count on getting back—from those whose bride they have received—an amount equivalent to what they gave to the family that took *their* daughter. Such arrangements, while rare among Brahmans in north India, are not uncommon among Hindu castes of middle and low rank.
3. For example, in Urdu the mother's brother is *māmā* rather than *māmā*, the father's younger brother is *cacā* rather than *cācā*. Some terms are entirely different: *e.g.*, mother's sister (Hindi *mausī*) is called by the (Arabic-derived) term *khālā*, the son-in-law (Hindi *jamāī*) by the (Persian) *dāmād* and the elder sister (Hindi *baṛī bahen—SV: didi?*) by the term *āpā*, which came into Persian from the Turkish and thence into Urdu. (See Ahmad [1977] for the etymology of these

and other Muslim kinship terms used by speakers of Urdu and other Indo-Aryan languages).

4. Note that his description of Muslim marriage preferences applies specifically to the so-called *āshraf*, those of superior social strata, who typically claim foreign rather than convert ancestry. The latter tend to follow the same rules of kin-group and village exogamy that their Hindu ancestors did before they converted to Islam.
5. Trautmann cautions that this preference is very different from the Dravidian one, inasmuch as north Indian Muslims consider *all* categories of cousins equally marriageable, while in the Dravidian system only the cross-cousins (mother's brother's daughter and/or father's sister's daughter) can be taken in marriage. Indeed, as I have noted, neither the Hindi nor the Urdu kinship terminologies even recognize the distinction between cross and parallel cousins that is so fundamental a feature of Dravidian kinship (Trautmann 1981: 109–10).
6. Such marriages are, for example, greatly favored both in theory and in practice by Punjabi-speaking Muslims in Pakistan (see Eglar 1960; Alvi 2007).
7. This is the case among Sunnis, the dominant sect in South Asia. In Shi'a marriages the *mahr* is more likely to be paid at the time of marriage.
8. The unpaid *mahr* also becomes a legal charge against the estate of a man who dies leaving a surviving widow. It is supposed to be paid out to her before the heirs are given their shares of the assets he has left behind. But in India the vast majority of widows waive—whether voluntarily or at the insistence of their in-laws—their right to claim it.
9. The Arabic language, in a variety of dialectical forms, is spoken throughout North Africa and the Middle East, not only by Muslims but also by Christians and adherents of other minority religions in the region. But, despite considerable linguistic variation, the basic structural features of the kinship terminology as I describe it here are fairly uniform throughout the Arabic-speaking world.
10. The only exception to this "descriptive" pattern is found in the terms for grandparents: i.e., Arabic has only one term for grandfather and another for grandmother. When necessary, the paternal and maternal grandparents can be distinguished from one another (just as they can

be in English) by means of a descriptive phrase: "father's father" and "mother's father."

11. Indeed many non-Muslims indigenous to the region share the same marriage preferences.
12. Large numbers of Arabs, mostly sea-faring merchants, did settle along the southern coasts of the subcontinent, beginning even before and continuing after the advent of Islam. Most of their descendants, like the Mappillas mentioned above, today speak languages belonging to the Dravidian family and follow Dravidian-type patterns of marriage and kinship classification. On the other hand, the Nawayats, who have similar origins and whom I discuss in some detail later in this paper, speak Urdu and have a kinship system very similar to that of upper-class north Indian Muslims.
13. Even in such a system, inconsistencies may occasionally arise when real people go about making real marriages. Someone, for example, may wish to arrange a son's or daughter's marriage with a person of the "wrong" terminological category. Thus Trautmann gives some examples of marriages between two distantly related persons who are classificatory brother and sister to one another, in which the solution was to find a roundabout way to reclassify them as cross-cousins, thus transforming a prohibited match into a perfectly appropriate one. I have written about a similar kind of manipulation, practised occasionally by north Indian Hindus in order to make possible the marriage of a man and woman sharing putative descent from a common ancestor, as members of the same patrilineal clan (*gotrā*) which in the Indo-Aryan Hindu marriage system is strictly exogamous. The solution is to make the bride into the fictive daughter of her mother's brother and then having him marry her—as they say—"from his *gotrā*" (Vatuk 1970).
14. Ghulam Mahmud's descendants use no common surname, nor is there any proper name by which they are collectively known. When they refer to themselves as a group they simply speak of "our family" (*hamārā khāndān*).
15. There are a few minor lexical differences, but the structure of the terminology is the same.
16. An underlying assumption of these rules is that when one is in the presence of a person of the opposite sex who is potentially

marriageable, there is a strong likelihood of being overcome by sexual desire and even impelled to act upon it. It is considered unthinkable, on the other hand, if the two are related in such a way that marriage between them is forbidden, that erotic feelings could possibly arise.

17. The bar to marriage with these people lasts only as long as one's marriage remains intact. They are distinguished from other *mahram* by the expression *nazar kā mahram*, from *nazar*, literally "sight" or "view."
18. This is called a "milk relationship", *dūdh kā rishta* (Arabic *ridā'a*—see Altorki 1980; Parkes 2005). Until the early twentieth century the use of wet-nurses was common in this *khāndān* and careful records were kept to prevent the inadvertent arrangement of a marriage between two relatives who had ever been nursed by the same woman.
19. If one wishes to be more specific, one can, of course, distinguish a cousin from a "true" (*sagā/sagī*) sibling by using a descriptive phrase such as *khālazād bhāī* (mother's sister's son), *cacāzād bahen* (father's brother's daughter), and so on.
20. It may be noted that the Dravidian kinship terminology is also incompatible with Arab Muslim marriage preferences. In these terminologies, cross-cousins (mother's brother's children and father's sister's children) are linguistically distinguished from siblings. But, parallel cousins (mother's sister's children and father's brother's children), who, as we have seen, in the Arab system are also preferred mates, are classed with brothers and sisters. At least some Dravidian-language-speaking Muslims have at some point in their history adjusted their marriage alliance patterns accordingly.
21. Alvi, writing about marriage to close relatives in Punjab, Pakistan, remarks in this regard: "for a woman every cousin is a brother, and when after marriage one of them becomes her husband, his affinal characteristic remains subordinated to the quality of siblingship" (2007: 668). However, she does not elaborate the point nor is it entirely clear how this "subordination" is manifested in either discourse or actual behavior. It may also be worth noting here that, unlike Urdu, the Punjabi terminology used by Alvi's informants has distinct terms of reference for each of the four types of first cousin: they are not simply referred to as brothers and sisters. Whether this has any

behavioral or other implications for a comparison between Muslim north India and the Pakistani Punjab remains to be explored.

22. Younger brothers may be referred to and addressed by their given names, while the kin term is usually employed—with or without the given name—as a sign of respect for those who are older than the speaker. Muslims consider it almost mandatory that the husband be older than the wife, though in this *khāndān* there are a few exceptional couples in which the wife is older. However, each of these cases involved a marriage of personal choice that was initially opposed by their parents and other family members for this very reason.
23. In any case, even among North Indian Hindus, the reference terms for conjugal kin (such as *sās* [mother-in-law], *sālī* [wife's sister] and so on) are never used in address. A Hindu woman would address her husband's mother either by the same term her husband uses or by some other "mother" term. She would call her husband's sister by one of the several "sister" terms that are available in the language, and so forth (see my discussion of Hindi address terminology in Vatuk 1992). If an Urdu-speaking Muslim woman is married to a *non-relative*, she will follow the same principle in addressing her in-laws.
24. This English word has nowadays almost replaced the word *zanāna* in conversational usage, even when people are speaking in Urdu. The corresponding term for the men's area of a house or other gathering place (such as a wedding hall) is "gents".
25. Two important ethnographic studies of Indian Muslims that have come out since that time are Rao's 1998 monograph on the Bakkarwals of Kashmir and Jamous' 2003 work (first published in French in 1991) on kinship among the Meo of Rajasthan. In addition, there have been a few monographs and scholarly articles on kinship and marriage among *Pakistani* Muslims that provide insight into some of the issues I have raised (see, for example, Donnan 1988, Alvi 2007).

REFERENCES

Ahmad, Aziz. 1977. "Muslim Kinship Terminology in Urdu." *Journal of the Economic and Social History of the Orient*, 20: 344–50.

Alam, Muzaffar. 1998. "The Pursuit of Persian: Language in Mughal Politics." *Modern Asian Studies*, 32: 317–49.

Alttrki, Sorayya. 1980. "Milk Kinship in Arab Society: An Unexplored Problem in the Ethnography of Marriage." *Ethnology*, 19: 233–44.

Alvi, Anjum. 2007. "India and the Muslim Punjab: A Unified Approach to South Asian Kinship." *Journal of the Royal Anthropological Institute*, n.s.13: 657–78.

Bourdieu, Pierre. 1977. *Outline of a Theory of Practice*, trans. Richard Nice. Cambridge: Cambridge University Press.

Casson, Ronald W. 1974. "Semantic Structure and Social Structure in a Central Anatolian Village."*Anthropological Quarterly*, 47: 347–73.

Das, Veena. 1973. "The Structure of Marriage Preferences: An Account from Pakistani Fiction." *Man*, n.s. 8: 30–45.

Davies, Rodger P. 1949. "Syrian Arabic Kinship Terms."*Southwestern Journal of Anthropology*, 5: 244–52.

D'Souza, Victor. 1955. *The Navayats of Kanara: A Study in Culture Contact*. Dharwar: Kannada Research Institute.

Dumont, Louis. 1962. "Le Vocabulaire de Parentī dans l'Inde du Nord." *l'Homme*, 2: 5–48.

———. 1966. "Marriage in India: The Present State of the Question." *Contributions to Indian Sociology*, 9: 90–114.

———. 1975. "Terminology and Prestations Revisited." *Contributions to Indian Sociology*, n.s. 9: 197–216.

Donnan, Hastings. 1988. *Marriage among Muslims: Preference and Choice in Northern Pakistan*. Delhi: Hindustan Publications.

Eglar, Zekiye S. 1960. *A Punjabi Village in Pakistan*. New York: Columbia University Press.

Gingrich, Andre. 1995. "The Prophet's Smile and Other Puzzles: Studying Arab Tribes and Comparing Close Marriages." *Social Anthropology*, 3: 147–70.

Goody, Jack and S. J. Tambiah. 1973. *Bridewealth and Dowry*. Cambridge: Cambridge University Press.

Goody, Jack. 1990. *The Oriental, the Ancient and the Primitive: Systems of Marriage and the Family in the Pre-Industrial Societies of Eurasia*. Cambridge: Cambridge University Press.

Holy, Ladislav. 1989. *Kinship, Honour and Solidarity: Cousin Marriage in the Middle East*. Manchester, Manchester University Press.

Jamous, Raymond. 2003. *Kinship and Rituals among the Meo of Northern*

India: Locating Sibling Relationship, trans. Nora Scott. New Delhi: Oxford University Press.

Jeffery, Patricia. 1979. *Frogs in a Well: Indian Women in Purdah*. London: Zed Press.

Karve, Irawati. 1939–1941. "Kinship Terminology and Kinship Usages of the Maratha Country." *Bulletin of the Deccan College Research Institute*, 1: 327–89, 2: 9–33.

Morgan, Lewis Henry. 1871. *Systems of Consanguinity and Affinity of the Human Family*. Washington: Smithsonian Institution.

Parkes, Peter. 2005. "Milk Kinship in Islam: Substance, Structure, History." *Social Anthropology* 13: 307–29.

Pastner, Carroll. 1979. "Cousin Marriage among the Zikri Baluch of Coastal Pakistan." *Ethnology*, 18: 31–47.

———. 1981. "The Negotiation of Bilateral Endogamy in the Middle Eastern Context: The Zikri Baluch Example." *Journal of Anthropological Research*, 37: 305–18.

Radcliffe-Brown, A. R. 1941. "The Study of Kinship Systems." *The Journal of the Royal Anthropological Institute of Great Britain and Ireland*, 71: 1–18.

Rao, Aparna. 1998. *Life Cycle, Gender and Status among Himalayan Pastoralists*. New York: Berghahn Books.

Raheja, Gloria Goodwin. 1988. *The Poison in the Gift: Ritual, Prestation, and the Dominant Caste in a North Indian Village*. Chicago: University of Chicago Press.

Roulet, Marguerite. 1996. "Dowry and Prestige in North India." *Contributions to Indian Sociology*, n.s. 30: 89–107.

Tambiah, Stanley J. 1989. "*Bridewealth and Dowry* Revisited: The Position of Women in Sub-Saharan Africa and North India." *Current Anthropology*, 30: 413–35.

Trautmann, Thomas R. 1981. *Dravidian Kinship*. Cambridge: Cambridge University Press.

———. 1987. *Lewis Henry Morgan and the Invention of Kinship*. Berkeley: University of California Press.

Vatuk, Sylvia. 1969. "A Structural Analysis of the Hindi Kinship Terminology." *Contributions to Indian Sociology*, n.s. 3: 94–115.

———. 1972. *Kinship and Urbanization: White Collar Migrants in North India*. Berkeley: University of California Press.

———. 1975. “Gifts and Affines in North India.”*Contributions to Indian Sociology*, n.s. 9: 155–96.

———. 1992. “Forms of Address in North India: The Family Domain.” In *Concepts of Person*, ed. A. Ostor, S. Barnett, and L. Fruzzetti, 56–98. 2nd ed. New Delhi: Oxford University Press.

———. 2005. “Moving the Courts: Muslim Women and Personal Law.” In *The Diversity of Muslim Women's Lives in India*, ed. Zoya Hasan & Ritu Menon, 18–58. New Brunswick: Rutgers University Press.

———. 2007. “The ‘Cancer of Dowry’ in Indian Muslim Marriages: Themes in the Popular Rhetoric from the South Indian Muslim Press.” In *Living With Secularism: The Destiny of India's Muslims*, ed. Mushirul Hasan, 155-176. New Delhi: Manohar Publishers and Distributors.

Vreede-de Stuers, Cora. 1963. “Terminologie de Parentīchez les Musulmans Ashraf de l'Inde de Nord.” *Bijdragen tot de Taal-, Land- en Volkenkunde*, 119: 254–66.

———. 1968. *Parda: A Study of Muslim Women's Life in Northern India*. Assen: Van Gorcum.

Wila, Aziz Jang. 1976. *Tārīkh-un Nawāyat*. 2nd ed. Hyderabad: Wila Akaidami.

Wolf, Arthur P. 1995. *Sexual Attraction and Childhood Association: A Chinese Brief for Edward Westermarck*. Stanford: Stanford University Press.

Ziadeh, Farhat J. 1957. “Equality (*Kafā‘ah*) in the Muslim Law of Marriage.” *The American Journal of Comparative Law* 6: 503–17.

Seeing the Precolonial through Colonial/Modern Eyes

6

Recovering Attestation Practices from the Footnotes of a Colonial History

The *Treatise of Mirasi Right* Revisited[1]

BHAVANI RAMAN

The British East India Company fundamentally reorganized attestation procedures that underwrote the credibility of documents in Madras at the turn of the nineteenth century. Soon after they assumed direct control of the Madras hinterland, Company men sought to monopolize notarial authority and verify written documents.[2] A new system of law courts, established in 1802, was quickly followed by the introduction of stamp duties.[3] The Madras Government redefined forgery and renewed their efforts to curtail the authority of notables.[4] Most importantly, when faced with collecting and verifying documentary evidence about land control and the legal adjudication of disputes, officials began to judge the credibility of written claims by privileging the legitimate use of the personal name in its most material form: the written signature.

The Company's pre-occupation with the signature's singular and personal qualities was not without its problems. The attempt to tie claims to individual authors rendered many inhabitants, who did not sign for themselves and who depended on professional scribes for document work, vulnerable to the collector's disfavor. At the same time, Company courts were overwhelmed with forged bonds and claims. Such problems of discerning and instituting the credibility of writing, common in the Company records from that time, in turn, present some intriguing questions: What was the nature of attestation protocols dismantled by the Company, given that personal inscription, as such, was not unknown in the Madras region? Can attestation protocols, a problem rarely studied by historians, enable us to understand the changing role of the signature? Why were attestation protocols so central to the recovery of the past and pacification in the present? What, in other words, was the afterlife of old regime attestation practices?

This essay proposes to engage with these questions by revisiting the footnotes of an influential colonial history, a well-known essay on *mirasi* rights to land written by the East India Company's leading Orientalist-bureaucrat in Madras, Francis Whyte Ellis. Indeed, any attempt to recover older practices of attestation in Madras must reckon with the moment of their transformation in the context of the colonial land settlement of the early nineteenth century. While Ellis wrote his masterly account about the ancient nature of *mirasi* proprietorship to argue against what he thought were wrongheaded Company interventions, I will examine the evidence he detailed in this text to glean preliminary answers to the issue of attestation practices and their relationship to the written signature, and to the production of Ellis's historical method. I will suggest that it is particularly important to pay attention to the evidentiary weight attributed to the idea of "usage" in Ellis' work to understand these connections.

Footnotes, as Anthony Grafton argues, beg scrutiny for they are a humanist's rough equivalent of scientific evidence, "revealing a staggering range of divergent practices under history's apparently stable surface" (Grafton 1997: 7). In Ellis's footnotes, attestation practices of the everyday world of the Madras region in the eighteenth century appear in their afterlife as the methodological basis for his scholarly investigations of land tenure arrangements. The footnotes form a repository of attestation protocols that were no longer the dominant judicial basis for resource management in the region. Ellis's methods embedded the production of the past in ideas of proprietorship in ways that tie both scholarly methods and governance to protocols of attestation.

Aside from his contribution to the idea of the autonomous roots of the Dravidian languages, the subject of a recent book by Thomas Trautmann (2006), Ellis was an important figure in the land tenure debates in Madras. He is best known for his monumental essay on proprietorship, written in 1814 with his primary assistant B. Sankariah and published in 1818 as *Replies to seventeen questions, proposed by the government of Fort St. George, relative to Mirasi right: with two appendices, elucidatory of the subject*.[5] The text has generally been called the *Treatise of Mirasi Right* and it is an extraordinarily important source for the reconstruction of South Indian agrarian history. Ellis argued that *mirasi* (Tamil: mīrācu) tenure, although bearing a name of Perso-Arabic provenance, was in fact an authentic system of ancient Tamil proprietorship called *kaniyatchi* (kāṇiyāṭci), which was worthy of official revival and preservation. More than anything else, Ellis positioned *mirasi* as peculiar to a region: the Madras hinterland or as it was called in classical Tamil texts, Tondaimandalam.

Ellis's arguments about the ancient institutions of Tondaimandalam were really a claim that usage or custom could be historically recovered through etymological and comparative methods—by tracing out and describing the elements of the words of land tenure in different South Indian languages with their modifications of form and sense through time. These arguments about usage's past derived from his ideas about law and language. As Donald Davis has argued, Ellis's views on law were comparable to the school of historical jurisprudence represented by Friedrich Carl von Savigny who held that custom evolved from the *volksgeist* (the spirit of the people) and derived its validity from historical processes (Davis 2009: 301, Gale 1982: 131).[6] Ellis's theory of custom, in consonance with his ideas about the autonomous basis of South Indian languages, went into the production of *mirasi* as a form of ancient usage in Tondaimandalam. In turn, Ellis produced a view of regional history derived from usage and a history of usage that turned ordinary land documents into legitimate sources of *volksgeist*.[7]

Ellis's arguments about *mirasi* usage, which he derived from an etymological analysis of the vocabulary of land use-terms, were sourced from contemporary and historical land documents rather than Sanskrit legal texts. They were culled from two sources collated in the early nineteenth century: a corpus of donative inscriptions from Colonel Colin Mackenzie's vast collection of South Indian historical texts, and the land deeds pertaining to the settlements of the city and its immediate hinterland, collected by the Madras collectorate.[8] The donative inscriptions taken from Mackenzie's collection broadly date to a period before the fifteenth century. Colonel Colin Mackenzie, the first Surveyor-General of India, collected several such texts in South India in the early years of the nineteenth century (Ellis 1852: 29–36).[9] Ellis's second set of sources, the land deeds from the Madras collectorate concerning the city and its hinterland, date from the seventeenth century onward.[10] All these documents pertain to families holding *mirasi* rights in settlements that the Company acquired as assigned villages, revenue farms, or "home farms" from the Nawab of Arcot (Crole 1879: 233). Given that his work as Madras Collector must have been closely tied to the larger interventions in property claims, what Ravi Ahuja has called a process of "expropriating the poor" from Madras city, we can safely assume the bulk of the land deeds pertaining to the city first appeared in the course of dispute adjudication in the Company's Madras Cutcherry (court or public office) or were specifically seen or requested by Company officers (possibly even by Ellis or Sankariah) in the course of the everyday work of land settlement (Ahuja 2001). But how were these documents, culled from quotidian work of pacification, turned into artifacts of usage that were legitimate by virtue of their production in another time?

For documents to become sources of ancient usage, chancery practices of discerning the credibility of writing had to be applied to the scholastic study of the evidentiary value of conveyances. South India easily produced the largest corpus of subcontinental inscriptions written on palm-leaf, stone, and metal, between the seventh and seventeenth centuries, making written inscriptions, "the 'central pillar' upon which the entire edifice of precolonial Indian history rests"(Wagoner 2003: 786). But exegeses on epigraphic methods in the subcontinent tend to invoke and treat diplomatics—the study of documents through assessing their provenance and authenticity—as a self-evident toolkit (Sircar 1965, Chhabra 1951).[11] Epigraphists and historians have tended to assume that their tools, first developed in the nineteenth century by Orientalist scholars, were simply derived from principles of document authenticity in the Sanskrit legal tradition, the Dharmasastra, and applied to historical materials to study the past. Recent research on Indian epigraphy's colonial past, however, has shown the need to recover the specificities of subcontintental epigraphic practices from chancery practices (Saloman 1998, Wagoner 2003).[12] As Phillip Wagoner persuasively argues, far from being a simple application of European scholarly norms to South Asian language materials or a self-evident application of Dharmasastra textual norms, colonial epigraphy is fundamentally indebted to the unacknowledged contributions of high-ranking Telugu Niyogi Brahmans who served as assistants to Colonel Mackenzie's survey. Formerly employed in the bankrupt Arcot court, Mackenzie's assistants ascribed serious evidentiary value to donative inscriptions in unearthing precedents for social arrangements. Their familiarity with lexical usage, along with their ability to identify handwriting and ascertain forgeries, provided epigraphy's methodological tools in South India to decipher and date inscriptions (Wagoner 2003). We can surmise that the active role of Niyogis illustrates how Arcot "diplomatics" was transposed from the ruins of a princely court to invigorate a colonial project of knowing the past of recently pacified regions.

In the *Treatise,* a parallel and complementary trajectory to the Niyogi story connects chancery practices to the recovery of the past. In this text, written conveyances were not so much a source for the historical chronologies of kings, but evidence of usage validated by historical processes. In the absence of support for usage in positive law, Ellis turned to documents recording *mirasi.*[13] He wrote "documents of this nature are the best proofs of the existence of rights, which are not always supported by positive law, as it is impossible, that deeds, conveying, limiting, extending, or transferring such rights, should in any country be in common use, unless the rights themselves were well known and generally recognized" (Ellis 1852: 12). In other words, he felt that *mirasi* could only be gleaned from documented sources of everyday land transactions. But in order to render written conveyances authentic sources of ancient usage, to render them as credible evidence and a substitute for positive law, Ellis was forced to engage with the problem of notarial authority and attestation that undergirded these written instruments.

Ellis used his understanding of attestation protocols and chancery skills that he acquired from different sources, to determine the credibility of written conveyances. He transformed these observations into a method for his scholarly investigations of past usage while leaving us with a rich picture of how attestation practices structured the credibility of documents and proprietorship prior to the introduction of Company law courts. In the process, he produced an invaluable resource: commentarial residues that observe the efficacy of scribal practices, while simultaneously enabling the content of the documents amenable to an analysis based on the historicity of language that was his overt concern.

Ellis's commentary then reveals the double story of attestation. The everyday work of colonial pacification rendered older practices of attestation irrelevant precisely when the efficacy of older written forms and the protocols of attestation engaged the interest of those officials like Ellis seeking credible sources with which to reconstruct the region's ancient past. For the purposes of my essay, then, the documentary appendix of the *Treatise* best reads as an "example book" of attestation practices, making Ellis our reluctant guide.

TREATISE OF MIRASI RIGHTS IN THE DEBATES ON PROPRIETORSHIP IN MADRAS

The *Treatise of Mirasi Right* was written in the context of an ideological battle in Madras over colonial land revenue policy, specifically Colonel Thomas Munro's advocacy of *ryotwari* tenure. Key aspects of the debate provide a context for the arguments and evidence in Ellis's text.[14] Munro's *ryotwari* model was based on his experience as Collector of Bellary, a district now in Karnataka and advocated a direct annual settlement between the Company and individual tillers, *ryots*, that would rest on comprehensively measured and assessed small landholdings. *Ryotwari* would do away with the large class of revenue intermediaries and revenue farmers to revive a system that would be true to the region's past (Mukherjee 1962). To Munro, this ancient past was a model of sovereignty in which the sovereign was regarded as the sole landlord, and tenants were tenants at will. In his view, landed notables were not absolute proprietors but holders of privileges that could be resumed by the sovereign. Munro's plan found favor with the Board of Control in London that was in search of a rational and territorially bounded land settlement in South India. They were sympathetic to his hostility to intermediaries and persuaded by his arguments favoring the sovereign's claim to sole proprietorship (Beaglehole 1966, Stein 1989).

Among Munro's opponents were the Madras *mirasidars*, who belonged to the mainly upper-caste non-Brahman Vellalar landholding castes. *Mirasi* privileges were held as individual shares in revenue entitlements spread over several villages. The entitlements were held jointly with kin, but individual shares were passed on, transferred, or mortgaged while the actual plots were periodically reassigned among the kin. *Mirasidar*s were also entitled to a variety of privileges over the productive resources of a settlement, including its agrestic slaves, but because they calculated these privileges as shares constrained by kinship and kin-based consent, these landholders would naturally oppose the *ryotwari* model of individual landholding based on the measured assessment of land and premised on the sovereign's claim to ultimate proprietorship.

In 1814, keeping in mind the Madras Board of Revenue's arguments that existing *mirasi* landholders (especially in the Madras hinterland) would object to the new system, London instructed Madras to institute *ryotwari* only if current landholders could be protected. The Madras Board of Revenue then issued a letter of inquiry to all its district collectors seeking a response to 17 questions pertaining to *mirasi* landholding. Ellis, then Collector of Madras, wrote a comprehensive scholarly response, the so-called *Treatise of Mirasi Right*. The text written in collaboration with his assistant B. Sankariah was considered worthy of publication by the Madras Board of Revenue and printed in 1818.

As Trautmann has argued, the disagreements between Ellis and Munro on proprietorship were grounded in a tacit difference in their methods to find evidence for usage in the past (Trautmann 2009). For Munro, direct observation formed the evidence of customary usage. He drew on his experience acquired in Bellary to oppose the model of proprietorship, "Permanent Settlement," that emanated from Calcutta, which he argued was fanciful and European. In contrast, Ellis' methods of textual analysis arrived at a historically grounded account of usage through the evidentiary value of records, which he placed in tandem with legal texts like the Dharmasastra to argue against the notion that the sovereign was the only landlord.

Munro's *ryotwari* became the official settlement, though in its practical workings, it did not succeed in displacing existing landholders (Mukherjee 1962, Frykenberg 1977). Ellis's *Treatise*, which claimed *mirasi* as a form of proprietorship, was in the meantime disregarded by the Company's highest offices. But the essay became an authoritative source for writing South Indian history. The 1818 edition was subsequently republished with notes by C. P. Brown in 1852, ultimately reappearing in Bayley and Hudleston's edited selections from the official record called *Papers on Mirasi Right* (1862). Since then it has been cited in standard studies of colonial land revenue policy pertaining to South India and of the history of the Madras hinterland, the Chinglepur region also known as the "Jaghire." So the text lived on in the official colonial record and left a series of intricately worked arguments about usage and the past that became a repository of facts for scholars of agrarian and social history.

Most importantly, Ellis's intellectual contribution lived on in historical and cultural arguments made by different groups who claimed to be the region's original settlers on the basis of ancient usage (Irschick 1994). Late nineteenth century officials like Tremenheere argued that Ellis's researches gave an impetus to the historical validity of *mirasi* system and the power of elite landholders at the expense of landless groups.[15] Ellis is categorical that his remarks on the area's settlement history apply to the country "as it formerly existed, *then as now* divided and in part possessed by tribes foreign to the original occupants" (1852: 51, my emphasis). Ellis believed that *mirasi* right was established in Tondaimandalam by the region's first Tamil settlers, and "judging from the permanency of Hindu institutions, it may be rationally inferred, [they] would have remained unaltered at the present day, had the country been preserved from the baneful effects of foreign conquest and despotic government" (1852: 61).[16] Usage and history were not only mutually constituted but had to be discerned from the distorting lens of post-conquest arrangements.

CONQUEST, LANGUAGE, AND USAGE IN THE "EXAMPLE BOOK"

Twenty-six documents written in the scripts of Kannada, Telugu, and Tamil interspersed with Sanskrit language verses, and an elaborate English translation provided in the Appendix, make up the sources of the *Treatise* (Ellis 1852: 29–50, 67–108). Ellis presents the documents in broadly chronological clusters to prove that these were not only sources to understand the arrangements of *mirasi* but also financial arrangements and general government "which prevailed in the Hindu States anteriorly to the Mohammedan conquest" (1852: iii). Thus, Ellis's argument about *mirasi*'s antiquity was illustrated through *mirasi*'s existence, albeit in a submerged manner, even after "foreign" conquest.

He argued that, despite the Arabic provenance of its current name, *mirasi* represented a set of coherent arrangements, namely the existence and transfer of a variety of proprietary rights held and administered conjointly by all the sharers, datable to a distant past. The word *mirasi* was prevalent among inhabitants from a very early date, but it was a term "probably introduced, with many Arabic terms now prevalent, into the dominion of the Moslem Princes of the Deccan, and from thence spread over the neighbouring countries" (1852:71). The antiquity of *mirasi* presented in this manner, rendered Tondaimandalam an ancient commonwealth or republic that was comprised of *kaniyakarars* (kāṇiyākarar), a word in Tamil that literally means those who possess shares (1852: 62). Ellis argued that "the character of nations is unchangeably maintained, it was invigorated by time, operates with unseen but irresistible force, even in countries long subject to foreign rule… In India, supported strongly by distinctions of caste and the characteristic attachment of all classes to the observances of their forefathers, however repressed by temporary circumstances, it has always existed in powerful operation" (1852: 65).[17]

Ellis further argued that distinctive arrangements of proprietorship marked the difference between the "the Tamil nations, the aborigines of Dravidam, the South-west division of India, and the Cannadiya and Telugu people, who, at an early period, were more inter-mixed from strangers from the north and centre of India" (Ellis 1852: 62). To him the model of proprietorship represented by Tondaimandalam *mirasi* was proof of a greater "degree of freedom" enjoyed by these groups compared to "the Telugu and Cannidiya people." These arguments led him to conclude the *Treatise* with the observation that *mirasi* resembled allodial land holding in Europe (Ellis 1852: 107).[18]

Such arguments linking kinship-based proprietorship to language and nation suggest that Ellis's claim for the long existence of *mirasi* was based on a notion of an ancient past discernable in present usage because it was anchored in a timeless caste feeling. Such assumptions also meant that Ellis was less interested in whether a document was forged and more in its verisimilitude. He wrote that absolute authenticity was not necessary because he wanted to use these sources

> not to prove the *fact* but the *thing*, not to prove the sale or mortgage of a property, but to prove that a property exists to be sold...nothing, therefore, short of proving the whole of the documents contained in the Appendix spurious, can invalidate their evidence on the several points of Mirasi right which they embrace (1852: 12, his emphasis).

By attributing verisimilitude with evidentiary value, Ellis wanted to judge written credibility by discerning the accuracy of the lexical form of the document. He abstracted inscriptions from their material culture to create a uniform document "series." Barring the first five documents from the Mackenzie corpus, Ellis does not explicitly remark on the materials used for the other documents.[19]

The *Treatise* privileges the capacity of language, especially grammar and vocabulary, to open up the worlds of the past and distill the cultural specificities of present speakers. Ironically these arguments relied greatly on the views of Ellis's assistant, the highly trained and knowledgeable Telugu Brahman *sastri*

B. Sankariah, a long-serving revenue accountant and manager (Trautmann 2009). Although Sankariah was a Telugu Brahman, an expert in Sanskrit legal texts and knew English in addition to Tamil, Sanskrit and Telugu, the *Treatise* emphasizes Sankariah's Tamil expertise at the expense of his other abilities (Trautmann 2009). Ellis was keenly invested in claiming that special access to the past was provided by a careful attention to "native" languages. But he did not conceive "native" languages as spoken by multilingual persons but as a means to make an autochthonous link between people and land, between ancient past and current usage, writing and spoken vocabulary.

The section by Sankariah (presented in Tamil and English "translation") strongly underscores the language of revenue terms in current use and frequently alludes to the antiquity of prevalent language use and land tenure practices. For example, Sankariah replies to a question regarding the recognition of *mirasi* rights by claiming that his knowledge was gleaned from "the well informed" (Ellis 1852: 23). The response essentially provides an account of *mirasi* practice purportedly in place since the original settlement of Tondaimandalam, with an elaborate gloss of revenue terms and privileges such as *ulcudi* and *payacaris*. Notably, there are no references to any words of Persianate provenance. Indeed, Sankariah notes, like Ellis, that *kaniyatci* was a native term, "for which the foreign word Mīrācu has in latter times been substituted" (1852: 23). Ellis calibrates everyday documents against the vocabulary of native speakers, in a way that made Sankariah's terms *and* the terms used in documents as a repository of an ancient past.

While Sankariah's Tamil may have anchored Ellis's scholarly credibility in this vernacular language, how are written conveyances, collected from a variety of colonial recordkeeping projects, taken to bear the documentary imprint of an ancient past? If conveyances were to serve the purpose of revealing the past by resonating with contemporary use, they had to be made to assume a documentary status. That is, written conveyances had to be anchored in time, represent a specific linguistic region and most important, they needed to represent normative custom.

LAW, USAGE, AND THE "SPECIAL PRACTICE" OF ATTESTATION

Other than calibrating documents against a vocabulary of ancient usage in Tamil, Ellis argued that these everyday transactions *met* the criteria of ancient usage because they agreed with general norms prescribed by classical legal commentaries in Sanskrit regarding conveyance and ownership. So Ellis did not reject classical commentaries or apply the commentaries blindly but used documents to render usage commensurate with classical texts. This was an essential step to make conveyances into documents that would be an acceptable substitute for positive law.

In response to the twelfth question, "Can *mirasi* be sold?," Ellis gave a long and learned response about legal usage in which he argued that *mirasi* was not supported by positive law but could be gleaned from everyday documents when set in relation to prescribed classical norms. *Mirasi* was a form of proprietorship because it could be transferred like property: with a written deed accompanied by the six formalities of consent set out in the Dharmasastra legal texts. Ellis notes that these six formalities were the consent of townsmen, of kindred, of the Lord (the king or his officers), and of heirs, and by the delivery of gold and water (1852: 14). Ellis's observations thus lay out the formal modes of consent in the lexical form of the documents in the region and their relationship to classical law.

Although Ellis relied on *A Digest of Hindu Law,* by the Calcutta-based Orientalist and Anglo-Hindu legal theorist Henry Thomas Colebrook, for purposes of comparing the documents to legal prescriptions, he differed from the Calcutta jurist on the matter of the sovereign's rights to proprietorship.[20] For example, Ellis differed from Colebrook when he suggested that the subject could assert his right to property transfer not at the sovereign's pleasure, but by invoking the sovereign's consent (1852: 12). He also suggested that individual consent could be direct or implied because the key aspect of the procedure of conveyance was witnessing (1852: 13).

The transfer of *mirasi* could be undertaken through auction, whereby the act of sale was collectively witnessed, or if the sale was private, those defined by law as interested parties had in some fashion assented to the transfer. These transactions allowed possessors of *mirasi* to enjoy their share in the same way as those who held actual land. That is to say, based on the formal contents of the documents, Ellis argued that *mirasidars* claimed the textually-sanctioned eight enjoyments of ownership called *ashtabhogam* even if *mirasi* only existed in "usage" (1852: 14). Ellis judged the documents' formal compliance with the categories of Dharmasastra law to argue that *mirasi* was a form of proprietorship, but that it was distinctly specific to Tondaimandalam.

The categories of possession, such as the six formalities of conveyance and the eight enjoyments, derived their efficacy not only from their mere invocation in writing, but because they were framed within salient attestation protocols. Did attestation and writing practices also conform to Dharmasastra prescriptions? Right after his discussion of the formal qualities of consent, Ellis makes a set of remarkable points about attestation by relating the form of the document to its efficacy (1852: 17):

> By the custom of the country the bill of sale must be drawn up by the *curnam* (accountant) of the village; it must be witnessed by two or more creditable persons, and countersigned by all or at least by the principal *Mirasidars;* it must state the exact share transferred, (or when land and right is sold, the boundaries toward the four cardinal points, sometimes also, it shows the measure and produce); it must contain a distinct date and the name of the reigning prince and one or more of his predecessors; the persons of the transferer [*sic*] and transferee must be clearly designated by the insertion of their father's name, their caste, tribe and place of

residence; and the transfer must be regularly recorded by entry of the new *mirasidar*'s name in the *pangu-malai* (compilation of shares) register.

So the six formalities and the granting of the eight enjoyments—legally sanctified ways of conveyance by the Dharmasastra for example—relied on certain "customs" of attestation to be efficacious. Here again Ellis understands attestation to be a form of usage that had a legal claim.

The source of these injunctions about attestation is unclear from Ellis's notes. Were these taken from written texts, like the Dharmasastra commentaries or did he receive this information in conversation with the experienced Sankariah, or from his work as revenue collector interacting with local accountants? Any of these could be plausible sources. Ellis, for example, drew deeply from Mackenzie's collection, and among that collection is an English fragment, purportedly a version of *Lekhītaprakaram,* that set out the "formulae of deeds of the Hindu Governments." [21] Furthermore, like in Calcutta, legal digests on litigation were composed in Sanskrit at the behest of Company patrons (Derrett 1968: 261–65, 270—73). It is also very likely that Ellis derived his knowledge of attestation from his own office work, or from the knowledge of Sankariah.

Although the origin of Ellis's observations is hard to pin down, his claim that attestation practices were anchored in usage resonates with standard injunctions on legal procedure in the commentarial literature on the Dharmasastra. According to S.C. Banerji, legal commentaries describe the administration of justice as resting on four feet. The foot of *dharma* rests on truth, *vyavahara* (procedure) on witnesses, *caritra* (customary law or conduct) on popular practice, and the royal edict on the King's commands (Banerji 1996: 1.15). The resonance between Ellis's observation and formal Sanskrit prescriptions anchors the authority of attestation practice in usage which implies that regionally varied practices of attestation were acceptable and indeed necessary to render documents credible prior to Company intervention.

Ellis's attention to the documentary form demonstrates that practices of document authentication were closely tied to regimes of discernment based on repeated appearances of words, subject arrangements and the like. For instance, he repeatedly noted that trained scribes used their knowledge of lexical usage to discern forgery. Ellis himself compared documents that were composed a few centuries apart and in different regions by frequently relying on lexical usage. He produced a check list of topic components that included "dates of the reigning prince, names and styles of the granters and grantees, purpose of the grant, specification of the land boundaries, conditions that the grantees are to perform, investiture of the grantees with prescribed formalities, verses of imprecation and execution of the deed" (1852: 69). The list of heads bears an uncanny resemblance to the core tenets of diplomatics outlined in foundational studies of the modern epigraphic method in the Indian subcontinent and resonate with the procedures laid out in the *smriti* texts (Sircar 1965, Chhabra 1951; Banerji 1996). This would suggest that these practices of discernment had legal status in the Sanskrit commentaries. We can surmise that if practices of discernment rather than particular words had legal sanction, then codes of attestation would have rested on the expertise of persons rather than solely on the individual signature alone.

DISCERNING ATTESTATION: THE ROLE OF EXPERTS

Ellis noted that the inscriptions he consulted from the Mackenzie corpus displayed great diversity: conveyances varied in form in various regions (1852: 72 fn. 10). Then how was credibility ensured? For example, subtle variations in form posed a particularly acute obstacle for discerning a deed's date of composition. The time of the deed's execution could be indicated in a variety of ways. Although the regnal year was considered the standard for displaying the date of execution, in many cases the regnal years were inaccurately noted. Ellis notes that the date could also be written as a *sancetam* or arrangement of syllables having a numerical value which was difficult to decipher (1852: 69 fn.1).[22] At times, only the month was mentioned without the year, suggesting that rights or revenue shares in question could be redeemed in any year on that month, the time coinciding with the harvest (1852: 97 fn. 2). But in general, Ellis notes that, in the Tamil speaking regions, all genuine documents bore the date derived by the solar computation of time which could only be provided by the astronomer of the settlement. This man, the "Almanac Brahman" or *pancangi*, would give the date based on his computation of an auspicious time from the almanac (1852: 89 fn. 5). The expertise of a few anchored the credibility of documents.

Expertise, however, was shaped by ties of intimacy and the reputation of individuals. Given that many did not write for themselves, a document's credibility rested with the document writer, most often the settlement's accountant who would also guarantee the authenticity of the document's writing. The knowledgeable, usually other accountants, discerned the credibility of the document despite the variation in form. Ellis notes the topics that made up a deed differed often in substance, but they were the same in number (i.e., all followed the limit of eight heads) and that these were a product of expert professional training. Faced with the variations in document form, Ellis, for instance writes, although he could not find a written precept on how to account for variations, "technical arrangements of this kind are not formed by chance, one must have existed by which notaries were guided" (1852: 84). We can read Ellis's observation as a clear indication of the enormous claim of expertise vested in the person of the *kanakkuppillai*.

Discerning correct usage was a subtle affair and intimately tied to the scribe's reputation. Ellis notes, for example, elaborate exordiums occurred only in grants deemed important enough to record on stone or copper or if they were royal in origin. They were uncommon in ordinary sale deeds. However, the appearance of one such elaborate exordium in an ordinary deed from Tondiarpet led him to conclude that the deed was not necessarily a forgery. This was because the deed was guaranteed by the village accountant or *kanakkuppillai* (1852: 88). The various specimens from the cluster of documents indicated, Ellis argued, that "the persons who were accountants in this village, Tandeiyarpet, Gurvappa and his son Pudavan Pillai, at the period when this deed was written, were remarkable for their strict attention to established forms and technical language" (1852: 88 fn.1). Furthermore, the *kanakkuppillai*'s credibility was derived from his lineage and expressed by invoking it. A document from the same settlement written in 1767 AD bears the attestation line from the accountant and reads "the integrity of this writing is attested by the son of Poduva Pillai, Guruvappen, the Village Accountant" (1852: 95). Commenting on this text, Ellis noted that grandsons often took the name of their grandfathers as a way to authenticate writing, an important feature which made the deed credible (1852: 95 fn. 3).

From the discussion so far, it is clear that the *kanakkuppillai*'s role in attestation practice was absolutely crucial because not only did he notarize deeds, he also composed them. This made him a remarkably important figure in the settlement when we consider that, in all these deeds, he would write down the identity of the executors and the parties to the deed by inserting their lineage and place of residence. In addition, he also kept land records, specifically an updated record of shares or the *pangu-malai* (compilation of shares) register.[23] In short, the *kanakkuppillai* managed the personal identities of individuals, in a situation where a personal name was not as important as claims to lineage. We might conclude that the efficacy of the deed rested on these two elements, the personal identity of the parties established through their lineage and the settlement's land register, both of which lay in the hands of the *kanakkuppillai* (1852: 17). The notarial authority vested in the *kanakkuppillai* was guaranteed in his expertise, his personal reputation and lineage, and his power to maintain the authoritative written record of lineage and property shares.

In this respect, the *kanakkuppillai* was different from the North Indian *qazi*, the Muslim judge of a locality, who attested paper documents with a personal seal. In the eighteenth century, all manner of individuals came to the local *qazi* to attest documents in regions as far apart as Gujarat and the Panjab (Hasan 2004, Grewal 1975, Bhatia 1982). In contrast, the *kanakkuppillai* was the settlement's revenue accountant *and* its primary document writer, as well as notary (Ellis 1852: 74 fn. 3).[24] It is not clear whether the *kanakkuppillai* used paper or seals for common transactions. Ellis's notes make no mention of seals, a surprising silence given that the earliest surviving seals in the Tamil region date as early as third century BC and both inscribed and un-inscribed seals were used to mark objects since then.[25] It is possible that seals in this region may have been pressed onto the fabric or string to tie documents or goods, rather than onto the palm-leaf itself. But in any case, we can conclude that the *kanakkuppillai*'s importance in attestation procedures demonstrates that the juridical value of the "customary" practice of credible writing was anchored in the authority of his person.

ATTESTATION AND THE PERFORMANCE OF CONSENT

The notarial authority of the *kanakkuppillai* seems to have been equally intertwined with elaborate codes of witnessing monopolized by the settlement's notables. All deeds, other than those issued by kings, required witnesses (Ellis 1852: 71, fn. 9). An example from the Tondiarpet document cluster translated by Ellis illustrates, for our purposes, the key role of witnesses in authenticating a document. The earliest document from that cluster dates to 1720 and records the transfer of *mirasi* in an auction by Arjunan Mudeli, who identifies himself as the son of Rakaippa Mudeli (1852: 88–92). The deed uses the word "Om" to denote consent (1852: 89):

> Arjuna Mudeli, the son of Rakiyappa Mudeli, one of the Mudelis of Tandeiyarpet and his parceners in the Nayeru Nadu in the Puzhel Cotam

in Tondaimandalam acquired by conquest in the kingdom of Chandragiri pronounce *Om!* Having proclaimed aloud in public auction...

Although Ellis used the English term *parcener*, he noted that the term in Tamil is "ullittar," which is not just a coparcener but a name for all those connected in any manner with the principal party (1852: 89 fn.6). Thus the collective declaration "Om!" implies the oral performance of solemn consent, in this case by Arjunen and his kin. In addition, the execution of the deed rested on an elaborate line that commented on its integrity and its attestation, followed by a list of witnesses, as shown below (1852: 91):

All blunders of the deed, arising from the quality of the cadjan (palm-leaf), errors in writing, mistakes in words, and interlineations, and from its being cut, split or worm eaten from erasements [*sic*] or breaks are not to be regarded.

Witnesses
Pudur Periya Catchiyappa Mudeiliyar
Connur Manasivaya Mudeiliyar
Naiyiniyappa Mudeiliyar
Poyadi Viraragava Mudeiliyar

With the knowledge of these the integrity of this writing is attested by the signature of the Puduven, the son of Guruvupa Pillai the Village accountant of Tondeiyarpet.

Signed
Varadappan the son of Rakiappa Mudeiliyar
Tiagappan the son of Toppei Mudali
Tiyaggappen the son of Culla Mudali
Nallen the son of Shinnanna Mudali
Periya Muttiappan
Periya Mudali
Periya Tambi
Arjunen
Tiyagappen the son of Shinntambi Mudeiliyar

The deed is interesting because the consenters agree that the efficacy of the deed did not rest on the material survival of the deed or mistakes in form. In fact, they considered the performance of consent and witnessing recorded in writing more important for the efficacy of the deed than its material *survival* in a record. The efficacy of deeds lay in their performative qualities, with appropriate marks of consent, properly witnessed in a way that marked them as events in the collective remembrance of the settlement. This is important if we consider that in prescriptive legal texts the claims to possession and dispossession, in addition to the structure of inheritance, were safeguarded by recollection. Ellis for example, noted that *mirasi* could not be regained by traditional law if it had passed on to another person after the third generation, or after the lapse of the period of memory determined to be a hundred years (1852: 6).

How was consent performed and who could witness documents? Who was in position to remember authoritatively, other than the *kanakkuppillai*? We note that the *kanakkuppillai* attested the deed with his signature, acknowledging the collective presence and consent of other landholding *mirasidars* of the settlement. The group marked "witnesses" did not have to sign in their own hand. But the accountant's authority to attest the document rested on the marking of their names in the document as witnesses. This remarkable procedure is explained by Ellis in terms of authority exercised by the settlement's notables. The witnesses in this document were "capable of attesting the integrity of writing ('eḷutiṇa naṇmai'), it having drawn by the notary in communication with them" (Ellis1852: 91fn. 24). These types of persons were different from ordinary witnesses who would affix their signatures to attest the execution of the deed. Ellis notes, in this particular case, the two were identical.

Notwithstanding these important variations, from this example and others in the Ellis Appendix, it is clear that all those with a share in the *mirasi* routinely appeared as consenters and the settlement's prominent men appeared as witnesses and co-attesters. Dharmasastra commentaries make it clear that witnessing was a highly regulated act. Credible testimony, for example, could only be given by people of the same lineage or invested in the same dispute, by those belonging to the same habitation, or by notable men of piety, charity, high birth, wealth and rank (Banerji 1996: 1.22). Juxtaposed with the prescription on the formal modes through which conveyances were deemed efficacious, we can surmise that consent and witnessing were closely tied and collective in nature. Testimonial credibility was thus conventionally limited to respectable society, suggesting that the pool of witnesses was highly restricted.[26] Already in the late Cola period, prominent people who received official temple positions as "honors" were not mere temple servants, but acted as witnesses or signatories in arrangements made by the temple. The ability to witness and give consent to written transactions resulted from respectable status (Orr 2000: 168). Ellis, commenting on what he knew in the early nineteenth century, suggests that in the Madras hinterland *mirasidars* were prized for their ability to give sureties. He observed that the possession of a *mirasi* was the evidence of the antiquity of a family and it conferred considerable personal credit on to the holder. In quotidian terms, this meant that the security offered by a *mirasidar* was readily taken (Ellis 1852: 20).

The ability to provide security or to witness emanated from socio-economic status but was also closely tied to juridical functions. Thus, the office of the *Nattan*, the head of a sub-region, was conferred on the principal Vellalar; we can assume that in the Madras hinterland, such a person would have been a large resource controller if not a member of a *mirasi* family. The *Nattan*, along with a *Desayi* (an appointed post that Ellis dates back to the time of the Bijapur sultans, which was usually given to a Telugu-speaking Baliga Chetty), and assisted by the principal *mirasidar*, claimed jurisdiction rights over several caste groups. The *Nattan*, in particular, claimed precedence in all assemblies composed of more than one caste, and most interestingly for our purposes, Ellis notes that the Company considered these individuals respectable sources of information on all revenue transactions (1852: 57).[27]

The close relationship between witnessing and social dominance suggests the degree to which attestation was intimately connected to resource control, restricted to the socially powerful, and a collective act among the prominent and the known. Its close connection with status meant, for instance, that witnesses were not required to take an exculpatory oath and that they always spoke from a position of authority. Indeed those with authority were often described as those who are "fit to speak."

Did low caste witnesses or signatories ever appear in deeds? Ellis's corpus provides no easy answers, but it does include two examples of bondage deeds ("aṭimaip pattiram") dating to the sixteenth century. One of them depicts a Dalit man of Paraiyar caste who, with the consent of his kin, sold his female kin to upper caste buyers. Although neither of the two deeds bear the *kanakkuppillai*'s guarantee, the witnesses in one case and the personal declaration of the Paraiyar seller stand in as attestation (1852: 102–5). I should note here as a caveat that Ellis would have been familiar with petitions written by low caste urban workers.[28] These petitions were quite commonly submitted in the vicinity of colonial port towns. Paraiyar caste leaders were important players in multi-caste assemblies. Within Company jurisdiction, they participated in legal procedures, proffered petitions, and gave testimonies to Company-sponsored commissions of enquiry (Balachandran 2008). But it is possibly fair to conclude that outside Company jurisdiction the collective nature of attestation, in general, restricted the pool of credible witnesses.

The specificities of witnessing that I have discussed so far has an important implication for personal inscription: documents bore personal inscriptions and marks as a form of collective attestation/ consent rather than as representations of individually verifiable signatures made in a signatory's own hand. On palm-leaf, marks were often indistinct, merely resembling a *kiral* or a scratch, and names were often written by the *kanakkuppillai* and framed by performative phrases. Words such as "kai eḷutu" (hand writing), "ippati ivai" (this is), or "nāṉ aṟiyêṉ" (I know this) followed the individual name, secured the deed's execution and the notarial attestation provided by the *kanakkuppillai*. Of these, *kai elutu* is routinely glossed by Ellis as signature. But some very important points indicate that the meaning of *kai elutu* in the documents did not resonate entirely with definitions of the signature that we hold today. In a context where a variety of performative phrases were used to mark witnessing and consent, *kai elutu* accompanied other forms of consent. It was sometimes secondary or equal in importance to oral consent forms such as declaring "om!" Furthermore, as the discussion so far indicates, attestation did not rest on the ability of individuals to sign in their own hand—the *kanakkuppillai*'s notarial authority and the variety of witness invocation, was materially crucial to secure the efficacy of documents. Scribes routinely wrote in the names of consenters, while sometimes consenters marked the deed under the word "*kai nattu*" (kai-nāṭṭu or "mark") distinct from "*kai elutu*" (signature). Finally, we might note that the documents listed in the Appendix were exchanged within a local context, guaranteed by the person of a small number of tightly restricted witnesses and the expertise of the *kanakkuppillai*, suggesting that social networks, even if they were geographically dispersed, guaranteed the credibility of the document. Writing was guaranteed by networks of trust cemented by personal reputation, credible witnesses, known associates who gave sureties and the expertise of scribes. Even if the use of the labels *kai elutu* (hand writing) or *kai-nattu* (mark) may indicate that witnesses or executors wrote or marked for themselves, the credibility of the document did not rest on the signature itself. Written instruments consequently represent not only a sophisticated tradition of scribal textual production, but they suggest that attestation practices were deeply mediated and not easily reducible to mere verification of personal authorship.

CONCLUSION

This essay has argued that the varied protocols of attestation deserve greater scholarly attention precisely because they enable an analysis of inscriptional texts in ways that show how they were generated into documents. If we consider that protocols of attestation are a mutable set of orientations towards the credible and the authoritative, then the multiple strands of mediation necessary to ensure the efficacy of written instruments open up to historical investigation. Ellis's footnotes reveal a rich source through which to conduct that investigation. They throw into sharp relief the Company's dismantling of attestation forms and how these forms were then folded into a methodical study of usage that constituted a written instrument as a source of the past.

The credibility of documents in the Madras region prior to Company interventions in the early nineteenth century did not lie in the strict adherence to one particular written form, even if lexical usage was crucial to its efficacy. Variations were regarded as authentic when undergirded by adherence to content ("topics" as Ellis calls them) and by the expertise of *kanakkuppillai*, along with the corroboration of genealogy and witnessing by credible persons—the most credible of whom were the *mirasidars* themselves. The discernment of credibility through attestation protocols lay in usage that was dismantled by Company interventions in the early nineteenth century.

Investigations into attestation protocols merit our interest in the light of recent debates on the production of knowledge disciplines under colonial rule.[29] The vast historiography around these concerns has largely debated the important issues of authorship, collaboration, or the power exercised by taxonomic categories in colonial governance. Attestation protocols are ignored in these studies, but they deserve attention because they underscore the role of evidentiary practice in the production of history.

NOTES

1. I am grateful to Thomas Trautmann for pressing me on the question of personal inscriptions and for sharing his interest in Francis Whyte Ellis. I thank the audience at Ann Arbor where a version of this essay was first presented, and S. Raman and Iravatham Mahadevan for invaluable advice. Cynthia Talbot, Samira Sheikh, Aparna Balachandran, and Francis Cody commented on a draft version of this essay which helped in its revision. I particularly thank Cynthia Talbot for sharing her insights on epigraphy.
2. Company presence in the Coromandel Coast dates to the early seventeenth century and it founded Fort St. George (Madras) around 1640. It expanded its control in the region in the eighteenth century through a combination of military victories and mortgage acquisitions from the local ruler, the Nawab of Arcot. By the end of the eighteenth century, the Company took advantage of Arcot's bankruptcy and established formal direct rule over the Madras hinterland, the region called the Jaghire.
3. Although the Company adjudicated disputes through institutions like the Mayor's Court in the town of Madras, the introduction of the new law courts in 1802 marked a new self-conscious interest and intervention in record keeping and notarial procedures.
4. As early as 1750, a Company lease abolished the punitive powers of individual renters of Trivendipuram over the "Company's inhabitants" thereby curtailing the judicial authority of leading inhabitants (Mizushima 1986, 344) even as its legal structures integrated collective assemblies to resolve urban disputes (Brimnes). After the formal acquisition of the Coromandel hinterland, the autonomy of multi-caste assemblies was greatly diminished with the expansion of the judicial powers of European officers and jurisdictional authority of Company moffusil courts.
5. First published in 1818 by the Government Gazette Office of Madras, the text was republished by C. P. Brown in 1852, along with papers by Thomas Munro, Lt. Colonel Blackburne. and Colonel Thomas Munro, as *Three Treatises on Mirasi Rights;* and then again in 1862 by Bayley and Hudleston, as part of a compilation called *Papers on Mirasi Right*. I have consulted it in the C. P. Brown edition.

6. Davis suggests that Ellis shares some important similarities with the school of historical jurisprudence. His emphasis on historically grounded and regionally variegated approaches to custom and legal texts differed from the increasingly influential Utilitarians who advocated codification. Ellis also believed in regional differences within the subcontinent on issues of substantive law. For this and other points of comparison with the Calcutta orientalists and the context of historical jurisprudence, see Davis (2009).
7. In this, Ellis seems to resonate with the historical school of jurisprudence in his interest in tying usage to historical processes. His views here should be placed in relation to the wide-ranging literature on customary practice in colonial law. Scholars of colonial law have frequently noted that official reification of customary usage drained those very practices of their political vigor (Cohn 1996, Dirks 2001). Davis has, in addition, argued that *acara* or "practice" in the Sanskrit commentaries refers to norms consciously and deliberately established by the elites of a group. It could refer to both norm and practice. Usually, a form of consensus could turn everyday practice into a norm (Davis 2004).
8. Recent scholarship on Mackenzie is detailed. See Dirks 1993, Mantena 2002, and Wagoner 2003. Wagoner offers a succinct survey of the debates on colonial knowledge.
9. Ellis appears to have consulted Mackenzie's papers in great depth, selecting these five out of a large corpus of 1700 such texts (1852: 72, fn. 10). Mackenzie's undertaking has been extensively discussed and vigorously debated in recent years as an exemplary project in the making of colonial knowledge.
10. A few of these documents may have well been taken from the Mackenzie archive, but most would have been collected in Madras in the course of everyday revenue work. Ellis does not remark on the provenance of each one of his sources.
11. See also Tirmizi 1982. Mohiuddin 1971 provides the only extended treatment of Persian documents that comprehensively treats their scribal production in the Mughal Chancellery.
12. Unlike the principles of diplomatics, the literary tone of inscriptions has received considerable theoretical attention. The importance of literary composition, the performative context, and political rhetoric

in the language of inscriptional records has been emphasized by many scholars. For extensive recent treatments for South India, see Dirks 1976, Heitzman 1987, Ali 2000 and Talbot 2001.

13. Positive law is distinguished from natural law. It is generally held to be the body of laws that have been enacted and upheld by the courts.
14. Thomas Trautmann's essay in *The Madras School of Orientalism* (2009) situates this important text in the British-Indian debates about revenue and oriental despotism.
15. See Irschick's (1994) treatment of the afterlife of Ellis's text in Tamil political and intellectual history, especially as it pertained to landless groups.
16. Ellis distinguished between the Deccani sultans—"Mohammadan conquest"—from the Mughal conquest which he dates to Aurangzeb's conquest of Golconda and Bijapur. The Sultans, he argued, respected the ancient usage of the "Hindu people," "it was the Mughals and their all devouring system of revenue which abrogated them" (Ellis 1852: 92, note 25).
17. In his view, proprietorship was so closely allied to kin-based decision making and possession that he argued that Dalit laboring groups could be understood as possessing *mirasi* right. This rather paradoxical separation of proprietorship from lordship allowed him to naturalize bondage as slavery, and further, as benign. Commenting on a sixteenth-century bondage-deed, Ellis argues that *mirasi* rights extended to Paraiyar agrestic groups because by law the head of the family could sell his kin. "The natural state of the Paraiyar is slavery," he argued and felt that, although they could be transferred like property, Hindu legal prescriptions paid humane attention to the condition of slaves because slaves could be only sold as family units and not individuals. Ellis insisted that this too was an instance where the customs of antiquity were praiseworthy and that many such praiseworthy customs had fallen into disuse (1852: 103–4). This controversial stance taken by Ellis was deeply criticized in the late nineteenth century by those who felt he had contributed to rendering slavery in South India "benign." See Irschick (1994) for an overview of this issue. Furthermore, many scholars have noted that, although the British viewed agrestic labor relations through the lens

of slavery, the internal dynamics of the system were quite different from plantation slavery (Ludden 1985: 93, Chatterjee and Eaton 2006: 1–16, 17–43).

18. Allodial tenure pertains to the holding of land in absolute ownership usually used in contrast to feudal tenure where the lord held all property. In medieval English law, allodial tenure denoted land ownership in the age before the Norman Conquest. Ellis' emphasis on allodial tenure kept more with his belief the *mirasi* system was evidence that the sovereign was not the landlord.
19. A variety of materials were, in fact used to write documents at this time in Madras. Although paper was not unknown in the immediate vicinity of European coastal enclaves and the Maratha and Arcot courts, several observers from that time note the widespread use of palm-leaf for textual copying and recordkeeping in Tamil. The Company's own efforts at tax collection depended on accountant-scribes, *kanakkuppillai* (kaṇakkuppiḷḷai), who kept Tamil records on palm-leaf and commonly wrote documents such as the ones in Ellis's appendix in a given settlement. It is quite possible then, that many of the Tamil documents from the Madras hinterland in the *Treatise* may have been first written on palm-leaf even if Ellis made use of paper transcriptions. In the course of a discussion on stamp duties, Ellis wrote a detailed letter to the Board discussing the use of palm-leaf for conveyances and deeds.
20. For an overview of Anglo-Hindu law in Calcutta under Company rule see Cohn 1996. On the problem of interpretation of Dharmasastra legal traditions in the medieval period and in contrast to colonial interpretations more generally, see Davis 2004 and 2005.
21. "Extract on Writing" in folder 10 (following a "History of the Bijapur Nabobs"), Mackenzie Misc. 169 (Asia, Pacific and Africa Collection, British Library, London). Brief prefatory comments attribute the text to Vidyaranya or Madhavacarya and present the text as the rules or "regulations of Lekhitapracaranum different ways of the Hindus or formula of deeds of the Hindus as reported in the vyavaharaconda."
22. In a perceptive section on the limits of epigraphy, D.C. Sircar notes that poetic eulogies and conventional elements overshadowed historically verifiable information. Further, he notes that many inscriptions did not bear dates and very few bore dates of popular eras because they

mostly aligned themselves with regnal years. Most importantly, he notes that astronomers calculated dates (Sircar 1965: 23–24).

23. This "register" provided a comprehensive record of shares possessed by *mirasidars,* their tenants, dependants, and the extent of cultivable lands for the current year. Ellis notes that these records were discarded by the East India Company in favor of certificates based on the register, distributed to individuals and detailing their possession (1852: 5).
24. C.R. Cheney argues that notaries emerged in England much later than in the continent because "customary law prevailed" and written records were more in the nature of precautionary evidences (Cheney 1972: 6–7). In contrast, Michael Clanchy suggests that the non-literates' distrust of written modes of proof may have prevented the proliferation of notaries and a continued use of seals (Clanchy 1979: 232–6). Both of these views of notarial practice assume a different understanding of notarial authority (premised on a distinction between public and private law) than that exercised by the *kanakkuppillai.* We should read Ellis's use of the term as an act of rendering the two equivalent, rather than a self-evident translation.
25. Scholarly research on South Indian seals in the seventeenth century is very sparse. I have relied on Ganesh 2008. By the seventeenth and eighteenth centuries, South Indian seals tended to be inscribed with images or names of a deity—usually, Shiva, Vishnu, or the Devi. Personal names began to proliferate much later. Sometimes seals were inscribed with the name of the saint, like a Nagari seal found in Belgaum that bore the text, "*Sri Vithal Jandev Thukaram,*" suggesting that a devotee or monastic institution following the saint Tukaram used it. From the metallic properties and carving of seals we can discern that they were used on wax to seal letters on paper or mark goods in the bazaar. From stray examples, it is possible to speculate that these sealings were exchanged in circles that used paper. The Company introduced the embossed seal on palm-leaf, but it is likely that prior to this innovation seals were not uniformly applied to minor conveyances.
26. See Shapin 1994 on the relevance of "Gentlemanly" credibility to the creation of scientific truth in England.
27. Ellis observes that multi-caste assemblies had greater juridical powers in the past, but that in the early nineteenth century were only

composed of groups belonging to the right hand faction under the direction of the *natu-desam* and deliberated only on the questions of caste (1852: 57). The place and power of the multi-caste assembly has intrigued historians and produced a large scholarly literature. Niels Brimnes (1999) offers a comprehensive overview of the multi-caste assemblies in the colonial port town in the eighteenth and early nineteenth centuries.

28. See Ravi Ahuja (1998, 1999, 2002), Niels Brimmes (1999), and Aparna Balachandran (2008) for discussions of the activities and political power of low caste groups in urban Madras.
29. Colonial knowledge/power studies is a vast field, but for a founding text and quick overview of the salient points of the argument, see Bernard Cohn's classic formulation, *Colonialism and its Forms of Knowledge,* 1996. Also see Nicholas B. Dirks, *Castes of Mind: Colonialism and the Making of Modern India,* 2001. For an overview of the problem of evidence as it pertains to different modern disciplines, see Chandler, Davidson and Hartoonunian 1991; and for the problem of evidence in historical method, see Ginzburg [1986] 1989. For a succinct overview of the debate over colonial knowledge production under Company rule in India, see Wagoner 2003.

REFERENCES

Ahuja, Ravi. 1998. "Labour unsettled: Mobility and protest in the Madras region, 1750-1800." *Indian Economic & Social History Review*, 35, no. 4: 381–404.

———. 1999. "The Origins of Colonial Labour Policy in Late Eighteenth-Century Madras." *International Review of Social History*, 44, no. 2: 159–95.

———. 2001. "Expropriating the Poor, Urban Land Control and Colonial Administration in Late Eighteenth Century Madras City." *Studies in History*, 17, no. 1: 81–99.

———. 2002. "Labour Relations in an Early Colonial Context: Madras c. 1750–1800." *Modern Asian Studies,* 36, no. 4: 793–826.

Ali, Daud. 2000. "Royal Eulogy as World History: Rethinking Copper-plate Inscriptions in Cola India." In *Querying the Medieval: The History of Practice in South Asia,* ed. Daud Ali, pp 165–229. New York: Oxford University Press.

Balachandran, Aparna. 2008. "Christ and the Pariah: Colonialism, Religion and Outcaste Labor in South India, 1780–1830." Ph.D. dissertation, Columbia University.

Banerjee, S.C. 1996. *Traditions of Hindu Jurisprudence*, Volume I and II. New Delhi: Sharada Publishing House.

Bayley, W.H., and Hudleston, W. 1862. *Papers on Mirasi Right: Selected from the Records of Government and Published by Permission*. Madras: Pharoah.

Beaglehole, T. H. 1966. *Thomas Munro and the Development of Administrative Policy in Madras, 1792–1818*. Cambridge University Press.

Bhatia, M.L. 1982. "Mode of Registration of Sale/Transfer Deeds: A Case Study in the Second Half of the 17th Century." *Indian History Congress: Proceedings* (Delhi), 43rd session: 263–69.

Brimnes, Niels. 1999. *Constructing the Colonial Encounter: Right and Left hand Castes in Colonial South India*. Surrey: Curzon Press.

Chandler, J., A. Davidson and H. Hartoonunian, eds. 1991. *Question of Evidence: Proof, Practice, and Persuasion across the Disciplines*. Chicago: The University of Chicago Press.

Chatterjee, Indrani, and Richard Eaton, eds. 2006. *Slavery and South Asian History*. Bloomington: Indiana University Press.

Chhabra, B.C. 1951. "Diplomatic of Sanskrit Copperplate Grants." *Indian Archives*, 5, no. 1 (January–June): 1–20.

Cohn, Bernard. 1996. *Colonialism and its Forms of Knowledge*. Princeton University Press: Princeton.

Crole, Charles Stewart. 1879. *The Chingleput, Late Madras, District. A Manual Compiled under the orders of the Madras Government*. Madras: Asylum Press.

Davis, Donald. 2004. "Dharma in Practice: Acara and Authority in Medieval Dharmasastra." *Journal of Indian Philosophy*, 32: 813–830.

———. 2005. "Intermediate Realms of Law: Corporate Groups and Rulers in Medieval India." *Journal of the Economic and Social History of the Orient*, 48.1: 92–117.

———. 2009. "Law in the Mirror of Language: The Madras School of Orientalism on Hindu Law." In *Madras School of Orientalism, Producing Knowledge in Colonial South India*, ed. Thomas Trautman, pp. 288–309. Delhi: Oxford University Press.

Derrett, J. Duncan M. 1968. *Religion, Law and the State in India*. The Free Press: New York.

Dirks, Nicholas. 1976. "Political Authority and Structural Change in Early South Indian History." *Indian Economic and Social History Review*, 13, no. 2: 125–57.

———. 1993. "Colonial Histories and Native Informants: Biography of an Archive." In *Orientalism and the Postcolonial Predicament*, eds. Peter van der Veer and Carol Breckenridge, pp. 279–313. Philadelphia: University of Pennsylvania Press.

———. 2001. *Castes of Mind: Colonialism and the Making of Modern India*. Princeton University Press: Princeton.

Ellis, Francis Whyte. 1852. "A Reply to the First Seventeen Questions Stated in a Letter From the Secretary to Government in the Revenue Department." In *Three Treatises on Mirasi Right by the Late Francis W. Ellis, Lt. Blackburne, Sir Thomas Munro with the Remarks made by the Hon'ble The Court of Directors*, ed. C.P. Brown. Madras: Christian Knowledge Society Press.

Frykenberg, Robert. 1977. "The Silent Settlement in South India, 1793–1853: An Analysis of the Role of Inams in the Rise of the Indian Imperial System." In *Land Tenure and Peasant in South Asia*, ed. Frykenberg, pp. 37–53. New Delhi: Orient Longman.

Gale, Susan Gaylord. 1982. "A Very German Legal Science: Savigny and the Historical School." *Stanford Journal of International Law* 18: 123-46.

Ganesh, K. 2008. *Seals of South India*. Bangalore: Published by the Author.

Ginzburg, Carlo. [1986] 1989. *Clues, Myths, and the Historical Method*. Johns Hopkins Press: Baltimore.

Grafton, Anthony. 1997. *The Footnote*. Cambridge, Mass.: Harvard University Press.

Grewal, J.S. 1975. *In the By-lanes of History: Some Persian Documents from a Punjab Town*. Simla: Indian Institute of Advanced Study.

Hasan, Farhat. 2004. *State and Locality in Mughal India: Power Relations in Western India, c. 1572–1730*. Cambridge, U.K.; New York: Cambridge University Press.

Heitzman, James. 1987. "State Formation in South India, 850-1280." *Indian Economic & Social History Review* 24, no. 1: 35–61.

Irschick, Eugene. 1994. *Dialogue and History Constructing South India, 1795-1895* Berkeley: University of California Press.

Ludden, David. [1985] 1993. *Peasant History in South India.* Princeton: Princeton University Press.

Mizushima, T. 2002. "From Mirasidar to Pattadar: South India in the late Nineteenth Century." *Indian Economic & Social History Review* 39, no. 2–3: 259–84.

Mantena, Rama. 2002. *"Vernacular Futures: Orientalism, History, and Language in Colonial South India." Ph.D. dissertation, University of Michigan.*

Mohiuddin, Momin. 1971. *The Chancellery and Persian Epistolography under the Mughals, from Babur to Shah Jahan, 1526–1658: A Study on Insha, Dar al-Insha, and Munshis based on Original Documents.* Calcutta: Iran Society.

Mukherjee, Nilamani. 1962. *The Ryotwari System in Madras 1792–1827.* Calcutta: Firma K.L. Mukhopadhyay.

Orr, Leslie. 2000. *Donors, Devotees and Daughters of God: Temple Women of Medieval Tamil Nadu.* New York: Oxford University Press.

Rao, Velcheru N., Sanjay Subrahmanyam, and David Shulman. 2001. *Textures of Time: Writing History in South India 1600–1800.* New Delhi: Permanent Black.

Salomon, Richard. 1998. *Indian Epigraphy: A Guide to the Study of Inscriptions in Sanskrit, Prakrit, and the Other Indo-Aryan Languages.* New York: Oxford University Press.

Shapin, Stephen. 1994. *A Social History of Truth: Civility and Science in Seventeenth-Century England.* Chicago: Chicago University Press.

Sircar, D.C. 1965. *Indian Epigraphy*. Delhi: Motilal Banarasidass.

Stein, Burton. 1989. *Thomas Munro: The Origins of the Colonial State and His Vision of the Empire.* Delhi, Oxford University Press.

Talbot, Cynthia. 2001. *Precolonial India in Practice: Society, Region, and Identity in Medieval Andhra.* New York: Oxford University Press.

Tirmizi, S.A.I. 1982. "Medieval Indian Diplomatics" *Indian History Congress: Proceedings* (Delhi) 43rd session: 211–31.

Trautmann, Thomas. 2006. *Languages & Nations: The Dravidian Proof in Colonial Madras*. Berkeley: University of California Press.

———. 2009. "Riot over Ryotwar." In *The Madras School of Orientalism,* ed. Thomas Trautmann, pp. 310–32. Delhi: Oxford University Press.

Wagoner, Phillip. 2003. "Pre-Colonial Intellectuals and the Production of Colonial Knowledge." *Comparative Studies in Society and History* 45, no. 4: 783–814.

7

Contesting Knowledges in Colonial India

The Question of *Prithviraj Raso*'s Historicity*

CYNTHIA TALBOT

In 1886 an article was published in the *Journal of the Asiatic Society of Bengal* with the lengthy title, "The Antiquity, Authenticity and Genuineness of the Epic called THE PRITHI RAJ RASA, and commonly ascribed to Chand Bardai."Despite its bland name, the article caused quite a stir because it forcefully repudiated the historicity of the *Prithviraj Raso* epic, which was widely regarded as contemporary to the late twelfth-century lifetime of its hero, Prithviraj Cauhan. The author laid out his position with admirable succinctness at the outset of the article, in these words (Syamaldas 1886a: 5):

"This famous Hindi epic—generally believed by scholars to be the work of Chand Bardai, the court bard of Prithi Raj Chauhan, and describing the latter's history from his birth to his death—is not *genuine*, but was, in

* I am grateful to Lloyd Rudolph for kindly sharing his unpublished conference paper on Syamaldas, and for encouraging me to write on him and other matters Rajasthani. I also thank Tom Trautmann, Bhavani Raman, and others in the audience at "Conceptualizing South Asia's Past: A Conference in Honor of Thomas R. Trautmann," a conference held in Ann Arbor in October 2007, for their helpful comments.

my humble opinion, fabricated several centuries after Chand's time, by a bard or bhat of Rajputana, to show the greatness of his own caste and of the Chauhans, who had come to the province from other parts of the country, and were not held in great esteem by the Princes of Rajputana." [italics in original]

This bold attack on conventional wisdom was controversial enough to provoke a rebuttal, called *The Defence of Prithiraj Rasa No. 1*, which was published the following year.[1]

The text under question, *Prithviraj Raso*, is a long poem composed in the Pingal literary language (a form of Braj Bhasa inflected by Rajasthani) that had circulated widely in Western India among aristocratic warriors of the Rajput community. It presented itself as an eyewitness account of the career of the Indian king Prithviraj Cauhan, best known for his defeat at the hands of Muhammad Ghuri in 1192. Since Muhammad Ghuri's conquests ushered in six centuries of Muslim political dominance in the subcontinent, Prithviraj Cauhan was repeatedly described as the "last Hindu emperor of north India" by Colonel James Tod in his authoritative *Annals and Antiquities of Rajasthan*, published in 1829–1832.

Echoing the view of the elite Rajputs with whom he associated for years, Tod also understood *Prithviraj Raso* to be "the heroic history of Prithiraj, the last of the Hindu sovereigns of Delhi, written by his bard Chand" (Tod [1920] 1990: lvii). The dynastic histories and genealogies that the Mewar and Marwar courts supplied to Tod in his early nineteenth-century quest to recover the Rajput past—"the annals" to which he often refers—did not date back nearly as far as the late twelfth-century lifetime of Prithviraj Cauhan. Tod therefore resorted to the *Raso* not only for its narrative of Prithviraj's career, but also for details on the early history of the various Rajput clans—their origins, migrations, feudal culture, and heroic activities(Talbot 2007b). Rejecting the *Raso*'s historicity thus meant rejecting a good deal of what had been written about medieval Rajput history, as well as about Prithviraj Cauhan's career, by Tod and subsequent scholars.

There was even more at stake in challenging the "authenticity" of *Prithviraj Raso* in 1886 than the issue of Rajput history and its implications for contemporary Rajput identity. If the *Raso* was not in actuality a twelfth-century work, it could no longer be considered the earliest surviving text in the Hindi language. The *Raso*'s status as first of its kind had been touted at least as far back as 1827, when William Price—a professor at the College of Fort William, the East India Company's school in Calcutta—identified the "writings of Chand" as the "oldest upon record" of any works in the Hindi language.[2] Price differentiated between Hindi (written in Nagari script) and Hindustani (written in Perso-Arabic script), but regarded them as dialects of the same language or "various forms of one common tongue" (Krishnacarya 1966: 187). From the 1860s onwards, however, the belief that Hindi and Hindustani/Urdu were two distinct languages with separate genealogies became increasingly appealing to non-Muslim residents of north India. *Prithviraj Raso* was the sole piece of vernacular north Indian literature that had been assigned to an era before extensive Muslim influence, thereby establishing the antiquity of Hindi and its independence from Hindustani/Urdu (Dalmia 1997: 193–95, 200). The assertion that the epic was "fabricated" hundreds of years after Prithviraj's lifetime thus seriously threatened a cornerstone of the Hindu nationalist sense of its own past that was just beginning to take shape in north India.

Syamaldas questioned centuries of certainty about *Prithviraj Raso*'s evidentiary status, in both the local knowledge of Rajasthani bards and the colonial knowledge of British administrator-scholars like James Tod. What makes this attack on a truth accepted equally by traditional and colonial authorities especially striking is the identity of its author: Syamaldas, who lived from 1836 to 1893 AD. Awarded the honorific title "Kaviraj" by the ruler of Mewar in recognition of his meritorious service as court poet, Syamaldas was a member of the Caran bardic community of Rajasthan. Even more surprising than his caste affiliation or his residence in a princely state, where traditional ways typically persisted with greater force than in British India, was Syamaldas's inability to write in English. He composed his article for the *Journal of the Asiatic Society of Bengal* in Hindi and had it translated into English by a Munshi Ram Prasad; the Hindi version was published the following year.[3] The rebuttal to Syamaldas's critique, on the other hand, was first written by Pandit Mohanlal Vishnulal Pandya in English and then rendered into Hindi. The English-educated Pandya was a Brahman from the Gangetic heartland of British India, although he was employed at the royal court in Udaipur just as was Syamaldas. Despite his greater exposure to Western ways, it was Pandya who upheld the established view regarding *Prithviraj Raso*, rather than the bard.

The dispute over the *Raso*'s credentials as a historic document offers an opportunity to apply, on a small scale, Thomas R. Trautmann's interest in the formation of colonial knowledge to the topic of historiography, in a foray away from the classificatory schemes relating to kinship, race, and language to which he has paid the most attention. Trautmann has focused on the early colonial period, when a basic framework for understanding India's society and history was being formulated. In his recent *Languages and Nations: The Dravidian Proof in Colonial Madras*, Trautmann asserts that "the new knowledge being produced in British India came about precisely because of the conjuncture of these two traditions of language analysis, European and Indian" (2006: 42). When analyzing Rajputs or Rajasthan instead of languages and nations, a comparable conjuncture of traditions can be located in the early nineteenth-century work of Colonel James Tod, even though aspects of it were eventually repudiated. As Jason Freitag has said aptly, "Tod's text straddles two historical worlds and finds a home in each" (Freitag 2007: 87). Reading *Annals and Antiquities of Rajasthan* as a product of a conjuncture of knowledge reveals the complexities of the intellectual environment of late nineteenth-century north India, for it means that Syamaldas was himself responding to the new knowledge formulated 60 years earlier by

Tod, which had been based on a reinterpretation, a recasting, of Rajasthan's bardic chronicles.

Syamaldas does not fit neatly into schemes such as the "dual economy of knowledge" that Christopher Bayly has described as emerging in India during the nineteenth century. In Bayly's words, there was "an 'advanced' sector, which used western forms of representation and communication subsisting within an attenuated but still massive hinterland employing the older styles of information and debate" (1996: 372). The newer and more authoritative system of knowledge was that created by British administrators and European scholars, with its own criteria for admissible evidence, modes of argumentation, and above all, an insistence on applying historical frameworks. The networks of communication and dissemination also differed greatly between the newer and older "information orders." By the 1860s and 1870s, at least some Indians participated actively in the British-style knowledge system as scholars, and as intellectuals within the adjacent sphere of the newly established vernacular newspapers and presses (Bayly 1996: 340–51). The vernacular print culture represents yet another "economy of knowledge," one that began superseding the older indigenous forms during the late nineteenth century.

Attesting to the existence of multiple networks of knowledge by the late 1880s is the fact that Syamaldas and Pandya each propagated his views in both English and Hindi. By publishing their assessments of *Prithviraj Raso*'s authenticity simultaneously in these two languages, they sought to influence audiences that encompassed north Indian intellectuals who were active mainly in vernacular circles, as well as those Indians and Westerners who participated in the more rarified sphere of English-language scholarship on India. Their dispute not only straddled linguistic boundaries, it also straddled the divide between British and princely India—while Syamaldas published his repudiation of the *Raso* in British India, Pandya's response (also issued in British

India) makes it clear that Syamaldas had angered sections of elite society in the state of Mewar.

In this essay, I take a close look at Syamaldas's challenge to the accepted truths of his age and also at the manner in which Pandya attempted to counter Syamaldas's critique. I ask what personal or social factors caused Syamaldas and Pandya to arrive at their differing positions on the historicity of *Prithviraj Raso*, positions that are diametrically opposed to what one might have assumed they would take. Their dispute over the value of this elite vernacular epic is but one of many episodes that went into the making of a modern Indian historiography, or rather the making of a *variety* of modern Indian historiographies. Thanks to Trautmann, Bayly, and others, the broad outlines of nineteenth-century knowledge formation have been sketched in; the present study is one step in the filling in of the general picture. By bringing to the forefront of our scholarly scrutiny two Indian intellectuals who took part in creating constructions of the Indian past that persist to this day, I hope to draw attention to the multiplicity of agents and convoluted pathways embroiled in the process(es) of writing history.

SYAMALDAS'S HISTORICAL SCHOLARSHIP

Syamaldas's "The Antiquity, Authenticity and Genuineness of the Epic called THE PRITHI RAJ RASA, and commonly ascribed to Chand Bardai" appeared in the *Journal of the Asiatic Society of Bengal*, the most prestigious scholarly outlet in the subcontinent. Founded over a century earlier, in 1784, the Bengal Asiatic Society was an entirely European enterprise until 1829, when the first Indian member was inducted (U. Singh 2004: 14). The proportion of Indians grew gradually until it comprised a quarter (83 out of 329) of the Society's membership by 1885, the year before Syamaldas published his critique of *Prithviraj Raso*.[4] Despite the presence of a fair number of Indians in the late nineteenth century, the Society was still dominated by Europeans. The preponderance of Europeans is especially evident in the pages of its journal: between 1865 and

1890, for instance, only 15 percent (18 out of 117) of the men whose articles were published there possessed Indian names.[5]

Many of the Indians whose scholarly work was published by the Asiatic Society were members of the colonial establishment, holding positions like deputy magistrate (e.g., Gourdass Bysack), deputy collector (e.g., Rangalal Banerjea), and deputy inspector of schools (e.g., Babu Sarat Chandra Das), or they were educators. They had been trained in the medium of the English language and generally instructed in Western subject matter; a few of them had earned college degrees. They were precisely the sort of "educated natives" or "Babus" against whom the European opponents of the Ilbert Bill of 1883 had recently mobilized. (The Ilbert Bill would have allowed Indian magistrates to try Europeans in rural localities where no European judge was readily available, but European antagonism led to the watering down of its provisions.) Syamaldas, on the other hand, apparently knew no English—it is this fact that differentiates him most from other contributors to the *Journal* in the late nineteenth century, rather than his Indian identity.

In "The Antiquity, Authenticity and Genuineness of the Epic called THE PRITHI RAJ RASA," Syamaldas engages in the most fundamental historiographic task of all—the verification of source material. He shared the late nineteenth-century distrust of the evidence of literary texts. In addition to the terms "authenticity" and "genuineness" that are featured in the title, his article makes liberal use of words like "spurious," "fabricated," and "forged." Syamaldas also refers repeatedly to the *Raso*'s "mistakes" and its "incorrect" dates. His language is highly judgmental and admits of no shades of gray—facts are either correct or inaccurate, a text is either genuine or false.[6]

The issue of dating was central to Syamaldas's repudiation of *Prithviraj Raso*. Only the first of the five sections into which Syamaldas divided his argument focuses on something other than correct chronology. In this first section, he looks rather at the linguistic features, noting that the use of Rajasthani words suggested a provenance in Rajasthan rather than in Delhi, which the epic identifies as Prithviraj's capital and place of residence. In the remainder of the article, Syamaldas examines the dates provided in the *Raso* in order to establish that it was composed considerably later than the twelfth century. He begins by quoting *Raso* passages containing dates for three events: Prithviraj's birth, his accession to the Delhi throne, and the final battle Prithviraj fought against Shihabuddin Muhammad of Ghur. "So that no one might argue that it might be a mistake of the scribe," Syamaldas takes pains to cite at least two instances of the *Raso*'s date for each event (1886a: 12).

Having shown that the epic was consistent in its dating, Syamaldas demonstrates in the third part of the article that these dates were inaccurate. He does so through comparison with the testimony of Persian texts, especially the mid thirteenth-century *Tabaqat-i Nasiri*, which contains the earliest detailed description of the hostilities between Prithviraj Cauhan and Muhammad of Ghur. Indo-Persian histories placed the final conflict between the two men in 1192–93 AD, some 91 years later than was specified in *Prithviraj Raso*, and there is no hesitation on Syamaldas's part as to which date was more credible. "The Muhammadans," he writes, "had a regular system of writing History, the Hindus had no such system; if there was anything of the kind, it was simply the genealogies, and very little, if any, historical accounts written in the books of the bards, or exaggerated poems of the time" (1886a: 16). Here Syamaldas reiterates the widespread Orientalist charge that Hindu India lacked a proper historical consciousness and had therefore produced little that could be considered historiography (see Thapar, this volume). In determining the date of Prithviraj's accession to the throne, Syamaldas similarly rejected the *Raso* in preference for another type of source material, the stone inscription. The privileging of inscriptions in chronological matters, along with Indo-Persian histories, was a well-established practice among scholars of India, and became especially prevalent after the systematic collection and publication of inscriptions was officially undertaken by the Archeological Survey of India.

Syamaldas explains the significance of *Prithviraj Raso*'s chronological inaccuracies in the fourth section of his article, for they had repercussions far beyond the reckoning of Prithviraj Cauhan's lifetime. The dates provided in the *Raso* had become temporal anchors for bardic genealogies composed hundreds of years later for the royal dynasties of Mewar, Marwar, and Amber, among others. That is, the rulers of these Rajasthani kingdoms were alleged to be descendants of warriors who had fought in Prithviraj's wars. Because the *Raso* placed Prithviraj almost a century earlier than he had actually lived, there was a considerable gap in the royal genealogies that later bards had to creatively adjust in some fashion, leading to numerous "mistakes." Thus, if one were to accept Syamaldas's assessment of the *Raso* as spurious, many of the dynastic histories of Rajasthan's ruling families would also have to be questioned. Syamaldas ends the article with a discussion of the *Raso*'s true date of composition, which he places between 1583 and 1613 AD.

The extensive use of primary sources is a hallmark of Syamaldas's historical scholarship. In order to make his points, he cites verses from *Prithviraj Raso* in full and explains their gist in English; passages from *Tabaqat-i Nasiri* are also quoted in translation. The most amply documented source material of all are the inscriptions Syamaldas relies on as proof of the true dates for Prithviraj Cauhan and for Samar Singh, the Mewar king who was allegedly Prithviraj's staunch ally.[7] Syamaldas is detailed in his descriptions, stating exactly where the epigraphs were situated and often commenting on the overall size of the written text, the number of inscribed lines, any peculiarities in orthography and the like—the standard features noted in the late nineteenth century as the professionalization of Indian epigraphy progressed. Aside from upholding his argument, the inscriptions also testified to Syamaldas's competence as a scholar.

The basic historical method employed by Syamaldas was comparison of several different *types* of primary sources pertaining to the same event or era. Although it appears routine to us today, such comparisons would have been much harder to carry out in the precolonial past, even had the inclination to do so existed. That is, European-style scholarship on India's past required a substantial collecting effort—a variety of different texts and documents had first to be gathered together. It also required the presence of investigators able to decipher and interpret both the language and the style of diverse historical materials.

These two conditions for modern historical research—a collection of primary sources and linguistic/technical expertise in dealing with them—were abundantly fulfilled in Syamaldas's case. An official History Department (*Itihas Karyalaya*) had been created in the mid-1870s by the Maharana of Mewar, Sajjan Singh, who allocated one lakh rupees for the purpose.[8] A staff of scholars was assembled to assist the head of the department, Syamaldas, in producing an official history of the princely state.[9] The team of assistants included specialists in Sanskrit, Arabic, Persian, Rajasthani, and English—the English expert was Ram Prasad, who translated all five of Syamaldas's articles into English for publication(Sharma 1992: 59). Access to the royal library, with its large collection of literary texts and official correspondence, was provided to Syamaldas. He also acquired a personal library of English-language books that contained items as current as the *Centenary Review of the Asiatic Society of Bengal*, published in 1885, or as old as Abbe Renaudot's *Travels of the Merchants Sulaiman and Abu Zaidul-Hasan*, from 1733.[10]

Syamaldas was in the enviable position, therefore, of having a stable of capable research assistants, like many eminent Western scholars in nineteenth-century India; and he could draw on the royal archive and manuscript library, in addition to his own library of secondary scholarship in English. Few other Indians in this time period would have had such parity in (both human and material) resources with the leading scholars of British India, nor did their job responsibilities typically involve the writing of histories. His physical location outside the boundaries of British India, and his sociological distance from the English-educated babus whom some Europeans so disdained, may well have gained Syamaldas more respect from his Western counterparts than would otherwise have been the case.

Before turning, in the next section, to further consideration of the courtly and colonial contexts within which Syamaldas operated, let me briefly introduce the eventual outcome of the Mewar historical project—the multi-volume text called *Vir Vinod: Mewar ka Itihas*. Syamaldas's article on *Prithviraj Raso* was a work in progress from that larger project, and it appeared in *Vir Vinod*(printed between 1886 and the mid-1890s) with only minor changes.[11]Written in Khari Boli Hindi with considerable use of Persian vocabulary, *Vir Vinod* is an impressively comprehensive survey of Mewar's political history that has been praised for its objectivity by modern scholars (Sinh 1978: 30–31; Sharma 1973: 285).

Although it is labeled a history of the Mewar kingdom, *Vir Vinod* begins with a universal perspective that quickly zooms down to the more restricted focus on the region. Its first hundred pages contain a sketch of world geography, followed by the geography of Hindustan. This spatial orientation is complemented by the inclusion of a chronological framework, a short summary of Indian history. Only after deploying these "technologies of location," to use Tom Trautmann's wording (2006: 2–13), does Syamaldas narrow his gaze to Mewar. While the introductory portion is reminiscent of puranic texts that begin with the origin of the cosmos, the influence of the colonial gazetteer as a model for Syamaldas is apparent in the next 150 pages, on the physical and cultural geography of Mewar. It is chock full of specifics on Mewar—its flora, fauna, climate, prevalent religions, festivals, and castes—the kind of intimate knowledge about localities that colonial authorities had accumulated in British India by this time. In contrast, much of the rest of this massive book, consisting of more than 2000 pages, is devoted to dynastic history—that is, the lives of the royal family and courtly elite.

The bulk of *Vir Vinod* resembles earlier histories composed by court bards in its almost exclusive attention to, and praise for, Mewar's ruling family. To be sure, Syamaldas occasionally condemns the conduct of a past king, and he often questions the dating of specific events and reigns. His emendations of the historical record were facilitated by his possession of a large number of primary source documents whose full texts were published in the book, as was the case in the *Prithviraj Raso* article. While the provision of primary sources and the attempts to establish a firm chronological framework definitively differentiate Syamaldas's endeavor from those of his bardic predecessors, it must be noted that Syamaldas kept his criticism well in check. For instance, he does not refute the many fabulous stories told about Bappa Rawal, the first king of the Guhila/Sisodiya line to supposedly conquer Chittor fort and subsequently rule beyond the borders of the Indian subcontinent. Even if this was not entirely true, writes Syamaldas, Bappa Rawal was without doubt a glorious and mighty emperor (1986: 254). Syamaldas is also careful to stress the longevity and greatness of Mewar's ruling lineage, and he cites a long list of European scholars in support of this assertion, presumably because they were more authoritative. The reliance on foreign testimony is another departure from earlier practice that would have had the added benefit of making Syamaldas appear objective. Overall, however, *Vir Vinod* has to be characterized as a somewhat transitional work: far more critical than Tod's *Annals and Antiquities of Rajasthan* in many respects, as we saw in the case of Syamaldas's assessment of *Prithviraj Raso*, yet still displaying considerable reverence for the foundational myths of Mewar's royal family.

SYAMALDAS, A BARD IN A MODERNIZING COURT

Syamaldas writes in *Vir Vinod* that he had no idea how to go about writing a history when he was first asked to do so in the 1870s, and had to consult several Persian chronicles in order to get started (1986: 182–83). How was it possible for a man like Syamaldas who lacked any formal training in Western historiography to display such a good grasp of modern practices only a decade later? In this section, I explore aspects of Syamaldas's social and political milieu for insight into the influences that shaped him and led to the production of Mewar's first modern historiographic work, beginning with his social identity as a Caran.

Syamaldas was proud of being a Caran, one of Rajasthan's two main groups of bards. He justifies the long account of his community (*qaum*) included in *Vir Vinod* on the grounds that authors should inform their readers about themselves, but it becomes an opportunity for him to extol the greatness of Carans as a whole (Syamaldas 1986: 168–80). During the era of Buddhist ascendance, according to Syamaldas, the Vedic *ksatriyas* were oppressed and had to flee to western India along with their Caran associates. The Carans helped their *ksatriya* patrons (*yajman*) in this time of calamity, by engaging in mercantile activity, but they lost their learning in the process and from that time on had to compose vernacular *dohas* (couplets) instead of Prakrit or Sanskrit *slokas* (verses). Although Syamaldas makes no direct mention of it, much of the early modern vernacular literature of Rajasthan was created by Carans and Bhats, Rajasthan's other bards. In the late seventeenth and early eighteenth centuries, Carans and Bhats were fixtures at the Mewar court and received land and valuables from the kings on ceremonial occasions; they vied with other literate/scribal groups of Brahman and Jain background for royal patronage.

Although Rajasthani bards also acted as messengers, witnesses to agreements and contracts, or guarantors of safe passage in travel,[12] what was important about Carans for Syamaldas was their long service to the ruling class. This may reflect the history of his own family, which had moved to Mewar during the fifteenth-century reign of Maharana Kumbha and received two villages from him. A descendant later received a village from Maharana Sanga as well.

Syamaldas, who was born in 1836, first attended the royal court in 1847 in the company of his father. We are not told where or from whom Syamaldas received his extensive but unfocused education, which covered not only poetry, the epics, and the Puranas, but also aspects of astrology, astronomy, medicine, and the occult (Syamaldas 1986: 180–82). No mention is made of specifically bardic training or of the vernacular languages; his education as described in *Vir Vinod* would equally have been suitable for a Brahman, perhaps because he was preparing himself for a life as courtier.

Indeed, Syamaldas was called upon to perform a variety of services on behalf of Maharanas Sambhu Singh (r. 1861–1874) and Sajjan Singh (r. 1874–1884), far beyond the role of bard.[13] He became quite close to Sambhu Singh, whom he accompanied on journeys and for whose pleasure he recited devotional poetry. In Sambhu Singh's era, Syamaldas was often involved in adjudicating disputes; he also assisted in famine relief efforts and organized various festival observances; in return he received a *haveli* mansion in Udaipur from the king. His duties were even more diverse under the next ruler, Sajjan Singh, for whom he acted as personal secretary. He advised the Maharana on many of the reforms being newly instituted in Mewar, and even accompanied court troops trying to quell an insurgency of Bhil tribals in the hills. Sajjan Singh awarded Syamaldas the honorary title of Kaviraj in 1878 (Somani 1985: 290–91); the king's regard for Syamaldas is evident in Syamaldas's appointment first to the state's Privy Council (*Ijlas Khas*) in 1877, and subsequently to its successor, the State Council (*Mahadraj Sabha*) in 1880.

Other Carans before Syamaldas had occupied positions of considerable political importance, but seldom in such a period of change. The reigns of Sambhu Singh and Sajjan Singh witnessed the first attempts to modernize the kingdom of Mewar in accordance with British ideas and policies, and Syamaldas was involved in myriad innovations as a consequence.[14] Under Sambhu Singh, Mewar's first public hospitals, pharmacies, and schools were established and some roads were built. Changes were made in the court system, a new code of law was introduced, and attempts were made to improve the sanitation system. Reforms proceeded at a faster pace during Sajjan Singh's reign, which witnessed the assessment of land revenues on crown land, the taking of a census, and the opening of a railway line in the eastern part of the state. Simultaneously, the state tried to discourage certain traditional practices that the British abhorred, especially those involving females, such as infanticide, sati, or witch-burning.

Mewar was not the only princely state to come under increased British pressure and surveillance in the post-1857 era, but it was particularly susceptible because Sambhu Singh and Sajjan Singh ascended the throne as young boys and were closely supervised by British political agents. The youth of these Mewar rulers also made them more receptive to new ways. The situation was to change dramatically under Maharana Fateh Singh (r. 1884–1930), who was also adopted but came to the throne as an (already conservative) adult and managed to impede most British influence and intervention. Thus the late 1860s through mid-1880s, the years when Syamaldas was at the height of his career, was simultaneously the period of greatest British influence in Mewar. Udaipur, famous for its beauty since the days of Colonel James Tod, attracted a succession of British visitors in this era, some as eminent as the Viceroy Lord Northbrook in 1875 or Viceroy Lord Dufferin and his wife in 1886.[15]

The creation of an official history of the Mewar state was one of the activities encouraged by the British. It was due to the urging of Mewar's political agent (later known as "resident") that Sambhu Singh set up a History Division (*Itihas Vibhag*) in 1871 in order to produce an authoritative account of the past. Syamaldas was soon appointed to the task along with Purohit Padmanabha and their collaboration led to an incomplete manuscript of 172 pages that covered events up to the reign of Maharana Udai Singh (Sharma 1987: 52). Maharana Sambhu Singh died in 1874, while Syamaldas was still collecting material—when describing this stage in his career, Syamaldas blames his own ignorance of the discipline of history for the slow progress. It was once again at British instigation that the history project received the attention of the next ruler, Maharana Sajjan Singh. When Colonel Impey, the new political agent, persuaded him that a new history of Mewar would enhance the kingdom's reputation, the scale of the effort was greatly expanded with the hiring of several assistants for Syamaldas.

The British also helped Syamaldas in acquiring the most current technologies of historical research, specifically in the field of epigraphy. Upon Syamaldas's request, Pandit Govind Gangadhar Deshpande was deputized by a certain Fleet Sahib to assist Syamaldas for a period of over a year (Syamaldas 1986: 184). This is presumably a reference to J. F. Fleet, who served as Epigraphist to the Government of India between 1883 and 1886 (U. Singh 2004: 126). Deshpande trained Syamaldas and his men in the latest practices (e.g., how to make estampages) and supervised the collection of many inscriptions. We have seen that Syamaldas made use of his newly gained expertise in epigraphic matters by publishing several inscriptions in his *Prithviraj Raso* article; he did so again in the Asiatic Society's *Journal* the following year. Syamaldas also became a member of the Royal Asiatic Society and a fellow of the Royal Historical Society, both of London, and he was awarded the title Mahamahopadhyaya by the British government (Syamaldas 1986: 184).

In spite of his location in a princely state, Syamaldas was clearly part of an international community of scholars interested in Indian culture and literature. He was acquainted with some of them only through correspondence but others personally experienced the warm hospitality of Syamaldas and his princely patron in Udaipur. Among them was Peter Peterson, who spent about 10 days in the Mewar region in October 1882. A professor of Sanskrit in Elphinstone College, Peterson was involved in the government-sponsored search for Sanskrit manuscripts in the Bombay circle and came to Mewar for that purpose. He gratefully notes the assistance extended to him by Syamaldas, whom he calls his "good friend," which enabled him to survey the royal collection and even borrow some 30 manuscripts (Peterson 1883: 54). Peterson also mentions that he lent several manuscripts to Kaviraj Syamaldas for use in preparing a history of Mewar (1883: 54 fn.).

We get more evidence of Syamaldas promoting his own work to European scholars from an account by Cecil Bendall (1856–1906) from the department of Oriental manuscripts and printed books of the British Museum. On his first visit to South Asia during the winter of 1884–85, Bendall's main objective was the acquisition of Sanskrit manuscripts in Nepal but he also stopped briefly in Udaipur. He speaks warmly of Syamaldas, "who lost no time in extending to me the right hand of fellowship" (Bendall [1886] 1974: 30). Bendall considered Syamaldas' historical research to be "very important" and devotes several sentences to its description. His remarks are worth quoting in their entirety, as the only extended contemporary commentary on the project:

The chief families of Rajputana have usually employed a herald or family bard, who has in some sort chronicled their deeds. Babu Śyamal Das has made a most fitting use of his position as royal herald in causing these to be collected and having digests made of their contents. From these, and from the general chronicles and royal *vamśavalis*, which are extant for the state of Oodeypore (or Meywar), the Kaviraj is compiling a history of this state. I was much surprised to find in his library a very fine collection of books in all the chief European languages bearing on the history and topography of Rajputana. Bearing in mind, however, how much history and panegyric run into one another in Eastern literature, it is most important to find that, supplementing his work, is a systematically collected series of inscriptions, which exist in such numbers in these parts. The growing interest (though still it is surprisingly small) felt by native scholars in their own ancient monuments and the records they bear, is one of the encouraging sides of the influence of Western thought in India, though one must confess that Europeans may still do much to make up for the influences, so deteriorating in many ways, which they and their civilization have brought to bear on native morality and native art (Bendall [1886] 1974: 30–31).

Bendall's comments testify to Syamaldas's utilization of recent texts written by European scholars as well as medieval Mewar inscriptions; they also reveal that "native scholars" such as Syamaldas who made use of a range of source materials were still considered very unusual.

Without the support of British officials and scholars, it is unlikely that a lengthy, Western-style history of Mewar like *Vir Vinod* would or could have been put together at such a relatively early date. Its creation must be regarded as another of the innovations being adopted by the young rulers of Mewar, who sought to improve their realm along the lines suggested by the colonial overlords. While *Vir Vinod*'s methodology and inclusion of extracts from original sources were a marked departure from earlier bardic practice, much of its subject matter resembled that of earlier bardic compositions: it was first and foremost a history of Mewar's kings. Syamaldas's text was thus reminiscent of an old type of courtly literature, while simultaneously also representing new knowledge and practices. Choosing a Caran to compose an official history was logical, given the bard's traditional responsibility to record and narrate the pasts of his patrons. Furthermore, Syamaldas was a close royal servant who could be trusted to represent the ruling family in a positive light, yet still discharge his obligation to produce a work that was scholarly by modern British standards. In the end, however, Syamaldas's historical scholarship was sufficiently novel to cause considerable consternation, as we shall see.

IN DEFENSE OF *PRITHVIRAJ RASO*: MOHANLAL VISHNULAL PANDYA'S REBUTTAL

Syamaldas's article on *Prithviraj Raso* evoked a strong response almost immediately, in the form of a rebuttal published the following year by Mohanlal Vishnulal Pandya, in both English and Hindi renditions. *The Defence of Prithiraj Rasa No.1*, is 50 pages long and appeared as a booklet from Medical Hall Press of Benares in 1887, as did its Hindi counterpart. Syamaldas and Pandya had known each other for years; at the time they publicly expressed their respective opinions on *Prithviraj Raso*'s historicity, both men were members of Mewar's *Mahadraj Sabha* or State Council. They had been particularly close to the previous Maharana, Sajjan Singh (r. 1874–84 AD), and served him in various capacities. Syamaldas and Pandya apparently shared Sajjan Singh's great enthusiasm for Swami Dayanand Saraswati, founder of the Arya Samaj, who spent a considerable amount of time in Mewar between late 1881 and early 1883 (B. K. Singh 1970: 72–79; Somani 1985: 291–92). This is reflected in Dayanand's will, which named Syamaldas as secretary and Pandya as assistant secretary of the committee to which he entrusted his possessions and affairs; the committee was convened soon after the Swami's death by poisoning (at the Jodhpur court) in late 1883.[16]

Although they operated in the same political circle and shared a reformist sympathy,[17] the two men came from very different backgrounds. Unlike Syamaldas, whose family had dwelt in Mewar for centuries, Pandya was a native of Mathura who moved to the Rajasthan region sometime in the early 1870s.[18] He was working for the Mewar court by 1880, as a manager looking after the affairs of the Nathdwara temple and as a member of the State Council (Somani 1985: 281–82, 284). A short satire titled *Angrez Stotra*, compiled by Pandya in 1873 suggests that one of his motivations for moving to Rajasthan may have been a desire to get out of British India. Modeled on Sanskrit hymns of praise addressed to popular deities, *Angrez Stotra*'s Hindi parody was more critical than humorous in tone. For example, it lauded the British as the Trimurti, the three great gods of Hinduism: (equivalent to) Brahma, because they were also the god Prajapati (i.e., in being masters of the subject-people); Vishnu, because they were the recipient of goddess Lakshmi's favor (i.e., were wealthy); and Siva, because their wife was goddess Gauri (i.e., the fair-skinned). The hymn, composed not by Pandya but most probably by Bharatendu Hariscandra, was said to be intended for the spiritual liberation of those who engaged in false flattery of the British (Pandya 1873: 2, 4).[19] Political overtones are also apparent in a play by Pandya published the following year.[20]

Another difference between the two men was Pandya's social identity as a Brahman, probably from a community that had originated in Gujarat.[21] Pandya was often addressed as pandit in recognition of his learning, which included some knowledge of Sanskrit. Like many other educated Brahmans in late nineteenth-century north India, Pandya also knew English. That Syamaldas and Pandya were addressing more than one audience is evident in their issuing of both English and Hindi versions of their pieces on *Prithviraj Raso*, but whereas Syamaldas needed someone else to translate his Hindi composition into English, Pandya wrote both himself, beginning with the English version (Pandya 1887b: 3). Pandya may have received some of his education in Benares, perhaps even at Jai Narayan's College where Dr. A. F. Rudolf Hoernle—described in Pandya's 1887 booklet as "my venerable tutor" and "my venerable teacher"—taught from 1869 to 1874 (Pandya 1887a: 38, 43).[22] The most famous of Pandya's Benares acquaintances was the acclaimed Hindi author Bharatendu Hariscandra (1850–85), at whose instigation Pandya culled the hymns in *Angrez Stotra* from the pages of *Kavivacansudha,* Hariscandra's first journal.[23] Hariscandra was the leading literary figure in Benares during the 1870s and early 1880s and is often regarded as the father of modern Hindi literature, due both to the range of his own writing (plays, poems, and prose) and the publications he supported. Pandya is known to have edited some issues of Hariscandra's second journal in the early 1880s (McGregor 1974: 85 n. 5). Around this time Hariscandra was invited to Mewar by Maharana Sajjan Singh and given Rs. 10,000 (Somani 1985: 293); it is likely that Pandya had some role in this honoring of a man he admired.[24]

As an English-educated Brahman from British India, one might not have expected Mohanlal Vishnulal Pandya to so vehemently uphold the traditional view on the *Prithviraj Raso*. In his response, it is striking that Pandya takes contention with virtually every aspect of Syamaldas's article, albeit in a disorganized and illogical manner. He spends much of his energy attacking minor points made by Syamaldas, rather than the more problematic issues of chronology. Eventually Pandya does have to address the discrepancies in dating that are so central to Syamaldas's critique, particularly regarding the reign of Mewar's Samar Singh whom the *Raso* depicts as a close ally of Prithviraj Cauhan. Pandya challenges "the testimony of the inscriptions," whose dates for Samar Singh he believes were recorded inaccurately due to scribal error (1887a: 20). Elsewhere, he asks whether certain inscriptions might not be counterfeit, or if "not false, we may think that they having been raised many years after the events recorded thereon had taken place might contain incorrect dates" (1887a: 21). He similarly casts doubt on the evidentiary value of Indo-Persian texts, saying:

> But how is it known that all the contents of these Persian histories are quite right? Is there nothing inaccurate in them? Were the writers infallible? If there is any mixture of truth and falsehood in them, how can they go to prove that the great Epic was a gross forgery? (Pandya 1887a: 36)

In place of inscriptions or Indo-Persian chronicles, which Western scholars regarded as far more trustworthy than literary texts composed in Indic languages, Pandya privileges the consensus of the learned. Especially authoritative "in historical and antiquarian matters" were the writings of Colonel James Tod, "whose work was a labour of love and who maturely weighed all matters given therein" (Pandya 1887a: 25, 17). Pandya repeatedly invokes Tod (and implicitly rebukes Syamaldas) with statements such as: "Cannot our author [Syamaldas] guess Colonel Tod's opinion of the authenticity of the date of the Prithiraj Rasa from the above foot-note?" (1887a: 17). Some 60 years after the publication in England of his *Annals and Antiquities of Rajasthan* (1829–32), Tod had thus attained a hallowed status in Rajasthan that no other author, Indian or Western, has equaled to this day (Rudolph and Rudolph 2003: 255). By the time Pandya wrote his rebuttal, Tod's romantic portrayal of Rajput history was already available in Bengali and Urdu translations and was rapidly being disseminated among the educated populace of British India (Freitag 2001: 232). Tod's was the final word on things Rajput; literally in this case, for Pandya concludes his defense with a long, appreciative quote about the *Raso* taken from Tod's *Annals*.

Pandya also has recourse to the testimony of Western scholars[25] who had worked on *Prithviraj Raso* more recently, such as John Beames, F. S. Growse, and especially Dr. A.F. Hoernle, who was at the time editing the epic for the Bibliotheca Indica series published by the Asiatic Society of Bengal.[26] In support of his views, Pandya additionally cites the "concurrence of many influential Chiefs, Pandits, Bhats, and Charans, the author's caste fellows" or consults "my friends, learned Pandits of Benares"(1887a: 20, 22)."Universally accepted proof," as when "every one in Mewar both high and low, rich and poor knows" something, is another measure of veracity, in Pandya's view (1887a: 24–25). Despite his impeccable control of the English language and his credentials as a former student of Dr. Hoernle (later to become a President of the Bengal Asiatic Society), Pandya makes little attempt to argue from the original sources in Syamaldas's empiricist fashion. On occasion, Pandya refers to material from a later date, such as the famous *Rajaprasasti* poem inscribed ca. 1680 at the command of a Mewar king, but he displays no understanding of the importance of documentary testimony that was more or less contemporary to Prithviraj Cauhan's twelfth-century lifetime. Instead, Pandya relies on the authority of the learned—that is, conventional wisdom—to make his case, just as pandits had for generations before him.

Why Pandya would have gone to the trouble of refuting Syamaldas at length is a fascinating question. None of Syamaldas's other articles provoked such a negative reaction, nor does Pandya seem particularly knowledgeable about historical matters, even if he was a pandit who knew several languages. He tells the reader in his essay that he originally "undervalued" the poem, and only came to appreciate it after spending some time in Rajasthan, where "I have seen the work read or heard with love and esteem by almost all the Rajas and nobles in all parts of the province" (1887a: 43). This led him to start reading the *Raso* with a famous poet of Kota, and "a new light dawned" (1887a: 44). In the preface to the English rendition of the essay, Pandya also states that: "Had it not been that the name of the prince of poets in India [i.e., Cand Bardai]—one who has been commanding the heart and homage of his countrymen for centuries—is unjustly in jeopardy, I would never have taken up the pen." In other words, he justifies his attack on Syamaldas (to whom he acknowledges a debt of gratitude) on the basis of the great regard he, and others, had for *Prithviraj Raso*. Pandya thus positions himself as a selfless individual, working for the benefit of all.

There is ample evidence to suggest that Pandya had additional incentives to uphold the historicity of *Prithviraj Raso*, beyond his admiration for its putative author, Cand Bardai. Motilal Menariya, a twentieth-century scholar long based in Mewar, believed that Pandya was incited to oppose Syamaldas by some court bards from the Bhat community, a group to whom Cand Bardai had allegedly belonged and who were quite distinct from Syamaldas's own Caran community (Menariya 1958: 35).This is a plausible scenario, for the Bhats may understandably have been incensed by Syamaldas' accusation that *Prithviraj Raso* was "fabricated several centuries after Chand's time, by a bard or bhat of Rajputana, to show the greatness of his own caste and of the Chauhans, who had come to the province from other parts of the country" (Syamaldas 1886a: 5). Syamaldas went on to state, "the poem appears to have been composed by some literate bard of the family of Kotharia or Bedla Chauhans, to prove that they were related to the kings of Rajputana," alluding to two of the most powerful subordinate lineages in the Mewar kingdom (1886a: 5).

In response to Syamaldas's allegation that the *Raso*'s actual author was most probably a Bhat from Rajasthan, Pandya implies that Syamaldas had an ulterior motive with these words: "To those who carefully read the paper, the drift of it does but plainly indicate that the author is not to a certain extent on terms of friendship with the Bhats in general and the Chohans of Bedla" (Pandya 1887a: 5). Pandya returns to this aspect of Syamaldas's critique more than once, as when he argues that there was no need to "fabricate" an epic in order to extol the greatness of the Kotharia and Bedla Cauhans, since their "high birth and power" were widely accepted (1887a: 8–9). That descendants of Cand Bardai still held *jagirs* (assignments of land revenues) in places like Bedla proved the poet's historicity, to Pandya's mind; and he felt that Rajasthani peculiarities in the *Raso*'s language were only to be expected, in light of the Rajasthani origin of both Cand Bardai and Prithviraj Cauhan, even though the *Raso* placed them primarily in Delhi (1887a: 10–11). Pandya also remarks that, during his stay in Rajputana, he had "come to know of the enimity [*sic*] existing between Charans on one side, and Raos, Bhats and Barwas on the other for many generations" (1887a: 43).

Tension between Syamaldas and other bards at the Udaipur court is not the only contemporary implication of Syamaldas's critique that becomes apparent in Pandya's response. Other groups in Mewar besides the Bhats had a vested interest in having *Prithviraj Raso* continue to be accepted as a valid record of the past. The longer recensions of the epic featured a king of Mewar, Samar Singh or Samarsi, as Prithviraj Cauhan's most valuable associate, so much so that Prithviraj gave his own sister Prithain in marriage to Samarsi (Talbot 2007a: 27–28). In return, Samarsi fought against Prithviraj's foes on several occasions, until his death in the final battle with Shihabuddin Muhammad of Ghur where Prithviraj was taken prisoner. Much of Syamaldas's article was dedicated to demonstrating that Samarsi had actually lived approximately a hundred years after Prithviraj Cauhan. Not only did this totally discredit any conceit that Mewar had played its part in resisting the Turkic conquest of north India, it also threatened the livelihood of numerous landed families in Mewar who held jagirs because their ancestors supposedly accompanied Prithviraj's sister, Pritha, when she came from Delhi as a bride. Pandya tells us these families, whom he specifies by name, "take it ill if any one question the truth of their coming over in Pritha's following—a fact which they look upon as a point of honor" (1887a: 24–25, see also 20). They no doubt fully supported Pandya's attempts to establish, *contra* Syamaldas, that "Samar Singh was a contemporary of his brother-in-law the Emperor Prithiraj Chohan of Delhie" (1887a: 20).

The internal evidence of Pandya's own statements reveals that he was indeed voicing the concerns of certain elements of Mewar society, for whom Syamaldas's repudiation of *Prithviraj Raso*'s historicity was far more than a pedantic exercise. While Pandya's adamant opposition may have been inspired in part by the socio-political repercussions of Syamaldas's stance within the princely state of Mewar, I believe he was committed to a late twelfth-century date for the *Raso* for an additional reason.

THE *RASO* AND HINDU NATIONALISM

Another indication of Pandya's motives is unveiled in the preface to the Hindi version of his essay, *Prithviraj Rase ki Pratham Samraksha* (Pandya 1887b). Pandya tells us that he first wrote his rebuttal of Syamaldas in English and then translated it into Hindi, perhaps because he wanted to communicate with the world of English-language scholarship as quickly as possible. In any case, the contents of the two essays are identical except for the prefaces, which are notably different. In Hindi, Pandya calls on the learned to read *Prithviraj Raso*, reflecting all the while on the superiority of its poetry and how it reveals the vigor, valor, and martial heroism of the ancestors of "our Aryas," before deciding whether his or

Syamaldas's argument is stronger (1887b: 1–2). There is a special reason for defending this great poem created by Cand Bardai, he goes on to say:[27]

Virtually no indigenous (*svadesi*) historical texts that narrate the heroism of the ancestors of our current kings exist; none among those works available under the name *khyat* etc. is as excellent or detailed as this text; in other words, when this is our only book (tantamount to the entirety of our possessions), if we should sit by quietly while public discussion proves it to be false and inauthentic, having been defeated, we will be forced to rely on Muslim chronicles (*tawarikh*) just as our Kaviraj-ji does, considering them as of the highest evidentiary value (Pandya 1887b: 1–2).

Pandya continues by saying how distasteful it would be to him to have the compositions of "our adversaries" (*hamare vimukhom*) regarded as truthful and deserving of acceptance, while such an invaluable repository of knowledge like the *Raso* from "our house" (*hamare ghar*) became the object of disrespect (1887b: 2).

In these statements, Pandya abandons any pretense of being objective and adopts a blatantly partisan position. Instead of dwelling on the merits of his argument for *Prithviraj Raso*'s historicity, Pandya emphasizes the negative consequences of accepting Syamaldas's position: the only reliable original sources remaining would be "Muslim" texts, not "indigenous" or "ours." As he had done once or twice in the body of the essay, Pandya again questions the veracity of Persian chronicles, but here he rejects them solely because they were produced by the "Others." Clearly Pandya needed to believe in *Prithviraj Raso*'s authenticity, no matter how marred by later interpolation, because there would otherwise be no valid attestation of Hindu martial heroism. The implication is that questioning *Prithviraj Raso*'s status, as Kaviraj Syamaldas did, was an unpatriotic act. Thus, Pandya states:

Whatever errors might be evident to us in our indigenous historical texts, those we should rectify, after careful thought, on the basis of the books of other communities (*jati*) and from new research. We should not, because of those errors, call our indigenous texts spurious, false, and inauthentic and thereby disrespect them (Pandya 1887b: 2).

The kind of problems Syamaldas identified in the *Raso* could be found in the books of Europe and elsewhere in the world, Pandya asserts, but the lack of freedom (*svatantrata*) in India led people to find the praiseworthy only in Europe.

In effect, Pandya admits in this preface that his defense of *Prithviraj Raso* was based not on scholarly reasoning but on a communal patriotism. He was, in the end, very much a product of the Benares intellectual circles of the 1870s and 1880s, which were characterized by a growing sense of distinct Hindu identity. The corollary was an increased antagonism (at least in public expression) toward Muslims, as is well evident in Pandya's repeated use of us-them oppositions and his hostility toward Persian-language histories. By this time, "the language question had become one of the key markers of Hindu identity" (Dalmia 1997: 230); that is, being Hindu for educated men in Banaras meant adopting a highly Sanskritized idiom in the Devanagari script (thereby establishing the Hindi language as separate from Hindustani or Urdu) and supporting the movement to make Hindi an official language in the law courts and offices of the Northwest Province & Oudh (King 1994: 126–41). Michael Dodson has recently suggested that the pandits and English leadership at Benares Sanskrit College, which had been advocating a Sanskritized Hindi for decades, may have contributed to the strength of the Hindi movement in Benares (Dodson 2007: 142). In this connection, it is noteworthy that Pandya makes extensive use of Sanskrit vocabulary, as well as extremely long sentences, in *Prithviraj Raso ki Pratham Samraksha*. Syamaldas's prose in "Prithviraj Rasa ki Navinta," the Hindi version of his *Journal of the Asiatic Society of Bengal* article, is only slightly less Sanskritized, although considerably more straightforward. He uses many more words of Perso-Arabic origin in parts of his magnum opus, *Vir Vinod*, however; leading one later scholar to remark that Syamaldas's language was actually a form of Urdu.[28]

The poor quality, in intellectual terms, of Pandya's "defense" of *Prithviraj Raso* becomes more comprehensible once we realize that Pandya was not principally motivated by scholarly concerns in his attempt to repudiate Syamaldas. An important impetus must have come from that segment of Mewar society whose socio-economic interests were threatened by Syamaldas's questioning of the *Raso*. Even more central in Pandya's reaction to Syamaldas, I would argue, was his Hindu nationalist leanings. The Hindi preface to his essay, presumably meant for an audience sympathetic to his own inclinations (who preferred to read and write a Sanskritized Hindi), was blatant in its assertion of an identity for "us" and for "Aryas" that was incompatible with that of "our opponents" and "other communities." Pandya's Hindu nationalism may have been rather early in date, but it was fully developed in its "othering" of Muslims and their historiography, in favor of histories that were "indigenous," no matter how flawed. In brief, Pandya's attitude toward *Prithviraj Raso* was entirely partisan; he approached it not as a scholar but with the reverence due to an ancient relic of a seemingly endangered cultural past. By applying modern historical methods of analysis to this living symbol of Hinduness, Syamaldas, in contrast, had betrayed his lack of patriotism.

THE FATE OF TWO TEXTS

Syamaldas prevailed in his dispute with Pandya, as far as scholarly opinion on *Prithviraj Raso*'s historicity is concerned. The Asiatic Society suspended its ongoing publication of the *Raso* after 1886—the year Syamaldas's article came out—even though only a fraction of the epic's total 69 chapters had been printed. Only because the epic was thought to be a product of the late twelfth century, and therefore the earliest known work in the Hindi language, had scholarly interest been focused on it from the late 1860s onwards. The scholarly turn against the *Raso* was accelerated by news from

Georg Buhler, who in 1893 announced the recent discovery of a Sanskrit text *Prithviraja Vijaya*, "whose author was certainly a contemporary of Prithviraja and one of his court poets." The Sanskrit author's "account of the Chauhans contradicts Chand's in every particular," leading Buhler to conclude in a letter to the Asiatic Society that the *Raso* was a forgery (1893: 94). English-language scholarship, whether conducted by Europeans or Indians, subsequently lost interest in the epic and virtually no studies of it have been conducted in English since the 1880s.[29]

This is not to suggest that Syamaldas was immediately or entirely successful in discrediting *Prithviraj Raso*. In 1906, 20 years after Syamaldas's article, Hoernle again referred to the epic as "the oldest work written in Hindi, or indeed in any of the modern North Indian vernaculars." He noted that the genuineness of the text was challenged by Kaviraj Syamaldas "and has since remained greatly suspect, on the ground mainly of the incorrectness of its dates" (1906: 500). But Hoernle believed that Syamsundar Das, a central figure in Nagaripracarini Sabha (the organization dedicated to promoting the Hindi language in Nagari script), had resolved the dating problems by suggesting that Chand Bardai had used a previously unknown Anand era, which began 90–91 years later than the Vikrama era. Echoing Pandya's view, Hoernle wrote that "it is not denied that the text has suffered by occasional interpolations of incidents as well as by modernization of the language" (1906: 501). The belief that *Prithviraj Raso* is at core a twelfth-century text which has been extensively revised in subsequent centuries still has a considerable number of adherents among Indian literary scholars.

Mohanlal Vishnulal Pandya, who had expressed such great admiration of *Prithviraj Raso* in his rebuttal to Syamaldas, retained his commitment to the text until the end of his life. His foremost objective was to make the *Raso* available in a printed edition, initially through Medical Hall Press, Benares. Although Pandya started publishing the epic in 1887, the project progressed very slowly until 1904, when the Nagaripracarini Sabha of Benares took it on. With the help of additional editors such as Syamsundardas and Radhakrishnadas, the entire text was published by 1912.[30] The Nagaripracarini Sabha edition was widely circulated in the early twentieth century and again in its recent 1993 reprinting; it is by far the best known version of the epic today. Although it took decades of effort, Pandya did manage to disseminate *Prithviraj Raso* to new circles and new audiences, even if the world of English-language scholarship was largely skeptical about its value as a historical document.

While Syamaldas's assertion that *Prithviraj Raso* was composed centuries after Prithviraj's time became the dominant scholarly position on the epic, his victory was bitter-sweet to say the least. His view on the *Raso* may have prevailed; on the other hand, Syamaldas's main project, the *Vir Vinod* history of Mewar, paid a heavy price for his boldness. By the time the first chapters of *Vir Vinod* were ready for printing in 1886, Maharana Sajjan Singh, Syamaldas's foremost royal patron, had been succeeded on the throne by Fateh Singh, a considerably more conservative ruler. Syamaldas suffered a serious stroke soon after finishing the text in 1892, and died two years later.[31] About the same time, Maharana Fateh Singh ordered that all copies of the text be confiscated and locked up in the palace, thus removing them from public circulation. Syamaldas had received 100 of the total press run of 1,100 copies, and distributed a few to friends and institutions like Nagaripracarini Sabha. Outside of this small group of scholars, his work—the result of more than a decade of effort—remained unknown.

It is not entirely clear why the Mewar ruler took such a drastic step. Some scholars believe that Syamaldas's enemies at court took advantage of his ill health after the stroke to conspire against him. Maharana Fateh Singh, who was suspicious by nature and tried to retain all power in his own hands, was persuaded by Syamaldas's enemies that *Vir Vinod* was potentially dangerous, since it could provide excellent ammunition for those of Mewar's aristocratic chiefs who sought to expand their power and privileges (Sinh 1986; Sharma 1987: 34). That is, it recorded events such as a chief's participation in a major battle and could therefore serve as grounds for various claims by his descendants, at the expense of the king. Another scholar suggests that the blame for the banning of *Vir Vinod* rests with Gaurisankar Hiracand Ojha, the eminent historian of Rajasthan who began his career working for Syamaldas (Jain1973: 301). It is well known that Ojha received a personal copy of *Vir Vinod* and that he drew heavily on Syamaldas's findings in writing his own multi-volume *Rajputane ka Ithihas*, published in the 1920s and 30s.[32] Ojha thus preserved the fruits of Syamaldas's labor, but did not—perhaps, could not—give Syamaldas the credit he deserved. Syamaldas's voice remained silent and suppressed until about 1945, when Maharana Bhupal Singh, Fateh Singh's successor, allowed the already printed copies of *Vir Vinod* to be sold (Sharma1973: 283).[33] Not until 1986, with the re-publication of the text by Motilal Banarsidass, did it become easily accessible—exactly one hundred years after it began its printed life.

CONCLUSION

That Kaviraj Syamaldas, a Caran bard from Rajasthan who wrote only in Hindi, should display a good grasp of modern historiographic practices is not so surprising once we situate him within the context of the Mewar court of the late 1860s through early 1880s. In this most reformist era in nineteenth-century Mewar history, Syamaldas was acting in concert with the desire of his young Maharana lords to embrace and emulate the ways of the British. Their receptivity to new modes of thinking and acting led Maharana Sambhu Singh and Sajjan Singh to welcome scholars and other foreign visitors, providing Syamaldas with numerous opportunities to build up a wide-ranging network of academic acquaintances. Because he was supplied with the type and scale of resources deemed necessary to pursue Western-style historical research, Syamaldas occupied a position much like that of an eminent British administrator-scholar, only in the parallel universe of a princely state. The respect extended to Syamaldas by the academic establishment, as exemplified in the publication of several articles in the premier periodical of the day, may derive at least partly from the fact of his location outside British India: Syamaldas was not directly subservient to any Englishman, but exerted much influence in the service of his princely patrons. A hereditary bard with no command of English, Syamaldas may have exemplified the virtues of the "traditional" India that, to the late nineteenth-century colonial mind, still persisted in the princely states.

The courtly context of Syamaldas's career shaped his historiography in negative as well as positive ways, as Lloyd Rudolph has observed perceptively (1993: 3–7, 19–23). Syamaldas could be quite rigorous in his methods, as we have seen in the case of *Prithviraj Raso*, and successfully overturn centuries of received knowledge(s) as a result; but he often chose not to do so. In his discussion of the royal genealogy, for instance, Syamaldas is definite that the dynasty's claim to be descended from the sun is sound, while at the same time expressing reservations about the accuracy of the king-list for the early historic period (1986: 231–34). In other words, Syamaldas aimed his skeptical scrutiny at topics that were rather tangential to royal interests, and not to anything that would greatly perturb his rulers. Or, at least, such it appears was Syamaldas's intention, for he carefully praises his patrons' longing for historical truth and consequent support for his efforts (1986: 253). The constraints imposed on Syamaldas by state patronage are cast into high relief during the reign of Maharana Fateh Singh, who suppressed Syamaldas's intellectual progeny, *Vir Vinod*, for decades. Unlike his British counterparts who could write what they wished about the Indian past with little fear of harmful repercussions, Syamaldas had no colonial authority to insulate him from the ill will of those whom he offended in local society. Being "objective" had its hazards for the native historian in colonial India and few rewards; Europeans had far more incentive to engage in critical historical scholarship.

Trained as a court bard and having access to the court's ample archive of genealogies, dynastic histories, and heroic tales, Syamaldas was in one sense a repository of the older, indigenous historiography. Yet the local understanding of the past had already been filtered through the European sensibilities of James Tod and reconstituted, before being transmitted back into the locality. While ostensibly merely transmitting the bardic works created for Rajput patrons in the seventeenth and eighteenth centuries Tod, in fact, transformed them through his attribution of new kinds of meanings to them. A significant difference resulted from Tod's reading of these accounts through the lens of race and nation (Peabody 1996), in a variation of the early nineteenth-century project to classify human groups that Tom Trautmann has written about in reference to the notion of Aryans (1997). What had been narratives of ancestral exploits relevant to a single lineage or clan became, in Tod's reformulation, the records of past activities that pertained to an entire category of people—the Rajput, Maratha, or Mughal race/nations, for instance. This represents but one of several ways in which Tod's *Annals and Antiquities of Rajasthan* can be construed as the outcome of a conjuncture of knowledges.

Tod's vision had so quickly and firmly become the (newly) established consensus on the Rajput past that Syamaldas was notably diffident in pointing out errors in Tod's dating of events. Indeed, he makes excuses for Tod, saying that "the Colonel is not to blame, because the '*Prithi Raj Rasa*' has caused mistakes of dates in the histories and annals of Rajputana; and it was difficult, rather impossible for him, to write otherwise, when materials for History were available with great difficulty" (1886a: 16). It was Hindu nationalists like Pandya who, in contrast to Syamaldas, embraced Tod's work with such approbation that he was placed beyond reproach.

Pandya, the English-educated Brahman from British India, wields Tod's name like a weapon in defending *Prithviraj Raso* and pointedly refuses to take Syamaldas's word over Tod's, for if Tod "had the least doubt in his mind and met with any conflicting opinion he would never have been satisfied until he had turned over all stones, sifted all matters and arrived at the truth" (Pandya 1887a: 25). The public adulation of Tod by Pandya and other nationalists was based on a fundamental transformation of his categories of analysis, however. In place of the multiplicity and diversity of races/nations that Tod saw populating the subcontinent, the Hindu nationalists saw only two: Hindus and Muslims. A past king like Prithviraj Cauhan was now regarded as a Rajput representative of the Hindu nation, and it was imperative, in Pandya's mind, that his epic story be regarded as truth. This conception of a (Hindu) nation encompassing all non-Muslim inhabitants of the subcontinent is what is modern about Pandya, not his historiographic practice.

Pandya and other early Hindu nationalists who wrote about the Indian past were not academically trained or professionally employed as scholars, and they often came from the ranks of the new vernacular print culture. Pandya's colleague Bharatendu Hariscandra is an excellent example of this type of early nationalist intellectual, who was foremost a literary figure writing in the vernacular. *Prithviraj Raso* was certainly known to Hariscandra, who referred to its dramatic finale in which the blinded king shoots the sultan to death with an arrow, in his famous speech on how India was to make progress delivered in 1884 (Dalmia 1997: 21–27). Dalmia (2001: 60, 68) has pointed out that Hariscandra and others of his Banaras circle drew freely on the more popular Sanskrit religious traditions like the Puranas as well as on local legends and genealogies in reconstructing the past, along with the inscriptions and Indo-Persian histories favored by the English-language scholarly establishment. Their variety of nationalism can be characterized as vernacular not only because it was typically expressed in the Hindi language press, but also because pride in the Hindi language was central to it, as expressed in the movement to have Hindi recognized as the language of schools, government offices, and legal courts.

Prithviraj Raso continued to be highly regarded among many vernacular nationalists, and especially among those who were engaged in literary studies. It had a place in the Hindi curriculum at Benares Hindu University in the 1920s, for instance, and also in the certification for proficiency in Hindi language administered by the Hindi Sahitya Sammelan (Orsini 2002: 108, 120 n. 223). In other words, the *Raso* lived on in vernacular educational programs and vernacular literary scholarship, although it faced near extinction in the world of English-language scholarship, especially in the field of history. Our fine-grained look at the debate over *Prithviraj Raso* has revealed the multiplicities of knowledges in late nineteenth-century India, which cannot be neatly categorized as old or new, traditional or modern, and indigenous or colonial. It also reveals the considerable variety in historiographical production, even within what might be broadly categorized as nationalist history. Popular, vernacular constructions of the past, in particular, have often proved remarkably resilient over time and resistant to scholarly revision—they and their genealogies deserve more sustained academic attention.

NOTES

1. Written by Mohanlal Vishnulal Pandya, *The Defence of Prithiraj Rasa No. 1* was published in Benares by Medical Hall Press (1887).
2. Cited in Krishnacarya 1966: 188. The quote comes from the introduction to Price's book, *Hindee and Hindoostanee Selections*, the first volume of which was published at Calcutta by Hindoostanee Press, in 1827.
3. This information is provided on the first page of the article (Syamaldas 1886a: 5). The Hindi version (Syamaldas 1959) was supposedly first published in 1887 (Bhatta 1959: 5–6), although I have been unable to find the text or even the exact details of its publication.
4. This statistic is based on my own quick reckoning from "List of Members of the Asiatic Society of Bengal on the 31st December, 1885," in *Proceedings of the Asiatic Society* 1886: iii–xvii.

5. These numbers are based on my own examination of the journal's table of contents. I did not include Pandit Harachandra Chakravarti (who transcribed an inscription), nor Babu Jogendra Nath Rae (who collected folk songs contributed by another); but I did count Sri Narayan Singh and Hiralal Kavyopadhyaya—who collaborated with G. Grierson—among the 18 Indians.
6. The censorious attitude conveyed in the English article is not quite as pronounced in the Hindi original, whose title can be rendered as "The Newness of *Prithviraj Raso*." Asserting something's relatively recent date is less offensive than describing it as inauthentic; similarly softer in tone is *asuddha*, meaning impure or imperfect, the Hindi word used by Syamaldas that was translated into English as "mistake," "incorrect," and "wrong."
7. Seven stone inscriptions are referred to in the body of the article, and an appendix that is almost 40 pages long contains the complete Sanskrit text of six of these, along with modern Hindi and English translations of the two longest inscriptions.
8. Mewar was likely the first among Rajasthan's princely states to establish such an office devoted to historical research, in Lloyd Rudolph's view (1993: 3).
9. According to Raghuvir Sinh (1978: 26), Syamaldas was appointed to write a history of Mewar in 1877; G.N. Sharma gives the date as 1875 (1992: 59).
10. A short printed booklet lists 82 scholarly books in Syamaldas's private library (Syamaldas 1886b).
11. The discussion of *Prithviraj Raso*'s historicity appears in the first volume of *Vir Vinod* (Syamaldas 1986: 1254–83). It differs from the *Journal of the Asiatic Society of Bengal* article mainly in that the epic's probable date of composition is stated to be from 1518 to 1613, rather than the earlier estimate of 1583 to 1613. Syamaldas also gives a better overview of his reasons for rejecting the *Raso*'s historicity in *Vir Vinod*.
12. For a discussion of bards, see Vidal 1997: 85–112 and Prabhakar 1976: 30–34.
13. In this paragraph, I rely primarily on Sharma 1987: 19–27.
14. On the various policies of Sambhu Singh and Sajjan Singh, see Paliwal 1971: 86–179.

15. It was perhaps through such official British contacts that Syamaldas came to participate in Edward Eastwick's literary project, the composition of a poem-cycle in praise of Queen Victoria titled *Kaisarnamah-i Hind, or Lay of the Empress,* with partial translations in Arabic, Hindi, and Sanskrit. The second volume of this project, with two cantos accompanied by Syamaldas's Hindi translation, was published in England in 1882.
16. For Dayanand Saraswati's will, see Prakash n.d.: 265–66; for more on his death, see B. K. Singh 1970: 81–90.
17. Syamaldas was also involved in the campaign against *tyag* and other customary payments made by Rajputs and other landholders to bards at weddings and funerals. *Tyag* was among the reasons why the costs of Rajput marriage were so exorbitant, which the British believed was largely responsible for the practice of female infanticide (Sharma 1987: 28–29).
18. Motilal Menariya calls Pandya a Mathura resident (1958: 36), as does Vishwa Prakash (n.d.: 81). In his essay, Pandya mentions that he had dwelt in various parts of Rajputana for about 15 years (1887a: 43).
19. R.S. McGregor ascribes the authorship of *Angrez Stotra* to Hariscandra (1974: 81) and it has been published in collections of Hariscandra's works. The title page of the publication says only that it was compiled by Pandya at Hariscandra's command.
20. Pandya wrote "on the mythological hero Prahlad with political overtones," according to Sisir Kumar Das (1991: 282). R.S. Mcgregor dates *Prahlad natak* to 1874 and also remarks on its political commentary (1974: 93).
21. Pandya's Brahman status is indicated by his occasional use of the suffix "Sharma" (e.g., Pandya 1905: 2); and the frequent prefix of Pandit which he is accorded by others. Pandya is a surname borne by some Gujarati Brahmans, and it is clear that Pandya had some connection with the region. He was, for example, a member of the Gujarat Vernacular Society. Interestingly, G.N. Sharma, a noted twentieth-century Brahman scholar from Mewar, accused Syamaldas of being biased in stating that the Brahmans of his day were largely ignorant in comparison to Carans (Sharma 1987: 54).
22. The information on Hoernle's career comes from Sweet 2006. A close relationship between the two men is also indicated by Hoernle's

four-page contribution to Pandya's essay, which attempts to identify the Muslim warriors mentioned in the *Raso* using Persian texts (Pandya 1887a: 38–42). In a book review published years later, Hoernle credits Pandya with discovering the clue to the problem of the *Raso*'s incorrect dates (Hoernle 1906: 500), which Syamsundar Das developed into a full-fledged hypothesis about the epic's use of an alternative, Anand, era. That is, Pandya (1887a: 44–45) offered a convoluted explanation for the roughly hundred-year discrepancy in the *Raso*'s dates, which he said resulted from mistakes made in the distant past when converting from the Saka to the Vikrama eras (which are actually 135 years apart).

23. *Kavivacansudha* is only mentioned in the short preface of *Angrez Stotra*.
24. Pandya is described as a follower of Hariscandra by Sisir Kumar Das (1991: 282).
25. Pandya did not confine himself to Western scholars. He once refers to R. Mitra (i.e., Rajendralal Mitra) as a "learned researcher" and solicited Raja Siva Prasad's opinion on Syamaldas's article (Pandya 1887a: 17, 5).
26. Beames edited the first section of *Prithviraj Rasau* published in 1873 in the Bibliotheca Indica series sponsored by the Asiatic Society of Bengal. Hoernle edited the subsequent five installments of the epic text from 1874 to 1886; Hoernle also translated a translation of one chapter, Revatata, in 1881. These appeared as Fasciculus I through V of Pt. II, *The Prithiraj (CT: Prithviraj?) Rasau of Chand Bardai,* Bibliotheca Indica new series nos. 269, 304, 408, 430, 452, 489, 577.
27. My translation.
28. This statement is ascribed to Motilal Menariya by G.N. Sharma (1987: 50). Sharma also feels that Syamaldas's language was unusual for its high degree of Persian vocabulary.
29. Perhaps the only exception during the colonial era is Halder 1927. Much of Halder's article is devoted to demonstrating that the dates of *Prithviraj Raso* are incorrect, even supposing its use of an Anand era that was 90 or 91 years off from the regular Vikrama era.
30. These are the dates given in the preface to the Nagaripracarini Sabha's second edition of the *Raso* (Pandya 1993: 3). Elsewhere the time span is said to extend from 1906 to 1913 (S. Singh 2000: 26–27).

31. I have relied primarily on Sinh 1978, Sinh 1986, and Sharma 1987 for the following statements on the fate of *Vir Vinod.*
32. K.S. Gupta (1992: 75) says that the second volume of this work, on Mewar, is taken primarily from *Vir Vinod.*
33. According to Lloyd Rudolph, copies of *Vir Vinod* were accessible after Fateh Singh's death in 1930, but were not publicly available for purchase until the eve of Indian independence (1993: 3). Raghuvir Sinh mentions that Maharana Bhopal Singh gave him a copy in 1933 in order to facilitate his research (1978: 32).

REFERENCES

Bayly, C.A. 1996. *Empire & Information: Intelligence Gathering and Social Communication in India, 1780–1870.* Cambridge: Cambridge University Press.

Bendall, Cecil. [1886] 1974. *A Journey of Literary and Archaeological Research in Nepal and Northern India During the Winter 1884–85.* Kathmandu: Ratna Pustak Bhandar.

Bhatta, Bhagavatilal. 1959. "Prastavana (Introduction)." In *Prithviraj Raso ki Vivecana*, ed. Mohanlal Vyas Sastri and Nathulal Vyas, 1–18. Udaipur: Sahitya Sansthan, Rajasthan Vidyapith.

Buhler, G. 1893. "Extract from Letter." *Proceedings of the Asiatic Society of Bengal*, 94–95.

Dalmia, Vasudha. 1997. *The Nationalization of Hindu Traditions: Bharatendu Harischandra and Nineteenth-Century, Banaras.* Delhi: Oxford University Press.

———. 2001. "Vernacular Histories in Late Nineteenth-Century Banaras: Folklore, Puranas, and the New Antiquarianism." *Indian Economic and Social History Review*, 38.1: 59–79.

Das, Sisir Kumar. 1991. *A History of Indian Literature, Vol. 8: 1800–1910.* Delhi: Sahitya Akademi.

Dodson, Michael S. 2007. *Orientalism, Empire, and National Culture: India, 1770–1880.* Basingstoke, Hampshire, New York: Palgrave Macmillan.

Freitag, Jason. 2001. "The Power Which Raised Them from Ruin and Oppression: James Tod, Historiography, and the Rajput Ideal." Ph.D. dissertation, Columbia University.

———. 2007. "Tod's Annals as Archive and History." In *James Tod's Rajasthan: The Historian and His Collections*, ed. Giles Tillotson, 86–97. Mumbai: Marg Publications.

Gupta, K.S. 1992. "Dr. G.H. Ojha as a Historian." In *The Historians and Sources of History of Rajasthan*, ed. G.N. Sharma and V. S. Bhatnagar, 71–80. Jaipur: Centre for Rajasthan Studies, University of Rajasthan.

Halder, R.R. 1927. "Some Reflections on the Prithviraj Rasa." *Journal of the Asiatic Society, Bombay Branch,* n.s. 3: 203–11.

Hoernle, A.F. Rudolph. 1906. "Notices of Books: Annual Report on the Search for Hindi Manuscripts, 4 vols." *Journal of the Royal Asiatic Society*, 497–503.

Jain, M.S. 1973. "Gaurishankar Hirachand Ojha." In *Historians and Historiography in Modern India*, edited by S.P. Sen, 291–304. Calcutta: Institute of Historical Studies.

King, Christopher. 1994. *One Language, Two Scripts: The Hindi Movement in Nineteenth Century North India*. Bombay: Oxford University Press.

Krishnacarya. 1966. *Hindi ke Adi Mudrit Granth*. Calcutta: Bharatiya Jnanpith Publication.

McGregor, R.S. 1974. *Hindi Literature of the Nineteenth and Early Twentieth Centuries*. History of Indian Literature vol. 8 fasc. 2. Wiesbaden: Otto Harrassowitz.

Menariya, Motilal. 1958. *Rajasthana ka Pingala Sahitya*. 2nd ed. Bambai: Hindi Grantha Ratnakara.

Orsini, Francesca. 2002. *The Hindi Public Sphere 1920–1940*. Delhi: Oxford University Press.

Paliwal, Devilal.1971. *Mewar and the British 1857–1921* AD. Jaipur: Bafna Prakashan.

Pandya, Mohanlal Vishnulal. 1873. *Angrez Stotra*. Benares: Chhannu Lall, 1873.

———. 1887a. *The Defence of Prithiraj Rasa No. 1*. Benares: Medical Hall Press.

———. 1887b. *Prthviraja Rase ki Prathama Samraksha*. Benares: Medical Hall Press.

———. ed. 1905. *Sri Govarddhananathaji ke Prakatya ki Varta*, by Hariraya. Bombay.

Pandya, Mohanlal Vishnulal, Syamsundar Das, et al., ed. [1904–1912] 1993. *Prithvirajaraso*. 2nd rev. ed. Varanasi: Nagaripracarini Sabha.

Peabody, Norbert. 1996. "Tod's Rajast'han and the Boundaries of Imperial Rule in Nineteenth-Century India." *Modern Asian Studies*, 30, no. 1: 185–220.

Peterson, Peter. 1883. *Detailed Report of Operations in Search of Sanskrit Mss. in the Bombay Circle, vol. 1 (Aug. 1882–March 1883)*. Bombay: Bombay Branch of the Royal Asiatic Society; London: Trubner & Co.

Prabhakar, Manohar. 1976. *A Critical Study of Rajasthani Literature*. Jaipur: Panchsheel Prakashan.

Prakash, Vishwa. n.d. *Life & Teachings of Swami Dayanand*. Allahabad: Kala Press.

Rudolph, Lloyd. 1993. "Tod's Influence on Shymaldass's Historiography in Vir Vinod." Unpublished paper presented at the Annual Conference on South Asia, Madison.

Rudolph, Lloyd I. and Susanne Hoeber Rudolph. 2003. "Writing and Reading Tod's Rajasthan: Interpreting the Text and Its Historiography." In *Circumambulations in South Asian History: Essays in Honour of Dirk H.A. Kolff*, ed. Jos Gommans, pp. 251–82. Leiden: Brill.

Sharma, G.N. 1973. "Kaviraj Shyamaldas." In *Historians and Historiography in Modern India*, edited by S.P. Sen, 281–90. Calcutta: Institute of Historical Studies.

———. 1987. *Kaviraja Syamaldas aur Unka Vir Vinod*. Parampara Nos. 82–83. Jodhpur: Rajasthani Sodh Sansthan Caupasani.

———. 1992. "Kaviraja Shyamaldas." In *The Historians and Sources of History of Rajasthan*, ed. G.N. Sharma and V.S. Bhatnagar, 57–70. Jaipur: Centre for Rajasthan Studies, University of Rajasthan.

Singh, B.K. 1970. *Swami Dayanand*. New Delhi: National Book Trust.

Singh, Shanta. 2000. *Chandbardai*. Delhi: Sahitya Akademi.

Singh, Upinder. 2004. *The Discovery of Ancient India: Early Archaeologists and the Beginnings of Archaeology*. Delhi: Permanent Black.

Sinh, Raghuvir. 1978. "Syamaldas Dadhvariya." Chapter 3 in *Rajasthan ke Pramukh Itihaskar aur Unka Krititva*, 26–33. Bikaner: Hindi Visvabharati Anusandhan Parishad.

———. 1986. "Bhumika (Introduction)." In *Vir-Vinod*, by Kaviraj Syamaldas, vol. 1. Jaipur: Mayank Prakashan.

Somani, Ram Vallabh. 1985. *Later Mewar*. Jaipur: Shantidevi Somani.

Sweet, William. 2006. "Hoernle, (Reinhold Friedrich) Alfred (1880–1943)." *Oxford Dictionary of National Biography*. Oxford University

Press. [http://www.oxforddnb.com.ezproxy.lib.utexas.edu/view/article/94419, accessed 25 February 2009]

Syamaldas, Kavi Raj. 1886a. "The Antiquity, Authenticity and Genuineness of the Epic Called the Prithi Raj Rasa, and Commonly Ascribed to Chand Bardai." *Journal of the Asiatic Society of Bengal* 55, pt. 1: 5–65.

———. 1886b. *Kavi Raja Shyamal Das Ji's Private Library*. Privately published.

———. 1959. "Prithviraj Rasa ki Navinta." In *Prithviraj Raso ki Vivecana,* ed. Mohanlal Vyas Sastri and Nathulal Vyas, 1–61.Udaipur: Sahitya Sansthan, Rajasthan Vidyapith.

———. 1986. *Viravinod: Mevara ka Itihas, Pt.1*. Delhi: Motilal Banarsidass.

Talbot, Cynthia. 2007a. "The Mewar Court's Construction of History." In *The Kingdom of the Sun: Indian Court and Village Art from the Princely State of Mewar*, ed. Joanna Williams, 12–33. San Francisco: Asian Art Museum.

———. 2007b. "Recovering the Heroic History of Rajasthan: Tod and the *Prithviraj Raso*." In *James Tod's Rajasthan: The Historian and His Collections*, ed. Giles Tillotson, 98–109. Mumbai: Marg Publications.

Tod, James. [1920] 1990. *Annals and Antiquities of Rajasthan*, ed. William Crooke. New Delhi: Low Price Publications.

Trautmann, Thomas R. 1997. *Aryans and British India*. Berkeley: University of California Press.

———. 2006. *Languages & Nations: The Dravidian Proof in Colonial Madras*. Berkeley: University of California Press.

Vidal, Denis. 1997. *Violence and Truth: A Rajasthani Kingdom Confronts Colonial Authority*. Delhi: Oxford University Press.

8

Astral Time

Almanacs and Colonial Modernity in Bengal

PARNA SENGUPTA

> The history of this Bengali almanacc [*sic*] stretches from a time when our country was reeling under the British rule... Codified religious canons and tenets, correct procedure of rituals and ceremonies found it impossible to bear the onslaught of "modernism" and "pragmatism" preached by the western Indians there was a void which had to be filled by an authentic religious manual. Thus was born the Gupta Press Directory Panjika.
>
> —Gupta Press Panjika website[1]

The Gupta Press, one of the most popular almanac publishers in Bengal, provides a wide array of astrological services on its website including methods for choosing children's names, auspicious times to move into a new office, and individual star charts. According to the website, the Gupta Press only began printing Bengali almanacs, or *panjikas*, in order to counter the attack of colonial era "modernism" and Western "pragmatism." The paradox of such an argument, in which an "authentic" religious manual of ancient religious canons and rituals appears on the worldwide web (also available on CD), seems irrelevant to the publishers of the Gupta Press Directory. Rather, the website claims that in spite of changes in the technology of almanac production, from manuscript to print to the web, the *panjika* (and the practice of astrology more generally) remains both unchanged and connected to India's pre-colonial past.

In this essay I want to trouble this assumption by analyzing the *panjika* as a historical problem. The Gupta Press, in spite of the fact that it only began publishing almanacs during the colonial period, wants to narrate its own historical emergence as a part of the great battle against the "onslaught of pragmatism and modernism." I argue instead that the printed astrological almanac was not so much a bulwark against colonial modernity but very much its product. In doing so, I explore the almanac as a distinctive kind of text and genre. In fact, my research suggests that the printed *panjika* was not produced to preserve an authentic tradition from the "onslaught" of colonial culture, but rather as a means to help individuals navigate that very world. In this way, the astrological almanac offers an important and understudied way to theorize the dynamic relationship between the past and the present—between pre-colonial forms of knowledge and the epistemological (and technological) changes wrought by colonialism.

This essay takes as its inspiration Thomas Trautmann's 2008 remarks to the University of Minnesota South Asia Seminar. Trautmann argues that much of the writing on colonial history is marked by "the sense that in the nineteenth century everything has been made thoroughly new, and discontinuous with the past; a growing belief that the deep past has nothing significant to tell us about the world we inhabit in the here and now" (2008: 3). For Trautmann, the historical investigation of the ancient past has been marked by theories of temporal rupture—the notion of the fundamental discontinuity of the colonial modern that transforms all that came before and ultimately shapes our ability (as historians) to even access that pre-modern past.

The flip side of this argument, Trautmann contends, are culturally conservative arguments (like those made by the Gupta Press) which also employ notions of fundamental discontinuity to argue for the existence of a core, unchanging "Indian" (often seen as coterminous with a Hindu) past that can and should be recuperated and protected. Trautmann proposes instead that we find the "just right" of narrating the colonial past that rejects both a notion of fundamental (and irrevocable) rupture between the pre-modern and modern as well as temporal models that argue for an unchanging cultural authenticity handed down from generation to generation.

My research represents a preliminary attempt to consider the emergence of the nineteenth-century printed *panjika* as a paradigm for understanding the continued relevance, and necessity, of older forms of knowledge to the modern colonial world. I am interested in the ways the *panjika* indexed multiple temporal models, especially the astrological and the scientific, and structured the ways time was imagined by ordinary people in colonial India. I use the term "ordinary" in a purposeful manner—the almanac was bought and consulted by diverse sections of colonial society: men and women, urban clerks and rural peasants, literate and non-literate populations, Hindus and Muslims. As a genre, this makes the almanac invaluable in helping us understand how a broad cross-section of colonial subjects continued to draw upon local cosmologies in order to be able to negotiate an increasingly expanding and bewildering imperial culture.

ALMANACS AND THE *LONGUE DUREĪ*

Almanacs have been indispensable as sources for historians interested in illuminating the social and epistemological worlds of early modern Europeans and Americans. Almanacs were used by Annales School historians to recreate the collective *mentalitī* of ordinary Europeans while later French and British historians focused on almanacs as part of an emerging book culture. Thus both the circulation of almanacs as well as their actual content and form became important to historians for exploring the complex ways in which astrological, religious, scientific, and environmental knowledge were assembled and connected by women and men in the past.

Historians of early modern Europe and America agree that by the nineteenth century almanacs began decreasing in popularity and (more importantly) their prophetic and astrological content came under attack from both the Church and those who subscribed to a more scientific (rather than "superstitious") view on the natural world. The reform of European and American almanacs was a cultural project aimed at shaping acceptable forms of modern knowledge and, by the nineteenth century, discussions of prophesy (commonly called judicial astrology) had been replaced by natural astrology. This meant that phenomena, such as eclipses, were not seen to have any astrological significance for "events on earth," but were merely occurrences that could be explained in astronomical terms. Cosmological events were no longer perceived to have any effect on the lives and futures of individuals themselves.

In contrast to historians of America and Europe, historians of India have done very little historical work on almanacs, in spite of their near ubiquity all over the subcontinent. Instead historians of South Asia have focused on various other efforts of the British to redefine native notions of time as a part of imperial dominance—from the insistence on European models of history writing to the introduction of the clock discipline of factory and office work. These analyses have overlooked astrology and astrological almanacs as providing a competing—and often more powerful—temporal paradigm. Astrology has been more commonly studied within the fields of religious studies and anthropology as part of Vedic science or popular religious culture. In exploring the *panjika* as a historical source, however, I am interested in what it tells us about the shifting social and imaginary world of nineteenth-century Bengalis.

THE HISTORY OF THE *PANJIKA*

In India, astrological time, as represented in the *panjika* or almanac, drew upon the ancient Hindu tradition of astrological prognostication or *jyotisha.* The science of astrology appeared during the Vedic period and its initial function was to determine the appropriate times for rituals performed by the *adhvaryu* priests. As a *sastra* or science, *jyotisha* was distinctive in terms of its more cosmopolitan development and character—qualities that I would suggest made it especially adaptable and more germane to individuals in ways that went well beyond its early ritual aspect.

Christopher Minkowski, drawing upon the seminal work of David Pingree, argues that *jyotisha* was more akin to "Ayurveda, the other Sanskrit technical art" than the more traditional *sastras* of language, hermeneutics or morality (2002: 495). The result, which is important in considering the later history of astrology, is that *jyotisha* had a more tenuous relationship with canonical Vedic knowledge and was also more open to "foreign" intellectual systems. Minkowski concludes that, by the seventeenth century, scholars of *jyoti-sastra* were connected "to networks of scientists outside the Sanskrit sphere," in particular "Arabic and Persian scientists." Moreover, the relative openness of scholars of astrology to the sciences of the "*mlecchas*" resulted in the acceptance of "observation as foundation for the 'improvement' of the astronomy"(Minkowski 2002: 509, 510).

Although the science of *jyotisha* was at the level of the cosmological, those that actually practised astrology tended to be preoccupied with more pragmatic issues. As Barry Friedman, in his wonderful ethnography of astrology in Bengal, notes, "astrological practitioners were concerned with the effects of celestial bodies on human life and affairs, and with the appropriate times for secular activity and religious ritual"(1986: 328).From the medieval period onward, astrologers were employed to cast horoscopes of newborn sons, determine auspicious days for marriages or journeys and practise other forms of divination.

As a Vedic science, *jyotisha* was a caste-based practise, but the Brahmans who plied their art straddled the high and low. Medieval epigraphic evidence indicates kings and wealthy landowners employed elite astrologers in their courts and households, while lower-level astrologers (who Friedman suggests were more akin to magicians or village priests) were employed in villages.[2] Court astrologers would give daily and annual readings while village astrologers might supplement their work with various kinds of divination and occult services for their local customers. Medieval astrologers, both elite and popular, plied their trade through the use of a *panji* or *pancanga*: manuscript almanacs that dealt with the five subjects relevant to astrological prognostication (solar days, lunar days, half-lunar days, *nakshatras* and conjunctions). The authority of *jyotisha* rested on both the person of the astrologer and the manuscript *pancanga*, which meant that astrologers were invested in retaining their privileged access to the interpretation of the text.

PANJIKAS AND MODERN TEMPORALITY

In the mid-nineteenth century, the manuscript *panjika* found itself eclipsed by the cheap print astrological almanac. After the 1850s, technological modernization led to the unprecedented expansion of vernacular publishing all over India. The changes in print technology made Bengali books more widely available and significantly cheaper (a book that cost 16 annas or one rupee, in 1825, cost 2 annas by 1855; Ghosh 2003: 30). The *panjika* soon became one of the few printed books that might be found in a nineteenth-century Bengali household—its sales far outpacing any other kind of vernacular text. The Battala Presses in Calcutta churned out large numbers of almanacs, but soon a few big publishing houses, like the Gupta Press, came to dominate the field.

In certain ways printed almanacs, like other nineteenth-century books, remained closely tied to their manuscript counterparts. The legitimacy of astrology depended on its connection to Hindu tradition, Brahmanical authority, and aristocratic patronage. The privileged access of particular classes of Brahman priests to the almanac did not seem fundamentally challenged by the print version, since these individuals retained their right to publish the "official" almanacs. Early *panjikas* continued to recognize a connection to an aristocratic patron and court-based practice—the earliest extant printed *panjika, Navadvipa Sammata Panjika* (1821), acknowledged the importance of the Raja of Navadip, Girishchandra, as its patron on its frontplate. Even later editions recognized his descendants in a similar manner, although by that point they had almost nothing to do with almanacs or astrology (Friedman 1986:200). Printed almanacs not only shared some of the same formal aspects as the manuscript versions, but, like earlier texts were routinely transmitted orally and communally, as when literate members of villages read the contents to their non-literate neighbors.

But in other ways, print transformed the content of the almanacs and democratized the practice of *jyotisha* itself. For example, publishers of the printed almanac began publishing Sanskrit astrology in Bengali script, increasing the accessibility of the literate population to astrology and clearly departing from the manuscript version. Moreover, by the twentieth century, non-Brahmins had taken up the science of *jyotisha* and effectively ended the Brahmanical monopoly on prophesy.

The most obvious change in the print (versus manuscript) *panjikas* was the influence of European almanac conventions among publishers and distributors. The Bengali *panjika* incorporated European-type calendars; lists of Hindu, Muslim and Christian festivals; agricultural advice; and postal rates. Modern printed almanacs also began to be used as vehicles for advertisements—clearly placing them within the bazaar economy of the late nineteenth century. In addition to the numerous ads for Ayurvedic medicines were ads for new astrological practitioners as well as books that detailed horoscopes. Astrology, like baldness remedies, was now a part of market exchange rather than a part of caste or religious work. Furthermore, the new advertising also led to a set of unanticipated changes in the visual material that was so central to *panjika* literature. Early *panjikas* had a number of wood block prints of deities that were immensely popular with the non-literate village populations. But the increase in secular advertisements within almanacs meant that the traditional print-maker suddenly found that he had to learn how to artistically represent everyday objects, like bottles and syringes. This represented an aesthetic as well as subject shift from the sacred to the mundane and from the flattened, two-dimensional images of Hindu gods to the three-dimensional realism of rubber stamps.[3]

In spite of the addition of advertisements and holiday calendars, the *panjika*'s main subjects remained prognostication and cosmological determination. The widespread popularity of Hindu astrology, as evidenced by the large numbers of printed almanacs printed and sold, demonstrates the continued belief among ordinary Bengalis that human experience was influenced by planetary movements and constellations. As a cultural system, *jyotisha* saw the heavens and stars as ordered in a particular way that, when appropriately interpreted, would result in the telescoping of time and predictions of the future.

Yet the notion of time rooted in Hindu astrology seemed fundamentally at odds with the notion of time represented by European calendars and holiday lists. Scientific notions of time were predicated on seeing it as a series of neutral, homogenous units that could be marked but not interpreted or predicted. The annual calendar, for instance, contained a series of months and days stretching into the future, but each of those months and days were blank. Scientific certainty assured that there would be a February 15 in 1890, but refused to speculate on what might happen on that day. In contrast, what was important in an astrological calendar was determining whether or not February 20 would be an auspicious day to name a child or change jobs or move.

The different relationship to the future symbolized by the European-style calendar and the astrological calendar were ostensibly at odds with one another. In Europe, this tension had resulted in the systematic marginalization of judicial astrology in favor of scientific ways of comprehending the world. One might expect, then, that in Bengal there would be a similar resolution to the issue of astrology within the almanac. But my study of *panjikas* suggests a more complex and interesting outcome.

The nineteenth-century printed *panjika* represented neither a complete rupture between astrological and scientific models of temporality nor the preservation of an authentically pre-colonial culture. Instead, the particular (and peculiar) exigencies of colonial society made the printed *panjika* more, not less, necessary. To illustrate this dynamic, I will take the example of travel. One of the main uses of the almanac and the astrological calendar was as a means to choose the best times to travel. Choosing an auspicious day to undertake a small or large trip was routinely decided through cosmological computations. Having an appropriate interpretation of the annual *panjika* was critical in order to ensure there were no harmful or malefic influences on a day chosen for taking a trip.

However, by the mid-century, a new template for choosing when to travel was introduced into almanacs: the railway schedule. Alongside the astrological maps, almanacs began publishing railway timetables that represented a more standardized means to select the date and time for a journey. In fact, the expansion of the railway in India (as in other parts of the world) was important more generally in standardizing time across the subcontinent. A railway timetable could be published annually and once an individual learned to read the table, there was no need for any specialized interpretation in order to decide when and where to catch the train. A cosmological determination of when was best to travel, on the other hand, could not be simply mapped onto a static chart. Astrology was dependent on an individual's birth chart; it was not a matter of determining "objectively" good or bad days, but a complex set of calculations and interpretations that allowed the astrologer to determine what was auspicious or malevolent for that particular person.

There is no evidence that the introduction of the railway timetable displaced the astrological chart. Instead, I would speculate that the two kinds of systems were used in tandem to ensure that an individual took a journey that was both efficient (the right time, the right station) and auspicious. There was no sense, within the almanac, nor within Bengali culture, of the two methods being at odds with one another. Indeed they both provided crucial and complementary kinds of information necessary in a rapidly changing society. In this sense, the *panjika* should not be read as an example of the arbitrary juxtaposition of temporal models, but as very much a text created to navigate colonial modernity.[4]

TRAUTMANN'S TIME

I would like to return to the theoretical challenge posed by Thomas Trautmann about the need to find new ways to think about the relationship of the deep past to the colonial (and post-colonial) present. The deep past, for Trautmann, can be described as "history over the *longue dureī*," a kind of history that serves as a "resource…rather than an end in itself" (2008:2). This essay has tried to suggest, in a very preliminary manner, that astrology, as represented in the Bengali *panjika*, is a part of India's "deep history." The science of astrology, upon which the *panjika* was based, was always a highly dynamic and cosmopolitan science, containing within it the historical traces of Hellenistic, Persian and Arabic scientific thought. In its encounter with colonial modernity, *jyotisha* proved similarly adaptable and flexible—quite the opposite of the "bulwark against modernity" suggested by the Gupta Press.

While this might suggest why *jyotisha*, among the Vedic sciences, proved so flexible, it does not answer why astrology continued to be relevant to people's lives. My initial research into the Bengali *panjika* demands that we interrogate any claims that modernity effectively made everything anew. While the nineteenth century was certainly a period in which scientific rationality was embraced against the "backward" intellectual and cultural ideas of the past, we should not dismiss the continued importance of older narratives and systems that made an unknown and difficult world comprehensible. Astrological time, unlike the European calendar or holiday list, provided a meaning for time. Time was not homogenous and empty but full of pitfalls and pleasures, malefic planets and benevolent stars, all of which had to be safely navigated with the right guide. It is incumbent upon us to take up Thomas Trautmann's challenge to illuminate how the deep past shaped and continues to shape our present.

NOTES

1. Gupta Press Panjika 2005.
2. D.C. Sircar notes, for instance, various epigraphic instances of kings employing astrologers to help them make important strategic decisions about their kingdom (1952: 346–47).
3. For a discussion of the place of woodcuts in the Bengali *panjika*, see Ashit Paul 1983.
4. My reading diverges from Pratima Banerjee's description of nineteenth-century almanacs which suggests that they packed together "newer and older time-reckoning and mismatched temporal duties" that were part of the "aporetic everyday" (Banerjee 2006: 45–46).

REFERENCES

Banerjee, Prathama. 2006. *Politics of Time: 'Primitives' and History-writing in a Colonial Society*. Delhi: Oxford University Press.

Friedman, Barry. 1986. *Negotiating Destiny: The Astrologer and His Art in Bengali Cultural History*. PhD dissertation, University of Chicago.

Ghosh, Anindita. 2003. "An Uncertain 'Coming of the Book': Early Print Cultures in India." *Book History*, 6:23–25.

Gupta Press Panjika. 2005. "A Brief Introduction to the Foremost Bengali Almanac." http://www.guptapresspanjika.com/index.htm.

Minkowski, Christopher. 2002. "Astronomers and Their Reasons: Working Paper on Jyothisastra." *Journal of Indian Philosophy*, 30: 495–514.

Paul, Ashit, ed. 1983. *Woodcut Prints of Nineteenth Century Calcutta*. Calcutta: Seagull Press.

Perkins, Maureen. 1996. *Visions of the Future: Almanacs, Time and Cultural Change, 1775–1870*. Oxford: Oxford University Press.

Sircar, D.C. 1952. "The Astrologer at the Village and the Court." *Indian Historical Quarterly*, 28: 342–49.

Trautmann, Thomas R. 2008. "Finding India's Deep History." Paper presented at the University of Minnesota South Asia Seminar, Minneapolis. (Published in *The Clash of Chronologies: Ancient India in the Modern World*. New Delhi: Yoda Press, 2009.)

9

Sex and the City

Debates over the Medieval Pasts of Khajuraho

ANNE HARDGROVE

> I took a look around—"Si monumentum quaeris, circumspice,"—and could not help expressing a feeling of wonder at these splendid monuments of antiquity having been erected by a people who have continued to live in such a state of barbarous ignorance. It is a proof that some of these men must then have been of a more superior caste of human beings than the rest... indeed, some of the sculptures here were extremely indecent and offensive...the religion of the ancient Hindoos would not have been very chaste if it induced people under the cloak of religion, to design the most disgraceful representation to desecrate their ecclesiastical erections... the female figure, that should be here has been taken away (confound the rascally despoilers), and nothing remaining of her beautiful form (for I am sure it must have been beautiful, judging from the rest), but two feet, and her hand which is posited upon the left throat or neck of the animal... I would willingly have given a hundred rupees (10£) to have had a good sight of the "Prithee" creature, (who has been taken away,) and that in a mutilated state too, as they have left her feet and one arm.
>
> T.S. Burt 1839: 162–66[1]

The tenth- and eleventh-century Hindu and Jain temple complexes known as Khajuraho are famous for their proliferation of erotic sculpture. From the British arrival onward, much of the commentary seeking to understand the sacred sexuality both derives from and contributes to emerging associations between obscenity, sexuality, and communalism in British India. This essay will trace the history of observations about the Khajuraho erotic sculpture. In considering the layers of meaning brought to the sublime erotic temple sculpture art at Khajuraho, I contend that it was the British visitors to Khajuraho, and not various waves of Muslim visitors (Burt's "rascally despoilers") who brought to the temples not just a Victorian discomfort about commemorations of the erotic, but indeed a sensibility embroiled in ideas about Hindus and Muslims and their relationship to sexuality. In making this assertion, I draw upon Charu Gupta's persuasive argument about the interconnectedness of obscenity, sexuality, and Hindu national identity in colonial India (Gupta 2002). As Niloufer Ichaporia (1983) notes in her insightful analysis of Khajuraho tourism in the 1970–80s, it was elite Christian education in colonial India that gave Hindu culture its Victorian sensibilities, leading anti-colonial nationalist leaders such as Gandhi to deny the place of Khajuraho's erotic imagery in the Indian nation. However, at its inception, British colonists ascribed the source of these attitudes to previous Muslim regimes. For early European visitors such as T.S. Burt, Muslims served as a convenient scapegoat for denying him his pleasure of looking at Hindu erotic imagery. Despite his proclaimed disgust at the indecency that he encountered, Burt clearly expressed his regrets over missing the opportunity to see the images, imagining himself happily offering the princely sum of 10 pounds sterling to satisfy his lustful gaze.

This essay examines how the written records left by visitors to Khajuraho grapple with understanding the temples for their own times, implicating sexuality and obscenity within the communal triangle of Hindu, Muslim, and British relationships. Though not explicitly set in Khajuraho, such fraught responses to sexuality entered into the literary imagination of colonial critics such as E.M. Forster, whose *Passage to India* (1924) depicts Miss Quested becoming disoriented by her encounters with religious erotica coinciding with her inauspicious visit to the mysterious caves, ultimately causing deep fissures between the Hindu, Muslim, and British in his fictional town of Chanderpore.

After India's independence from colonial rule, and especially with the proliferation of tourism in the 1960s and 1970s, Khajuraho was reclaimed by the Indian state as an essential and welcome part of its ancient heritage, becoming a "must-see" World Heritage site attracting hoards of foreign and Indian tourists each year. Today, the erotic sculptures often strike visiting observers, both Indian and foreign, as an anomaly to contemporary Indian culture. Indeed they do stand out in a country better known for traditional gender roles and a strict sexual morality. Like the comments of visitors to modern Athens who marvel how the brilliance of the ancients has been lost to the chaos of the modern nation-state, and as T.S. Burt himself commented for Khajuraho, such reasoning represents a post-Orientalist move to appropriate civilizational artifacts for one's own narrative of global progress. Yet as Tapati Guha-Thakurta (2004) asserts, the new postcolonial respectability of Khajuraho stands in contrast to erotic representations produced by Muslim artists, such as M.F. Husain, who have been singled out and targeted by Hindu nationalists on the charge of creating obscenity and indecency.

By looking at changing understandings of Khajuraho, from Arab, Chinese, Hindu, British, nationalist, and postcolonial observers, the history of writings on Khajuraho serves as a microcosm of north Indian historiography, delineating viewpoints that say as much about the understandings of India's history in the contemporary society in which they were written as they do about understandings of erotic sculpture.

THE TEMPLES OF KHAJURAHO

Located in what is today a still somewhat isolated area of Madhya Pradesh, the archaeological site known as Khajuraho has been famous since British colonial times for its collection of erotic sculpture featured on the facades of Hindu and Jain temples dating back to the Chandella dynasty of the tenth century. The two dozen-odd temples stand in clusters described by archaeologists as the Western, Eastern, and Southern Groups that surround the modern town. The architectural styles are relatively consistent with one another, with each temple being a compact yet tall style set onto platforms, and allow visitors to circumambulate the walls as they move their gaze upward through the receding horizontal layers of ornate carvings of the *sikhara* (spire). Reading from the bottom up, the intricate carvings on the slabs depict gods, goddesses, maids and servants, royalty, and even animals engaged in a variety of acrobatic sexual acts, with the upper layers presenting various stages of post-coital bliss.

It is estimated that it took about 250 years, from roughly 900 to 1130 AD, to complete the 85 temples built on the site. Of these original temples, just 25 remain today. The extent of the site is far from fully excavated, and the Archaeological Survey of India continues to locate, survey, and restore additional temple structures found in the immediate region. One facet that makes the Khajuraho complex unique is that it is an example of a multi-sectarian religious space, shared by followers of Vishnu (Vaishnavites), Siva (Saivites), and also Jains. Though the Jain shrines are curious for their unusual mimicry of ornate Hindu erotic imagery, I will leave aside that sectarian debate and concentrate my analysis primarily on the Hindu temples of the Western Group.

Understanding the time-line of their construction is an important point of discussion. As fascinating as the issues of eroticism and sexuality are in themselves, the grafting of communal chronologies onto the temples of Khajuraho also make for an interesting story. One of the flashpoints in the debates over Khajuraho is that the

Hindu and Jain temples of Khajuraho were constructed in the early medieval period, coinciding with the beginning of the spread of Islam across north and central India after the initial Arab conquests of Sindh in the eighth century. The period when Muslim rulers established polities, from the ninth to mid-nineteenth centuries, is often mislabeled as the "Muslim period" in the broader history of South Asia, with the "British period" beginning with the arrival of Europeans, whose rule was made concrete by the English victory in the 1757 Battle of Plassey. Such periodization schemes immediately raise questions about how modern scholars, both implicitly and explicitly, theorize the Indian "medieval" in broader narratives of Indian history. Indeed, one guidebook author writing on the history of Khajuraho, and clearly invested in the Hindu/Muslim/British school of chronology, actually refers to this time as the "late Hindu" (Punja 1995). Other scholars label the time period of the ninth and tenth centuries as the "late Golden Age" or "Post-Gupta" period, attempting to draw ties to the highly caste-conscious classical age of the Gupta dynasty of the fourth to sixth centuries AD.[2]

After Burt's re-discovery of the Khajuraho temples, a major question arises as to who might have built the temples. In order to address this question, it is necessary to consider the broader regional, political, and material contexts of Chattarpur district in Madhya Pradesh. The Khajuraho temples are among a series of physical artifacts in the state from India's ancient and medieval past, ranging from stone-age cave paintings dating back thousands of years, to Buddhist monuments, including Sanchi, dating from 200 BC to 200 AD. The region was conquered by the Gupta Empire (320–550 AD), which united much of northern, central, and eastern India under a single administration. After the waning of the Gupta Empire, northern India decentralized into a number of smaller polities, ruled by local lords and rulers. Until the ninth century, a dynasty known as the Prathiharas held power, building temples nearby in Gwalior and towards Jhansi, that have survived to the present.

Most accounts of the history of the Khajuraho temples say that they were built by the Chandella dynasty that emerged as a regional powerhouse in the area following the decline of the Prathiharas in the tenth century. The only scholars who actually dispute the Chandella building of Khajuraho are Asher and Talbot (2006:15–16), who point out that there is actually no direct evidence of who might have built the largest temple at Khajuraho, Kandariya Mahadeva, dedicated to the god Shiva, although they acknowledge that most scholars presuppose that it was commissioned by the Chandella rulers. The Chandellas, as their origin myth relates, are purported to be one of the 36 Hindu Rajput clans tracing their mythical lineage from the sun, the moon, and the sacred fire.

Though historians agree that the Chandellas became the next ruling power of the region from the tenth through twelfth centuries, there are competing ideas about Chandella origins and how they succeeded in rising to preeminence. Here, two major accounts diverge. The first tradition states that the Chandellas are descendents of Rajput clans, the traditional warrior caste. According to the mythology, a high-caste Brahman woman gave birth to a boy in Khajuraho, after having had a short affair with the god of the Moon. While pregnant, she was told that by going to Khajuraho, her child would become a powerful king and rule over a vast kingdom. Inscriptions in stone and copperplate found at Khajuraho maintain that the kingdom takes its name from the teacher Chandratreya, descendent of the teacher Atri, and ultimately from the Moon. These inscriptions would serve to collaborate the rulers' Rajput origins, since their clans typically claim descent from either the sun or the moon (Punja 1995).The second, and considerably less respectable story of Chandella birthright, places their origins in the local tribes of the region, outside the fold of caste Hinduism. These rulers, proponents of the theory maintain, fell under the influence of the mysterious, virulently anti-Brahman sect known as Tantra, who flouted high-caste superiority by, among other things, eating meat and indulging in promiscuous sex.

More broadly, coinciding with the Chandellas' rise to regional power, is the beginning of the spread of Islam across northern and central India. Many historians of medieval India have chosen to portray the advent of Islam in India in a negative light, emphasizing conflict, stagnation, and repression over adaptation and collaboration. This historical bias was especially true amongst British writers of the colonial period, but still has many adherents among nationalist historians. By writing of Muslim savagery amidst Hindu victims, this trope of history helped legitimate British rule in India, insinuating that the British were there to help ward off Muslim influence and return India to its imagined Hindu origins. The British depicted Muslims as enemies of Hindu India, and helped promote the idea that Muslims routinely desecrated Hindu places of worship, while the British always maintained that they took a more neutral and detached stance on religious policy.

The British popularized a controversial chronology of Indian history separating out ancient (Hindu), medieval (Muslim), and modern (British) periods. This division of time along the lines of religious identity gives the impression of an imagined homogeneity to each period, clearly denying the diversity of polities, sects, and practices in India's history. Most importantly, besides the anomaly of juxtaposing two religious identities with the "neutral" religious identity of the colonial British, as Asher and Talbot (2006) point out, this periodization also tends to emphasize a viewpoint of history which lays stress on an imagined "clash" of history and civilizations. Asher and Talbot propose a consideration of the encounters between religions as a kind of bilateral "revitalization" rather than some essentialized communal struggle. What is most fascinating about the writing of Chandella history is how modern interpretations of the erotic figures found on the Khajuraho temples re-inscribe such competing narratives of medieval history. Questions of sexuality, caste, and communal Hindu-Muslim tensions all come into play in the reporting of Khajuraho's pasts.

In describing the dynasty that built the Khajuraho temples, scholars of the modern era have struggled with how to characterize the patron's preferences for the carving of loving couples known in Sanskrit as *mithuna* over the exterior and interiors of the temple structures. There are a number of theories purporting to explain the erotic sculptures of the temple complex, and scholars extrapolate from their chosen theory to make claims about the identities and interests of their builders. This is where the history-making again gets really interesting, as contemporary scholars rewrite the past according to their own understandings and intellectual placement of erotica within the Indian tradition. What scholars do agree upon is that the granite and sandstone temples of Khajuraho served as the religious center for the ruling dynasty, and that their government and other so-called secular buildings, made of brick and wood, have not survived to the present time. Beyond this, however, narratives diverge.

Two competing theories for Khajuraho's erotic art are the "high culture" or "low culture" schools of thought. The divide between these schools illustrates the significance of the competing narratives over the ethnogenesis of the Chandellas. Authors interpret the temples to be part of the high-culture Sanskrit cosmopolitan—to paraphrase the words of Sheldon Pollock (2002)—or part of the prevailing regional subculture of anti-Brahman tantric practices including meat-eating and sacred fornication. Depending on the interpretation of the Chandellas, the significance of the temples is markedly different.

The high-culture perception of Khajuraho casts the Chandellas as descendents of the Rajputs, and makes implicit claims about the accessibility of the world of Sanskrit learning to the Chandellas and their court. Ruling kings in India certainly collaborated with Brahmans to establish their social legitimacy, and even if the rulers did not themselves read and understand Sanskrit, they would have had access to court pandits.[3] This high-culture explanation often includes the theory that the carvings are a celebration of ancient

Hindu sexuality, literally the *Kama Sutra* etched in stone. The noted art historian Ananda K. Coomaraswamy exemplifies this high-culture view when he writes of the decoration of medieval temples such as Konark in Orissa and Khajuraho, commenting that "much of the sculpture may be described as a detailed illustration of the *Kamasastra*" (1999: 57). Though this view is widely accepted in western popular culture (indeed a recent "Lost Cultures" documentary on the History Channel again reasserted this claim), there is little evidence to substantiate the theory. In the first decades after independence, as colonial interpretations of India's heritage made way for progressive popular writers such as Mulk Raj Anand (1968), a movement began to embrace ancient erotica as an essential part of India's glorious past, neither maligning nor blushing about the images, but celebrating these forms as part of the shining constellations that make up Indian civilization. A wave of popular books on Indian eroticism emerged as part of the corpus of Indian culture, of which Khajuraho formed an essential part. Photographs of Khajuraho are used to illustrate the numerous editions of ancient erotic literature aimed at westernized readers, especially translations of the fourth-century *Kama Sutra*.

It is postcolonial archaeological specialists on Khajuraho including Krishna Deva and Devaganga Desai who have best succeeded in lifting off Victorian veils of disgust and indecency to discuss Khajuraho. Their work builds upon the extensive survey done by British archaeologist Alexander Cunningham, under whom British-supervised crews did extensive although somewhat careless restoration. Crews often bungled their repairs, inserting friezes wherever convenient, without consideration of their relative narrative position to other sculptures. British supervisors used the restoration effort as an opportunity to collect pieces of friezes and sculpture for their personal collections. Krishna Raj (1959) was the first Indian archaeologist to lead an extensive survey of Khajuraho between 1956 and 1962, initially publishing his findings in the

Archaeological Survey of India's journal *Ancient India*. In the introduction to his two-volume compilation *Temples of Khajuraho*, Raj glosses over the issue of temple erotica with his sweeping statement that "with an enormous array of lovely sculptured forms ever present, the texture of the Khajuraho temple vibrates with a rare exuberance of human warmth, which is unparalleled in any other art" (Raj 1990: 17). Throughout the text, Raj employs the controlled tone of archaeology's scientific objectivity, providing detailed descriptions of the temple architecture and sculptures with rather technical language.

Devangana Desai's brilliant contributions to our understandings of Khajuraho build upon Krishna Raj's work, focusing on the development of cultural interpretations which place the meanings of the temples and their forms at the center of her analysis. Desai's approach to the temples is to de-emphasize the obvious erotic aspects of the temples, arguing instead that they should be considered as part of a broader, pre-existing tradition of temple erotica ranging from Ellora to Konark.

While accepting Khajuraho's place in the "high culture" of royal and Sanskrit courtly life, Desai repudiates the "*Kama sutra*" and "free love" theories of the temples, doubting that a secular interest in sex manuals would lead to religious motifs, and in her words, offer a "sex education" to visiting religionists (Desai 2000: 35). Desai also dismisses the "low culture" theory that the temples are tied to Tantric sects of the broader region. Instead, Desai's major contributions to the study of Khajuraho focuses on understanding the relative positions of sculpture, particularly the corner niches, in creating a symmetry drawing upon a deeper symbolism of philosophy. While providing enjoyment for visitors, the sculptures also contain evil-fighting structural qualities embedded, for example, in messages encoded by the sculptures, in particular, the upside down head postures. Desai also draws connections from the sculptures to underlying principles of yoga, exploring aspects of spiritual non-duality.

In order to consider the variety of narratives written about the history of Khajuraho and its erotic temples, let us now return to the narratives that observers wrote about the temples themselves. Though we lack direct literary evidence from the time period and region when and where the temples were built, it is useful to consider what was written about Khajuraho in the centuries before and after its ninth–eleventh-century prominence as a temple town in central India.

EARLY OBSERVERS OF KHAJURAHO

Since foreign observers wrote of the religious center of Khajuraho even before it became the thriving Hindu and Jain temple complex and religious center of the builders of erotic sculptures, it is clear that the site itself was already considered sacred. The Chinese explorer Xuanzang is credited with being the first writer to mention the place Khajuraho, referring to it as the "country of Chi-Ki-to" (2000: 271). Xuanzang visited India in the early decades of the seventh century AD (641–642), and on his voyage he was most concerned with collecting Buddhist texts and visiting sites of importance to the Buddhist tradition. Xuanzang notes:

> The soil is celebrated for its fertility; it is regularly cultivated and yields abundant crops; it is specially adapted for beans and barley; it produces abundance of flowers and fruits. The climate is temperate; the people are naturally virtuous and docile; most of them believe in heretical doctrine, a few honour the law of Buddha. There are several tens of sangharamas with few priests. There are about ten Deva temples, which some thousand followers frequent. The king is of the Brahman caste. He firmly believes in the (three) precious ones; he honours and rewards those who are distinguished for virtue. Very many learned men from distant countries congregate in this place (Xuanzang 2000: 271).

Here, Xuanzang mentions the existence of Buddhist "brethren" in monasteries but makes it clear that Brahmanical Hinduism is the predominant religious practice of the site. At the time of Xuanzang's visit, it appears that the contemporary temple complex had not yet been initiated, although the area was already established as an important religious center. The *Imperial Gazetteer*, following up on Xuanzang's interest in Buddhist practices in the region, comments on a massive Buddha containing "the usual" inscriptions from the seventh and eighth centuries on the location, yet oddly dismisses the evidence and maintains that "there are no Buddhist remains on the spot" (Meyer et al. 1909: 217).

After Xuanzang, the next observations of Khajuraho are from a few centuries later, after the construction and consecration of the primary temples at Khajuraho. Al-Biruni (sometimes called Abu Rihan), the famous Muslim historian traveling with Mahmud of Ghazni, visited "Kajuraha" in 1022 AD and mentioned the town as the capital of the region ruled by the Chandella kings. He writes of Khajuraho not as a center of religious piety, as he does with other place-names, but as an important political center:

> Marching from Kanoj towards the south-east, on the western side of the Ganges, you come to the realm of Jajahuti, 30 *fursakh* from Kanoj. The capital of the country is Kajuraha. Between this town and Kanoj there are two of the most famous fortresses of India, Gwalior and Kalanjar (Al Biruni 1910: 202).

Al-Biruni's patron, Mahmud, in fact laid siege to the Chandella forts of Gwalior and Kalanjar in 1022–23, as part of a broader campaign against North Indian regional rulers. Khajuraho was later overtaken by Aybak in 1202–3 (Wink 1997: 146). By the early thirteenth century, however, it is likely that the temple patrons had already left the Khajuraho temples in advance of the campaigns of Turkish soldiers.

What evidence do we have of temple destruction, which prevented T.S. Burt from viewing the beautiful woman he almost encountered in the jungles of the site? Subsequent visitors to Khajuraho provide seemingly contradictory evidence about the condition of the temples. Much has been made of temple demolition in Indian history, especially in the eyes of Hindu nationalists who disparage the effect of Muslim culture on the subcontinent, asserting that Muslims indiscriminately desecrated temples as part of their intolerance for local culture. However, historian Richard Eaton (2000) argues that far from indiscriminate attacks on Hindu temple structures, Muslim state-building involved temple desecration only when the political authority of local rulers was vested in the local temple. By displacing a state-identified deity of Vishnu or Siva within a prominent temple, the political legitimacy of a local kingdom could be shaken. However, Hindus still saw this as a desecration.

The next traveler to Khajuraho who recorded personal observations was Ibn Battuta, who visited in 1335, and wrote of matted-haired Jogis discussing philosophy and performing their purported magic. The passage as rendered by Samuel Lee, one of his earliest translators to English, states that:

> We then proceeded from the city of Barun to the stage of Kajwara, at which there is a lake about a mile in length; and round this are temples, in which there are idols. At this place resides a tribe of Jogees, with long and clotted hair. Their colour inclines to yellow, which arises from their fasting. Many of the Moslems of these parts attend on them, and learn (magic) from them (Ibn Battuta [1829] 1971: 162).[4]

Interestingly, Lee's harder-to-find 1829 translation does not include any information about temple desecration. The situation Ibn Battuta discusses reads more like our knowledge of pacifist Sufis and yogis, who integrate themselves into their local surroundings. It is fairly clear that he is describing Khajuraho, with his mention of a mile-long pond surrounded by tall temples with idols, which later scholars, including Scotsman Hamilton Alexander Rosskeen (H.A.R.) Gibb, take to mean the Shivsagara water tank.

But the translations of Ibn Battuta diverge tremendously on some important details, reflecting a number of issues of colonial translation. First of all, H.A.R. Gibb's accessible and lucid translation is almost universally credited by both popular and scholarly writers on Khajuraho as the source of the comment about the yogis' matted hair, what we might now characterize as dreadlocks, even though this aspect is clearly missing from his text. For Gibb's sentence on Khajuraho as seen by Ibn Battuta reads:

> We went from Parwan to Kajarra, where there is a large tank about a mile long having on its banks temples with idols, which have been made examples of [i.e., mutilated] by the Muslims. Thence we journeyed (Ibn Battuta 1929: 226).[5]

This issue of temple desecration is a major source of disagreement between scholars. Krishna Raj conjectures that Sikandar Lodi may have damaged the temples in 1495, but does not provide the reference to his source(1990:4). While both Lee and Gibb concur on Ibn Battuta's comment on the idolatrous temples, they diverge widely on the issue of any damage to the structures, presumably by Muslims. Whereas the early nineteenth-century Lee does not mention Muslim damage, the early twentieth-century Gibb, writing in the heydey of British colonialism, leaves out physical descriptions of the yogis, and makes a point about Muslim desecration. What I found instructive, in my research on this issue, is that many modern scholars writing on early explorations to Khajuraho combine the two readings of Ibn Battuta and attribute their source to Gibb, mentioning both matted hair (which Gibb omits) and temple desecration (which Lee omits), apparently without checking carefully either source.

Without access to the manuscripts of Ibn Battuta's text, it is difficult to know whether Lee simply ignored a remark about temple desecration, considering it unworthy of translation, or whether this was an assumption made on the part of Gibb and written into the work as Ibn Battuta's own words. Because Burt's account was written at approximately the same time that Lee translated Ibn Battuta, it is clear that the British were familiar with the concept of Muslim temple destruction. It is significant to note that desecration would have been far more politicized in 1929 (the date of Gibb's translation) than in 1829 (when Lee translated Ibn Battuta), due to the increase of communal tension during the anti-colonial nationalist movement.

While it is unclear whether Ibn Battuta's journal excluded references to desecrating, it is very clear that he omitted descriptions of the erotic images. Here we have two versions of a description by a foreign visitor who chose not to describe, much less condemn, any erotic statuary. This does not mean, however, that such temple carving was not visible, far from it. Ibn Battuta characterized the temples as idolatrous, for Islam frowns upon any graven images. Indeed perhaps from his worldview the very fact that they were images of people was more disturbing than any acts they may be engaging in. Still we are left with two visitor accounts of Khajuraho where no mention of the eroticism of the temple carvings is made. In summary, early Arab writers verify archaeological and inscriptional evidence that Khajuraho was an important and thriving political and religious center of Central India. At the same time, they do not specifically mention erotic images, referring only to idolatrous decoration. Their descriptions of the complex are notable for what they do not include—any reference to the erotic nature of the sculpture. We can see here that what was obvious and shocking to British surveyors was not worthy of note to Muslim visitors. Notably, by the time of the *Ain-i Akbari*, the official account of the Mughal empire's territories and resources in the late sixteenth century, there are no contemporary references to Khajuraho, although nearby forts are mentioned.[6] Most likely, by this time dense forests covered the area, rendering it inaccessible. As far as we know, there are no additional commentaries on Khajuraho for the next 300 years, until the serendipitous arrival of Bengal Engineer T.S. Burt.

THE EUROPEAN REDISCOVERY OF KHAJURAHO

It was not until the early nineteenth century that the Khajuraho temples were re-discovered in modern times, after probably lying abandoned for several hundred years. Like many archaeological finds in India and Pakistan, it was not seekers of religion, architecture, or antiquities, but rather an engineering crew doing survey work who described the temple structures for Europeans. Khajuraho had in fact been marked as a place-name on European maps of India, after Lt. William Price deciphered an inscription mentioning the Chandella dynasty, placing its name in the annals of European cartographic knowledge. The first known European description of the Khajuraho temples comes from Captain T.S. Burt of the Bengal Engineers. Burt's visit to the temples, and the descriptions that he subsequently published, drew attention to Khajuraho, and his views helped to establish an interpretation of Khajuraho as a strange enigma that juxtaposed the finest temple art with the most explicit and lewd imagery.

Burt's report on his findings at Khajuraho, published by the Asiatic Society in 1839, is replete with details of colonial power relations. Riding in a palanquin, Burt notes that one of his so-called "Palky-Bearers" told him about the wondrous sights of "Khajrao," and Burt decided to make a visit there. Having arrived at his destination Chatterpore twelve hours early, Burt instructed his bearers to carry him throughout the night to the site, in order to reach the place they called Khajrao by sunrise the next morning. He mentions that he traveled directly to the temples without stopping at the nearby village, clearly showing that the location was well-known to people in the broader region. Burt emerged from his palanquin only to have to push through a dense undergrowth of trees to reach the covered temples.

Burt's first response was to express delight at seeing the numerous temples and ruins, marveling at how the tops of the temples rose above the treetops of the surrounding jungle. He makes clear that his first task, after finishing his breakfast, was to search for Sanskrit inscriptions. In his account, Burt elaborated on his meticulous technique for transcribing the inscriptional text he discovered. On top of the 20 square feet of stone, Burt spread out a sheet of white paper. Using wet towels he pushed the sheet into the cavities made by the lettering. He then spread over this another long scroll of paper that was covered with ink to make an exact impression.[7] Having finished what seemed to be—in his mind at least—the essential task of recording the inscription, Burt proceeded to explore the material structures, but almost as an afterthought.

The rough manner in which Burt first reached the interior of the temple structure he found would shock modern conservationists. In order to explore the temples' upper stories, after his bearers could find no doorway or stairs, Burt followed one of his bearers to the roof by scaling up the exterior images of the temple using the sculptures as toe and hand holds, in his words "laying hold of the leg of one god, and the arm of another, the head of a third, and so on" in order to reach the top when he found an opening to squeeze himself into (Burt 1839: 164). Upon entering the temple, unattended except for the pungent smell of bat and monkey, Burt's professional skills in engineering led him to consider the construction of the temple architecture, and he marvels at the solidity and lasting structures, commenting upon the builders' lack of masonry and plaster. Burt excused himself from describing the sublime sculptures of the site, saying that he lacked the resources, but identified the major gods of the temples, expressing his astonishment at the exquisite carvings and especially the size of an ox, of which he takes careful measurements of dimensions and weight.

What does Burt have to say about the erotica on the temple walls, which have been the focus of so much interest by subsequent visitors? Burt writes:

> I found in the ruins of Khajrao seven large Diwallas, or Hindoo temples, most beautifully and exquisitely carved as to workmanship, but the sculptor had at times allowed his subject to grow rather warmer than there was any absolute necessity for his doing; indeed, some of the sculptures here were extremely indecent and offensive; which I was at first much surprised to find in temples that are professed to be erected for

good purposes, and on account of religion.... The palky bearers, however, appeared to take great delight at the sight of those to them very agreeable novelties, which they took good care to point out to all present. I was much struck with the beauty of the inner roofs of the temples, which were circular, and carved in the most elaborate style (Burt 1839: 163–64).

Here, Burt admired the structure of the temples, but felt compelled to offer a disclaimer in order to distance himself from the erotic subject matter. Despite his self-stated Victorianism, it is clear that Burt responded to the sexuality of the images in a positive way. At the same time, Burt expressed the inculcation of his own desire in subsequent remarks about a curious but incomplete serpentine sculpture carving. He lamented the absence of a female figure near a well-formed snake, blaming it on "rascally despoilers." His personal disappointment at not seeing the female nude is expressed in monetary terms when Burt places a value on what he missed, saying he would have gladly surrendered a hundred rupees or ten pounds sterling in order to get a good look. Here we see Burt touching on the commodification of the female image in a colonial context.

After lamenting his loss, he proceeded to another temple to obtain a measurement of an exceptionally tall Shiva lingam, which he was informed was the largest in India and much venerated. He was told that a light burned there throughout the night, perhaps indicating its use as an active place of worship. Intending to measure the height of "the gentleman," Burt ran into local resistance when he refused to remove his work boots upon entering the temple. Rather than suffer such inconvenience, Burt sent in a bearer to measure and ascertain its height at eight feet and its diameter four feet, and calculated its weight at about seven-and-a-half tons. Towards the end of his short stay at Khajuraho Burt ran into further difficulties. Having misplaced his pencil, and deputizing several persons to look around for it without success, Burt was unable to make sketches of some stone lions fighting human wrestlers which appear at the entrance to a temple. At the end of the journal entry included in the Asiatic Society publication, he noted the presence of a large tank, albeit with very little water in it at the time of his visit.

Burt's visit to Khajuraho gives us an opportunity to consider the two enduring "puzzles" of the remarkable temple site, namely, the question of the eroticism of the temples, and the evidence of destruction wrought to the site some time after its period of greatest popularity but before European contact. Burt in fact combines the two, twice begrudging the actions of (presumably Muslim) destroyers for interfering with his own commodifiable enjoyment of the female Hindu form. 10 quid! After Burt's visit, the local Maharaja Pratap Singh tried to repair some of the temples in the 1840s, using brick and lime, but to no lasting success. When the Archaeological Survey took over administration of the site in 1904, they were compelled to undo many of the repairs that the Maharaja's staff had attempted.

British archaeologist Alexander Cunningham's work in the 1850s provides much more detailed descriptions and illustrations of the temples as they began to be excavated, but it is Burt who embarked upon an essential interpretative problem that remains with us to this day, namely, the simultaneity of the erotic along with the religious in the temple carvings, or as Burt ironically puts it, "ecclesiastical erections" (1839: 163). What we see in Burt's writing is a particular way of talking about religious erotica, establishing a basic intellectual problem about Khajuraho that scholars and visitors—both Indian and foreign—grapple with when trying to make sense of Khajuraho's erotic temple architecture. This question has morphed over time, but essentially asks: How could medieval Indian society create something erotic in the name of religion? In modern incarnations, this question has also become, how could a society as prudish as India have produced such explicit images for public viewing?

Burt's sentiments are echoed by the British archaeologist Alexander Cunningham who came to Khajuraho in 1852. He devised the directional classification scheme for Khajuraho, differentiating the "Western Group of Temples" from the "Eastern Group of Temples," which is still in use today. Cunningham's own writing about the erotic sculpture of the temples has a unique dialectical tension. Echoing the engineer Burt's comments, Cunningham writes about "highly indecent" and "disgustingly obscene" figures on the temple walls, but then in the same sentence normalizes the same temple sculptures to be "ordinary representations of the Hindu gods and goddesses, in different positions and under various forms" (Cunningham 1872: 420). As historian Upinder Singh notes in her fine work on the history of archaeology in India, Cunningham's reactions may be described as "controlled disapproval" (Singh 2004: 75). Indeed, in subsequent writings on the site, Cunningham maintains a dual consciousness of finding Khajuraho simultaneously to possess both the most sublime and magnificent forms of temple architecture in Central India, and yet be the most "indelicate" and "grossly bad" in terms of the erotic content. An undercurrent of misogyny extends through many of his observations, including his references to *yogini* sculptures as "female goblins" (1872: 416–17) and maligning the numerous female figures that are shown dropping their clothes and "purposely exposing their persons" (1872: 423).

Other official European views on Khajuraho extend these interpretations. The *Imperial Gazetteer of India* makes note of the curious fact that Jain temples follow the same sculptural precedents of the Hindu temples of the region. The description contains the usual colonial tropes of disparagement in describing the structures, referring to "heaps of ruin" and considering the erotica to be a "defect." As the authors note, "the carving is exceedingly rich and covers every available inch of space, but many of the figures are highly indecent, not a usual defect in Saiva temples" (Meyer et al. 1909: 218). There is also evidence of British views of medieval Hindu-Muslim relationships. In commenting and elaborating on the writings of Ibn Battuta, the *Imperial Gazetteer* conjectures that "*even* Muhammadans resorted [to the matted-haired jogis] in order to learn magic" [emphasis mine]. It further comments that "it seems probable that the partial demolition of its temples and consequent loss of importance dates from 1494–95, when Sikandar Lodi, after his expedition into Panna and Baghelkhand, retreated through this region and sacked the country as far as Banda."[8] Even in the case of indelicate and grossly indecent temple complexes, no opportunity is missed to point out the destruction visited on India by Muslim rule.

NATIONALIST FRAMES

I have already mentioned how postcolonial popular writers worked to reclaim Khajuraho as a respectable piece of India's past. Indian leadership had divergent opinions on the complex. It is widely rumored in many writings about Khajuraho, but I have yet to see properly substantiated with documentation, that Gandhi disapproved of the erotic sculptures of Khajuraho, writing to the Government of India asking them to cover up the most lurid bits in an attempt to sanitize Indian tradition. Blaming both Muslim and English puritanism, Alain Danielou claims that Gandhi sent armies of his followers to destroy the erotic carvings found on the temples, but was persuaded by Rabindranath Tagore to stop this program (1994: 10). Many popular writers maintain that Gandhi hoped to cover up the statues with mud, with the idea that the temples could be viewed by experts when necessary, but should not be available to the general public. As for Nehru, Danielou goes on to claim (again without citing evidence) that Nehru disapproved of Danielou's publication of photographs from Khajuraho depicting homosexual activity, since Nehru took a hostile stance towards same-sex love, preferring to think of it as a foreign poison infiltrating a heterosexual India.

In 1950–51, the first President and Prime Minister of independent India, Dr. Rajendra Prasad and Jawaharlal Nehru, respectively, visited Khajuraho, drawing attention to the site as an important part of India's heritage. Nehru wrote Khajuraho into his five-year plans to develop the tourism sector of the Indian economy, in the protectionist nation's desperate search for foreign currency. In 1952 a Circuit House was built to house visitors to the area, when the Government of Madhya Pradesh nominated Khajuraho as one of four tourist centers to be promoted internationally. This rustic accommodation remained the only housing available for visitors until 1969, when the first hotel "Hotel Chandella" opened as a commercial establishment to house overnight guests (Chopra 1991: 52).

There is evidence of divergent viewpoints about the erotic temple sculptures of India, raising questions about whether it should be considered obscene. Khajuraho became the focus of a legal battle in newly-independent India, in a case concerning the publication of a book which included pictures of the erotic content of its temples. A question was proposed to bring up in the Rajya Sabha as to whether or not a book containing images of the temple sculptures at Khajuraho should be declared obscene. The question arose in 1957, when Delhi magistrate Shri Baldev Raj delivered a judgment convicting publishers of a book on Khajuraho for obscenity (Home Political 8/22/59). In this case, the magistrate rejected arguments raised that such images were themselves available for purchase from the Archaeological Survey of India, and that the Govt. of India Publication Division itself had produced a film on the Khajuraho temples, and disregarded testimony from officials from the Archaeology Department that such images were not obscene.

In the judgment on the case, it was ruled that only the temples themselves were exempt from anti-obscenity statutes, and that publications of the images could in fact be classified as obscene. In considering the plea to admit the case into the Rajya Sabha discussion, the aforementioned picture book on Khajuraho was borrowed from the Delhi administration. The question was ultimately disallowed by the Ministry of Law, though not before the *Statesman* and the *Times of India* published scathing editorials on the subject, pointing out the "ludicrous" implications of the case. As an editorial to the *Indian Express* pointed out:

> that the Khajuraho sculptures are valued as a rich heritage of art of which the country is proud has not prevented the court from holding the reproduction of these arts pieces as obscene.... One should have thought that Khajuraho, and many other great works of art bequeathed to us by our forbears [*sic*] had once for all established the legitimacy of the explicit representation of sex as an artistic enterprise...we have been undergoing for nearly a century now a process of knowing ourselves through others' eyes (Mubarak 1959: appended in Home Political 8/22/59).

The challenges faced by India's own government and courts in finding a balance between the heritage of the temple complex and their own social mores is only the latest challenge presented by Khajuraho. The temple complex defies periodization by standing as a multi-sectarian religious space that withstood the advance of Muslim rule. Yet the portrayals of the erotic carvings seem to defy not only British, but also nationalist perspectives of what Hinduism is. The problem has been reduced in the western worldview to the *Kama Sutra* etched in stone, a celebration of a libertine spirituality lost long ago, first to Muslim and later to British prudishness. Even this view, however, is undermined by the description of Muslim visitors, who noted religious practice but had nothing to say about the sculptures.

Though we have written evidence of what medieval visitors recorded about the temples, it is only through European colonial interpretations that we find the first evidence of people characterizing the art as "obscene," and calling attention to the explicit sexual depictions in the carvings in the temple facades. It is remarkable that this perspective on Khajuraho came about, it seems, some eight hundred years after the temple's construction and consecration. By pursuing an understanding of Khajuraho, and of how it has been seen over the centuries, the question of juxtaposing sexuality with Hindu religious practice is better understood as an extension of the Orientalist trope of British imperialism. In Khajuraho, the sexual dimension of the temples has become embroiled in the implied relationship between Hindu and Muslim. Indeed, many of the interpretations of the Khajuraho temples emphasize the struggle between Hindu and Muslim, even though we do not see this in the writings of Muslim visitors themselves. The fact that only upon the British uncovering of the temple statues did their reputation as erotic sculpture develop seems to say more about Victorian England than about early medieval India.

NOTES

I am grateful for the comments given to me by Cynthia Talbot, Jennifer Joffee, David Libby, colleagues at UTSA and members of the audience at the Trautmann conference organized by Cynthia Talbot and held at the University of Michigan.

1. Among other things, Burt comes across as something of a dilettante in his quotation of the inscription at Sir Christopher Wren's tomb at St. Paul's. Literally translated, the Latin expression means "if you seek his monument look round about you."
2. One note on chronology is pertinent here: While the formal Gupta Empire lasted from 320 to 600 AD, and is considered India's Golden Age due to the excellence of its Sanskrit literature and other arts, I have been quite fascinated to see how some scholars have stretched that golden age for nearly one thousand years, from the Laws of Manu through the end of the Chandella kingdom in 1150. From Manu's perspective, however, the age is golden only if you are male and Brahman.
3. Professor Madhav M. Deshpande, personal communication, 2 October 2007.
4. Lee is rather unclear about the exact location of this site, stating in his note on the place-name Kajwara that "the Kitchwara of Rennell is a province, and seems to be too far to the south-west to be the place here intended. Gajara, or Kurrera, seems more immediately in the route of our traveler" (1971: 162 note).

5. In his note to this passage, Gibb remarked, "As regards Kajarra, there can be no question that this is Khajuraho, 27 miles E. of Chhatarpur and 25 N.W. of Panna, in spite of the detour which it involves on the journey" (Ibn Battuta 1926: 226). The description given by Ibn Battuta is in complete agreement with the description of the site contained in Sir Alexander Cunningham's official reports (Cunningham 1872: 412–39).
6. For example, *Ain-i Akbari* refers to the fort at Gwalior.
7. The article focuses on the inscription, and its translation by J.C.C. Sutherland, with the intention of identifying and charting the genealogy of the erstwhile kings of that region.
8. *Imperial Gazetteer*, Vol. 15, p. 217.

REFERENCES

Abu al-Fazl ibn Mubarak. 1894. *A'in-i Akbari vol. 3*, trans. H. Blockmann. Calcutta: Asiatic Society of Bengal.

AlBiruni, Muhammad ibn Ahmad. 1910. *Alberuni's Indiavol. 1*, trans. Edward C. Sachau. London: Kegan Paul, Trench, Trūbner & Co.

Anand, Mulk Raj. 1968. *Khajuraho*. Bombay: Marg.

Asher, Catherine and Cynthia Talbot. 2006. *India Before Europe*. Cambridge: Cambridge University Press.

Burt, T.S. 1839. "Khajuraho."*Journal of the Asiatic Society of Bengal,* 8: 158–84.

Chopra, Suhita. 1991. *Tourism and Development in India*. New Delhi: Ashish Publishing House.

Coomaraswamy, Ananda K. 1999. "Mediaeval Sculpture (AD 850–1200)." In *Introduction to Indian Art*. Delhi: Munshiram Manoharlal.

Cunningham, Sir Alexander. [1872] 2000. *Four Reports Made during the Years 1862–63–64–65,* vol. 2. New Delhi: Archaeological Survey of India.

Danielou, Alain. 1994. *The Complete Kama Sutra*. Rochester, VT: Park Street Press.

Desai, Devangana. 2000. *Khajuraho: Monumental Legacy*. New Delhi: Oxford University Press.

Eaton, Richard M. 2000. "Temple Desecration and Indo-Muslim States." In *Beyond Turk and Hindu: Rethinking Religious Identities in Islamicate*

South Asia, ed. David Gilmartin and Bruce Lawrence, 246–81. Gainesville: University Press of Florida.

Forster, E.M. 1924. *A Passage to India*. NY: Harcourt.

Guha-Thakurta, Tapati. 2004. *Monuments, Objects, Histories*. Delhi: Permanent Black.

Gupta, Charu. 2001. *Sexuality, Obscenity, Community:Women, Muslims, and the Hindu Public in Colonial India*. Delhi: Permanent Black.

Xuanzang. 2000. *Si-Yu-Ki: Buddhist Records of the Western World*, trans. Samuel Beal.NY: Routledge. Originally published in 1889.

Ibn Battuta. [1829] 1971. *The Travels of Ibn Batuta*, trans. Samuel Lee. New York: Burt Franklin.

———. 1929. *Travels in Asia and Africa 1325–1354*, trans. H.A.R. Gibb. London: George Routledge & Sons, Ltd.

Ichaporia, Niloufer. 1983. "Tourism at Khajuraho: an Indian Enigma?" *Annals of Tourism Research* 10: 75–92.

Meyer, William Stevenson et al. 1909. *Imperial Gazetteer of India*. Oxford: Clarendon Press.

Mubarak. "What is Obscenity?" *The Indian Express*. 7 July 1959.

Pollock, Sheldon. 2002. "Cosmopolitan and Vernacular in History." In *Cosmopolitanism*, ed. Carol Breckenridge, Sheldon Pollock, Homi K. Bhabha and Dipesh Chakrabarty. Duke University Press.

Punja, Shobita. 1995. *Khajuraho and Its Historical Surroundings*. New Delhi: Gulmohur Press.

Raj, Krishna. 1959. *Ancient India*. New Delhi: Archaeological Survey of India.

———. *Temples of Khajuraho*. 1990. New Delhi: Archaeological Survey of India.

Singh, Upinder. 2004. *The Discovery of Ancient India: Early Archaeologists and the Beginnings of Archaeology*. Delhi: Permanent Black.

Wink, Andre. 1997. *Al-Hind: The Making of the Indo-Islamic World Vol 2: The Slave Kings and the Islamic Conquest 11th–13th Centuries*. Leiden: Brill.

10

Hindu Sects and Hindu Religion

Precolonial and Colonial Concepts

DAVID N. LORENZEN

The modern study of Indian history, Indian religions, Indian languages and other aspects of Indian society and culture essentially dates back only to the formation of the Asiatic Society by Sir William Jones and his colleagues in 1784. These European scholars, the so-called Orientalists, and their mostly anonymous and more traditional Indian teachers revolutionized both the content and the epistemological methods and models used for studies of Indian history and culture. Among contemporary scholars, Thomas Trautmann has long been at the forefront of those who have been re-examining the contributions of the early Orientalists and their Indian colleagues to this revolution in the way Indian society and culture has been studied.

One of the chief aims of Trautmann and of others who agree with his main arguments, myself included, has been to try to find a middle way between scholars influenced by postmodern and postcolonial approaches and the more traditional (although also modern) views associated with scholars not influenced by these approaches. Postcolonial scholars often argue that the epistemological break introduced in the early British colonial period was so dramatic as to virtually create or invent Indian institutions of all sorts—social, religious, political, and economic—both in the sense that new institutions were, in fact, created and in the sense that existing institutions were reconceptualized in so radical a fashion that they too became something quite different and, in a certain sense, new. Institutions and cultural categories such as Hinduism, Indian history, and even caste have come to be seen, conceptually at least, as recent and essentially European inventions. More traditional contemporary scholars have generally considered such conclusions as hyperbole disguised as insight and have gone about their business as usual. What Trautmann and those who follow him have done is to try to identify and compare what was new and what was not new, the continuities as well as the discontinuities, in the way that the Orientalists—and by implication virtually all modern scholars, postcolonial ones included—have looked at Indian history, Indian society, and Indian culture.[1]

Trautmann's more recent work has been mainly on the ways in which the early Orientalists, especially Sir William Jones in Calcutta and F. W. Ellis in Madras, changed our views of the deep history of Indian languages. This was done with the collaboration of the Indian scholars with whom they worked. The Europeans added something new to this study, but also did not ignore the powerful insights of pre-modern Sanskrit and Tamil grammarians, most notably Panini, into the science of linguistics (Trautmann 1997, 2006). That these European scholars rarely if ever publicly acknowledged their debt to their Indian collaborators is a sad product of imperial hubris, but this does not substantially change the fact of what happened.

My own work has concentrated more on the contributions of the early European missionaries and Orientalists to the study of Indian religions and religious history rather than historical linguistics (Lorenzen 2006a, 2006b, 2011). Much of this work has tried to show how early European missionaries and Orientalists built on previously existing Indian concepts of Hindu religion in their own modern conceptualizations of this religion. Here in this essay I want to extend this line of research to consider the ways in which pre-modern intellectuals writing in Indian languages and missionaries and Orientalists writing in European languages conceptualized the relation between the major religious traditions that have come to be called Brahmanism, Buddhism, Jainism and Hinduism on the one hand, and, on the other, the smaller Brahmanical, Buddhist, Jain and Hindu sects that have historically made up a substantial part of the major traditions.

My main argument here is that, starting from pre-modern scholars right through to twentieth-century Orientalists, there has been an awareness of a dynamic and historically changing relation between religious sects and the larger religious traditions with which they were associated. Each important author nonetheless gave his own slant on the nature of sects and on how their relation to the larger traditions should be conceptualized. Early Sanskrit texts described different sects principally in terms of their metaphysical doctrines. Vernacular texts like the *Bhaktamals* turned to hagiographies of the founders of the various sects. The studies introduced by the Orientalists, on the other hand, emphasized an empirical, historical, and ethnographic epistemology, sometimes highlighting the relation between sect and caste. These changing views about the nature of sects, and their relation to wider traditions, undoubtedly reflect the differing concerns of the authors of the texts, but they also provide evidence about the historically changing nature of the sects and traditions themselves.

The views discussed here will include those of Asoka, Madhava, Anantanandagiri, Nabhadas, Raghavdas, Roberto de Nobili, Horace Hayman Wilson, Sir R.G. Bhandarkar, and J.N. Farquhar.[2] For the most part I will not pay much attention to the contributions of Christian missionaries, except insofar as they can be classed primarily as Orientalists. This omission is merely intended to better focus the discussion and not to deny the importance of missionary criticisms of Hindu religion in influencing the responses of colonial-period Hindu intellectuals.[3]

ASOKA MAURYA

By the time of King Asoka (ca. 269–232 BC), we find already in place a clear division between *brahmanas* and *sramanas*, between those who followed Vedic tradition and those who followed newer religions that did not recognize the authority of the Vedas, meaning principally the Buddhists, the Jains, and the Ajivikas. At the least, this division into *brahmanas* (Brahmans) and *sramanas* implies that the Vedic tradition was still more or less intact and clearly distinguished itself from Buddhism, Jainism, and other non-Vedic religions. In addition, Asoka proposed a still broader religious concept that he called *dhamma* that was apparently meant to bring social harmony among smaller sects and even between the Brahmans and *sramanas*.

Among Asoka's inscribed edicts, a key text with regard to what his *dhamma* actually meant in terms of human conduct is his fourth major rock edict (Thapar 1961: 251; Goyal 1982: 43):

> In the past, the killing and injuring of living beings,[and] lack of respect towards relatives, brahmans, and *sramanas* had increased. But today, thanks to the practice of *Dhamma* on the part of the Beloved of the Gods, the king Piyadassi [i.e., Asoka], the sound of the drum has become the sound of *Dhamma*, showing the people displays of heavenly chariots, elephants, balls of fire, and other divine forms. Through his instruction in *Dhamma*, abstention from killing and non-injury to living beings, deference to relatives, brahmans, and *sramanas*, obedience to mother and father, and obedience to elders have all increased as never before for many centuries. These and many other forms of the practice of *Dhamma* have increased and will increase.

The scope of Asoka's *dhamma* has been much debated among modern historians. Some identified the *dhamma* fairly closely with Buddhist doctrine, the Buddhist *dhamma*, but the Asokan texts clearly suggest that Asoka regarded his *dhamma* as something more general, a doctrine that encompassed not only Buddhism but also other religious groups including the Brahmans and the non-Buddhist *sramanas*. Other scholars attempted to give Asoka a decidedly secular and practical purpose. Romila Thapar, the leading historian of Asoka's period, argued that Asoka's *dhamma* is basically an attempt to find a common religious morality that can help overcome sectarian conflict. Thapar called this "a policy rather of social responsibility... a plea for the recognition of the dignity of man, and for a humanistic spirit in the activities of society" (Thapar 1961: 3).

Amartya Sen recently attempted to secularize Asoka and his *dhamma* still further, arguing that Asoka was a sterling example of a champion

> of tolerance and freedom ... who during the third century BCE covered the country with inscriptions on stone tablets about good behavior and wise governance, including a demand for basic freedoms for all—indeed, he did not exclude women and slaves as Aristotle did; he even insisted that these rights must be enjoyed also by 'the forest people' living in pre-agricultural communities distant from Indian cities (Sen 2005: 284).

Although Thapar's and Sen's appreciations of Asoka have a slightly anachronistic flavor, there is no doubt that Asoka's principal concern was to avoid conflict between the Brahmans and *sramanas*, and among the smaller groups or "sects," through the promotion of a policy of religious tolerance and harmony. In his twelfth major rock edict, for instance, Asoka advocates "the essential doctrine of all sects" (Thapar 1961: 255; Goyal 1982: 58–62):

> The Beloved of the Gods, the king Piyadassi, honours all sects and both ascetics and laymen, with gifts and various forms of recognition. But the Beloved of the Gods does not consider gifts or honor to be as important as the advancement of the essential doctrine of all sects (*saravadhi asa savapasamdanam*). This progress of the essential doctrine takes many forms, but its basis is the control of one's speech, so as not to extoll one's own sect or disparage another's on unsuitable occasions, or at least to do so only mildly on certain occasions.... Many are concerned with this matter—the officers of *Dhamma*, the women's officers, the managers of the

state farms, and other classes of officers. The result of this is the increased influence of one's own sect and glory to *Dhamma*.

The word here translated as "sect" is, in Asoka's original Prakrit text, *pasanda*. Scholars are divided about whether this word is related to Sanskrit *parsada* (*parisad*) ("assembly, council") or to Sanskrit *pasanda* (a word that later comes to mean "heretic," often referring to Jains and Buddhists). *Pasanda* seems the more likely candidate. Asoka does not specify whether by *pasanda* he is referring to groups associated with the Brahmans or the *sramanas* or with both, but in any case he tells them to behave toward each other in a courteous manner, a plea that clearly implies that they did not always do so. Kautilya's *Arthasastra* and the *Manusmrti* are early Sanskrit works that contain interesting references to *pasandas*, apparently in the sense of heretics, especially Buddhist and Jain monks.

MADHAVA AND ANANTANANDAGIRI

The most important catalogues of religious and metaphysical traditions found in pre-modern Sanskrit literature are two texts: Madhava's *Sarvadarsanasamgraha* (1882, 1964) and Anantanandagiri's *Samkaravijaya* (1971). Both these works were written in southern India and in a historical environment that probably had only a small Muslim and Christian presence. The dates of both texts are somewhat uncertain, but the text attributed to Madhava probably dates from about the fourteenth century while Anantanandagiri's text is more recent, perhaps belonging to the sixteenth or seventeenth century. Later pre-British catalogues of Hindu sects were mostly written in vernacular or foreign languages. I will discuss some of these texts shortly.

The catalogues of sects and religions described in the *Sarvadarsanasamgraha* and the *Samkaravijaya* are quite different from each other, as are the strategies that authors used in organizing them. The *Sarvadarsanasamgraha* comprises a set of quite detailed descriptions of the sixteen different metaphysical systems or doctrines (*darsanas*). These are, in the order of the text: the Carvaka system, the Buddhist system, the Arhata (or Jain) system, the Ramanuja system, the *Purnaprajña* system (associated with the Vaishnava dualist Madhvacarya), the Nakulisa-Pasupata system, the Saiva system (meaning the mainly south Indian Saiva-siddhanta system), the *Pratyabhijña* system (a Tantrik Saiva school associated with Abhinavagupta of Kashmir), the Rasesvara system (a school of alchemy), the Aulukya (or Vaiseshika) system, the *Akshapada* (or Nyaya) system, the Jaimini (or Mimamsa) system, the Panini system (centered on grammatical and semantic analysis), the Samkhya system, the Patanjali (or Yoga) system, and finally the Samkara (or Advaita Vedanta system).

Apart from the fact that the first three non-Vedic systems mentioned by Madhava—namely, the Carvakas, the Buddhists, and the Jains—are clearly considered by the author to be the worst and the final Advaita system was considered to be the best, the content and order of the list of doctrines appears to be rather haphazard. It includes, in addition to three non-Vedic schools, the traditional six systems of Brahmanic metaphysics (Samkhya-Yoga, Vaiseshika-Nyaya, and Mimamsa-Vedanta), with Vedanta represented in three variants (Ramanuja's, Madhva's, and Samkara's), three Saiva systems (Pasupata, Saiva-siddhanta, and *Pratyabhijña*), and the rather anomalous grammatical and alchemical systems. The Buddhist, Jain, and Carvaka systems are attacked from time to time throughout the rest of the work and in the final chapter expounding the Advaita system (not included in the Cowell and Gough translation). The author also criticizes the Samkhya and Mimamsa systems at length.

The *Sarvadarsanasamgraha* offers little information about the extent to which Madhava regarded the Vedic/Brahmanic philosophical schools to be part of a single religion. In all chapters of the work, the discussion is consistently focused on metaphysics and has virtually nothing to say about issues of religious practice and community identity. Metaphysical concepts and views were, in fact, freely debated among Jains, Buddhists, and the followers of Vedic schools, and they frequently borrowed from each other. That Samkaracarya's use of ideas derived in part from Buddhist Madhyamika philosophers is only the most obvious example. What Madhava does do, however, is accept Vedic statements as a legitimate source of authority or *pramana*. In this way the *Sarvadarsanasamgraha* draws a reasonably clear distinction between what are called *nastika* traditions—such as those of the Carvakas, Jains, and Buddhists—that do not accept the Vedas as eternal and divine and the *astika* traditions followed by all the schools and sects that do accept the divine authority of the Vedas.[4]

Anantanandagiri's *Samkaravijaya* is a quite a different text. Its criticisms cover more than just the metaphysical views of various sects and schools. It also criticizes aspects of their religious ethical practices. The number of sects and schools criticized is also much larger than in the *Sarvadarsanasamgraha*. Anantanandagiri's work is divided into seventy-four chapters, a majority of which relate the victory (*vijaya*) of the Advaita philosopher Samkaracarya over the leaders of various sects. In total Samkara's encounters with about fifty rival groups are described. The basic principle of organization is, at least in theory, geographical and historical. Samkara one by one meets representatives of the different rival sects in the course of his "tour of victory" around the Indian subcontinent. In practice, however, these rival sects are grouped together in smaller sets.

The non-Vedic Carvakas, Jains, and Buddhists are placed in chapters 25–28. Sects devoted to a series of relatively minor deities (Mallari, Visvaksena, Manmatha, Kubera, Indra, Yama, Varuna, Vayu, Bhumi and Jala, and Varaha) follow in chapters 29–39. The adherents of the classical Brahmanical schools of Samkhya, Yoga, Nyaya, and Vaiseshika form another subset (chapters 40–42). The fifth of the six classical schools, Kumarila Bhatta's Mimamsa, is set apart in its own chapter (chapter 55). Several different sects devoted to Vishnu (the Bhagavatas, Pancaratras, the Vaikhanasas, and the *Karma-hina* Vaishnavas) form another category (chapters 6–10), as do a variety of groups devoted to Ganesa (chapters 15–18) and several types of Saktas (chapters 19–22). Other sects and schools mentioned in the text include various Saiva sects (chapters 4–5), the sect of the Kapalikas (chapters 23–24), and those of the worshippers of the Pitrs, Sesha and Garuda, the Siddhas, the Gandharvas, and the Bhutas and Vetalas (chapters 47–51).

A principal aim of both the *Sarvadarsanasamgraha* and the *Samkaravijaya* is to demonstrate the superiority of Samkaracarya's Advaita Vedanta. In the case of the *Sarvadarsanasamgraha,* all the rival schools whose views are discussed (with the possible exception of the Carvakas) really existed. In the case of the *Samkaravijaya*, however, many of the sects mentioned, most notably those dedicated to minor deities, probably never existed. The author's purpose in including these imaginary sects is not clear. Perhaps he simply wished to disparage any sort of worship directed at these minor deities. Notable in both works is the absence of any mention of Christians or Muslims. Some Christians were present in south India from the third or fourth centuries and possibly even earlier and some Muslims were in the same region (chiefly in Kerala) from the eighth or ninth centuries.

VERNACULAR HAGIOGRAPHIES

The *Sarvadarsanasamgraha* and the *Samkaravijaya* were both written in Sanskrit. When we come to literature about religious sects written in Indian vernacular languages, we find that a quite different sort of text predominates. At least in northern India, the basic model was established sometime during the late sixteenth century by Nabhadas in his *Bhaktamal* and its later commentaries. Here the emphasis is placed squarely on hagiography, the life stories of individual religious poets and saints.[5] Many saints described by Nabhadas are not closely associated with any sectarian groups, but at least a few were the reputed founders of lasting sectarian movements. These include Nimbaditya, Ramanuja, Vishnusvami,

Madhva, Samkaracarya, Ramananda, Kabir, Caitanya, and Vallabha. With the notable exception of Samkaracarya, virtually all the saints described by Nabhadas were Vaishnavas of one sort or another.

Other texts similar in many respects to Nabhadas's *Bhaktamal* include Anantadas's *paracai* legends of various saints (composed ca. 1600), Raghavdas's *Bhaktamal* (ca. 1720), and Mahipati's Marathi *Bhaktavijaya* (1762).[6] Although all these texts have a strong bias in favor of Vaishnava religion, none of them restricts the stories to the founders of a single sect. Mahipati and Raghavdas even include descriptions of Saivite Nath saints such as Matsyendranath and Gorakhnath. Raghavdas's encyclopedic *Bhaktamal* also includes some Jain, Buddhist, and Muslim saints, although Raghavdas himself is explicitly a follower of the *nirguni* (worshipping a formless god) Vaishnava saint Dadu Dayal.

Caturdas, who wrote his commentary on Raghavdas's text in 1800 AD, begins with a verse that offers homage to "the millions of Hari devotees, the Dasanami *samnyasis,* the Jains and the lords of Yoga, the blissful *jangama* ascetics, the Buddhists and the dervishes, the nine Naths and the eighty-four Siddhas, the Muslim teachers (*pir*) and prophets (*paigambar*), Brahma, Vishnu and Siva" (Raghavdas 1969: 6). Only the Christians are missing.

A text in many ways in a class by itself is Muhbad Shah's *Dabistan.* This seventeenth-century text, written in Persian by a Parsi author, contains stories about a great number of medieval Indian saints from various sects and both Muslim and Hindu religions. An English translation of this text was published in 1843. The late Aditya Behl (2008) wrote an important essay on the text and its author. Nonetheless, further work on it is still needed.

Other texts that might be discussed in this context include South Indian Tamil and Kannada hagiographies such as Cekkilar's twelfth-century *Periya Puranam* and the fifteenth-century Virasaiva *Sunyasampadane.*[7] These texts are similar to the *Bhaktamals* in that they contain hagiographies of large numbers of saints, but are different in that all the saints belong to, or are posthumously associated with, a single religious sect. In northern India, the same can be said of Gokulnath's sixteenth-century text, *Caurasi Vaishnavan ki Varta,* containing stories about saints associated with the Vallabha sect.[8]

In India, hagiography can, of course, be traced back long before Nabhadas. The legendary lives of Buddha and of Mahavira and other Jain saints, in particular, were integral parts of Buddhism and Jainism. Vedic and early Puranic tradition, however, never paid much attention to this genre. The Puranas certainly did present detailed narratives of the lives of gods, especially Vishnu's avatars, but the avatars are more mythological than historical or even legendary figures. Their mythological status is suggested by the fact that several of the main ten avatars are non-human (Fish, Turtle, Boar, Manlion) and by the fact that all of these avatars (including Vamana, Parasurama, Rama and Krishna) lived in former *yugas* or ages (except for the Buddha and the yet-to-appear Kalkin). Puranic stories about the ancient *rishis* (seers) also seem to be basically mythological, and none of these *rishis* are known to be the founders of historical religious sects in any case. The *Samkaravijaya* and other collections of legends about Samkara do contain many stories about the historical Samkara, but it is not clear if these texts are substantially older than vernacular hagiographies like that of Nabhadas. In addition, the Samkara hagiographies do not contain stories about the lives of multiple saints as is the case in Nabhadas's *Bhaktamal* and similar texts.

What produced this medieval explosion of hagiographic texts containing legends about historical poets and saints? Was this explosion simply the result of a mostly spontaneous change of literary fashion, or do these texts reflect important historical changes in the nature of Hindu religion? One possible answer is that the turning away from a reliance on the eternal and impersonal authority of the Vedas in medieval *bhakti*-based Hinduism, particularly among more radical sects such as those of the followers of Kabir, Nanak, and Dadu, led to a reliance on the words and persons of the founders of these sects, the guru and his *bani,* as sources of divine authority. The Vedas existed from the beginning of time, but *bhakti* sects were founded by historical persons. When these sects ignored or rejected the Vedas, they replaced Vedic authority with that of the guru, his words and the lessons of his legendary life story (Lorenzen 1996: 155–56).

The authors themselves generally have surprisingly little to say about why they wrote their texts. Nabhadas, however, comes close to explaining why he wrote his *Bhaktamal* in four *doha* verses near the beginning of the text (Nabhadas 1969: 37–42):

> The devotees (*bhakta*), devotion (*bhakti*), the Lord (*bhagavanta*) and the guru. These are four in name only, in fact they are one. When one offers homage to their feet, many obstacles are destroyed.
>
> Thinking about auspicious things is splendid. The devotee of God (*harijan*) who sings about the fame of the devotees (*jan*) becomes auspiciousness itself.
>
> All the saints (*santan*), the Vedas (*sruti*), the Puranas, and history (*itihas*) have declared that one should worship both God (*Hari*) and God's servants (*Haridas*).
>
> [My guru] Agradev commanded me: "Sing about the fame of the devotees. There exists no other means to cross the ocean of existence."

There are in fact several things that the authors of these texts tend to have in common besides their taste for hagiography. All of them support a religion based on devotion (*bhakti*) to Puranic gods (Vishnu, his avatars, Siva, or Sakti) and to the human saints themselves. Few of the authors seem to be learned in Sanskrit. Few demonstrate much interest in or knowledge of the Vedas or the six traditional *darsanas* (the hagiographers of Samkara and of the yogic Naths are notable exceptions). Many of the authors are probably not Brahmans (e.g., Nabhadas, Raghavdas, Anantadas, Muhbad Shah). Few have any known association with specific temples (the early Alvars and Nayanars and the somewhat later early Virasaivas are exceptions).

The overall picture suggests both a gradual breakdown in traditional Brahmanic and Sanskrit learning and a general lessening of the importance of big temple and *matha* (monastery) complexes. Implicit in the process is also an increasing importance of religious sects and the founders or leaders of these sects. Nonetheless, most of these authors do not discuss the sects per se or their relation to larger religious categories such as, for lack of a better term, religious currents (chiefly Vaishnavism, Saivism, and Saktaism) or the Hindu religious tradition as a whole.

ROBERTO DE NOBILI

Roberto de Nobili was an Italian Jesuit who worked as a missionary in southern India in the period from 1605 until his death in 1656. This makes him slightly later than Nabhadas but earlier than Nabhadas's commentator Priyadas. De Nobili is now famous for his scholarly works on Hindu religion and for his advocacy of a policy of Christian accommodation to Hindu customs that, in his view, were not clearly religious, most notably the use of the sacred thread. During the seventeenth century, he was the Christian missionary in India who made the most serious studies of Indian religions and his views on these religions and their sectarian and theological divisions are worth a closer examination.[9]

De Nobili's most accessible work on Indian religions is his *Informatio de Quibusdam Moribus Nationis Indicae,* edited and translated from Latin into English by S. Rajamanickam as *Roberto de Nobili on Indian Customs* (1972). De Nobili here divides Indian religions into three "sects" (he reserves the term "religion" for the "one true religion," namely, Christianity). These three sects are the Buddhists or Atheists, the "Gnanis" (i.e., the Jains or Tamil Siddhas?), and the Idolaters (i.e., the Hindus). De Nobili states quite clearly that these three "sects" had little or nothing to do with each other, in other words, that they were, in our terms, independent religions:

> Again, that the sect of the Atheists cannot be said to be an unorthodox offspring of the sects of idolaters is clear under yet another head, namely

the fact that these sects do not agree in any of their tenets, just as the sects of the Gnanis have nothing in common with these same idolaters (1972: 36–37).

De Nobili in turn divides the Idolaters into their own sects, the main ones being four. The first of these he calls the "Mayavadis," those "who hold in equal honour the three gods *Brumma, Visnu,* [and] *Rudhren.*" The second sect is called that of the Xaivas, the third is that of the Vaishnavas, and the fourth is that of the "Tadvavadis." The members of the first are said to be followers of "Ciancaraciarier" (i.e., Samkaracarya), the second of "Civen" (Siva?), the third of Ramanuja, and the fourth of "Madhuva" (i.e., Madhva). These groups or sects are clearly those more properly known as the Advaita Vedantins or Smartas, the Saiva-siddhantins, the Sri-Vaishnavas, and the Dvaitins or followers of Madhva. De Nobili also mentions the existence of minor Idolater sects including the "Logaidas" (Lokayatas), the "Sciandra vadis" (worshippers of the Moon), the "Suria vadis" (Sauryas or worshippers of the Sun), the "Mavivadis"(?), the "Vamas" who follow the god "Siacti" (Sakti, i.e., the Saktas), and the "Aginager"(?).

On the whole, this analysis of the Hindu sects of seventeenth-century southern India seems to be reasonably complete and accurate, at least as far as sects led by Brahmans are concerned. What is important for this discussion is the fact that de Nobili clearly saw all these Idolater sects as members of one big "sect" or religion which is clearly distinguished from that of the Buddhists and the Gnanis. It is also interesting that de Nobili did not seriously attempt any historical or geographical analysis of Idolater religion and its composite sects, a type of analysis that H.H. Wilson and other later Orientalist scholars generally thought was necessary. For the most part de Nobili adopted a model similar to that found in the *Sarvadarsanasamgraha* and the *Samkaradigvijaya.* I strongly suspect that de Nobili was following a classification system offered to him by some learned Brahman interlocutor, perhaps one acquainted with the texts by Madhava and Anantanandagiri.

WILSON, BHANDARKAR, AND FARQUHAR

What happens when we come to the English Orientalist, H.H. Wilson (1786–1860)?[10] Although the earliest British Orientalists like Sir William Jones and H.T. Colebrooke were also interested in Hindu religion and Hindu mythology, Wilson was the first Orientalist to look at the beliefs and practices of Hindu sects in detail. Wilson's "Sketch of the Religious Sects of the Hindus," first published in 1828 and 1832, begins with a discussion of the lists of sects in the *Sarvadarsanasamgraha* and in the *Samkaravijaya*. In later chapters in several places he makes use of Nabhadas's *Bhaktamal*. Wilson also claims to have based his essay largely on two Persian language texts by Hindu authors, one text by Sital Singh, munshi to the Raja of Banaras, and one by Mathura Nath, a librarian at the Hindu College in the same city. Wilson does not mention the title of either work, and I have not been able to identify them. Wilson apparently did not make use of the *Dabistan*.

Wilson was, of course, not a Hindu and had no interest in showing that Advaita Vedanta was superior to all other sects and schools. He also had no interest in inventing sects centered on minor deities. The opening paragraph of his essay states his aim as follows (1828: 1): "The Hindu religion is a term that has been hitherto employed in a collective sense, to designate a faith and worship of an almost endlessly diversified description: to trace some of its varieties is the object of the present enquiry."

The most obvious thing to note about this statement is that Wilson is affirming both the great diversity and an implicit underlying unity in Hindu religion. Since this text was written in the period of what Thomas Trautmann (1997) calls the shift or transition from Indomania to Indophobia among British-born scholars of Indian history and culture, and since Wilson belongs more to the Indophiles than to the Indophobes, his recognition of the underlying unity of Hindu religion deserves more attention than the view of missionary scholars like Alexander Duff (1839), who also saw in Hindu religion a unity, but the unity of a giant conspiracy against Christian reason and morality.

The actual procedure of Wilson differs from his Indian pre-colonial predecessors most notably in his reliance on a fairly strict empirically-grounded historical methodology rather than an emphasis on metaphysics or on hagiographic legends. He also shifts the emphasis of his descriptions onto the religious communities. Where and how did they originate? Where are their chief centers located? What social groups belong to them? How numerous are their supporters? What are their religious rituals and customs? All these questions are discussed only in passing by earlier authors, but in Wilson's text they move center-stage. The later authors I will discuss here are J.N. Farquhar and R.G. Bhandarkar. They mostly follow Wilson in employing such an empirical historical methodology, but they also each apply particular emphases to their discussions.

Let us take as an example of Wilson's methodology, his treatment of the Kabir Panth. Nabhadas's commentator, Priyadas, was mostly content to narrate a series of legends that together amounted to a legendary biography of Kabir, without questioning the historicity of these legends. Wilson, in his "Sketch of the Religious Sects of the Hindus," begins by briefly summarizing a few key legends about Kabir, but he also indicates several times that he doubts that the legends are historically true, using phrases like "according to them [the Kabir Panthis]," "the story...perhaps not literally true in any fashion," "according to one account," and "it is said."[11] Wilson then passes to a discussion of the Vaishnava affiliation of the Kabir Panthi followers of Kabir and of the various customs, rituals, and dress adopted by members of the sect. Next he presents a detailed discussion of the literary texts of the Kabir Panth including those composed by Kabir and by later authors. Wilson also gives some translations of selected passages from the *Kabir bijak*, the text considered authoritative by the Kabir Panthis, most notably of Kabir's *sakhis* (verse couplets), and also a summary of a Kabir

Panthi (Dharamdasi) work titled *Sukh nidhan*. Finally Wilson gives a short historical summary of the branches of the Kabir Panth: who founded them, where their chief centers are located, and an estimate of the numerical size of their ascetic and lay followers.

To a considerable extent, the model set by Wilson in 1828–32 for discussing the Kabir Panth and other sects was followed by virtually all subsequent scholars. Nonetheless, the information available to later scholars about Hindu sects increased in exponential fashion. In at least this respect, the differences between Wilson, on the one hand, and R.G. Bhandarkar and J.N. Farquhar, authors who published surveys of Hindu sects in 1913 and 1920 respectively, on the other, amount to a sea change in the academic study of Indian religions. When Wilson wrote in the first half of the nineteenth century, much basic information about the history of Indian religions was still unknown to European scholars. For instance, in his first Oxford lecture on the "Religious Practices and Opinions of the Hindus," delivered in 1840, Wilson notes ([1862] 1976: 44): "The oldest monuments of the Hindu religion are the Vedas. It is much to be regretted that we have not a translation of these works in any of the languages of Europe." In fact, several Vedic translations and Sanskrit editions were published in Europe in the 1840s and 1850s, including Wilson's own translation of the first four books of the *Rg-veda* (done from 1850 to 1857). By the time that Bhandarkar and Farquhar wrote their surveys, most Vedic literature had already been published in editions and translations by European and Indian Orientalist scholars.

Another significant difference between Wilson, on the one hand, and Bhandarkar and Farquhar, on the other, centers on their respective attitudes towards Sanskrit and the vernacular languages. Wilson—like H.T. Colebrooke and Sir William Jones before him—had a decided prejudice in favor of Sanskrit and against vernacular languages. It must be noted that Wilson did make use of some vernacular-language texts in his 1828–32 essay on Hindu sects, as in his translations of some of Kabir's *sakhis*. Nonetheless, in his discussion of Hindu sects in his 1840 essay, Wilson had this to say about their vernacular literature ([1862] 1976: 72–73):

> Such literature as they occasionally cultivate—and it is one of the means by which they act upon the people—is vernacular literature, compositions in the spoken languages. These are mostly songs and hymns addressed to Vishnu, Krishna or Radha, tales and legends of individuals celebrated amongst them as saints, always marvelous, mostly absurd and not infrequently immoral, and vague and dogmatic expositions of elements of belief.

Compare this with what Farquhar wrote about vernacular religious texts in the following passage in which he also moves toward attributing an overall coherence to all the religions and sects born on Indian soil ([1920] 1967: x): "The three religions [Hindu, Buddhist, and Jain] are moments in a single religious movement; and they have reacted on each other throughout their history. Vernacular religious books are as truly a vital part of the growth of the sects as their more formal Sanskrit manuals are. For a full understanding of the history, the whole must be envisaged as one great movement."

Chronologically, the next important survey of Hindu sects published after Wilson's *Religious Sects of the Hindus* was Sir R.G. Bhandarkar's *Vaisnavism, Saivism and Minor Religious Systems,* first published in 1913.[12] Bhandarkar was a Maharashtrian Brahman who had fully appropriated the historical methodology of the European Orientalists. Bhandarkar's survey of Hindu sects is much more contemporary in style and content than Wilson's. Bhandarkar does perhaps display a preference for Sanskrit as the language of religious authority, hardly surprising in a Brahman Sanskritist, but he also makes ample use of vernacular sources. *Vaisnavism, Saivism and Minor Religious Systems* also offers almost no theoretical statements about the ways in which sects are articulated with the larger category of Hindu religion. Bhandarkar's own ambiguous situation as an Indian Hindu writing in English and using a western intellectual methodology undoubtedly had much to do with his reluctance to theorize. Another factor was probably the constraints of colonial politics and censorship.

One text by Bhandarkar that does give us at least some idea of his personal and theoretical views about Hindu religion is a talk he gave at the Hindu reformist organization he supported, the Prarthana Samaj, in 1883. In this talk he attempted to characterize the metaphysical organization of Hindu religion and the need for Hindus to defend their religion from foreign criticism. He says (1928: 604):

> The prevailing Hindu Religion is a religion in which we find various shades of belief and modes of action confused together. We cannot say it is not monotheism, we cannot say it is not polytheism or even fetishism. It is neither simply a religion of external observances nor is it a religion enjoining purity of heart only. We are dissatisfied with this state of things and have been seeking a more consistent and rational system of religious faith and action. A foreign religion has for some time been knocking at our door and claiming admission. If we have deliberately refused to admit it we must give our reasons.

J.N. Farquhar first published his book *An Outline of the Religious Literature of India* in 1920, only seven years after Bhandarkar's survey. By this time, Farquhar felt that ([1920] 1967: ix):

> the Vedic literature has been studied with the utmost care by a company of brilliant scholars; certain sections of the philosophical literature have been critically examined; the classical Sanskrit literature is well known; and portions of the literature of Buddhism and of Jainism have been carefully described; but on the mass of the books produced by Hindu sects and on great sections of Buddhist and Jain literature very little labor has yet been expended.

In other words, Farquhar viewed the study of vernacular texts (including those written in Buddhist Pali and Jain Apabhramsa) as important not only in their own right, but also because he felt that Vedic and classical Sanskrit texts had already been amply studied.

A curious difference between Wilson and Farquhar concerns the ways they each negotiated the Christian prejudices of their English and European readers. Wilson—who in fact personally seems not to have been very religious—felt obliged to pay homage to the anti-Hinduism sentiments of the Christian establishment in his 1840 Oxford lecture. For instance, in this address Wilson mentions, with apparent approval, an

> invitation which has been addressed to the University by the Bishop of Calcutta.... The task that has been proposed to the members of the University is twofold. They are invited to confute the falsities of Hinduism, and affirm to the conviction of a reasonable Hindu the truths of Christianity ([1862] 1976: 40–41).

Farquhar, in contrast, wrote his *An Outline of the Religious Literature of India* with hardly any kowtowing to common Christian prejudice. On the other hand, Farquhar was himself a missionary and his most popular book, *The Crown of Hinduism* (1913), does argue that Hindu religious beliefs and practices were inferior to those of Christianity. Nonetheless, in at least his *Outline,* his approach differs radically from that of earlier, more polemical and anti-Hindu missionary scholars such as W. Ward (1822) and A. Duff (1839). Here Farquhar clearly belongs with the Orientalists, not with the missionaries.

CONCLUSIONS

What I have tried to do here is use historical evidence to indicate a path between the extremes of the claim that Hindu religion was invented, conceptually at least, in the eighteenth or nineteenth centuries, largely through the agency of foreign missionaries and Orientalists, on the one hand, and the claim that Hindu religion has some sort of absolute historical continuity that has survived from Vedic times until the present. I prefer to argue that the history of Hindu religion can be compared to the Buddhist conception of the person. Hindu religion has no eternal essence, no soul, no *atman,* but over time it is constantly being constructed, deconstructed, and reconstructed. It has no essence, but it does have causal continuity over time, stretching back even to Vedic times. Its present character may have little resemblance to that of its distant past, and Vedic religion certainly bears little resemblance to modern Hindu religion, but the causal genealogy does reveal a continuous chain of historical metamorphoses, some slow and some rapid.

One central element in this chain of metamorphoses has been the dialectic between sectarian and universally-shared Hindu identities. Asoka contrasts two general categories, *brahmanas* and *sramanas*, but he also complains about the conflicts among smaller sectarian groups, the *pasandas*. By the early centuries of the Christian era, the religion of the Brahmans had metamorphosed into that of the Puranas. Here again we have little historical information about the specific sectarian groups within Puranic religion, but the evidence does certainly suggest that some such groups did exist. At the same time there was a broader general division into the followers of Vishnu, Siva and Sakti. Nonetheless, all these gods were clearly part of a single pantheon whose myths are all interrelated and told, with varying emphases, in the same Puranas.

By early medieval times we have a much clearer picture of what seems to be a virtual explosion of sectarian groups. This explosion is evidently not just an artifact created by more historical information. Political, social, economic, and demographic changes appear to have fostered the creation of smaller, more tightly organized Hindu sects in both northern and southern India. Clear evidence is found in Madhava's *Sarvadarsanasamgraha* and Anantanandagiri's *Samkaravijaya*. Although these texts take as their primary purpose the descriptions of this sectarian diversity, they also register a difference between *astikas* and *nastikas*, those groups that accept the Vedas as a source of divine authority and those that do not (the Carvakas, Buddhists, and Jains).

By about 1400 if not before, there is clear evidence of the existence of a conscious religious identity among the followers of "Hindu *dharma*" (explicitly so-called). Usually this Hindu identity is contrasted to the Muslim identity of the followers of a "Musalman" or "Turk *dharma*." The early collections of songs and verses by the religious poet Kabir (ca. 1440–1518) are full of attacks against the religious practices of both the Hindus and the Turks or Musalmans. Many other such references are found in the compositions of other early *nirguni* poets, including those attributed to the Nath yogi Gorakhnath and those of Guru Nanak and other Sikh gurus.[13]

At the same time, some of these same poets seem to have been striving for a more complex personal religious identity which somehow went beyond Hindu, Musalman, and Yogi identities. This was done without any hint of an attempt to create "Hindu-Muslim unity" (Hedayetullah 1977) or "inter-religious tolerance" (Sen 2005: 19), as some modern scholars have claimed. Nonetheless, a curious verse attributed to Gorakhnath offers an unusual comment on one possible way to combine these multiple religious (and not just sectarian) identities: "I am a Hindu by birth, I am a Yogi in my maturity, and by intellect I am a Muslim. Recognize, Oh Kazis and Mullahs, the path accepted by Brahma, Vishnu, and Mahadev."[14]

The early Jesuit missionary Roberto de Nobili described Hindu religion pejoratively as the "sect of the Idolaters," but he did so in fairly accurate fashion with a metaphysical emphasis somewhat similar to that of Madhava and Anantanandagiri. The English, European, and Indian Orientalists, on the other hand, introduced a new way of describing Hindu religion based on an empirical historical methodology. This new historical methodology, exemplified in the work of scholars such as H.H. Wilson, R.G. Bhandarkar, and J.N. Farquhar, saw the interplay of religious sects and currents within Hindu religion as a historical phenomenon that depended not just on theological debates and charismatic leaders but also on political, economic, and social changes including the arrival of new political elites from distant regions. These colonial-period scholars did not, however, thereby invent Hindu religion. Hindu religion had already long since been invented.

On the other hand, the Christian and rationalist biases and criticisms of the Orientalists and also of Christian missionaries in India, coupled with the scientific, political, economic, and social changes being introduced by the modern world dominated by Europe, certainly did produce dramatic changes in the nature of Hindu religion. Other scholars have done much to identify the major contours of these changes.[15] Nonetheless, this is an area of research that remains relatively underdeveloped, and much work remains to be done.

NOTES

1. The discussion here is obviously very general and does not attempt to enter into the many associated debates. The published materials related to these debates are enormous, and there is little point in trying to offer a full guide here. Good starting points to lock at the differing views involved are the books by Chaturvedi 2000, Dube 2004, Llewellyn 2005, Nanda 2003, the various volumes of the series *Subaltern Studies,* and back issues of the journal that Trautmann edited for many years, *Comparative Studies in Society and History*.
2. The key original texts are found in Thapar 1961; Madhava 1882, 1964; Anantanandagiri 1971; Nabhadas 1969; Raghavdas 1969; De Nobili 1972; Wilson 1828 & 1832, 1862; Bhandarkar 1913, 1928; and Farquhar 1920.
3. For the missionary contribution to the dialogue, see especially Oddie 2006, Young 1981, Dalmia 1999, and Lorenzen 2006a.
4. It should be noted, however, that the text explicitly uses the term *nastika* only for the Carvakas, who are called "crest-jewels among the *nastikas.*" Nonetheless, the *nastika/astika* distinction was in common use among Brahmanic-tradition metaphysicians like the Vedantins in this period.
5. A fair amount of work on the hagiography of Indian saints has been done in recent years. For a general introduction, see the articles in Callewaert and Snell 1994.
6. On Anantadas, see Callewaert 2000 and Lorenzen 1991.
7. On Cekkilar's text, see Peterson 1991. On the *Sunyasampadane*, see Michael 1992.

8. On this Vaishnava sect and its hagiography collections, see Barz 1976.
9. On De Nobili, see Zupanov 1999. I have discussed De Nobili's description of "Idolater" religion further in Lorenzen 2007. Other missionaries who did some scholarly or semi-scholarly work on Hinduism in the 1500s and 1600s include the Jesuits Gonçalo Fernandes Trancoso (d. 1621), Henrique Henriques (or Anrrique Anriquez, 1520–1600), Andrew Freyre (1625–92), Jacomé Fenicio (1558–1632), Antonio Rubino, Diogo Gonçalves (1561–1640), Francisco Garcia (1580–1659), and Thomas Stephens (1549–1619), the Augustinian Agostinho de Azevedo, and the Franciscan Francisco Negrão. On this topic see Rubiés 2000: n.b. 315–17.
10. Interest in the Orientalists has increased dramatically since the publication of Edward Said's seminal work, *Orientalism,* in 1978. Many of these recent studies tend to vitiate their usefulness through their authors' attempts to extend Said's Foucault-based claim that the Orientalists *created* the Orient, in some ontological sense. A more reasonable view, in my opinion, is that the Orientalists simply projected deeply-rooted stereotypes, sometimes positive but more often pejorative, onto Oriental peoples and cultures. Two important exceptions to this Foucault-mania are the fine historical studies on the Orientalists by T.R. Trautmann (1997, 2006).
11. It is also worth noting that Wilson refers to a legend of Kabir being born from a Brahman virgin widow and claims that the story is "told in the *Bhakta Mala.*" In fact this story is not found in Nabhadas's *Bhaktamal* or in Priyadas's commentary. It is not clear where Wilson got the legend. It also appears in Westcott's 1907 monograph on the Kabir Panth and in many subsequent scholarly texts (but not in most texts by Kabir Panthi authors).
12. This is not to say that there were no significant books and essays on Hindu religion published by European Orientalist scholars in the interim. Among the authors who published such studies can be mentioned Max Müller, H.H. Wilson himself, A. Barth, M. Monier-Williams, E.W. Hopkins, E. Hardy, and H. Oldenberg. On this topic, see Dandekar 1979: 229–31.
13. For a more detailed discussion of these references to Hindus and Turks, see Lorenzen 1999 and 2011.

14. Gorakhnath 2004: 26 (my translation).
15. On the topic of colonial and postcolonial changes in Hindu religion, and especially Hindu sects, see, as a useful sample of the better works so far published, Babb 1987, Dalmia 1999, Dube 1998, Jones 1976, Juergensmeyer 1982, Thapar 1985, and Young 1981.

REFERENCES

Anantanandagiri. 1971. [*Sri*] *Sankaravijaya*, ed. N. Veezhinathan. Madras: University of Madras.

Babb, Lawrence. 1987. *Redemptive Encounters: Three Modern Styles in the Hindu Tradition*. Delhi: Oxford University Press.

Barz, Richard. 1976. *The Bhakti Sect of Vallabhacarya*. Faridabad: Thomson Press.

Behl, Aditya. 2008. "Pages from the Book of Religions: Comparing Self and Other in Mughal India." Unpublished manuscript.

Bhandarkar, R.G. [1913] 1965. *Vaisnavism, Saivism and Minor Religious Systems*. Varanasi: Indological Book House.

———. 1928. *Collected Works of Sir R.G. Bhandarkar*, Volume 2. Poona: Bhandarkar Oriental Research Institute.

Callewaert, Winand M., ed. and trans. 2000. *The Hagiographies of Anantadas: The Bhakti Poets of North India*. Richmond: Curzon.

Callewaert, Winand M. and Rupert Snell. 1994. *According to Tradition: Hagiographical Writing in India*. Wiesbaden: Harrassowitz Verlag.

Chaturvedi, Vinayak, ed. 2000. *Mapping Subaltern Studies and the Postcolonial*. London: Verso.

Dalmia, Vasudha. 1999. *The Nationalization of Hindu Traditions: Bharatendu Harischandra and Nineteenth-century Banaras*. Delhi: Oxford University Press.

Dandekar, R.N. 1979. *Insights into Hinduism*. Delhi: Ajanta Publications.

De Nobili, Roberto. 1972. *Roberto de Nobili on Indian Customs*, ed. and trans. S. Rajamanickam. Palayamkottai: De Nobili Research Institute.

Dube, Saurabh. 1998. *Untouchable Pasts: Religion, Identity and Power among a Central Indian Community, 1780-1950*. Albany: State University of New York Press.

———, ed. 2004. *Postcolonial Passages: Contemporary History-writing on India*. New Delhi: Oxford University Press.

Duff, Alexander. [1839] 1988. *India and India Missions: Including Sketches of the Gigantic System of Hinduism Both in Theory and Practice*. Delhi: Swati Publications.

Farquhar, J.N. [1913] 1971. *The Crown of Hinduism*. New Delhi: Oriental Books Reprint Corp.

———. [1920] 1967. *An Outline of the Religious Literature of India*. New Delhi: Motilal Banarsidass.

Gorakhnath. 2004. *Gorakh-bani*, ed. with modern Hindi commentary Pitambaradatta Badathval (Barthwal). Allahabad: Hindi Sahitya Sammelan.

Goyal, Sriram. 1982. *Pracin Bharatiy Abhilekh Samgrah* [A Collection of Ancient Indian Inscriptions]. Jaipur: Rajasthan Hindi Granth Akadami.

Hedayetullah, Muhammad. 1977. *Kabir: The Apostle of Hindu-Muslim Unity*. Delhi: Motilal Banarsidass.

Juergensmeyer, Mark. 1982. *Religion as Social Vision: The Movement against Untouchability in 20th century Punjab*. Los Angeles: University of California.

Jones, Kenneth W. 1976. *Arya Dharm: Hindu Consciousness in 19th Century Punjab*. Berkeley: University of California.

Llewellyn, J.E. 2005. *Defining Hinduism: A Reader*. London: Equinox Publishing Ltd.

Lorenzen, David N. 1991. *Kabir Legends and Ananta-das's Kabir Parachai*. Albany: State University of New York Press.

———. 1996. *Praises to a Formless God: Nirguni Texts from North India*. Albany: State University of New York Press.

———. 1999. "Who Invented Hinduism?" *Comparative Studies in Society and History* 42: 630–59.

———. 2006a. "Marco della Tomba and the Brahmin from Banaras: Missionaries, Orientalists, and Indian Scholars." *The Journal of Asian Studies* 65, no. 1: 115–43.

———. 2006b. "Religion, Skin Colour and Language: Arya and Non-Arya in the Vedic Period." In *Who Invented Hinduism? Essays on Religion in History*, 144–71. New Delhi: Yoda Press.

———. 2007. "Gentile Religion in South India, China, and Tibet: Studies by Three Jesuit Missionaries." *Comparative Studies of South Asia, Africa, and the Middle East* [Toronto] 27, no. 1: 205–15.

———. 2011. "Religious Identity in Gorakhnath and Kabir: Hindus, Muslims, Yogis and Sants." In *Yogi Heroes and Poets. Histories and Legends of the Naths*, ed. D. Lorenzen and A. Muñoz, 24–50. Albany: State University of New York Press.

Madhava or Madhavacarya [attributed]. [1882] 1961. *Sarva-Darsana-Samgraha* [A Collection of All Doctrines], trans. E.B. Cowell and A.E. Gough. Varanasi: Chowkhamba Sanskrit Series Office.

———. 1964. *Sarvadarsanasamgraha*, ed. with modern Hindi commentary Umasamkarasarma "Rsi." Varanasi: The Chowkhamba Vidya Bhawan.

Mahipati. [1930] 1982. *Stories of Indian Saints* [*Bhaktavijaya*], trans. J.E. Abbott and N.R. Godbole. 2 vols. in 1. New Delhi: Motilal Banarsidass. The original Marathi text was written in 1762.

Michael, R. Blake. 1992. *The Origins of Virasaiva Sects*. Delhi: Motilal Banarsidass.

Muhbad Shah (often wrongly attributed to Muhsin Fani). 1843. *The Dabistan: or, School or Manners* [*Dabistan-i Mazahib*], trans D. Shea and A. Troyer. Paris: Oriental Translation Fund of Great Britain and Ireland. Perhaps written about 1665.

Nabhadas. 1969. *Sribhaktamal*. With verse commentary of Priyadas (1712) and modern Hindi prose commentary. 5th impression; Lucknow: Tejkumar Press. Written about 1600.

Nanda, Meera. 2003. *Prophets Facing Backward: Postmodern Critiques of Science and Hindu Nationalism in India*. New Brunswick: Rutgers University Press.

Oddie, Geoffrey A. 2006. *Imagined Hinduism: British Protestant Missionary Constructions of Hinduism, 1793–1900*. New Delhi: Sage Publications.

Peterson, Indira Viswanathan. 1991. *Poems to Siva: The Hymns of the Tamil Saints*. Delhi: Motilal Banarsidass.

Raghavdas. 1969. *Bhaktamal*. With verse commentary of Caturdas (1800) and modern Hindi prose commentary of Narayandas. Jaipur: Dadudayalu Mahasabha.

Rubiés, Joan-Pau. 2002. *Travel and Ethnology in the Renaissance: South India through European Eyes, 1250–1625*. Cambridge: Cambridge University Press.

Sen, Amartya. 2005. *The Argumentative Indian: Writings on Indian History, Culture and Identity*. New York: Farrar, Straus and Giroux.

Thapar, Romila. 1961. *Asoka and the Decline of the Mauryas*. Oxford: Oxford University Press.

———. 1985. "Syndicated Moksha?" *Seminar*, September: 14–22.

Trautmann, Thomas R. 1997. *Aryans and British India*. Berkeley: University of California Press. Reprinted by Yoda Press, Delhi, in 2004.

———. 2006. *Languages and Nations: The Dravidian Proof in Colonial Madras*. Berkeley: University of California Press.

Ward, William. 1822. *A View of the History, Literature, and Mythology of the Hindus*. 3 vols. New edition; London: Kingsbury, Parbury, and Allen.

Westcott, G.H. [1907] 1953. *Kabir and the Kabir Panth*. Calcutta: Susil Gupta.

Wilson, Horace Hyman. 1828 & 1832. "Sketch of the Religious Sects of the Hindus." *Asiatic Researches* 16: 1–136 & *Asiatic Researches* 17: 169–313. [Later published in book form as *Religious Sects of the Hindus*.]

———. [1862] 1976. *Essays and Lectures on the Religions of the Hindus. Volume 2, Miscellaneous Essays & Lectures*. New Delhi: Asian Publication Services.

Young, Richard. 1981. *Resistant Hinduism: Sanskrit Sources on Anti-Christian Apologetics in Early Nineteenth-Century India*. Vienna: Indological Institute of the University of Vienna.

Zupanov, Ines G. 1999. *Disputed Mission: Jesuit Experiments and Brahmanical Knowledge in Seventeenth-Century India*. New Delhi: Oxford University Press.

Taking the Long Perspective

The Precolonial Past

11

Was There Historical Writing in Early India?

ROMILA THAPAR

A couple of hundred years ago it was stated that Indian civilization was unique in that it lacked historical writing and implicitly a sense of history. With rare exceptions there has been little attempt since to examine this generalization and it is taken as given. I would like to suggest that while there may not be a conventional form of historical writing in the early period there are, nevertheless, many texts that reflect a historical consciousness. This subsequently came to constitute a historical tradition which in the first and second millennia AD is reflected in distinctive forms that approximate historical writing.

My intention in this essay is to argue that, irrespective of the question of the presence or absence of historical writing as such, an understanding of the way in which the past is perceived, recorded, and used affords insights into early Indian society. It is worth investigating what was written on the past and why and what were the dialogues and debates that occasioned this writing. Ascertaining the degree of historicity would be the subsequent step.

Societies need to construct a past, or rather their many pasts, for the past has a social function. Such constructions narrated in sequential order claimed that what they narrated happened in the past, a claim that differentiates them from fiction. Communities have constantly to situate themselves in relation to the perceived past (Hobsbawm 1972), which therefore becomes a dimension of social identity although its construction, form and content might change with new definitions of identity. This is sometimes demonstrated in variant readings of the past which indicate plurality and is particularly apparent when there is an official version that can differ from other versions. New demands on power and legitimacy change existing forms. Thus, what came to be required of conventional history a couple of centuries ago was closely tied to nationalism, which tends preferably to tidy up variety into a single identity within the nation. The recognition of plurality is more recent.

My concern therefore is less with whether or not early Indian society produced a specific historical literature of the conventional kind to record the past, but rather with trying to understand the variety of texts that purport to represent the past. This involves many questions: why they took the form they did; what from the past was of relevance to their author; and why particular types of records were maintained. It seems to me that three aspects need enquiry. I would first like to ask why it was necessary to argue that Indian civilization lacked a sense of history. This was largely but not entirely a colonial argument with an emphasis that derived in the main from the way Enlightenment-thinking defined history. The second aspect is to recognize that historical traditions emanating from diverse cultures will inevitably differ and comparisons have to be more precise than they have tended to be so far. The third, which is in effect the most substantial, is to enquire into the nature of the representation of the past in the texts that are linked to the early Indian historical tradition.

INDIA'S ALLEGED LACK OF HISTORY

The search for indigenous histories of early India began in the late eighteenth century. European scholars, conscious by now of historical literature as a distinct category recording the past, looked in vain for recognizable histories from the literature in Sanskrit. Indian culture, and particularly the Sanskrit articulation of what came to be called Hindu culture, was therefore defined as ahistorical. William Jones, the leading Indologist of the late eighteenth century, suspected that some texts, even if including the myths and legends of the Hindus, probably contained the core of a history (Jones 1799). Most scholars tended to disagree. But even Jones quotes only the *Rajatarangini* of Kalhana, as acceptable historical writing.

A century later MacDonell's searing remark that "early India wrote no history because it never made any" was modified by others such as Rapson, who granted the making of history but regretted the absence of a systematic record (MacDonell 1900: 11; Rapson 1922: 57). Comparisons with the Chinese chronicles of Ssu-ma-ch'ien and the Arabic writings of Ibn Khaldun or even the Biblical genealogies, not to mention Greco-Roman texts, strengthened, if only in contrast, the axiom of Indian society denying history. Such comparisons made no reference to the historiographical contexts of any of the other histories.

The officers of the East India Company derived their data on law and religion from their Brahman informants so the centrality of the texts important to Vedic Brahmanism had priority. These were the *Dharmashastras* and later the *Vedas*, and to a lesser extent, the *Puranas*, the last of which they regarded as second order knowledge. Other systems of knowledge—Buddhist and Jaina—assessed as inferior branches of Hinduism, were initially given little importance. That these might earlier have been alternate systems of knowledge was hardly conceded. Even with the prominence this gave to a limited upper-caste Hinduism, there was little attempt at a discourse with Indian scholars on the wider context of the texts and their authors.[1]

Other theories emerged from the European excitement at discovering what many believed might be an Oriental Renaissance bringing innovative knowledge similar to the earlier revival of

Classical European learning (Schwab 1984). That religion and mysticism were characteristic of Indian culture, to the virtual exclusion of rational ways of organizing knowledge, was reinforced by the ideas of German Romanticism (Halbfass 1988). The argument that in India caste, viewed as civil society, overwhelmed the state further underlined the notion that without a state there could be no history. For Hegel, therefore, India was a land without recorded history (1958: 140–41, 162–64).

The enthusiasm for Sanskrit literature in some circles fed into what was emerging in the nineteenth century as the influential theory of the origins of language and culture, and came to determine the ideological context of early Indian history. The theory of Aryan race was woven into the readings of the *Vedas* and history lay in the foundations of Aryan culture. This explanation of origins presupposed that Vedic Brahmanism was to be equated with Aryan culture and since Vedic Brahmanism has little concern for history, there was a general absence of a sense of history. The entirely different Puranic projection of historical beginnings was ignored.

A different reconstruction of Indian history in the nineteenth century drew on other premises deriving from Utilitarian thought. This precluded the need for a historical tradition or even a concern for the past in the indigenous tradition. It underpinned the requirements of colonial policy in a changing relationship between the colonial power and the colony (Thapar 1992: 1–22). A denial of a sense of history was implicit in the theory of Oriental Despotism articulated at length in what became the hegemonic text on Indian history, James Mill's *The History of British India* (Majeed 1992; Inden 1986; Inden 1990). Mill's view was seminal to arguing that Indian society was static, registering no change, and therefore had no use for recording the past, one of the functions of the past being to legitimize the present (Mill 1968: 1.33 ff.). This stasis could only be broken by British administration legislating change and thus introducing the notion of history. Mill's *History* was defining a new idiom for imperial control.

The argument was that if the past is not recorded then despotic power cannot be accused of violating tradition, nor can any appeal be made to thwart despotism in the name of the past. History was a record of change and its teleology lay in the notion of progress. India's endemic despotism governed by custom rather than law and, lacking rationality as the motivating force, represented the reverse of progress. Since neither law nor rationality prevailed, history too was absent.

The absence of history had the practical advantage of allowing the formulation of a history for the colony that would underpin colonial policy. Colonial attitudes to knowledge pertaining to their colonies assumed that such knowledge was a form of control (Said 1978). Thus William Jones wrote of the *itihasas* and *puranas* being "in our power," and decades later Lord Curzon saw the intellectual discovery of the Orient as the necessary furniture of empire. History was the portal to knowledge about the colony. Every aspect of colonial activity was formulated as a history of that activity. This would be enhanced if it could be maintained that even the awareness of the colony's past had to be provided by the colonial power.

Assisting this process was the almost virtual obsession with the Orient being necessarily "the Other" of Europe. Statements on "Otherness" were foremost in the writings of Karl Marx and Max Weber. For Weber part of the "Otherness" was a lack of transition to capitalism which he attributed to a failure of economic rationalism. For Marx the static Oriental society was characteristic of the Asiatic Mode of production and in this there was an emphatic denial of history.

Meanwhile, throughout the nineteenth century, the collection of manuscripts and artifacts for the reconstruction of Indian history continued apace. Equally impressive were the results from the decipherment of the *brahmi* script which revealed the new resource of epigraphic data, and from archaeology, which was largely the collecting of artifacts and recording of monuments. Both were essential to the construction of early history. However, in the reconstruction and interpretation of the larger flow of history, European models and preconceptions hovered and comparisons with Europe were unavoidable. But the comparison was superficial and even the changing historiography of European history was ignored by colonial historians. For European historians the past of the non-European world was, even metaphorically, another country. The intellectual intensity of the discussion on the nature of history in Europe in the nineteenth century had little impact on Indologists and colonial historians.

The interest in the largely oral compositions of the bards was actively pursued by James Tod (1829–32) and Tessitori (1914, 1919, 1920). But they were inadequate in their understanding of the status of the bard in Indian society, a status that was special yet separate even when the Brahman took over the compositions of the bard (Havale 1946; Ziegler 1976). That the recording of the past could be a separate occupational function within the parameters of a caste society was not fully recognized. The bardic keepers of the tradition were alien to modern historians.

Indian historians, by and large, initially subscribed to the colonial view and accepted that Indian society was ahistorical. Their own social background did not encourage them to question the premises of the interpretations which followed largely from the perspective of the social elite.

THE DIVERSITY OF HISTORIOGRAPHY

The existence or lack of a historical tradition in early India has been the subject of passing comments in recent times. One argument is that a historical tradition did exist but that it was a weak tradition, and despite high intellectual levels in other aspects of thought, in this it never developed into a major tradition. This has been attributed to the decentralized nature of political institutions, to the role of the priestly elite in fabricating genealogies for rulers, and to the exclusive control of the Brahmans over the transmission of the tradition (Stein 1969). Another explanation points to the bifurcation between the keepers of state records, largely the scribal castes, and the Brahmans from whom a critical intellectual assessment might have been expected (Kulke 1979). More defensive views maintain that history as a discipline has been formatted through modernization and Indian civilization has been unconcerned with this (Nandy 1995; Narayana Rao et. al 2001; Deshpande 2007; Guha 2004; Lal 2003).

Such explanations are hardly adequate particularly in light of recent historical research which has questioned the earlier stereotypes about the Indian past being that of a static society. Indian society was clearly subject to change although the nature of such change was not uniform in time and space. This constitutes a radically different view of the Indian past. Change is a nodal point in history when new identities can emerge and the past can be reformulated for the purposes of the present. Two historical processes were tied into the question of perceptions of the past. One was the mutation of clan societies into castes, which was part of a bigger change of the assimilation of such societies into a state system, generally a kingdom. Kinship ceased to be crucial to the pattern of polities and new features emphasized social hierarchy and differential access to resources. The second process was the transformation of early kingdoms into more complex state systems. Both processes are reflected in what is referred to as the *itihasa-purana* tradition and in the genres of texts that recorded its articulation. Some represent historical change in a covert manner, others do so more openly.

Detailed explorations of the texts which claim to incorporate historical perspectives are necessary. Some studies of this theme have been made but they tend to remain sporadic. An initial foray was a collection of essays, where there were a few fresh ideas although by and large the older thesis tended to be repeated (Philips 1961). An attempt was made later to introduce a category of texts as distinctively historical but without much discussion to support this claim (Warder 1972). An important discussion elsewhere of one category of such texts, the *charita* literature of historical biographies, can be regarded as a study of substance relating to early Indian historical traditions, although limited to the one genre (Pathak 1966).

But before I speak about forms of historical consciousness I would like to consider the second aspect that I mentioned earlier. This concerns our changed understanding of history itself and the centrality of historiography in this change. Let me go back a bit in time to the Enlightenment.

History as defined by the Enlightenment was thought of as central to civilization. Every branch of knowledge had to have a history. Consequently a people without history were a people without knowledge. The history of civilizations also derived from humanist traditions which maintained that for Europe there was a unified European identity, with continuity from the Greeks to modern Europe and accessible in European literature (Ahmad 1992). The same was sought from other civilizations.

There emerged from this a rather literal view of Greco-Roman historical writing and a susceptibility to treating narrative accounts as historical. There were at the time no analytical studies such as those which have recently re-examined Greek and Roman historical writing. These have pointed to the interweaving of fiction and history in the representation of the past. The term *historia* in Greek referred originally to an enquiry into a matter and this could incorporate hearsay (Cornford 1907). It has been said that "if one starts by distinguishing between Oriental or mythical or mythologizing historiography and a rational and scientific historiography which strictly sticks to sources and facts, it is questionable whether Thucydides can be counted among the latter" (Boer 1968: 65). This may be too harsh a judgment, but Herodotus was frequently accused of lying perhaps because he drew heavily on oral data and later writers such as Manetho and Plutarch did not accept his statements (Momigliano 1958). History was a narrative of persons and events, some recalled from the past through oral and written sources and some witnessed in the present.

Parallel to the late Greco-Roman notion of history was the altogether different Jewish tradition, antecedent to the Christian. The Greco-Roman notion was virtually set aside with the coming of history infused with Judeo-Christian views. This began with Jerome and culminated in Augustine. History was no longer just a narrative of the past. It was now the record of the power of God and of Christ as reflected in the actions of the Christian Church. This was a departure which was contrasted in Renaissance writing drawing on Greek and Latin texts. It took a more secular form with the Enlightenment explaining human activity as the pivot of society. Historiography became decisive to Europe with the Judeo-Christian religions claiming the historicity of persons and events. History also provided a community identity for the nations of Europe as they emerged in recent centuries.

The recognition of historiographical mutation is a necessary part of history. Apart from the narrative of events, the explanation of events as forming a causal pattern ranges from commonsense observations to ideological perspectives. The change in European historiography needs underlining. Generalizations can hardly be made about the single, unified sense of history of the West. In Europe the change was from the Greco-Roman to medieval Christianity to the Enlightenment, each born of distinctly different historiographies and formulating diverse historical traditions. Some attempts were made to associate antiquity with new historiographies and to re-orient Greco-Roman ideas. Arnaldo Momigliano writes that Greek models became transformed into a Jewish apocalypse (Weinberg 1991: 19). Historical consciousness is understood in a different sense now as compared to a century ago.

Islamic historiography is also treated as uniform and seen from the perspective of religious texts. Yet there are distinct ideological variations that gave shape to the writings that emerged. The Arab discourse was imprinted with facets of Judaism and Christianity, even if what eventually emerged was the distinctive ideology of Islam. The Persians internalized their legacy of Zoroastrianism and Manichaeism. The difference within the Islamic tradition is apparent if one compares the representation of the past in Firdausi's *Shah-nameh* or the writings of the Ghaznavid scribe Baihaqi with Ibn Khaldun's *Muqadimmah*. Such diversity would have produced histories with variable nuances.

The historiography most frequently taken as the measure of historical writing is the Judaeo-Christian and Islamic. This has a clear eschatology narrating the beginning and end of humankind with a teleology built into it, and time is seen largely as linear. Other historiographies where this is not so evident are the Greco-Roman, the Chinese, and the Indian. Eschatology in these traditions is not definitive. Time concepts take various forms—linear, spiral, and cyclic. The Greco-Roman is treated as foundational to European historiography yet it has little in the way of common premises with the Judaeo-Christian.

We now recognize that history lies not just in a sequential narrative set in a chronological framework but also in enquiry and explanation. This implies that a comment on the presence or absence of a sense of history in a particular society also requires some familiarity with the genres of texts incorporating historical consciousness and these are not identical across its constituent cultures. Thus Al-Biruni visiting India in the eleventh century writes that Hindus do not pay much attention to the historical order of things and are careless in narrating the historical succession of their rulers (Sachau 1964: 10–11). Al-Biruni appears to be unaware of any Indian historical tradition and was probably seeking a parallel to the Islamic. His comments seem to follow from partial information and that too from Brahmanical sources.

Al-Biruni came from a society in central Asia familiar with Buddhist thought, and he mentions the importance of the *shramanas/shamaniyyas* to Indian religion, noting the hostility between them and the Brahmans. Yet his informants seem to have been Brahman ritual specialists and a few others knowledgeable about astronomy and the calendar. He was aware of Puranic chronology being unreliable but he also knew of the calculation of some aspects of historical chronology which was reliable. What were missing for him were possible parallels with Islamic historiography. Had he conversed with other scholars or with court scribes, he might have come to know about inscriptions as annals and their focus on dynastic events and succession, not to mention their calculation of chronology, or about epics such as the *Gaudavadha* of Vakpatiraja.

In a sense Al-Biruni was the forerunner of the seventeenth-century Indian historian Firishta who perhaps initiated European comments on a lack of history. Firishta's dismissal of historical writing from the earlier period was a view that contributed to the colonial writing on India and was quoted through Alexander Dow's rendering of Firishta in the *History of Hindostan* (Firishta 1768). However, the more interesting question is why, in each case, they were so selective about whom they consulted.

Diverse historical traditions have narratives relating the past. The way the narrative is formulated reflects not just a curiosity about the past but also has to do with the historiography that it represents. This draws from the tradition and from political economies and religious-ideological concerns that had currency at the time. The form of the narrative changes when political economies and religious concerns change and therefore there is more than one genre of text encapsulating the past.

The context is what allows us today to observe the complexities of the past looking at its own earlier past. We need to be aware of what is selected and what is left out, of the audience directly addressed and the presumed audience, of the awareness of political organization and its possible collaboration with the author, and finally knowing whose cultures are being discussed (Momigliano 1974; Momigliano 1975). Narratives claiming that the events they relate happened in the past make for historical consciousness but historical writing requires more than just this claim.

Essential to history is the shape and accounting of time. A distinction can be made between the past and the present which is initially often through symbols but gradually comes to incorporate measurements of time. Much has been made of the lack of history in India being tied to a cyclic concept of time, an insistence which continues despite research to the contrary (Eliade 1959; Thapar 1996). This is contrasted with the linear time of the Semitic tradition which is said to provide a necessary factor for historical thinking. Yet linear time in India is manifested in the extensive incorporation of genealogies, in the use of the *samvat* eras, and in the precise dating of inscriptions; and even more so in the shift in astronomy from lunar to solar reckoning. Stating in detail the time of an action is essential to recording gifts of land, rituals, accessions, and such like, as is evident in the many inscriptions intended for this purpose.

A sharp dichotomy between linear and cyclic time is not feasible since some elements of each are often parallel although pertaining to different functions. The Greeks observed categories of time in cycles as did the Indians and the form of time varied according to its function. Cyclic time is often viewed as cosmological time whereas the more measured time in human terms is linear and records generations and individual chronologies. Where cyclic time takes a spiral form, it can be seen as almost linear when sufficiently stretched. These variations are present in Indian texts and suggest an almost heterogeneous time calculation. Even in cyclic time the present is not a repetition of the past as has been maintained. The end of one cycle by-passes its beginning when transmuting into the next cycle. Each cycle records change and this too is represented in various ways. The notion of a past that is different from the present also assumes a future that is different from both.

Eschatology, both Buddhist and Puranic, is inherent in cyclic time but the pattern is unlike the more linear eschatology of the

Judeo-Christian tradition. The perfection of the first of the four *yugas* (cycles, ages) gradually degenerates, largely because of the distancing from norms and beliefs and the increase in non-meritorious behavior. Eventually the catastrophic end is so imminent that it requires the savior figure. This was the Brahman Kalkin—the final incarnation of Vishnu, or Maitreya—the Buddha to come, who would in each case restore the universe or the faith to its pristine condition. Even when a catastrophic end is spoken of, there is an assumption that a new cycle would emerge.

CHANGES IN EARLY INDIA'S REPRESENTATION OF THE PAST

Let me now turn the focus away from the rather dog-eared arguments about the absence of historical writing in early India and consider what I regard as the more relevant question of how the past was perceived and recorded. Answers to this question even if partial, might provide insights into early Indian society. Such a perspective is possible now that the understanding of history has itself undergone change.

The early Indian historical tradition has two distinctly different historiographies. One emerges from what might be called a Puranic framework. This draws on narratives and ideologies deriving from Vedic sources and the emergence of new sects and social movements in the first millennium AD. These historical traditions are encapsulated in one section of the early *Puranas*. The second historiography draws from ideologies that evolved from a questioning of, if not opposition to, Brahmanism, such as the Buddhist and the Jaina and what are included under the umbrella term of Shramanic. The ideological underlining of each was different as is reflected in the choice and representation of events and personalities that each highlight from the past or else represent in different forms. Alternate positions, although not always stated as such, are nevertheless reflected either in diverse formulations or in contradiction.

The awareness of the past seems to be represented in two forms suggesting perhaps a differentiation between historical consciousness and historical traditions. The first I would like to refer to as forms in which historical consciousness is embedded. Here the historical consciousness is subterranean as it were, being subordinated to other functions, for example, as references to events which occur in ritual hymns. The second category is forms that embody this consciousness and give expression to it as overt historical traditions. These occur in genres of texts, specific to this category. The forms are therefore embodied or externalized and recognizable as such. The texts themselves constitute new genres and their primary function is as expressions of a historical tradition. There is a shift from a representation of historical consciousness to the externalizing as it were of this consciousness in specifically historical traditions. This allows us to ask why there was a shift and what were the new genres required in the writing of history.

The two terms associated either separately or conjointly with traditions relating to the past are *itihasa* and *purana*. *Itihasa* literally means "thus indeed it was" and has come to be used now to mean history, but earlier it was not history in any modern sense of the term. *Purana* refers to that which belongs to ancient times and includes a medley of events and stories believed to go back to the early past and some that we would now call myths. *Itihasa-purana* taken together (and also the *Natyashastra)* is described as the fifth *Veda*, a phrase that refers to knowledge that is outside the *Vedas* but nevertheless important.[2] The label carries an oblique reference to divine sanction and constant recitation (Pollock 1985). The embodied forms are not Vedic categories.

THE EMBEDDING OF HISTORY

The origins of the Puranic framework of the *itihasa-purana* tradition go back to forms that are embedded in various texts such as the *dana-stuti* hymns in the *Rigveda* (Thapar 2000a). These have little ritual function *per se*. They are in praise of contemporary heroes and chiefs of clans and their generosity in giving gifts to the composers of the eulogies celebrating a successful raid or victory. Association with the sacrificial ritual perhaps gave these hymns greater credence and certainly ensured their continuity. They could well have been inserted at a later stage of the compilation of the hymns.

The context for these compositions was clan societies and the narratives associated with them are more extensive in the epics, the *Mahabharata* and the *Ramayana*. Action moves from raids and skirmishes to the formal battle, and the politics is complicated by the incorporation of new societies. The epics introduce new features since the appeal to the past can be to fix a precedent for action in the present. The *Mahabharata* as *itihasa* was used on occasion for this purpose to legitimize the induction of hitherto unknown clans and their social custom (Thapar 2000c). The central narratives described the confrontations between clans, some of which were older confederacies and some new upstarts. The *Ramayana* differs in as much as the conflict is between a newly emerging kingdom of Kosala with its capital at Ayodhya and the clan society of Lanka, the latter demonized as *rakshasas* (Thapar 2000d). Interestingly, both epics are recited at a sacrificial ritual, almost as if the earlier tradition was being continued even if the compositions themselves did not initially have the status of ritual texts.

The embedded history in the Vedic and epic texts relates to the first process of change that I referred to earlier. They represent clan societies and the epics register the gradual coming of kingdoms. Could we ask whether for historical purposes this might have been the function that had priority and persons and events helped to remember this past? There is some awareness of the difference between *itihasa*, that which is claimed to have happened, and narratives that are fictional, but the difference is not deeply impressed. The authors are looking back nostalgically to the past. Perhaps for historical purposes this might have been the priority in the function of the compositions. Historicity of person and event was less the essential concern where the intention was rather to evoke a past society. Composed as oral traditions, they are now seen as repositories of historical consciousness whereas societies without literacy were earlier said to be without history (Vansina 1965; Vansina 1985; Henige 1974; Henige 1982; Shah and Shroff 1959; Ziegler 1976b).

This was the raw material that was reformulated into a long-distance view of the past as in the *vamshanucharita*, or succession lists, of the *Vishnu Purana*.[3] Although constituting a section of the *Purana*, the *vamshanucharita* is ill-suited to the Puranic format of being a sectarian text and could again have been an insertion into such texts to ensure centrality and continuity. Scattered material from Vedic and epic sources and possibly other oral traditions was drawn together and a pattern worked out. This was marked by distinctive phases in the mapping of the lineages and their genealogies, to which were then attached lists of dynasties from the sixth century BC up to the Gupta period in the fourth century AD. The latter are largely historically attested. Clan societies, recorded as *vamshas* (lineages), succeeded by dynasties, would appear to have been a way of representing the mutation of clan societies to kingdoms.

Another indicator of the transition from clan to kingdom was the change from *kshatriya* lineages to non-*kshatriya* dynasties described as either *shudra* or Brahman. What is perhaps being stated in this format is that the legitimacy of kin relations among *kshatriya* chiefs had been undermined by upstarts of low status such as *shudras* appropriating power through a change in the priority from chiefship to kingship. The *kshatriyas* of earlier times were the logical ancestors to royal dynasties but there seems to have been a break, perhaps encapsulated in the battle at Kurukshetra where the *kshatriya* clans destroyed each other, and there was the subsequent emergence of political authority in the form of dynasties. These should have been of the *kshatriya* caste according to the normative codes but frequently were not.

The *vamshanucharita* was essentially history in a genealogical mode of thinking with the recording of succession and caste. It becomes a data-bank for families of obscure origin in post-Gupta times wishing to latch themselves onto a lineage and thereby claim *kshatriya* status. It was not intended to be taken literally, generation by generation, nor to be interpreted as racial identities as was done by modern scholars.

NEW HISTORICAL GENRES

From the perspective of the *itihasa-purana* tradition, the Gupta period starting in the fourth century AD marks a water-shed between history that is embedded from the articulation of the historical tradition in the post-Gupta period in embodied forms. The hint of historical consciousness is now embedded less in ritual texts and more in creative literature, as in some of the works of Bhasa and Kalidasa or the more overtly historical play, the *Mudra-rakshasas* of Vishakhadatta. This is the prelude to more specifically historical genres. The occasion is now the court and not a ritual or the gathering of the clan. This historical consciousness is made apparent in other more striking ways, for example in the re-use of objects from the past known to have had historical value.

The most dramatic example of such re-use is the pillar erected by Ashoka Maurya now located in the Allahabad fort. It carries a series of inscriptions each of a different millennium and in a different language—the Pillar Edicts of Ashoka; the long *prashasti*, "eulogy", on the Gupta emperor Samudragupta; and an inscription of the Mughal emperor Jahangir. Evidently there was a perception of its encapsulating history and the legitimacy that history provides, hence the deliberate choice of the pillar even though the reasons for eulogizing Samudragupta's fiercely violent campaigns were contrary to the ethics of the Ashokan edicts which endorsed non-violence. Gupta *brahmi* was probably still close enough to Ashokan *brahmi* for the earlier inscriptions to be read. Was it a response to the mute testimony of an earlier *chakravartin*, universal monarch, or was it the claim of a Gupta king to greater authority and the establishing of a new ideology?

The construction of the past now moved out of the chrysalis of embedded form whether ritual or literary and came to be expressed in genres specifically recording history. These were the embodied forms—the *charitas* or biographies of kings and ministers; the *vamshavalis* or regional chronicles; and royal inscriptions, some of which are in effect dynastic annals. The change of forms, information on authorship, and distinct ideological perspectives, signal the importance of the historical tradition to post-Gupta society. There is an awareness of sources in varying degrees and the specificities of space and time. What was subterranean now surfaces and takes visible new forms.

Kingdoms, of which there were many more, were being transformed into more complex state systems and their take on the past was necessarily different from before. A new form of kingship was symbolic of the polity, requiring additional mechanisms of legitimacy and representations of state power. Kings are occasionally said to be incarnations of deities but as such they were not even a pale shadow of the articulation of Divine Will familiar to us from other historiographies. Incarnations did not direct events; they shored up the claims of the ruler. The role of human agency remains primary. Association with a deity enhanced the value of the *prashasti* eulogy, and the early *prashastis* were included in inscriptions since such inscriptions were in effect annals.

Inscriptions, and particularly the *shasanas* (orders of the king), have their own format. The *prashasti*, in Sanskrit, is largely formulaic: the opening benediction is followed by a statement on the origins and achievements of the dynasty and of the reigning king, followed by stating the purpose of the inscription, and concluding with the name and designation of the official who composed it, the scribe who wrote it, and the engraver. The precise date of the king's order is given in detail in the prevailing era, generally the Vikrama and Shaka *samvats*. Inscriptions recording grants of land provide qualifications of the donee and the details of the land granted. Ministers and wealthy householders also issued votive and other inscriptions but less frequently than royalty. Genealogies move from desirable links to actual descent. Some statements are rhetorical but some allow of a historical narrative, set for the most part in a precise chronology. The section in the regional language addresses the legal aspects of the donation and the local administration. These could probably be read with profit in a comparative manner with texts in the same language claiming to be histories.

The *charitas*, or biographies, are of contemporary kings but include the historical antecedents of both subject and author. The focus is on a particular problem, such as an aspiration to spectacular power as can be argued for Banabhatta's *Harshacharita*, a biography of the seventh century king of Kanauj, Harshavardhana; or quelling a revolt of the *samantas* (feudatories), as in Sandhyakara-nandin's *Ramacharita*, a similar work on the Pala king Rampala. The intention is to give the official version justifying the king's action. This could have been a response to the questioning of the action. This becomes more likely in view of the biographies not being a narrative from birth to death but focusing on specific events of contemporary interest and how they evolve. The response would be relevant even to future readers. New powers claimed by kingship in new societies are being invoked and justified.

The *vamshavali* chronicle, of which the finest example is the twelfth-century *Rajatarangini* of Kalhana, was the document establishing the legitimacy of the kingdom and its rulers. As such they were composed in various kingdoms and some continued to be updated into later centuries. Origins tend to be linked to the Puranic *kshatriya* descent lists. But there is much that accounts for persons and events, largely of the past and some of the present, that approximates historical writing. They are valuable in tracing the process of state-formation and the establishing of kingdoms and the nature of the dynasties to which they refer as, for example, in the case of the *vamshavali* from the kingdom of Chamba in Himachal Pradesh (Thapar 2008). The *vamshavali* continued to exist as a genre of historical writing in later times, but such chronicles came to be written in the regional languages once they became a necessity in every new kingdom. Comparisons can be suggested with Buddhist monastic chronicles and medieval European chronicles.

These perceptions were predictably different in the parallel Jaina and Buddhist writing although the difference narrows in later times. Texts from these traditions were regarded as heterodox by Brahman authors of the Puranic tradition. The Shramanic tradition sometimes contested the representations from Brahman authorship. For example, the earliest Jaina version of the *rama-katha*, Vimalasuri's *Paumachariyam,* of about the third century AD, contradicts other versions and insists on its historicity (Jacobi 1914; Chanda 1970). A political dialogue is implied in these confrontations. The choice of subject in later Jaina biographies and chronicles highlights those who were their patrons and the style is not too dissimilar from other biographies and chronicles. The writing of *prabandhas* in the Jaina tradition was similar to chronicles. A clearly historical example is Merutunga's *Prabandhachintamani* which follows the format of the chronicle but with a distinctly Jaina view of the Chaulukya dynasty of Gujarat.

The Buddhist narratives of the history of Sri Lanka, in the monastic chronicles of *Dipavamsa* and *Mahavamsa* of the fifth and sixth centuries AD, begin with the earliest kingdoms in the Ganges plain and continue to draw on the history of the subcontinent up to the end of the Mauryan Empire. The Indian link is because of the Buddhist connection. These chronicles have a different focus on events and personalities from those in the Puranic king-lists. For example, Ashoka is a mere name in the latter but in the chronicles he is both a powerful monarch as well as the exemplar of a royal patron to the Buddhist Sangha (Geiger 1964; Oldenberg 1992; Strong 1983). The reason for the difference is ideological.

For the pre-Buddhist period the narrative draws on some sources that were common to the *itihasa-purana* traditions. Subsequent to the establishment of Buddhism, history is determined by persons and events in relation to the Buddhist Sangha. The interface between political authority and the Buddhist Sangha has no echo in the Puranic perspective. The Sangha's attempt to ensure authority included correlating the succession of monastic elders to successive rulers.

These heterodox traditions, as they have been called, have a sharper understanding of the centrality of a historical perspective. The reasons can be many. Literacy for them meant not only writing and copying the Pali, Prakrit, and Sanskrit Canons but also commentaries on the Canon, on the monastic chronicles that record sectarian developments and dissidence, as well as the biographies of the founders and the Elders who were historical figures. The records of monastic properties had also to be maintained. Events were generally related to the central date commanding their chronology, the date of the death of the Buddha (486/483 BC), or in the Jaina tradition the date of the death of Mahavira (527 BC). Within their own chronological structure their dates are consistent even if modern scholars argue that the actual date may not be precise.

A new and distinctive kind of historical consciousness emerges with these changes of form. Some links with the embedded tradition are present but their role is different. Forms such as the *charita* biographies and *vamshavali* chronicles carry traces of the Shramanic tradition, with its biographies of Elders of the Sangha and of patrons and its narratives of sectarian movements. Emergent Puranic sectarianism may have noticed the effectiveness of such literature in claiming a past to assert a particular present. At the same time inscriptions issued by Jaina patrons imitated the *prashasti* style and adopted the calendar of the *samvat*. To some extent therefore, there is a coming together of the forms, although the ideologies remain demarcated. These were forms that continued into medieval times—inscriptions, biographies, chronicles—claimed by various dominant social groups and often written in the regional language. Their assessment as history draws on both the *itihasa-purana* tradition and Sultanate and Mughal historiography. To these were added the epics of local heroes which were indirectly a commentary on local rulers and had perceptions that were different from the official version of events.

All these texts can be looked at afresh and in a comparative way because historians are now turning to themes which had earlier been precluded from history (LeGoff and Nora 1985). It is recognized that groups in society have their own versions of history which reflect the perception of their past as viewed by particular authors. Even what we regard as a fabricated version is of historiographical interest in its claiming to be historical. Fabrication is often the rhetoric of ideology, therefore the reason for the fabrication has to be sought as indeed the degree to which it is also an attempt to by-pass the problematic (Hobsbawm 1972; Errington 1979; Siegal 1979; Sahlins1985).

A view of the past becomes pivotal at times of transition when the past can either be rejected or can be used to legitimize the changing present. A significant function of history has been to legitimize those in power by providing origins and antecedents. What others had to say has largely to be extrapolated from these statements or from alternate sources where they exist.

Any codification of the past tends to be selective and the reasons for making a particular selection are significant. The *itihasa-purana* tradition in both its Puranic and Shramanic forms came to constitute the core of the constituents of historical thinking. A heroic phase moved to a courtly phase, or a king had an interface with the Sangha. The ideology of the Shramanic perspective was different from the Puranic although some of the data could overlap. Other parallel traditions incorporating a historical consciousness took other forms. The bardic tradition, the retrieval of which is problematic, was among these and the tension between the Brahmanic and the bardic remained an undercurrent.

In looking at the *itihasa-purana* tradition my intention is not to try and reinstate an indigenous interpretation of early Indian history or to argue that there is an "authentic" version of Indian history, an Indian view of India, in such sources. I am arguing that an awareness of the perceptions which earlier authors had of the past could be a way of illuminating our understanding of early society. Such perceptions would relate to the creation of variable identities and to social hierarchies of dominance and subordination that involved differentiated access to economic resources as well as claims to ritual status. It is for us as historians to recognize the manner in which these early writings record and explain how their authors perceived the processes of historical change. What I am arguing for is that we interrogate earlier traditions to ascertain if there is a coherent view of the past, analyze their constituent forms, and perceive the relation that these have with the society from which they emerge. Such an interrogation might help us to recognize the nature of historical consciousness that went into the making of historical traditions and in some instances of historical writing.

NOTES

1. The Asiatic Society, founded in 1784 to encourage Indological research, remained closed to Indians for almost half a century (Kejriwal 1988: 153).
2. See Chandogya Upanishad 7.1. 2. 4, in Radhakrishnan 1953.
3. See Wilson 1961, Book IV; Thapar 2000b.

REFERENCES

Ahmed, A. 1992. *In Theory: Classes, Nations, Literatures*. London: Verso.

Boer, W. den. 1968. "Greco-Roman Historiography in its Relation to Biblical and Modern Thinking." *History and Theory* 7: 60–75.

Chanda, R.K. 1970. *A Critical Study of the Paumachariyam*. Muzaffarnagar: Research Institute of Prakrit.

Cornford, F.M. 1907. *Thucydides Mythhistoricus*. London: Lawrence and Wishart.

Deshpande, P. 2007. *Creative Pasts: Historical Memory and Identity in Western India, 1700-1960*. New York: Columbia University Press.

Eliade, M. 1959. *Cosmos and History: The Myth of the Eternal Return*. New York: Bollingen Series.

Errington, S. 1979. "Style in the Meaning of the Past." *Journal of Asian Studies* 38, no. 2: 231–44.

Firishtah. 1768. *A History of Hindostan* [*Tarikh-i Firishtah*], trans. Alexander Dow. 2 vols. London: T. Becket and P.A. de Hondt.

Geiger, W. 1912. *The Mahavamsa*. London: Luzac and Co.

Guha, S. 2004. "Speaking Historically: The Changing Voices in Historical Narration in Western India, 1400–1900." *American Historical Review* 109, no. 4: 1084–1103.

Halbfass, W. 1988. *India and Europe*. Albany, NY: State University of New York Press.

Havale, S. 1946. *The Pradhans of the Upper Narbada Valley*. Bombay: Asia Publishing House.

Hegel, G.W.F. [1847] 1958. *The Philosophy of History*. New York: Dover Publications.

Henige, D.P. 1974. *The Chronology of Oral Tradition*. Oxford: Oxford University Press.

———. 1982. *Oral Historiography*. London: Longman.

Hobsbawm, E.J. 1972. "The Social Function of the Past: Some Questions." *Past and Present* 55: 3–18.

Inden, R. 1986. "Orientalist Constructions of India." *Modern Asian Studies* 20, no. 3: 401–46.

———. 1990. *Imagining India*. Oxford: Oxford University Press.

Jacobi, H., ed. [1914] 1962. *Paumachariyam of Vimalasuri*. Varanasi: Prakrit Text Society.

Jones, Sir William. 1799. "On the Chronology of the Hindus." *Asiatic Researches* 2: 111–47.

Kejriwal, O.P. 1988. *The Asiatic Society of Bengal and the Discovery of India's Past*. Delhi: Oxford University Press.

Kulke, H. 1979. "Geschichteschreibung und Geschichtesbild in Hinduistechen Mittelalter." *Secculum* 30: 100–13.

Lal, Vinay. 2003. *The History of History*. Delhi: Oxford University Press.

LeGoff, J. and P. Nora, eds. 1985. *Constructing the Past*. Cambridge: Cambridge University Press.

MacDonell, A.A. 1900. *History of Sanskrit Literature*. London: W. Heinemann.

Majeed, J. 1992. *Ungoverned Imaginings. James Mill's The History of British India and Orientalism*. Oxford: Oxford University Press.

Mill, J. [1817] 1968. *The History of British India*. 6 vols. New York: Chelsea House Publications.

Momigliano, A. 1958. "The Place of Herodotus in the History of Historiography." *History* 43: 1–13.

———. 1974. *Historicism Revisited*. MKN, Akademie van Wetenschappen, afd. Letterkunde, deel 37, no. 3: 63–70. Amsterdam: North-Holland Pub. Co.

———. 1975. "Polybius and Posidonius." In *Alien Wisdom: The Limits of Hellenisation*, 22–49. Cambridge: University of Cambridge Press.

Nandy, A. 1995. "History's Forgotten Doubles." *History and Theory* 34, no. 2: 44–66.

Narayana Rao, V., D. Shulman and S. Subrahmanyam. 2001. *Textures of Time*. Delhi: Permanent Black.

Oldenberg, H. [1879] 1992. *Dipavamsa*. Delhi: Asian Educational Service.

Pathak, V. S. 1966. *Ancient Historians of India*. Bombay: Asia Publishing House.

Philips, C. H., ed. 1961. *Historians of India, Pakistan and Ceylon*. London: Oxford University Press.

Pollock, S. 1985. "The Theory of Practice and the Practice of Theory in Indian Intellectual History." *Journal of the American Oriental Society* 105, no. 3: 499–519.

Radhakrishnan, S., ed. and trans. 1953. "Chandogya Upanishad." In *The Principal Upanisads*. London: George Allen and Unwin.

Rapson, E.J. 1922. *The Cambridge History of India*, vol. 1. Cambridge: Cambridge University Press.

Sachau, E. 1964. *Alberuni's India*. Delhi: Chand and Co.

Said, E. 1978. *Orientalism*. New York: Pantheon Books.

Sahlins, M. 1985. *Islands of History*. Chicago: University of Chicago Press.

Schwab, R. 1984. *The Oriental Renaissance: Europe's Rediscovery of India and the East 1680–1880*, trans. G. Patterson-Black and V. Reinking. New York: Columbia University Press.

Siegal, J. 1979. *Shadow and Sound: The Historical Thought of a Sumatran People*. Chicago: University of Chicago Press.

Shah, A.M. and R.G. Shroff. 1959. "The Vahivanca Barots of Gujerat: A Caste of Genealogists and Mythographers." In *Traditional India,* ed. M. Singer, 40–70. Chicago: University of Chicago Press.

Stein, B. 1969. "Early Indian Historiography: A Conspiracy Hypothesis." *Indian Economic and Social History Review* 6, no. 1: 41–60.

Strong, J. 1983. *The Legend of King Asoka*. New Jersey: Princeton University Press.

Tessitori, L.P. 1914. "A Scheme for the Bardic and Historical Survey of Rajputana." *Journal of the Asiatic Society of Bengal*, n.s. 10: 373–410.

———. 1919. "A Progress Report on the Work done during the year 1917 in connection with the Bardic and Historical Survey of Rajputana." *Journal of the Asiatic Society of Bengal*, n.s. 15: 5–79.

———. 1920. "A Progress Report on the Work done during the year 1918 in connection with the Bardic and Historical Survey of Rajputana." *Journal of the Asiatic Society of Bengal*, n.s. 16: 251–79.

Thapar, Romila. 1992. "Ideology and the Interpretation of Early Indian History." In *Interpreting Early India,* 1–25. Delhi: Oxford University Press.

———. 1996. *Time as a Metaphor of History*. Delhi: Oxford University Press.

———. 2000a. "*Dana* and *Daksina* as forms of Exchange." In *Cultural Pasts,* 521–35. Delhi: Oxford University Press.

———. 2000b. "Genealogical Patterns as Perceptions of the Past." In *Cultural Pasts,* 709–53. Delhi: Oxford University Press.

———. 2000c. "The Historian and the Epic." In *Cultural Pasts,* 613–29. Delhi: Oxford University Press.

———. 2000d. "The *Ramayana*: Theme and Variation." In *Cultural Pasts,* 647–79. Delhi: Oxford University Press.

———. 2008. "The Vamshavali from Chamba: Reflections of a Historical Tradition." In *India and Indology, The Professor Sukumari Bhattacharya Felicitation Volume,* ed. D. Bhattacharya, 581–94. Kolkata: National Book Agency.

Tod, J. 1829–1832. *Annals and Antiquities of Rajasthan.* 2 vols. London: Smith, Elder, and Co.

Vansina, J. 1965. *Oral Tradition*. Chicago: University of Chicago Press.

———. 1985. *Oral Tradition as History*. London: James Curry.

Warder, A.K. 1972. *An Introduction to Indian Historiography*. Bombay: Popular Prakashan.

Weinberg, J. 1991. "Where Three Civilizations Meet." *History and Theory* 30, no. 4 (Beiheft 30: The Presence of the Historian: Essays in Memory of Arnaldo Momigliano): 13–26.

Wilson, H.H., ed. and trans. 1961. *Visnu Purana*. Calcutta: Punthi Pustak.

Zeigler, N. 1976a. "Marvari Historical Chronicles." *Indian Economic and Social History Review* 13, no. 2: 219–50.

———. 1976b. "The Seventeenth Century Chronicles of Marvara: A Study in the Evolution and Use of Oral Tradition in Western India." *History in Africa* 3: 127–53.

12

Local Histories and Historical Narratives in the Central Tungabhadra Region of South India

Carla M. Sinopoli

Both archaeologists and historians explore the human past through accessing the partial evidence that has survived the vagaries of time: whether texts, inscriptions, constructed landscapes, monuments, or trash. All of these sources bring their own evidentiary and methodological constraints and interpretive challenges. My intent in this essay is not to rehearse the relations between archaeology and history in South Asia,[1] but instead to employ both to address another topic that has been a focus of Tom Trautmann's recent writings—time and its constructions (Trautmann 1997, 2008; Owen Hughes and Trautmann 1995). I do this through an examination of the long-term histories (and prehistories) of a small region of southern India. The region, of approximately 2000 square kilometers, is situated along the central reaches of the Tungabhadra River in inland north Karnataka (modern Koppal, Bellary, and Raichur districts; Figure 5), and extends from the fourteenth- to sixteenth-century imperial capital of Vijayanagara in the west toward the modern city of Bellary some 60 kilometres in the east. Within this

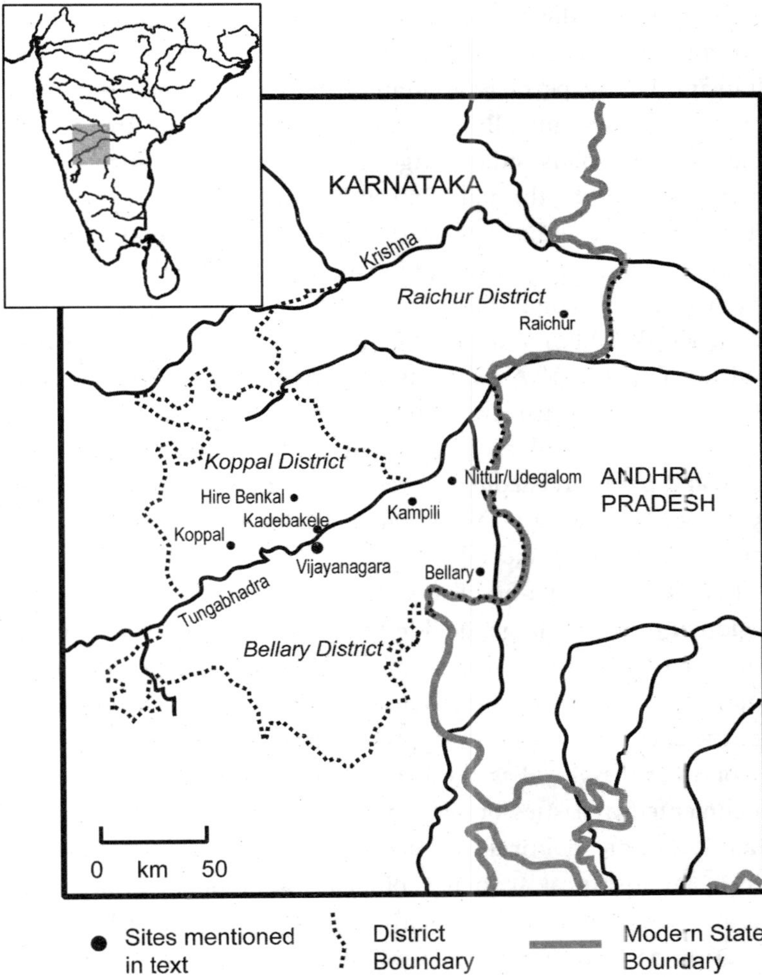

Figure 12.1 The central Tungabhadra region

relatively small area, the most comprehensively documented area is the ca. 450 square kilometer area surrounding the imperial city of Vijayanagara, which has been the focus of several decades of systematic archaeological research. I draw heavily from that work in this essay.

Geologically, this is the inland Karnatak Plateau (or Southern Deccan) plateau, characterized by a hot semi-arid climate and dramatic landscape of large granitic hills (inselbergs) separated by areas of low-lying alluvium. Archaeologically, the area is best known to historians and the larger public for the magnificent ruins of the fourteenth- through sixteenth-century imperial capital of Vijayanagara. To archaeologists and others interested in the region's deeper history, the Tungabhadra River Valley is also known for the distinctive archaeological features of the South Indian Neolithic (ca. 2800–1400 BC) and Iron Age (ca. 1200 BC–0 BC/AD) periods, and for a cluster of Asokan inscriptions that marks the region's entry into written history. A bit to the north, in Gulbarga District, recent archaeological research has dated South India's earliest stone tools and other archaeological remains to more than one million years ago (Paddayya 1997; Petraglia et al. 1999)—tracing a very long human history indeed.

Beyond focusing a fine lens on the long history of a very small region of India, my larger goal in this essay is to consider how this particular local history intersects (or fails to intersect) with larger "master" narratives of the Indian past and how the narratives we construct condition how we approach those regions and times that lie on their margins. Based on empirical evidence—of historically documented dynasties or sequences of ceramic types, sculptural traditions, or political formations—these master narratives create an historical sequence of neatly bounded chronological periods and, often, a directional trajectory, whether of historical progress or historical decline. While continuous in time, such narratives are almost inevitably discontinuous in space, favoring temporal continuities over geographic ones—for example, in the eastward shift of scholarly focus from the Indus Valley in the third millennium BC to the Ganges Basin in the second and first millennia BC as we recount the sequence of the "rise of Indian civilization." Master narratives also, not surprisingly, favor apogees—periods and locations of maximal complexity and power, rather than the histories of stable or marginal areas on the edges of such centers. Useful as these master narratives are, it is readily apparent that such constructions cannot possibly encompass the extraordinary complexities and richness of the Indian past and, that in their telling, they at worst erase and at best homogenize significant portions of sequences and regions whose histories lay outside of whatever criteria define the period under study.

Inland northern Karnataka in the southern Deccan is a particularly fertile setting in which to consider both local and larger scale historical narratives. As Richard Eaton has noted in his recent survey of Deccani history from 1300 to 1761 AD (Eaton 2005), the larger Deccan region (of which my study area is a part) has traditionally lain outside of the master narratives of Indian history. These have focused on what Eaton calls "core areas" including North India, Bengal and Tamil Nadu, regions that are characterized by durable nucleated political cores. In contrast, Eaton suggests the Deccan "has no enduring political or cultural center" (Eaton 2005: 1). Instead, the polities and their centers were relatively short-lived and their locations shifted across the region. Nonetheless, the long history of archaeological and (to a lesser extent) historical research in the region has created a rich and temporally deep record of human occupation. And over at least the last 5000 years, the region has experienced periods of intensive occupation, rapid change, and political dynamism interspersed by intervals of low populations and "marginality" in relation to other areas of the South—moving in and out of a more central position in larger South Indian and pan-Indian historic trajectories.

Below, I briefly review the history and larger context of archaeological and historical research in the central Tungabhadra region, before turning to the evidence of the past that such work has provided and a consideration of how that past intersects with larger narratives. I primarily focus on the period from ca. 3000 BC to ca. 1000/1300 AD and rely heavily on archaeological evidence. I address the Vijayanagara period only briefly, as it is well known to scholars and both Vijayanagara archaeology and historiography have been extensively discussed in a number of recent archaeological and historical writings. The abundance of writings on Vijayanagara owes to the fact that this was a time when the Tungabhadra region was a "core area" in the sense that Eaton discusses. Frequently portrayed as the last and largest "Hindu" empire of India, Vijayanagara has played a prominent role in larger and more familiar narratives of empire, religion, and resistance.

ARCHAEOLOGICAL RESEARCH IN THE TUNGABHADRA REGION

As in so many things, Sir Colin Mackenzie was among the earliest "collectors" of archaeological information along the Tungabhadra. This work began with the production of maps, drawings, and descriptions of the dramatic ruins of Vijayanagara at the end of the eighteenth century.[2] Interest in the monumental and romantic ruins of Vijayanagara continued into the early nineteenth century and, indeed, until the present (see below). The relatively new medium of photography was introduced at Vijayanagara in the 1850s by Sir Alexander Greenlaw (Nagaraja Rao 1988), generating evocative images of the ruined city decades before the first conservation or excavation work was conducted by the Archaeological Survey of India and Archaeological Survey of Madras and Coorg (1904, 1910; see Michell 1985). Interest in Vijayanagara continued in the first half of the twentieth century, with scholarly attention shifting from Vijayanagara's monumental ruins to the period's rich inscriptional and textual record (see Longhurst 1917; Historical Research Society of Dharwar 1936; Nilakanta Sastri 1966). After an interlude of several decades that saw relatively little new research, Vijayanagara studies (and South Indian historiography more broadly) were re-energized in the late 1970s as a result of influential publications by Burton Stein (1979), R. Champakalakshmi (1981) and others, and by the designation of Vijayanagara as one of six sites of national importance by the Archaeological Survey of India (ASI) in the mid-

1970s. In addition to the ASI excavations, archaeological work at the imperial capital was initiated in the late 1970s by the Karnataka Directorate of Archaeology and Museums (KDAM); collaborative research by Indian and foreign scholars at Vijayanagara began at this time as well. All of these efforts continued uninterrupted until the late 1990s, and ASI and KDAM work continues today, albeit at a somewhat reduced pace (see Sinopoli 2011 for an overview of the history of Vijayanagara research).

While Vijayanagara-period remains dominate the material evidence from historic (i.e., post third century BC) periods along the Tungabhadra, numerous temples, monuments, and inscriptions from earlier (and subsequent) historic periods have also been documented (see below and Patil 1992 for a discussion of temple architecture from the ninth through twelfth centuries AD in the region). Perhaps best known among the historic remains from pre-Vijayanagara times is a cluster of innocuous-appearing inscriptions found at more than a dozen sites that date to the very beginnings of written "history" in the region. Most important for this discussion are the inscriptions located some 60 kilometers to the northeast of Vijayanagara near the small villages of Nittur and Udegalom.

Crudely carved, small, and indistinct (Figure 6), these inscriptions have gained enormous significance as the earliest written texts in South India and as products of the third century BC Mauryan emperor Asoka. Mackenzie recorded one of these inscriptions, at Rajula-Mandagiri, some four decades before Prinsep's monumental decipherment of the Brahmi script in 1837. However, it was not until the late nineteenth century that the significance of the southern cluster was understood, following the 1892 discovery by Lewis-Rice of similar edicts at Brahmagiri, Jatinga-Ramesvara, and Siddapur, and their recognition as being associated with the ancient north Indian emperor Asoka (Sugandhi personal communications, from Falk 2006; see also Sugandhi 2008). Other discoveries followed—at Maski (1915), Gaimath (1931), Nittur (1977), Udegalom (1978), and Sannati (1989).

Figure 12.2 Detail of Asokan inscription, Udegalom, Karnataka

As noted above, this localized cluster of Asokan inscriptions in Karnataka has traditionally been taken to mark the Deccan's entry from "prehistory" into "history." This is not entirely accurate, as we have no evidence that the region's inhabitants could read or understand these Prakrit texts or the Brahmi script they were written in. Nor is there evidence, as I discuss below, that writing quickly became important among local communities following the inscriptions' production, or that dramatic social, political, ideological or other changes followed upon the Mauryan presence in the region. Indeed, the earliest documented Kannada inscriptions date to mid first millennium AD, some 700 years after the Asokan edicts were inscribed. Nonetheless, the recognition of Asokan inscriptions so far from the Gangetic imperial heartland had two important consequences for Indian historiography. The first lay in their contributions to understandings of the Mauryan Empire as India's first pan-subcontinental state, a perspective that has had tremendous resonance in Indian historiography and politics ever since. Second, the Mauryan presence in this distant region helped to bring the Dravidian-speaking South into the larger and dominant historical narrative of ancient (Indo-Aryan speaking) India and into interests in the spread of Buddhist religious traditions (and northern political or religious forms) that dominated the early history of Indian archaeology (see Singh 2004).

Scholarship on the region's prehistory has a similarly long path as interests in historic periods, beginning with the work of Colonel Meadows Taylor and his contemporaries in the 1840s, more than a decade before the "Darwinian revolution" extended human time for western scholars beyond biblical chronologies (Trautmann 2008: vi–vii). Most important for early prehistoric work in Karnataka were the extraordinary and prolific contributions of Geological Survey of India officer Robert Bruce Foote in the second half of the nineteenth century (Foote 1887, 1914, 1916; see Korisettar et al. 2001). Foote was a remarkable scholar, about whom a serious biography has yet to be written. We don't know whether he read Darwin's writings, but Foote was clearly influenced by larger archaeological discussions and debates in Europe, which had separately been constructing a much expanded time-depth for humanity in the early to mid-nineteenth century. He applied the then well-established "three-age" system (i.e., the "Stone Age, Bronze Age, Iron Age" sequence first developed in the 1820s by Danish archaeologist Christian Jürgensen Thomsen; Trigger 1989: 75) to his characterization of Indian prehistory (Korisettar et al. 2001: 153). Foote was the first to correctly identify Paleolithic artifacts in India in 1863 and, over the course of 33 years, identified nearly 500 archaeological sites dating from the Paleolithic through Iron Age across southern India (Korisettar et al. 2001: 153). Arguably, his most important discoveries in the Tungabhadra region date to the South Indian Neolithic period (ca. 2800–1200 BC)—including ashmounds, settlements, quarries, and rock art sites, to which I return below.

Along with his role in discovering sites and artifacts and amassing collections for museums in Madras, Calcutta, and Europe, Foote thought deeply about the significance of these materials and of South India's deep past. In a contribution published in the *Journal of the Asiatic Society of Bengal* in 1887, Foote challenged scholars who posited a short chronology for the "Paleolithic" (flaked stone) and "Neolithic" (polished or ground stone) tools and sites that were by then being discovered across South India. Foote was particularly critical of an 1878 presentation by a Mr. Valentine Ball, who argued that differences in stone tool types were racial rather than temporal; that is, that the different categories of stone tools were produced by contemporaneous "races" with different innate civilizational and technological capacities, rather than being indicative of temporal depth and technological change over time (see discussion in Korisettar et al. 2001). Foote also criticized functional interpretations of the differences in the stone tools that were also based in a short chronology, i.e., the view that the flaked and ground stone tools were contemporary but were used for different tasks.[3] With his familiarity with literally hundreds of archaeological sites and thousands of artifacts and his analytical acumen, Foote instead argued that the distinctive spatial distributions, raw materials, and other attributes of these artifacts indicated that they dated to very different periods and provided incontrovertible evidence that the occupation of India extended back into very deep prehistory.

Archaeological work on the prehistory of the Tungabhadra region continued throughout the twentieth century, under the aegis of both state and national archaeological departments, with additional research by university departments (especially Deccan College and Karnataka University) and by foreign scholars. Field projects continue in the twenty-first century and are made increasingly urgent by the intensifying threats to archaeological sites from industrial and agricultural expansion. The contributions of many of these efforts will be referenced below.

The result of more than two centuries of research is a rich and detailed archaeological and historical sequence, albeit one marked by discontinuities. As noted above, while the Tungabhadra region has a long record of human occupation, it is also the case that the record is uneven. In some periods (e.g., the Neolithic, Early Iron Age, Vijayanagara) the region appears to have been densely settled, a dynamic site of innovation, social experimentation, and cultural change. In others (e.g., the Early Historic, first millennium AD), archaeological and inscriptional sources are much scarcer, suggesting comparatively sparse occupation and a less consequential human presence (re: larger scale developments) relative to other contemporary regions of South India. Any focus on the local histories of the Tungabhadra region thus obliges us to examine the larger dynamics that contribute to these large-scale shifts in the centrality of some regions over others. Interpretations of local historical trajectories and transformations along the Tungabhadra likely lie in a combination of local and pan-regional political, economic, and environmental developments.

FIVE THOUSAND YEARS OF HISTORY IN THE CENTRAL TUNGABHADRA REGION

Archaeologists work in long time scales. The archaeological record is, in essence, a palimpsest, comprised of the residue of countless events and individual actions that form archaeological deposits. Ideally, these deposits (usually stratified layers of sediments, sometimes standing monuments or features constructed over greater or lesser time spans) can be subdivided into temporal ranges that inform on periods of human activities at a particular location in space (an archeological site). In South India, we have yet to develop very refined archaeological chronologies; as a result, our periods can span a thousand or more years, even for the not-too-distant past (by archaeological reckoning). While new efforts are underway to refine these chronologies (see especially Fuller et al. 2007; Bauer in preparation), our current chronologies force a very broad and not entirely satisfying reckoning of the complex social, political, and economic conditions and changes that characterized each period, as well as the nature of the transitions between them. Nonetheless, what our current understandings lack in historical specificity they make up for in temporal range, allowing us to explore historical developments and transformations over millennia. Below, I provide a very rough schematic of the last five thousand years in the Tungabhadra region, before returning to my interest in the region's place in larger historical narratives.

THE SOUTH INDIAN NEOLITHIC

In the early third millennium BC, communities throughout South India began adding domesticated plant and animal resources to the gathering and hunting of wild plants and fauna. These additions, initially of locally domesticated millets and pulses, and later of non-local crops including African millets and Near Eastern wheat (Fuller and Korisettar 2004) and of domestic cattle, sheep, and goat, were accompanied by technological innovations including the appearance of pottery vessels and groundstone axes. The communities that cultivated these resources and made the pottery, stone tools, and personal ornaments were likely small. Archaeologists have recovered the remains of village settlements, often located on sheltered terrace areas at the tops of high outcropping hills, with single room structures and sub-floor burials. The extent to which these communities were fully sedentary or semi-mobile remains unresolved, and likely varied both regionally and over time. There is no evidence of durable social inequalities or dramatic differences in access to key economic or symbolic resources.

While Neolithic communities were widespread across South India (see Paddayya 2002), the inland Karnatak plateau region, including the central Tungabhadra area of interest here, appears to have been an area of particularly dense Neolithic settlement during a 1600-year period from ca. 3000–1400 BC. Indeed, Korisettar et al. (2001: 174) have referred to this as the "core area" of the "Southern Neolithic" tradition (including also portions of the Krishna and Bhima river drainages). The inhabitants of this region were the builders of the Neolithic's only cluster of monumental constructions—the much-discussed "Neolithic Ashmounds" (Figure 7; see Newbold 1836; Taylor 1851; Allchin 1961, 1963; Paddayya 1973, 1991–92, 2002; Johansen 2004; Boivin 2004; Korisettar et al. 2001). More than 200 ashmound sites have been documented and many more likely existed in the past that were destroyed by subsequent human activities (a process that continues today, as the ashy deposits are mined for fertilizer). The ashmounds themselves typically contain relatively few artifacts or other materials (such as animal bone); some, but not all, are located near Neolithic settlement sites (though of uncertain contemporaneity).

Considerable debate continues about the use of ashmounds and their association (or lack of association) with permanent settlements, as well as their temporality. Scholars disagree on whether individual mounds were constructed in a small number

Figure 12.3 Kudatini, Neolithic ashmound

of discrete events or are the result of longer-term accretional activities; whether their use or production spanned the entire Neolithic or only a portion of the period; and about their association with nearby settlements. It is unlikely that a single answer to any of these questions applies to all ashmound sites. An important recent study by Fuller, Boivin and Korisettar (2007) has attempted to resolve some of these questions through the application of a Bayesian statistical model to the analysis of 116 radiocarbon dates from 23 Neolithic sites. Without going into detail on their analysis, they conclude that the construction of ashmound features occurred throughout the entire ca. 1600-year Neolithic period. However, individual ashmounds tended to be generated relatively quickly—in a small number of events over as little as a few generations; and ashmound construction typically *preceded* permanent settlement in a location and ceased once such settlements were established. They argue that this practice of initially defining a place through ritualized activities involving the burning of cattle dung may have been "an element of local 'performances' that set the stage for the establishment of village sites" (Fuller et al. 2007: 773); that is, these were foundational events to a more permanent territorial claim. If this preliminary interpretation proves correct, then Fuller and colleagues are describing a remarkably long-lived cultural tradition with practices (if not necessarily the precise beliefs that surrounded them) that persisted little changed for roughly 1600 years.

Like Fuller and colleagues, most contemporary scholars interpret the ashmounds as monuments that marked and defined the Neolithic landscape, and as products of ritual burning events and associated activities (e.g., Paddayya 1991–92; Johansen 2004). Why such monuments and the ritual practices that produced them were limited to only this small region of South India rather than the larger geographic expanse where Neolithic sites are found is less clear. Functionalist interpretations might suggest that the seemingly higher population densities or perhaps greater commitment to agricultural/pastoral production in the environmentally harsh Tungabhadra area were met by more dramatic responses to materializing community territories and group identities than occurred in areas that were either less densely settled or more ecologically favorable. At present, however, we lack adequate survey data to know if the Tungabhadra region was truly more densely populated than other regions or if, because of its unusual archaeological features, it has merely been the focus of more intensive documentation. It does, however, appear to be the case both that this distinctive form of monumental construction was restricted to only a limited geographic region and that during the third and second millennia BC, this region was an area of relatively dense populations and early cultural innovation, including possibly local domestication of plant species. In that sense, during the Southern Neolithic the Tungabhadra River Valley can be viewed as an area of cultural innovation and centrality in the larger South Indian social landscape. However, if Fuller et al. (2007) are correct, the period of initial ritual innovation—of new practices of place-making through ashmound construction—may have occurred very early in the Neolithic, and was followed by a long period of reenactment of similar rituals throughout the area as new places and territories were claimed.

LATE PREHISTORIC (IRON AGE)

The South Indian Neolithic lasted some 1600 years and we lack clear understandings of the pace and nature of changes within it. At about 1200 BC (or a bit before), we see some fairly dramatic material changes, marked by the appearance of new kinds of ceramic wares, iron technologies, and burial practices. These changes mark the beginning of the next archaeological period, commonly referred to as the "Iron Age" (*note*: I prefer the term "Late Prehistoric" to avoid privileging the appearance of iron over other criteria in its definition). Beginning and ending dates for the transitions that mark the Late Prehistoric period remain difficult to pin down and no doubt varied from place to place; a reasonable estimate for the Central Tungabhadra region is from ca. 1200 BC to an entirely arbitrary 0 BC/AD. The initial appearance of the new material forms that define the period seems to occur a bit to the north of the Tungabhadra region somewhat before this—during what Fuller et al. (2007) have called a "transitional" Neolithic-Megalithic period—starting at around 1400 BC.

While older interpretations (e.g., Leshnik 1974) saw the beginnings of the South Indian Iron Age as the result of the migration of new (North Indian) communities to the region, thus replacing local Neolithic traditions and communities, scholars now see these transitions as primarily a local South Indian development. This is not to say that contact with northern regions and peoples did not occur during this period. Indeed, there is important evidence for increased interactions across the entire subcontinent in the Late Prehistoric period, including the movement of valued commodities such as lapis lazuli and horses, as well perhaps as some exchange of technological knowledge (e.g., wheel-throwing of pottery?) and subsistence resources. However, while some people surely traveled over long distances, there is no evidence for large-scale population movements or in-migration to the south. Again, our archaeological chronologies are not yet refined enough to allow us to assess the precise pace and nature of Late Prehistoric changes. However, it does appear that both technological and associated sociopolitical transformations of the Late Prehistoric/Iron Age period began first in northern Karnataka and the greater Tungabhadra region and then spread toward coastal areas and to the south (Moorti 1994: 5).

The material transformations that mark the beginning of the Late Prehistoric/Iron Age period were part of a suite of larger and ultimately more significant changes—in the organization of labor (i.e., the emergence of specialized craft production and likely other economic specializations), in changing human relations with the landscape, and, in at least some regions, sociopolitical transformations and the creation of new kinds of hierarchical political and social formations. Some of these transformations are manifest in the nature and prevalence of Late Prehistoric monuments. In the Tungabhadra region the production of ashmounds of the South Indian Neolithic largely disappeared (though ash features of some form, perhaps not mounds, may persist as late as the eleventh century BC, for example at the site of Bukkasagara in Bellary District; see Johansen 2008; Morrison et al. n.d.). Monuments of ash, products of collective and probably community-wide ritual activities, were replaced by monuments of stone—megalith features used primarily in mortuary ritual (Figure 8). These monumental and highly visible graves, located in specialized site types (i.e., cemeteries) as well as in settlements, replaced earlier Neolithic burial practices that involved subfloor burial within domestic structures. Moorti (1994) and Brubaker (2000–2001), among others, have argued that burial in a megalithic feature was associated with new hereditary status relations, and

Figure 12.4 Megalithic features at Hire Benkal

that this period marked the emergence of durable relations of social inequality in many areas of southern India.

Megaliths are the most dramatic and visible human constructions of the Late Prehistoric period; indeed, they are so characteristic of this time that some scholars also refer to it as the "Megalithic Period." Smaller in individual scale than the ashmounds, many thousands of these stone features—cairns, dolmens, and other constructions—were constructed for the interment of a single or small number of individuals (a mean of 2.3 individuals per grave in excavated graves in the Tungabhadra region; Brubaker 2008); a significant number also appear to be commemorative features containing no human remains. Sites containing megaliths (exclusively or in association with other remains) are far more common than ashmound sites—in geographic extent, in absolute number, and in the number of identified sites. In a recent analysis of Late Prehistoric sites along the Tungabhadra River (and a small portion of the Krishna), Robert Brubaker reported on 309 documented archeological sites. Some 240 of these are megalithic mortuary sites (others are settlements, often with megaliths or rock art sites, or cannot be categorized from published sources; Brubaker 2008), with the number of megaliths per site ranging from one to more than a thousand.

Eventually, the practice of marking individual burial sites with stone monuments and the placement of burials in formal cemeteries, often set apart from settlements, was adopted across all of peninsular India, and more than 2000 such sites have been documented in Karnataka, Kerala, Andhra Pradesh, Tamilnadu, and Maharashtra (see Moorti 1994). Thus, the specific ritual practices with which megaliths were associated—burial and commemoration of a subset of the population—were far more widely adopted and transmitted throughout South India than were the practices that produced the earlier ashmounds. If the southern Neolithic was a local tradition, then the Iron Age mortuary practices were associated with much larger scale ritual, social, and arguably political phenomena.

Along with the dense distribution of mortuary sites, other archaeological features also suggest that the Tungabhadra region was especially densely occupied during the Late Prehistoric period. Prior research by Foote, Sundara, Allchin, and others has identified numerous sites with characteristic Late Prehistoric remains. And ongoing systematic regional archaeological research (the Late Prehistoric/Early Historic Landscapes of the Tungabhadra Corridor project; LP/EHLTC) in a ca. 37 square kilometer region along the Tungabhadra by the Karnataka Directorate of Archaeology and Museums, the University of Michigan, and University of Chicago, has identified more than 20 Late Prehistoric sites in a sample survey of this relatively small area, including several sizeable settlements (see Sinopoli, Morrison, and Gopal 2008; Sinopoli 2009; Morrison et al. n.d.; Sinopoli et al. n.d.). Kadebakele, the largest of the settlements and the focus of ongoing excavations, was many times the size of known Neolithic villages. Nearby, an ongoing archaeological survey directed by Andrew Bauer in an area adjacent to the LP/EHLTC project area has revealed, if anything, even higher densities of settlements and intensive land-use. Among the sites documented by Bauer are megalithic cemetery sites, rock art sites, large settlements, and probable shorter-term encampments possibly associated with pastoral activities (Bauer, personal communications). Bauer's work is particularly interesting in that it focuses on a hilly region away from the Tungabhadra (between our large settlement of Kadebakele and the enormous megalithic site of Hire Benkal, the latter known to scholars for more than a century). This area witnessed much less intensive Vijayanagara and subsequent occupation and land use than irrigable areas near the river, and its higher density of sites may well be a result of this. Taken together, both areas close to and away from the river show surprisingly high site densities during the Late Prehistoric period that appear to indicate that the central Tungabhadra region was an area of unusually high populations at this time.

We do not have comparable intensive survey data from other areas of the southern Deccan. However, even along the Tungabhadra, settlement was not uniformly dense. Namita Sugandhi has recently completed a small survey project in an area approximately 60 kilometers to the northeast of the Kadebakele area described above (Sugandhi 2008). Her work has focused on the region adjacent to and surrounding the Asokan inscriptions at Nittur and Udegalom and the large previously excavated Neolithic site of Tekkalakota. The sites identified by Sugandhi are mostly contemporary with these previously documented features, dating to the Neolithic and Early Historic periods. Remains of the Late Prehistoric period, while present, are much less common than in our research area, located a mere 60 kilometers away. This comparison points to uneven, variously dense, and shifting settlement across the region, though not to its causes.

While our understandings of society, politics, and economy in the Tungabhadra region during the late prehistoric period are at best preliminary, some general conclusions can be drawn. First, as noted above, the region was, in general, densely populated, with a diversity of settlement types and settlement scales, including pastoral camps, small agricultural villages, and a small number of significantly larger residential sites (towns?). Second, the economy during this period was becoming increasingly specialized and intensive with formal craft specialization in iron working, ceramic production, and probably other crafts, and a diversified agricultural economy, including dry farming of millets and other crops, wet rice farming, and pastoral production of cattle. Third, there is some evidence of social differentiation and emergent social inequalities, manifest in the mortuary data and possibly in settlement variation. Based on our current understandings, we can tentatively envision a political landscape of small territorial hierarchical polities unevenly distributed across the inland south that were engaged in trade and other interactions over long and short distances as well, no doubt in conflict and competition. A range of other more mobile communities which were also less complex in organisation, might also have been part of this diverse social landscape.

Early Historic and Early Medieval Periods

In the third century BC, we have evidence for new visitors to the Tungabhadra area. As noted earlier, a cluster of lithic inscriptions dating to the reign of the Mauryan emperor Asoka has been documented at 11 sites in southern India (Figure 9). Several of

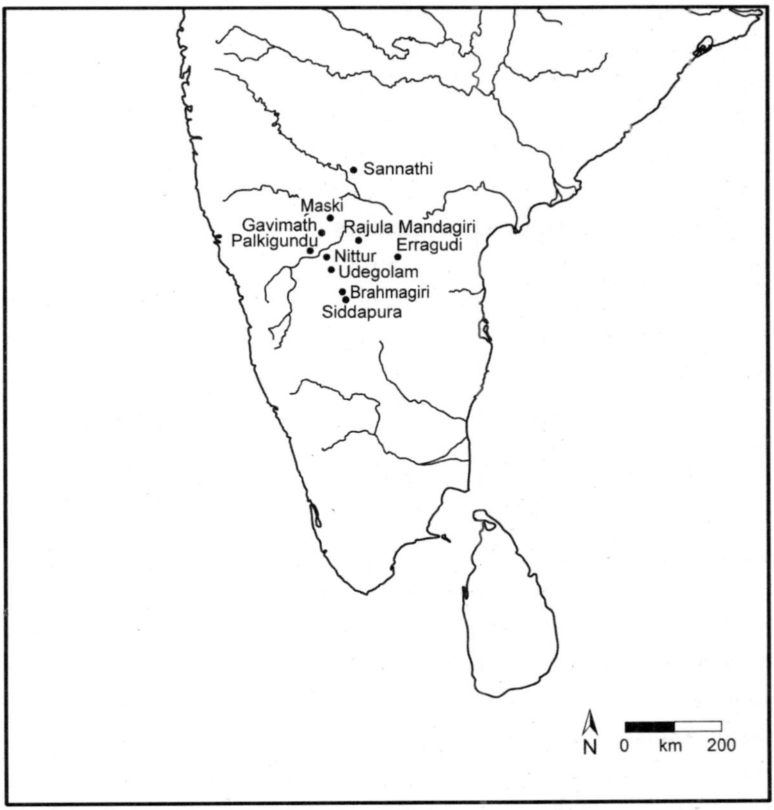

Figure 12.5 Southern cluster of Asokan inscriptions

these (e.g., Nittur, Udegalom, Koppal) fall directly in the Central Tungabhadra region that is the focus of this essay; the others lie nearby. These inscriptions are the earliest written texts in South India (though an increasing number of pottery fragments with Brahmi characters have been recovered at sites in Sri Lanka and Tamilnadu, and may date as early as the fifth century BC and certainly to the fourth century and provide evidence for longer standing peninsula-wide contacts than previously assumed). With the exception of the inscriptions at Erragudi and Sannati, all of the sites in this southern cluster contain variants of the two Minor Rock Edicts, which date to 258 BC and are largely concerned with the Buddhist *sangha* and practice of *dhamma* (R. Thapar 1997; Sugandhi 2008). There is no other evidence that Buddhism had reached the Tungabhadra region in any significant way at this time, and most of the remains at the monastic site of Sannati on the northern edges of the area date a few centuries later.

While the inscriptions themselves have been much discussed, our understandings of their larger material contexts remain limited. Some (e.g., those at Brahmagiri and Maski) are located at major and relatively well-studied population centers (e.g., Krishna 1934 and Wheeler 1947 at Brahmagiri, and B.K. Thapar 1957 at Maski); others, such as those at Nittur and Udegolam, are located in sparsely populated areas that lack major settlements (Sugandhi 2008). Little work has been done at Koppal; it may also have been a fairly sizeable center, but more research is required to confirm this.

Apart from the texts themselves, there is little other material evidence for the Mauryan presence beyond the occasional coin. Few northern artifacts have been found in the south, and those that have (e.g., Northern Black Polished Ware ceramics, lapis lazuli beads) could have moved through any number of exchange mechanisms not requiring imperial intervention. Nor is there evidence that the brief arrival of Mauryan representatives had any discernible impact on local communities or ways of life. Was this just a brief engagement by local communities with a few northern representatives that resulted in a small number of inscriptions propounding Asoka's religious ideology? Or were there longer term and more systemic interactions with the empire that involved economic or other exchanges that leave no obvious material traces? We cannot fully answer these questions with current data, but the lack of evidence for dramatic changes in site distributions, content, or economic practices suggests that the consequences of the Mauryan imperial presence in the southern Deccan were limited at best.

This sparse archaeological evidence stands at odds with the important place the southern cluster of Asokan inscriptions has occupied in historical narratives constructed by colonial, nationalist, and post colonial historians. For scholarship that privileges texts (see Trautmann and Sinopoli 2002), the inscriptions provide critical evidence for an integrated and politically unified India—when the peripheral inland south was first integrated into the much larger coherent pan-Indian Mauryan world. The region and the inscriptions have thus been important to Indian historiography even as the realities of the Mauryan presence in the Tungabhadra region remain difficult to decipher.

Whatever the answer, at the local level it does seem to be the case that populations and socioeconomic practices instantiated during the earlier Iron Age continued with little change during the late centuries BC and into the early centuries AD. Indeed, while the region was once a precocious center of agricultural invention and monument-building (South Indian Neolithic) and of emergent social and economic differentiation and intensification (early Iron Age), by the end of the first millennium BC and throughout much of the first millennium AD, the central Tungabhadra region appears to have become a periphery of developments occurring in other areas of the south. Throughout this lengthy time span, numerous more complex sociopolitical formations (states and empires) and urban centers rose and fell in other areas of the south, especially on the Tamil and Andhra coast. Buddhism, Jainism, and ultimately Hinduism and associated ideologies and ritual and monumental practices were adopted by the new elites in coastal and inland centers. Exactly why the center of gravity shifted during this period remains to be determined, but judging from available archaeological evidence, the Tungabhadra region appears to have been marginal to (though certainly not fully isolated from) many of the changes occurring elsewhere in the peninsula.

In the area around Vijayanagara that has been systematically surveyed, the "Early Historic" and "Early Medieval" periods have relatively low archaeological visibility compared to both earlier and later periods. This decline may, admittedly, be more apparent than real, based on the uneven intensity of archaeological research and the challenges of archaeological chronologies. And even if it were real, this is not to suggest dramatic depopulation of the region during this span. The site of Kadebakele, for example, appears to have a long occupational history and may have reached its maximal extent as a sizeable town in the early first millennium AD. Similar small centers and territorial polities no doubt existed throughout the region, and rose and fell, and engaged in complex material and social relations with each other and with larger neighbors, though without inscriptions we cannot precisely identify their names or affiliations. Nonetheless, it does seem to be the case that the Tungabhadra region lay on the peripheries of the many emergent states and empires of the period and was no longer a central place in South Indian political, economic, or technological developments.

The Early Second Millennium and the Vijayanagara Empire

To a considerable extent this pattern persisted throughout the first three centuries of the second millennium AD as the powerful Chalukya of Kalyani dynasty (ca. 973–1200 AD) came to power to the northwest of the Tungabhadra and the Cholas (850–1279 AD) reigned in the south. The successors of the Chalukyas, the Hoysalas and Kakatiyas, flanked the Central Tungabhadra on the southwest and southeast respectively. Numerous smaller dynasties, many tributary to more distant imperial states, are also documented in Karnataka during this period: the Haihayas of Morata, Kadambas of Kariadikallu, the Kalachuris, Nolambas, Sindas of Kurugodu, Pandyas of Uchchangi, the Kadambas of Kadambalige, and, based in the heart of the region considered here, the short-lived Kampili dynasty (Patil 1992: 12–14), ruled by Kampili Raya from AD 1280–1327. He reigned from several large fortified centers, including the hilltop fort of Kumattadurga, located in the high hills just north of the Tungabadhra River, less than 10 km from the riverside location where Vijayanagara would soon take form. The inscriptional and material record from the dynamic period that preceded Vijayanagara's emergence point to a heavily fortified and political unstable landscape. This fluctuating political scene and diverse claimants to authority in the central Tungabhadra is further confirmed by C.S. Patil's study of temple architecture and inscriptions (Patil 1992). Patil documented 76 eleventh-through early-fourteenth-century temples in Bellary and Raichur Districts (the latter was subsequently subdivided into Raichur and Koppal districts). The majority of these were presumably located in or nearby major settlements, though these were not documented in detail. Many of the temples contain inscriptions that reference the ruling dynasty under which they were constructed. Over fewer than three centuries, there are references to six dynasties: the Chalukyas of Kalyani (n=16, eleventh and early twelfth c.), Kampiladeva (n=4, early fourteenth c.), the Sindas of Korugudu (n=9; twelfth c.), the Haihayas of Morata (n=3, late twelfth-early thirteenth c.), the Kalachuris (n=2; twelfth c.), and Hoysalas (n=1; thirteenth c.). The relatively sparse and isolated populations of the central Tungabhadra and their local rulers no doubt experienced significant changes in political affiliation and perhaps, economic and service demands during this tempestuous period. However, by and large, the region continued to lie on the edges of major centers of power and outside of the grand trajectories of South India's major states and empires. As such, we know relatively little about either local political formations or the experiences of the communities that inhabited the central Tungabhadra region. This would change dramatically within a few decades.

Vijayanagara

In the wake of the turmoil caused by the expansion of the Delhi sultanate into South India, by the early fourteenth century all of the major (and many minor) polities mentioned above had collapsed. Vijayanagara was founded in this political vacuum, and quickly grew to be South India's largest city and the center of the largest pre-colonial empire to ever rule the peninsula. The emergence and expansion of Vijayanagara once again brought the Tungabhadra region into a central place in South Indian history and to Indian historiography. The founding and rapid expansion of Vijayanagara have been much discussed in recent publications (see especially, Stein 1989; Michell 1995), both from historiographic and archaeological perspectives, and need not be repeated in detail here. Urban growth in the capital was explosive and populations flowed into the city from throughout the region and, no doubt, throughout the peninsula. By the end of the fourteenth century, Vijayanagara was likely the largest city in South India and by the early sixteenth century was one of the largest and most densely occupied urban centers in the world.

As the center of empire, Vijayanagara lay at the nexus of major peninsular trade routes and exchange networks, and was a cosmopolitan and affluent city, visited by merchants and ambassadors from China, Portugal, the Arabian Gulf, and throughout India. Intensive investment in irrigation facilities transformed the local environment (Morrison 1995, 2009) and numerous suburban settlements of agriculturalists and artisans contributed to dramatically expanded populations throughout Vijayanagara (Sinopoli and Morrison 2007). Both within and beyond the capital, in Vijayanagara's many tributary centers, we see the creation of new styles of sacred (Michell 1995) and administrative (Michell 1992) architecture, constituting a distinctive imperial style that expressed Vijayanagara power and authority.

Vijayanagara's end was even more abrupt than its emergence. In 1565 AD, in the face of a military defeat against forces of the united Deccani sultanates and internal stresses throughout the empire, the city of Vijayanagara was abandoned. Populations in the Tungabhadra region declined precipitously as the capital of the waning empire shifted southward and the irrigation and other infrastructure and defensive features that supported the city were no longer maintained. Across the south, many of Vijayanagara's former tributaries reclaimed their autonomy (e.g., the *nayaka* states of Gingee, Mysore, Madurai, Thanjavur, Keladi-Ikkeri, as well as numerous smaller "little kingdoms" (sensu Dirks 1987), and the Tungabhadra region, while never fully depopulated, once again became a marginal sparsely populated region on the peripheries of larger political dynamics.

CONCLUSION

In this essay, I have attempted to provide a brief overview of the long history of a small region. A focus on thousands of years of "archaeological time" rather than the much shorter time spans of text-based historical research calls attention to the very long human histories of all regions of India and the fact that patterns, events, and practices established in the distant past can have important repercussions for subsequent local histories and practices. This study also serves as a reminder that the vast majority of the human past lies beyond the scope of written documentation and that even for those periods for which written records potentially existed, both the sources and historiography have tended to privilege major centers and "big events" rather than areas that lay on their peripheries. As a result, these latter areas where significant portions of India's population lived and died become largely invisible in our larger understandings of India's past. Collaborations between archaeology and history can play important roles in enhancing our ability to explore local histories at various temporal and spatial scales.

The central Tungabhadra area experienced dramatic fluctuations in its centrality and dynamism throughout the roughly 5000 years explored in this essay. During the lengthy Neolithic period and early centuries of the Late Prehistoric period, the Tungabhadra appears to have been a dynamic and comparatively densely populated region, a center of social, political, ideological, and technological invention and adoption. The later centuries of the millennium-long Late Prehistoric (Late Iron Age) and Early Historic periods are less well understood, but it appears that during these times the center of gravity shifted to other inland and coastal areas to both the south and north. Life and change continued in the semi-arid uplands along the Tungabhadra River as small polities rose and fell, and their inhabitants interacted with each other and with other regions across the peninsula and beyond in complex ways. This fluid pattern continued until the formation of Vijayanagara. The inhabitants of the central Tungabhadra certainly participated in these larger scale processes and dynamics to varying extents—they were taxed by larger polities and may have served in distant armies or building projects, temples were built in non-local styles, and material forms and economic practices no doubt changed in response to both local and larger scale conditions. However, it was not until the mid-fourteenth century that the region again appears as a "central place"—both in peninsular-wide developments and in historiography, and the region reappears in larger historical narratives.

The central Tungabhadra region is but one of thousands of regions whose local histories merit consideration. Its fluctuating status over long time spans and the intensity of archaeological and historic research in the area make it a useful one to consider for the purposes of this essay. In the tradition of Indian historiography, "big histories" are about big events and kings and courts, and these are certainly important. In this essay, I have paid heed to these big stories—of agricultural invention, emergent social inequality, and empire formation—while also trying to attend to the times, spaces, and lives in between.

ACKNOWLEDGMENTS

Thanks to Cyndy Talbot for her support as the Editor of this volume. Acknowledgments too to the Archaeological Survey of India, Karnataka Directorate of Archaeology and Museums, and American Institute of Indian Studies for facilitating my many years of archaeological research along the Tungabhadra River, and to all of the students and collaborators who have participated in that work. A special acknowledgment to Tom Trautmann, teacher, mentor, friend, and scholar extraordinaire. For many years, Tom has been my role model of the ideal scholar for both his personal and intellectual kindness and generosity and his extraordinary scholarship on ancient and colonial India.

NOTES

1. See Trautmann and Sinopoli 2002; Trautmann 2005 for discussions of this topic.
2. Michell 1985; also see the map reproduced as the frontispiece in "Homage to Hampi," *Marg Magazine,* 1985 (Marg Publications, Mumbai).
3. This view is not entirely without merit, but Foote was, overall, correct in his critique as regards these particular materials.

REFERENCES

Allchin, F. Raymond. 1961. *Utnoor Excavations*. Hyderabad: Andhra Pradesh Government Publications.

———. 1963. *Neolithic Cattle Keepers of South India: A Study of the Deccan Ashmounds*. Cambridge: Cambridge University Press.

Archaeological Survey of Madras and Coorg. 1904. *Annual Progress Report for the Year 1903–04*. Madras: Government Press.

———. 1910. *Annual Progress Report for the Year 1909–10*. Madras: Government Press.

Bauer, Andrew. In preparation. "Socializing Environments and Ecologizing Politics: The Production of Nature and Social Differentiation in Iron Age North Karnataka." PhD dissertation, University of Chicago.

Boivin, Nicole. 2004. "Landscape and Cosmology in the South Indian Neolithic: New Perspectives on the Deccan Ashmounds." *Cambridge Archaeological Journal* 14: 235–57.

Brubaker, Robert P. 2000–2001. "Aspects of Mortuary Variability in the South Indian Iron Age." *Bulletin of the Deccan College Post-Graduate and Research Institute* 60–61: 253–302.

———. 2008. "Regional Perspectives on Megalithic Landscapes: Investigating the Socio-Political Dimensions of Late Prehistoric Sites in Central Karnataka and West Andhra Pradesh, India." *Antiquity* 82 no. 317, electronic supplement. http://www.antiquity.ac.uk/ProjGall/brubaker/index.html.

Champakalakshmi, R. 1981. "Peasant State and Society in Medieval South India: A Review Article." *Indian Economic and Social History Review* 18: 411–26.

Dirks, Nicholas. 1987. *The Hollow Crown: Ethnohistory of an Indian Kingdom*. Cambridge: Cambridge University Press.

Eaton, Richard. 2005. *A Social History of the Deccan 1300–1761: Eight Indian Lives*. Cambridge: Cambridge University Press.

Falk, Harry. 2006. *Asokan Sites and Artefacts: A Sourcebook with Bibliography*. Mainz: Phillipp von Zabern.

Foote, Robert Bruce. 1887. "Notes of Some Recent Neolithic and Paleolithic Finds in the South." *Journal of the Asiatic Society of Bengal* 56: 259–82.

———. 1914. *Prehistoric and Protohistoric Antiquities of India*. Madras: Government Museum.

———. 1916. *The Foote Collection of Indian Prehistoric and Protohistoric Antiquities: Notes on Their Ages and Distributions*. Madras: Government Museum.

Fuller, Dorian R. and Ravi Korisettar. 2004. "The Vegetational Context of Early Agriculture in South India." *Man and Environment* 29: 7–27.

Fuller, Dorian Q., Nicole Boivin, and Ravi Korisettar. 2007. "Dating the Neolithic of South India: New Radiometric Evidence for Key Economic, Social, and Ritual Transformations." *Antiquity* 81: 755–78.

Historical Research Society of Dharwar. 1936. *Vijayanagara Sexcentary Commemoration Volume*. Dharwad: Vijayanagara Empire Sexcentenary Association.

Johansen, Peter. 2004. "Landscape, Monumental Architecture and Ritual: A Reconsideration of the South Indian Ashmounds." *Journal of Anthropological Archaeology* 23: 309–30.

———. 2008. "A Political Economy of Space: Social Organization and the Production of an Iron Age Settlement Landscape in Northern Karnataka." PhD dissertation, University of Chicago.

Korisettar, Ravi, P.C. Venkatasubbaiah, and Dorian Fuller. 2001. "Brahmagiri and Beyond: The Archaeology of the Southern Neolithic." In *Indian Archaeology in Retrospect: Volume 1: Prehistory*, ed. S. Settar and R. Korisettar, 151–38. New Delhi: Indian Council for Historical Research and Manohar.

Krishna, M.H. 1934. *Excavations at Chandravalli*. Supplement, Annual Report of the Mysore Archaeological Survey for the Year 1929. Mysore: Directorate of Archaeology and Museums.

Leshnik, L. 1974. *South Indian "Megalithic" Burials: The Pandukal Complex*. Wiesbaden: Franz Steiner Verlag.

Longhurst, A.H. 1917. *Hampi Ruins Described and Illustrated*. Calcutta: Government Press.

Michell, George. 1985. "A Never Forgotten City." In *Vijayanagara: City and Empire*, ed. A.L. Dallapiccola, 196–207. Franz Steiner Verlag, Wiesbaden.

———. 1992. *The Vijayanagara Courtly Style*. New Delhi: Manohar.

———. 1995. *Architecture and Art of Southern India: Vijayanagara and the Successor States*. The New Cambridge History of India I: 6. Cambridge: Cambridge University Press.

Moorti, U.S. 1994. *Megalithic Culture of South India*. Varanasi: Ganga Kaveri Publishing.

Morrison, Kathleen D. 1995. *Fields of Victory: Vijayanagara and the Course of Intensification*. Berkeley: Archaeological Research Facility, University of California.

———. 2009. *Daroji Valley: Landscape History, Place and the making of a Dryland Reservoir System*. New Delhi: Manohar Publishers.

Morrison, Kathleen D., et al. n.d. "Early Historic Landscapes of the

Vijayanagara Corridor: 2005 Preliminary Report" Unpublished manuscript.

Nagaraja Rao, M.S. 1983. *Vijayanagara: Progress of Research, 1979–1983*. Mysore: Directorate of Archaeology and Museums.

———. 1985. *Vijayanagara: Progress of Research, 1984–1985*. Mysore: Directorate of Archaeology and Museums.

———. 1988. *Vijayanagara Through the Eyes of Alexander Greenlaw 1956, John Gollings 1983*. Mysore: Directorate of Archaeology and Museums.

Newbold, T.J. 1836. "Note on the Occurrence of Volcanic Scorious Ashes in Southern India." *Journal of the Royal Asiatic Society of Great Britain and Ireland* 7: 129–36.

Nilakanta Sastri, K.A. 1966. *A History of South India from Prehistoric Times to Vijayanagar*. 3rd ed. Madras: Oxford University Press.

Owen Hughes, Dianne and Thomas R. Trautmann, eds. 1995. *Time: Histories and Ethnologies*. Ann Arbor: University of Michigan Press.

Paddayya, K. 1973. *Investigations into the Neolithic Culture of the Shorapur Doab, South India*. Leiden: E.J. Brill.

———. 1991–1992. "The Ashmounds of South India: Fresh Evidence and Possible Implications." *Bulletin of the Deccan College Post-Graduate and Research Institute* 51–52: 573–626.

———. 2002. "The Problem of Ashmounds of Southern Deccan in Light of Recent Research." In *Recent Studies in Indian Archaeology*, ed. K. Paddayya, 81–111. New Delhi: Munshiram Manoharlal.

Paddayya, K. and M.D. Petraglia. 1997. "Isampur: An Acheulian Workshop Site in the Hunsgi Valley, Gulbarga District, Karnataka." *Man and Environment* 22: 95–100.

Patil, C.S. 1992. *Temples of Raichur and Bellary Districts Karnataka 1000–1325 AD*. Mysore: Directorate of Archaeology and Museums.

Petraglia, Michael D., P. La Porta, and K. Paddayya. 1999. "The First Acheulian Quarry in India: Stone Tool Manufacture, Biface Morphology, and Behaviors." *Journal of Anthropological Research* 55: 39–70.

Singh, Upinder. 2004. *The Discovery of Ancient India: Early Archaeologists and the Beginnings of Archaeology*. Delhi: Permanent Black.

Sinopoli, Carla M. 2003. *The Political Economy of Craft Production: Crafting Empire in South India 1350-1650 AD*. Cambridge: Cambridge University Press.

Sinopoli, Carla M. 2009. "Late Prehistoric Landscapes of the Tungabhadra Corridor: Recent Excavations at Kadebakele (Koppal District, Karnataka)." In *Recent Research Trends in South Asian Archeology: Proceedings of the Professor H.D. Sankalia Birth Centenary Seminar*, ed. K. Paddayya et al., 279–294. Pune: Deccan College Post-Graduate and Research Institute.

———. 2011. "Vijayanagara Research: A Template for Interdisciplinary Scholarship on India's Past." In *South India under Vijayanagara: Art and Archeology*, ed. Anila Verghese and Anna L. Dallapiccola 13–24. New Delhi: Oxford University Press.

Sinopoli, Carla M. and Kathleen D. Morrison. 2007. *The Vijayanagara Metropolitan Survey, Vol. 1*. Ann Arbor: Museum of Anthropology, University of Michigan.

Sinopoli, Carla M., Kathleen D. Morrison and R. Gopal. 2008. "Late Prehistoric and Early Historic South India: Recent Research along the Tungabhadra River, Karnataka." *Antiquity* 82, no. 317, electronic supplement. http://www.antiquity.ac.uk/ProjGall/sinopoli/index.html.

Sinopoli, Carla M., et al. n.d. "Early Historic Landscapes of the Tungabhadra Corridor: 2003 Preliminary Report." Unpublished manuscript.

Stein, Burton. 1979. *Peasant State and Society in Medieval South India*. Delhi: Oxford University Press.

———. 1989. *Vijayanagara*. Cambridge: Cambridge University Press.

Sugandhi, Namita. 2008. "Between the Patterns of History: Rethinking Mauryan Imperial Interaction in the Southern Deccan." PhD dissertation, University of Chicago.

Taylor, Meadows. 1851. "Ancient Remains at the Village of Jiwargi near Ferozabad on the Bhima." *Journal of the Bombay Branch of the Royal Asiatic Society* 3: 179–96.

Thapar, B.K. 1957. "Maski 1954: A Chalcolithic Site in the Tapti Valley." *Ancient India* 20: 1–157.

Thapar, Romila. 1997. *Asoka and the Decline of the Mauryas*. Rev. ed. Delhi: Oxford University Press.

Trautmann, Thomas R. 1997. *Aryans and British India*. Berkeley: University of California Press.

———. 2008. *Lewis Henry Morgan and the Invention of Kinship*. New ed. Lincoln: University of Nebraska Press.

Trautmann, Thomas, ed. 2005. *The Aryan Debate*. Delhi: Oxford University Press.

Trautmann, Thomas R. and Carla M. Sinopoli. 2002. "In the Beginning was the Word: Excavating the Relations between History and Archaeology in South Asia." *Journal of the Economic and Social History of the Orient* 45, no. 4: 492–523.

Trigger, Bruce G. 1989. *A History of Archaeological Thought*. Cambridge: Cambridge University Press.

Verghese, Anila. 1995. *Religious Traditions at Vijayanagara as Revealed through Sculpture*. Manohar Publishers, New Delhi.

———. 2000. *Archaeology, Art, and Religion: New Perspectives on Vijayanagara*. Delhi: Oxford University Press.

Wheeler, R.E.M.1947. "Brahmagiri and Chandravalli Excavations." *Ancient India* 4: 181–310.

13

Secondary Cities and Urban Networking in Cola-era South India

KENNETH R. HALL

STUDYING EARLY SOUTH ASIAN URBANISM

Post-World War II Western and Western-trained scholars studying urbanism in the Indian Ocean realm initially focused on the networking between large urban centers and villages, although with the common acknowledgement that intermediate urban centers assumed importance in the development of national cultures. These studies derived from the University of Chicago-based concern for cultural interactions between the city and the village that shaped Asia's "Great Traditions" and "Little Traditions" (Cohn and Marriott 1958; Stein 1977). In the 1960s, G. William Skinner's "Marketing and Social Structure in Rural China" initiated a new trend in the study of Asian urbanism, and what was called "central place theory," by proposing that Asian urban centers and villages were networked in a hierarchical relationship to imperial capitals, based more on bureaucratic/political administrative than economic needs (Skinner 1964). My 1975 dissertation, written under the direction of Thomas Trautmann, applied the Great and Little Traditions and Central Place Theory models, in addition to the writings of Marcel Mauss (1967), Karl Polanyi (Polanyi, et. al. 1957), and Marshall Sahlins (1972) on gift-giving and reciprocity, redistribution, and marketing networks to depict the development of pre-1500 sovereignty in south India, and demonstrated how the Cola state (ca. 600–1300 AD) could be better understood by focusing on the development of hierarchical market networks rather than the emergence of bureaucratic authority (Hall 1975).

Since the 1980s, scholars have paid greater attention to cultural formation, to the production of social space, and to the importance of place. A variety of scholarship commonly addresses the origin of urban communities relative to movements of commercial commodities, confrontations between alien cultures, formation of plural societies, dual loyalties, and multiple affiliations, and as demonstrations of globalization. Taking their cue from post-modernism, scholars now present urban identities and forms as cultural constructions constantly in the process of being refashioned. The concept of space has gained increasing currency in the last two decades, notably among "production of space" theorists who approach space as something more than the background scenery for social activity. They examine urban social spaces as human creations with competing sets of meanings inscribed in them. By closely exploring the process of creating and defining these and other urban spaces, scholars try to better understand the identities, relationships, and experiences of urban dwellers (Lefebvre 1991; Foucault 1986; Wright and Rabinow 1982; Hayden 1995; Castells 1978; Castells 2000).

This study will address these new urban history issues by examining south Indian epigraphy from the ninth- through the thirteenth-century Cola age, to make an analysis of a representative Cola-era secondary urban center. Two books by Cola-era specialists James Heitzman (1997) and R. Champakalakshmi (1996) are foundational to this study. Heitzman and Champakalakshmi incorporated the revisionist urban studies literature to reexamine Burton Stein's (1980) and Noboru Karashima's (1984) seminal and

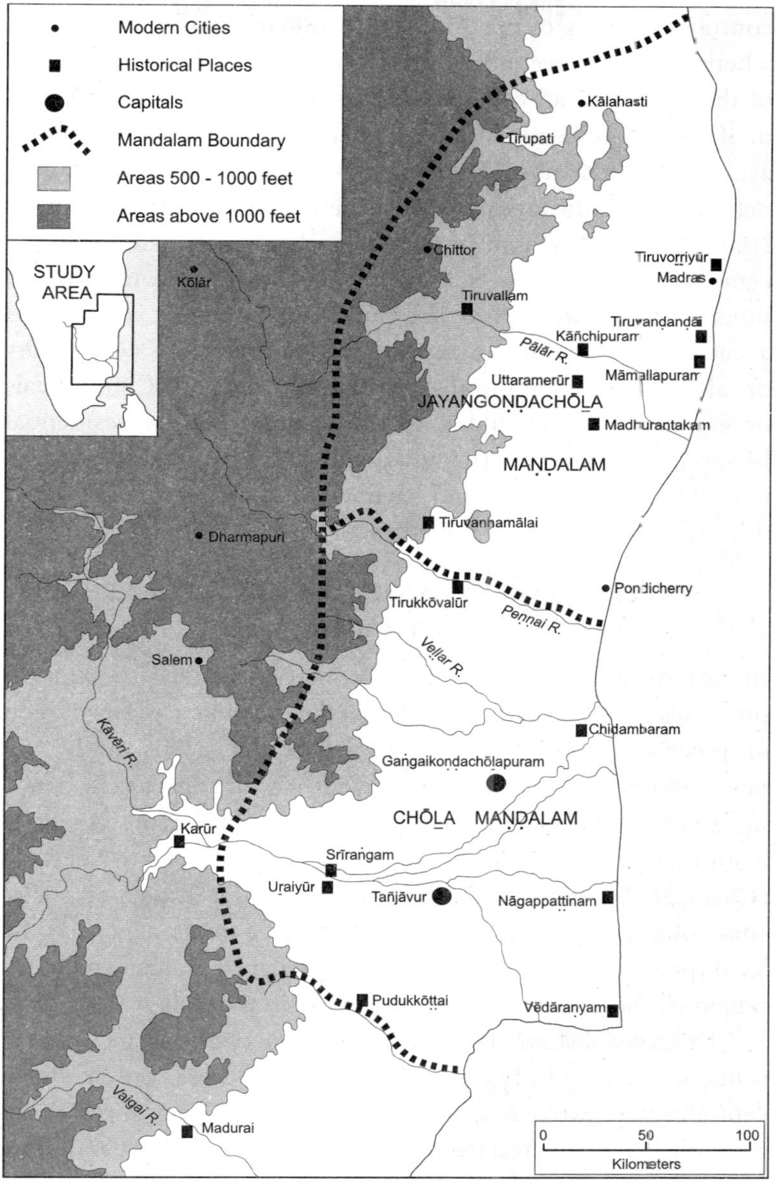

Figure 13.1 Cola-era south India

contrasting views of pre-1500 south Indian history, in debating whether Cola-era secondary cities acted as the intermediary agents of the metropolitan centers' temples, courts, and marketplaces, or if they instead advocated on their local community's behalf against the demands of outsiders—among these royal courts, networked Hindu temples, and itinerant merchant associations (Hall 2001b). The issue is whether these intermediary urban centers exploited their bottom up, top down, or long-distance links to their own residential community's benefit, perhaps as a cooperative venture in the interest of the entire community or, alternatively, serving the specialized interests of individuals or groups that contributed to the creation of new residential hierarchies. Above all, Heitzman and Champakalakshmi agreed that the scale, timing, and character of the secondary cities differed from that of the big cities.[1]

PATTERNS OF URBANIZATION IN COLA-ERA SOUTH INDIA

In current understanding, the Cola era was marked by multiple processes of cultural centralization that included the evolution of preexisting and new societal institutions. This study will not address the controversial evidence of developing caste hierarchy in Cola-era south India, which documents the early institutionalization of "right-hand" and "left-hand" caste hierarchy (Champakalakshmi 1996: 218, 229). Instead, it focuses on a case study of a representative secondary Cola-era urban center, as the local epigraphic evidence highlights the wider centralizing political, religious, and commercial forces at work in the Cola realm.

Champakalakshmi asserts that urban networking in Cola-era south India was of four sorts. In the first of these, Cola political centralization was based in a "sacred sovereignty" hierarchical network that emanated from a magnificent royal court and drew preexisting and newly constructed temples and urban centers in as its political and ritual secondary and subordinate centers

(Champakalakshmi 1996: 331–66). The foremost examples are the single-temple centered court cities of Tanjavur, the magnificent capital of Rajaraja I (r. 985–1014), and Gangaikondacolapuram, the imperial capital of his successor Rajendra I (r. 1012–1044) (Champakalakshmi 1996: 424–41; Heitzman 1997: 121–42). In each case the court was dominant over the capital city's temple. This is best shown in Rajaraja's inscriptions, in which he reassigned temple staff from throughout his realm to his new court temple, in a conspicuous attempt to promote his court temple's supremacy as the ritual center of his state. Tanjavur and Gangaikondacolapuram were "instant" cities, with supportive marketplaces and artisan communities instituted by the Cola king to supply the consumptive needs of the royal capital. Champakalakshmi asserts that Rajaraja purposefully instituted a *nagaram*, an institutionalized marketplace, as a dependent of the king rather than having the Tanjavur *nagaram* naturally evolve in agency with the surrounding rural community, as was the case in Kancipuram and other *nagaram* communities that pre-date Rajaraja's reign. The Tanjavur *nagaram* community was thus, like everything else in the capital city, subject to the authority of the king from its inception, rather than having a previous history of local accountability or autonomy.[2]

In their conquest of new territories, Cola kings regularly established local Saivite temples that in some way were ritually linked to the Cola capital's temple or other significant Cola-patronized temples, and which, like the temple at the Cola capital, supported the development of local marketing and other urbanism. Champakalakshmi makes the case that the first epigraphic records of *nagaram* in newly conquered regions demonstrate Cola efforts to promote local and long-distance trade coincident to Cola political initiatives to incorporate the region. She argues that Rajaraja I and his successors regularly established *nagaram* to institutionalize marketplace activity, and are equally paired with Cola efforts to institutionalize the region's ritual linkages into the Cola political hierarchy (Champakalakshmi 1996: 203–310).

A second type of urban networking had its foundation in preexisting major temples, such as Cidambaram and Srirangam, which were the single-temple centered urban centers of south Indian Saivism and Vaishnavism. Both were major pilgrimage centers, with numbers of temple staff and supportive urban institutions, including resident *nagaram* and artisan communities, which had evolved to serve the temple community and its numerous pilgrims (Hall 2001a).

A third urbanization is demonstrated in the evolution of periodic regional fairs and markets into urban commercial centers (Heitzman 1997: 37–81; Champakalakshmi 1996: 206–8). These were supported by surrounding productive agrarian societies, local Brahman and non-Brahman communities in the traditional rural districts (*nadu, kottam*). *Nadu/kottam* included *brahmadeya* "villages," as indicated by the suffix *chaturvedimangalam* that was attached to their name, which often linked an honorific reference to their initial royal patron.[3] Brahmans dominated these incorporated *brahmadeya* rural "village" communities, which they governed as members of village *sabha* assemblies. Incorporated non-Brahman villages were administered by hereditary communal, dominant peasant landholder, and kinship-based elites as members of *ur* assemblies (Stein 1980; Hall 1982).

As these local agricultural communities became productive, it was logical to have a corporate marketing center that centralized regional exchanges. One may characterize early Cola-era *nagaram* as locally imbedded and institutionalized town marketplaces on the edges of the developing Cola realm, which were subject to multiple opportunities that encouraged them to evolve into secondary urban centers in a hierarchical urban network that centered on a few primary urban centers. As I documented in my 1975 dissertation, *nadu* commonly incorporated a *nagaram* commercial center—one per *nadu*, except in a major commercial center, such as Kancipuram, where there might be several incorporated *nagaram* marketplace communities (Hall 1975; Champakalakshmi 1996:

203–310). Incorporation of a *nagaram* allowed the local agrarian elite to exercise administrative control in partnership with a local merchant community ("guild") to supervise the local exchange process, and to guard against illicit and immoral marketplace exploitation. My dissertation addressed whether the *nagaram* remained locally imbedded and accountable to their surrounding agrarian community, or whether heightened external commercial and political potentials increased the likelihood that a *nagaram* would link with an external political (Cola kings) or commercial (itinerant merchant guilds) agency to the potential detriment of local authorities.

A fourth urbanization is represented by Kancipuram, which was a multi-centered city that had well-established institutional roots as the historical center of Pallava political authority, a religious center that included several major networked Hindu, Buddhist, and Jain temples, and a merchant and craft center that was the gathering point for regional production and the redistribution source for imported luxuries. Pallava kings incorporated the Kancipuram commercial community as a *managaram* ("great" *nagaram*) in recognition of its supra-regional commercial importance. In the Cola era, Kancipuram's continuing importance as a major political and religious center was paired with its increasing prominence as the market source of south Indian cotton products, which were in high demand internationally. Kancipuram's Cola-era marketplace was the intermediary center where regional weavers sent their products for wider market distribution, and was also a major weaving center itself. It had well-established weaving neighborhoods, including one that was incorporated as a specialized *nagaram* dominated by *saliya nagarattar* ("cloth merchants"), enterprising local weavers who had become specialists in the marketing of cloth. There were other resident merchant and artisan specialists, including "oil mongers" who produced and marketed coconut-derived oils that were used in lamps, food preparation, and cooking (Hall and Spencer 1980; Heitzman 2001; Champakalakshmi 1996: 391–98).

In the past decades, south India specialists have intensified their study of south Indian inscriptions, literary sources, and architecture, to be better able to periodize rather than generalize these critical Cola-era societal and institutional transitions as they would become foundational to subsequent south Indian society and culture (Trautmann et. al. 1985; Hall 2001b). There is now wide acceptance that there were three phases of Cola sovereignty. The first, from 850 to 985., is the initial period in which Cola sovereignty was established and the earliest institutionalized networking took place, most notably set in motion by the conquests and inclusion initiatives of Parantaka I (r. 907–955). The second, 985–1150, was the pinnacle of Cola authority, marked by the leadership of aggressive kings such as Rajaraja I (r. 985–1014), Rajendra I (r. 1012–1044), and Kulottunga I (r. 1070–1120). In this age Cola conquests were paired with numerous royal initiatives, which included the financing of construction, reconstruction, and major additions to selected and strategic temples; the implementation of a functional though not pervasive royal administration; and the promotion of commerce, through the implementation of a system of monetary exchange sustained by the issue of royal coinage; foreign diplomacy and military intervention, if necessary, to promote their realm's international commercial interests in the Bay of Bengal region, Sri Lanka, and Southeast Asia; and their generalized if not direct support in initiating marketplace institutions. The third period, from 1150 to 1279, is a period of diminishing fortune and fragmentation, including periods in which there were regular dynastic crises, regular invasions of the Cola heartland by neighbors, and Cola re-conquests. The most recent work on this late Cola era has centered on the negotiation of new networks and institutions, privatization, militarization, and the institutionalization of new relationships that were foundational in the transition to subsequent Vijayanagara authority (Heitzman 1997; Heitzman 2008).

TIRUVORRIYUR IN THE COLA AGE

Tiruvorriyur, on the northern edge of modern-day Chennai (Madras), was a representative Cola-era south Indian city. In the Cola age, as in the previous era of Pallava rule, it was a secondary urban center networked with the former Pallava capital and continuous primary urban center of Kancipuram to its southwest (Hall and Spencer 1980; Heitzman 2001). The Colas called the former Pallava realm Tondaimandalam, which was north of their Colamandalam heartland in the Kaveri River basin (see Figure 10). When the celebrated Saivite saint Appar visited the shrine in the seventh century, Tiruvorriyur—also called Orriyur in early Cola epigraphic records in honor of the father of the founder of the Cola imperial dynasty (180 of 1912)—was a notable south Indian center for the worship of Siva, though not one of the seven most sacred south Indian sites listed in the *Devaram* ("saint singer") hymns. Subsequently Sundaramurti Nayanmar, the eighth-century Saivite saint, worshipped there, as did Adi Sankaracarya (b. 805), the legendary reformer of Saivite ritual traditions and founder of Saivite monasticism (Raman 1959: 13).

In Saivite lore, Sankaracarya performed a miracle on the local goddess of the Tiruvorriyur temple similar to that he had previously used to gain the submission of the presiding fertility goddess of Kancipuram, Kamakshi, who was then incorporated into Hinduism as a divine form (*avatara*) of Siva's consort Parvati (still worshipped in Kancipuram's Kamakshi Amman "mother goddess" temple). Hearing that the local Tiruvorriyur goddess was fierce and that she demanded animal and human sacrifices, Sankara converted her to the *Bhakti* ritual forms. Purged of its unacceptable local animistic rituals, Tiruvorriyur became a center of Tantric asceticism and scholarship, and during the Cola era was categorically affiliated with the Kalamukha Tantric Saivite sect.[4] Tiruvorriyur's central icon, a product of the Cola age, is an eclectic composite of the Siva, Vishnu, and Brahma trinity, with the latter two submissive in their worship to Siva's supremacy.

The Tiruvorriyur temple became the worship center for the adjacent and widely-respected educational facility (variously referenced as a *ghatika*, "seminary," and *matha*, "monastery"), where the curricula extended beyond sacred Vedic knowledge to include the study of medicine, poetics, and other arts. Brahmans controlled the temple and monastic compound; Brahman teachers instructed in the Sanskrit language, and most students had a valid Brahman genealogy. Tiruvorriyur became the center of a Saivite order (*sampradayam*) that became popular in the neighboring Kerala and Karnataka regions to the west after their conquest by the Colas, as a consequence of Cola patronage.

Tiruvorriyur's Saivite Pasupata school was accountable to a line of teachers titled Caturanana Pandita, who presided over the temple and its monastic compound (177, 181 of 1912); Parantaka I (r. 907–955) and Uttama Cola (r. 970–985) financed a major tenth-century expansion of the temple, which added *mandapas* (pillared pavilions) around the main shrine. The central shrine was rebuilt during the reign of Rajendra I (r. 1012–1044), and later temple additions were financed by Cola royalty and subordinates (104, 126 of 1912; Raman 1959: 198, 228).

At Kancipuram and elsewhere Cola kings were great patrons of major temple compounds, which were focal in the Cola "sacred sovereignty" ritual network that reached its pinnacle in the eleventh century (Stein 1980). Through the Cola era, Tiruvorriyur remained a secondary subsidiary to Kancipuram in the Cola ritual network. But Cola kings readily affiliated with Tiruvorriyur's Pasupata teachers, which resulted in a trail of evidence that includes a number of grants made by Cola kings and their subordinates to the temple and its Brahman priests who recited the scriptures and performed its rituals (Raman 1959: 228). Tiruvorriyur's distinguished Brahmans assumed special importance during the reigns of Rajendra I and Kulottunga I (r. 1070–1120), who financed the founding of new Pasupata temples in their post-conquest Kerala and Karnataka territories (Kaimal 1996; Ogura 1999).

Cola inscriptional honorifics (*prasasti*) highlight the grants made by kings while dining with the Tiruvorriyur temple's Brahmans, with a focus on the ritual legitimacy derived from the dining event. In contrast, most royal inscriptions of that era focused on the Cola army's aggressive conquests. These grants were said to have been proclaimed while the king was "in camp" somewhere on the campaign trail and recount the king's most recent victories to justify subsequent royal authority. Instead, the Tiruvorriyur inscriptions portray the intimacy between the Cola king and the distinguished religious leaders, resident *brahmadeya* ("Brahman community") leaders of adjacent and nearby agricultural lands, and learned Brahmans in the king's service. Shared food-taking with Tiruvorriyur's Brahmans validated the king's high ritual status as appropriate to one who claimed the stature of a *ksatriya* warrior/ruler. In these instances, the celebration of the royal relationship with individuals of high secular stature would seem to have been less important to Cola kings than their demonstrable association as patrons of the inclusive highly respected networked Tiruvorriyur community of Brahman learning. Celebrations of a local ritual network's incorporation into the hierarchically-linked Tiruvorriyur ritual community would have symbolically overridden previous local ritual autonomy, in sustaining royal institutional authority in newly-annexed regions.

Cola rulers might have appreciated Brahmanical learning for its own sake, in which case the Tiruvorriyur epigraphic evidence demonstrates proper regal (*rajadharma*) behavior in support of claims that the Colas were members of the solar clan of *ksatriyas*, and were thereby entitled to perform the Vedic *ksatriya* ritual of the *asvamedha* that was allegedly done by Rajadhiraja I(r. 1018–1054), Rajaraja's grandson (*ARE* 1899, 1: 53; Nilakanta Sastri 1955: 259, 279 n. 86). Only a powerful king could initiate the *asvamedha,* "horse sacrifice." It was an egotistical and risky public proclamation of royal power, glory, sovereignty, and the general prosperity of the kingdom. A horse that was eventually sacrificed was turned loose to wander initially in a northeast direction, and thereafter followed a course associated with the sun's yearly progression. Anywhere the horse wandered was subject to a king's authority, to be validated by his conquest or by the peaceful submission of neighboring populations to his sovereignty.

A symbolic story told in a temple inscription provides the legendary details of the origin of the special relationship between Cola kings and the Tiruvorriyur monastic community (181 of 1912; *ARE* 1912: 2, 17; *EI* 27: 293). In the early tenth century Caturanana Pandita, the reigning leader of the ascetic order, formalized the temple's links with the Cola kings, who had a special interest in the Tiruvorriyur temple because of its earlier association with Orriyuran, the father of Vijayalaya (r. 849–870), the founder of the resurgent Cola monarchy (Nagaswamy and Majeed 1979: 26–27). Caturanana Pandita was said to have previously been the close civilian advisor (*samanta*) to Rajaditya, son of king Parantaka I (r. 907–955), prior to becoming a member of the ascetic order—at that time Parantaka ("who took Kancipuram and made himself master of the northern districts of the Cola kingdom") was incorporating Tondaimandalam into his expansive Cola realm (Nilakanta Sastri 1935: 127–28). Caturanana Pandita was the son of a family of chieftains from Kerala, who as a youth had mastered the arts and sciences, and then, answering a Divine call to serve humanity, traveled east to the Cola realm where he became the friend of Rajaditya. Due to other responsibilities he did not die with his friend on the battlefield. In grief, he withdrew to become an ascetic monk at Tiruvorriyur. There he rose through the monastic order and became the head of its monastic community, and was the first among the vital clerical legitimizing agents of Cola sovereignty.

Tiruvorriyur's Institutional Foundations in the Late Pallava Era

Temple inscriptions dating from 870 to 912 document the spatial composition of the Tiruvorriyur community immediately prior to

Parantaka Cola's conquest of Tondaimandalam. Several inscriptions identify the Adambakkam *brahmadeya*, said to be the incorporated suburban community affiliated with the temple (158, 161, 163 of 1912). In that time a representative *amrita-gana*, "management committee," was accountable for the administration of offerings and temple lamps. This *brahmadeya*'s committee system is reminiscent of the well-documented *sabha* village management committees in the contemporary Tondaimandalam Uttaramerur *brahmadeya* near the Kancipuram urban center (Gros and Nagaswamy 1970). The Adambakkam *sabha*'s management committee received several substantial deposits of gold from politically-connected women, including a mistress of a local chieftain (158 of 1912) and a Pallava queen (163 of 1912), and agreed to burn perpetual temple lamps financed by the interest accruing from the *sabha* committee's investments of these sums, with a guaranteed interest rate return of 15% (161, 191 of 1912; see also Orr 2001). In contrast, another individual identified as a visiting chief deposited a substantial sum with the *karmakkilvar* of Tiruvorriyur, the temple's management committee, the accruing interest to fund assorted offerings including rice, ghee, plantains, sugar, vegetables, areca nuts, betel leaves, tender coconuts, sandal paste, and camphor (159 of 1912).

A second *brahmadeya*, Manali, said to be a "hamlet" of Tiruvorriyur, also received substantial gold donations on the temple's behalf. In return its management committee agreed to finance perpetual lamps at the temple on guaranteed interest of 15% (189, 190 of 1905). This networked community was also responsible for the construction of an outer shrine (*prakara*) around the central shrine by "purchase" of income rights to 20,000 *kuli* of the community's lands, future income from which was to pay for the subsequent upkeep of the shrine. The transaction was administered by the "village headman" (*madhyastha*, "unconcerned/ neutral person"). In another record, the *ur* assembly of Vaikkattur (a non-Brahman agrarian community assembly) received a sum of gold from the wife of a chief from the Kodumbalur region to the south (Pudukkottai) and in return promised to provide offerings to the Mahadeva at Tiruvorriyur on a specified ritual day (174 of 1912).

Tiruvorriyur under Cola Sovereignty

In the Cola age Tiruvorriyur was located in Pulal kottam, with neighboring Puliyur and Paiyur kottams the northernmost administrative regions of the Cola polity between the tenth and thirteenth centuries. There are no epigraphic references to the *sabha* of Adambakkam in the Cola-era inscriptions. Instead, the *brahmadeya* of Manali, otherwise known in Cola-era records as Singavisnu Caturvedimangalam, was the dominant landholding community associated with the Tiruvorriyur temple complex. An inscription reports that the late eleventh-century urban community of Tiruvorriyur consisted of several residential quarters (*perunderu*) that surrounded the temple: one for *manradis*, a special category of shepherds who cared for temple livestock; one inhabited by sculptors and artisans; and a third inhabited by merchants and weavers who were members of the Tiruvorriyur *nagaram* (136 of 1912). An inscription dating shortly after includes two *ur* village communities of non-Brahman cultivators in the local *kottam* ("district") as actively involved in support of the temple, in addition to two other *ur* villages from an adjacent district (106 of 1892/*SII* 3: 64; 131 of 1912/*ARE* 1913, 2: 6, 33).

As previously noted, Tiruvorriyur in the Cola age was prominent due to its association with the primal ancestor of Cola kings, Orriyuran, the father of Vijayalaya (r. 849–870), the founder of the resurgent Cola monarchy (Nagaswamy and Majeed 1959: 26–27), and its importance as a center of Pasupata-Kalamukha Saivism (Lorenzen 1972: 166–67). From the time of Parantaka I (r. 907–955), whose conquest of Tondaimandalam annexed the former Pallava territorial base into the Cola realm, every subsequent Cola king reaffirmed their monarchy's ritual links with the Tiruvorriyur temple. Through the Cola age the Tiruvorriyur temple and its associated monastic community remained an important center of Saivite scholarship, with extensive ritual links that attracted pilgrims from distant places. Some stayed to study, while others were wealthy patrons who provided substantial endowments to support the diverse activities of the temple and its resident staff (137, 142, 197 of 1912). During the Cola era Tiruvorriyur prospered, as it became a multi-dimensional urban center of political, economic, commercial, and religious importance.

Politically, Tiruvorriyur was secondary to Kancipuram in its role as a Tondaimandalam Cola administrative center. There Cola officials monitored the affairs of the Tiruvorriyur temple, and supervised and audited the income and expenditures of other regional temples (*SII* 3: 145; 103, 130, 136, 146 of 1912; 386 of 1958–1959). Cola kings, queens, sons, chiefs, military leaders, and dignitaries were among the temple's visitors and benefactors.

Local inscriptions report the temple's acquisition of over 10 productive *devadana* villages, and the numerous assignments of income rights to lands in over 20 other places distributed among the three noted *kottams* and lands in the neighboring Colamandalam, the Cola political and economic core (*ARE* 1912–1913, *passim*). The resulting agricultural productivity and the affairs of the temple required the services of professional merchants, whose *nagaram* commercial quarter is first recorded in local inscriptions dating to the beginning of the eleventh century, at the beginning of the "golden age" of Cola sovereignty (132 of 1912)

Local merchants were prominent managers of temple endowments, delegated by the temple to receive substantial monetary payments that they invested on the temple's behalf. They provided guaranteed annual rates of return in money and products to meet the temple's ritual and residential needs (132, 140, 141 of 1912). By the late eleventh century Tiruvorriyur's marketplace was prosperous enough to support resident craft specialists (weavers, artisans) and those who sold animals and their byproducts, who also provided for the consumptive needs of the temple and its supporting urban community (136 of 1912). Local merchants were linked to major external marketplaces, such as the regional marketing center *managaram* Kancipuram (129 of 1912) and its Tiruvandandai seaport (261, 267, 274 of 1910). A late twelfth-century inscription reports that the Tiruvorriyur *nagaram* was one among 10 networked marketplaces in the northern Cola realm (120 of 1930). Despite its noted external commercial networking, there is no evidence that Tiruvorriyur's merchant community or its marketplace were directly linked to the major international merchant associations of that age (Abraham 1988). It would seem that Tiruvorriyur's marketplace was most important as a secondary and designated marketplace for its immediate *kottam* region, and was a destination rather than a product source or service center for long-distance trade.

The Tiruvorriyur temple was the primary institutional base for local urbanism. Cola monarchs from the time of Parantaka I acted as patrons of the Tiruvorriyur temple to sustain their claims of royal legitimacy, and supported the spread of the temple's Pasupata-Kalamukha Siva cult in newly conquered regions in neighboring Kerala and Karnataka (Prasad 1989). Inscriptions of Parantaka I (r. 907–950), Kulottunga I (r. 1070–1120), and Rajaraja III (r. 1216–1256) provide examples of direct patronage from the monarch that financed major Tiruvorriyur temple construction projects, which greatly enhanced the grandeur of the temple complex (187, 200, and 211 of 1912). The Tiruvorriyur temple was richly endowed with land. Early agents of the king regularly intervened on the temple's behalf to mandate that previously uncultivated community lands were to be brought into production to provide additional temple funding, as also to insure that these and other newly developed lands not previously assigned to the temple remained free of Cola taxation (103, 128, 228 of 1912). In several late Cola-era inscriptions royal officials, faced with heightened court expenses, rescinded some of the temple's *devadana* land tax exemptions (199 of 1912). Money and gold were equally common gifts to finance the purchase of sheep—as a source of ghee, wool, and meat (138 of 1912))—and to sustain the variety of temple activities and needs such as festivals (140 of 1912), musical performance, dance, and public recitals of scripture (128 of 1912), daily rituals (129 of 1912), temple lamps (164, 170 of 1912), and subsidized the expenses of temple priests, resident ascetics, and the temple school (133, 202 of 1912).

The Tiruvorriyur secondary urban center exemplifies urbanism that was a byproduct of the preexisting sacred temple center and political expansionism. The appropriation of the Tiruvorriyur temple complex as the foundation for early Cola-era ritual networking initiatives, which led to linked urbanized religious and political institutional hierarchies, provided the opportunity for local economic growth. Increased agricultural productivity and specialized craft production (notably cotton weaving) mutually supported the emergence of Tiruvorriyur as a networked secondary marketing center to Kancipuram and its nearby coastal ports, which specialized in long-distance and international trade. While it might be concluded that the diversity of Tiruvorriyur's urban networking roles substantially improved and sustained local welfare, a late Cola-era inscription demonstrates that the increased local productivity also encouraged the exhaustive tax demands by revenue-starved Cola kings. Consequently, an inscription dating to the reign of Kulottunga III (r. 1178–1218) relates that some of the local population, when unable to make a required tax payment, had to relinquish some privately held land rights to the temple to cover their unpaid taxes (202 of 1912/*ARE* 1913, 2: 39).

SECONDARY URBANISM IN THE COLA ERA

This study of secondary urbanization in Cola-era south India has addressed the role of the creation of urban networking and hierarchies in the culturally-influenced formation of productive space. Tiruvorriyur's Siva temple was foundational to its community's continuing evolution from an exclusively temple town into a multi-dimensional urban center of greater size and complexity. In the early tenth century Tiruvorriyur consisted of its temple and monastic scholastic complex, which had its immediate needs supplied by two self-governing *brahmadeya* agricultural communities, one a "hamlet" and the other a "suburb" of the temple, neither of which lay immediately adjacent to the temple complex. There was also a self-governing *ur* community of non-Brahman agriculturalists in the local *kottam* ("agricultural district"), who similarly supplied the temple (see Figure 11). Each of these rural-based communities was administratively autonomous of the temple, which was governed by its chief cleric and administered by a temple management committee that was exclusively composed of temple clergy. Each of these local corporate communities, the temple, the *brahmadeya*, and the *ur*, had its own productive space, yet depended on the others in meaningful ways.

The Brahman and non-Brahman agricultural communities

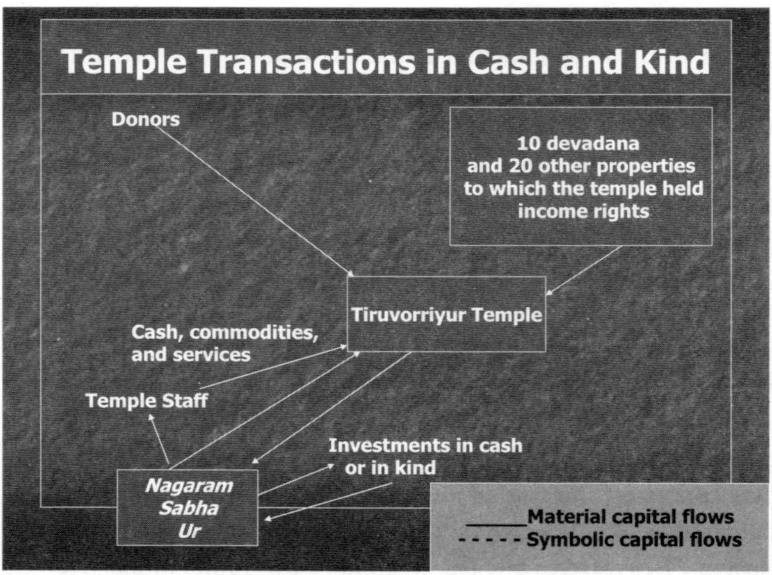

Figure 13.2 Tirruvorriyur temple economic networking

supplied the temple with produce, at contracted rates of return as interest payments on invested capital. The invested capital consisted of cash, bullion, or marketable commodities that had been donated to the temple, but were reassigned to Tiruvorriyur's networked communities in return for their contracted commitment to supply the temple with its annual food and ritual needs. These initial linked transfers and those that would follow had multiple sets of meanings. These were economic and ritual transactions that returned both material goods and "symbolic capital" (Bourdieu 1977: 159–97). In addition to their economic fulfillment, the linked agricultural communities received the psychological satisfaction of their service to Lord Siva, as certified for eternity in the temple's inscribed record. Political authorities also benefited, since many inscriptions detail the specific involvement of officials. Above all, their epigraphic transaction records acknowledged the current monarch's reign, as a statement of local political submission if not networked partnership.

By the eleventh century Tiruvorriyur was a complex urban center, with several residential neighborhoods (*perunderu*) that by then surrounded the Tiruvorriyur temple. One was the urban space delegated to those who tended temple livestock, another was the residence of the sculptors and artisans who worked on temple restorations and new temple additions, and the third was inhabited by merchants and weavers who were members of the newly incorporated Tiruvorriyur *nagaram*. The creation and existence of the *nagaram* reflects Tiruvorriyur's new urban stature, as also the evolution of the local *kottam* commercial exchange network, which could now and required a designated commercial center. The resident merchants brokered major temple financial transactions, and connected the local community to Kancipuram and other external primary centers of regional trade. That weaving specialists were residents indicates that the Tiruvorriyur temple and its community were sufficiently large to support a resident community of full-time weavers rather than depending on imported textiles to supply local demand. A non-urban resident *brahmadeya* suburban area and two rural *ur* in the local *kottam* had a continuing linkage with the temple, and as in the pre-urban era were still the recipients of sizeable cash and gold endowments in payment for their supply of agricultural products to the temple.

Eventually the Tiruvorriyur temple controlled the resources of 10 rural *devadana* agricultural communities and substantial income rights to lands in over 20 distant locales. Tiruvorriyur also prospered due to its enhanced role as a networked subsidiary center of Cola political authority, and as the continuing beneficiary of Cola monarchs and their loyal subordinates who were instrumental in financing significant reconstruction and expansion of the temple and its compound.

The epigraphic evidence conclusively demonstrates the continuing creation and defining of Tiruvorriyur's urban space and an evolving urban-rural relationship during the Cola era. The remaining temple inscriptions provide the details relative to the movement of commodities and people. They document Tiruvorriyur's evolution into a pluralistic community inclusive of resident priests, artisans, merchants, herdsmen, and agriculturalists, with a regular mix of itinerant pilgrims and other diverse visitors. While Tiruvorriyur had become an urban center of note, it still retained its rural roots and local accountabilities, as represented in its continuing institutionalized interactions with adjacent *brahmadeya* and *ur* agriculturalists and the failure of its *nagaram* merchants to associate with the powerful itinerant merchant associations of that age. In contrast, Tiruvorriyur's inscriptions also record the community's multi-dimensional external networking with Kancipuram and other primary regional political, economic, and religious centers of that age. In sum, Tiruvorriyur is representative of other single-temple towns that evolved into pluralistic urban centers during the era of Cola rule, and its epigraphic records document the wider secondary urbanism and networked and hierarchical urbanism (Morillo 2008) that was coincident to and the consequence of Cola sovereignty.

NOTES

ABBREVIATIONS

ARE – *Annual Reports on Epigraphy*, Archaeological Survey of India.
EI – *Epigraphica Indica*. Archeological Survey of India.
SII – *Annual Reports on South Indian Epigraphy/ South Indian Inscriptions*. Archaeological Survey of India.
Inscriptions listed by number and year of collection.

1. Heitzman cautions that even the so-called primary urban centers of the Cola age numbered no more than 1,000 residents. Thus population density was a marginal factor in the creation of productive space in a Cola-era urban center (Heitzman 1997: 114).
2. In the south Indian inscriptions *nagaram* has multiple meanings. In some instances it identified collective communities that were inclusively composed of those who derived their income from commercial activity (e.g., merchants, artisans, and their dependents, who might be cross-referenced as *nagaratar*); in other instances it was more specific in reference to merchants, notably merchant elites, who were members of a *nagaram* corporate administrative assembly, which had administrative authority over the wider *nagaram* community and the *nagaram* marketplace. *Nagaram* was also referential to a designated and legally incorporated space, whether a commercial "quarter" within a larger city or an inclusive and freestanding urban center (Hall 1975, Hall 1980).
3. As described, *brahmadeya* rural communities were controlled by those of Brahman ritual stature in the Indian caste hierarchy. Their origin was associated with assignments of income rights to subsidize the expenses and ritual activities of distinguished Brahman ritual specialists and temples. *Brahmadeya* were frequently "temple lands," or associated with those of Brahman caste stature who were actively engaged as priests. But they were also subject to Brahman landholders who actively engaged in cultivation, or supervised the cultivation of their dependent landed tenants. Historians debate their origin in south

India, but generally agree that they were a creation of the unsettled post-Gupta age when a number of Brahmans migrated to south India, where local political elite patronized them and their Hindu religious tradition, and provided them assignments of income rights to previously uncultivated lands these income entitlements were in exchange for their bringing prior borderlands under cultivation—to the Brahmans' and their monarch patron's mutual economic and political benefit. This is also seen as variously empowering Brahmans to the disadvantage of prior non-Brahman residents, who were associated with the rival *ur* village assemblies (Stein 1980; Karashima 1984).

4. Raman (1959: 196) suggests that though the offending goddess's icon, a remnant of earlier animism, was destroyed she was still worshipped locally. Similarly, the implementation of a Bhakti Saivite sect did not necessarily end the local tradition of sacrificial rituals. David Lorenzen (1972) traces the eleventh- through thirteenth-century development of the Kalmukha (Kalamukha) Saivite ascetic sect, which was a south Indian outgrowth of the *Pasupata*, considered the earliest Hindu sect to worship Siva as the supreme divinity. Due to the large number of epigraphic records recording donations to Kalamukha temples and monastic compounds (*mathas*) in Karnataka, Lorenzen concludes that these ascetics must have had considerable influence in the northern- and western-south Indian regions of Cola sovereignty. Kalamukha ("black faced"), who marked their foreheads with a black streak, were closely related to contemporary ascetic *Kapalikas*, "skull-bearers/bearers of the skull-bowl" and esoteric worshippers of Tantric Buddhism, as these groups collectively employed the imagery of death and cannibalism in their rituals. The Kalamukha sect derives from its association with Lord Bhairava, the fierce (Tantric) manifestation of Siva associated with annihilation, who vowed to cut off one of Lord Brahma's five heads in retribution for Brahma's unjustified claim to have supremacy over Siva (thus Brahma was thereafter depicted in iconography as four-headed). Consequently Lord Bhairava became an outcast and beggar, who, wearing only a garland of skulls and ash from a funeral pyre, frequented cremation grounds and marginally settled borderlands and wastelands (as highly appropriate to the sect's association with the expansive Cola state's incorporation of its prior frontiers). Remnants of the sect may be found in contemporary

Tamil Saivite cults that worship the goddesses Ankalaparamecuvari, Irulappasami, and Sudalai Madan. Each of these cults is known to have historically practiced ritual cannibalism, and still center their rituals around a ritual object known as a *kapparai*, "skull-bowl," representative of Siva's (Lord Bhairava's) begging bowl, decorated with a flower garland and the faces of the dead. K.A. Nilakanta Sastri, a conservative Brahman, negatively characterized Cola-era Tiruvorriyur Tantric Saivism in his classic study of Cola-era history (1935: 648–49), as its syncretic cult was in his view inconsistent with his own commitment to mainstream non-Tantric Brahman ritual tradition. Subsequent to the Cola era, followers of Tiruvorriyur's Pasupata Saivism worshipped Siva as the "Lord of Cattle" and "Lord of Souls," wherein Siva was the supreme cause of personal existence and the human soul (Raman 1959: 196–97).

REFERENCES

Abraham, Meera. 1988. *Two Medieval Merchant Guilds of South India*. New Delhi: Manohar.

Bourdieu, Pierre. 1977. *Outline of a Theory of Practice*. Cambridge: Cambridge University Press.

Castells, Manuel. 1978. *City, Class, and Power*. New York: St. Martins Press.

———. 2000. *The Rise of the Network Society*. Cambridge, MA: Blackwell.

Champakalakshmi, R. 1996. *Trade, Ideology, and Urbanization: South India 300 BC to AD 1300*. New Delhi: Oxford University Press.

Cohn, Bernard S. and McKim Marriott. 1958. "Networks and Centres in the Integration of Indian Civilization." *Journal of Social Research* (Ranchi) 1: 1–9.

Foucault, Michel. 1986. "Of Other Spaces." *Diacritics* (Spring): 22–27.

Gros, Francois and R. Nagaswamy. 1970. *Uttaramerur, Legends, Histoire, Monuments*. Pondichery: Institut fransais d'Indologie.

Hall, Kenneth R. 1975. "The *Nagaram* as a Marketing Center in Early Medieval South India." PhD dissertation, University of Michigan.

———. 1980. *Trade and Statecraft in the Age of the Colas*. Delhi: Abhinav.

———. 1982. "Peasant State and Society in Cola Times: A View from the Tiruvidaimarudur Urban Complex." *Indian Economic and Social History Review* 18, nos. 3–4: 393–410.

Hall, Kenneth R. 2001a. "Merchants, Rulers, and Priests in an Early South Indian Sacred Center: Cidambaram in the Age of the Colas." In *Structure and Society in Early South India,* ed. Kenneth R. Hall, 59–116, New Delhi: Oxford University Press.

———. 2001b. "Structural Change and Societal Integration in Early South India: An Introductory Essay." In *Structure and Society in Early South India,* ed. Kenneth R. Hall, 1–27.

———. ed. 2008. *Secondary Cities and Urban Networking in the Indian Ocean Realm, c. 1400-1800.* Lanham, MD: Lexington Press/Rowman and Littlefield.

Hall, Kenneth R. and George W. Spencer. 1980. "The Economy of Kancipuram: A Sacred Center in Early South India." *Journal of Urban History* 6, no. 2: 127–51.

Hayden, Dolores. 1995. *The Power of Place: Urban Landscapes as Public History*. Cambridge, MA: MIT Press.

Heitzman, James. 1997. *Gifts of Power: Lordship in an Early Indian State.* New Delhi: Oxford University Press.

———. 2001. "Urbanization and Political Economy in Early South India: Kancipuram During the Cola Period." In *Structure and Society in Early South India,* ed. Kenneth R. Hall, 117–56.

———. 2008. "Secondary Cities and Spatial Templates in South India, 1300–1800." In *Secondary Cities and Urban Networking in the Indian Ocean Realm, c. 1400–1800,* ed. Kenneth R. Hall, 303–34. Lanham, MD: Lexington Press/Rowman and Littlefield.

Kaimal, Padma. 1996. "Early Cola Kings and 'Early Cola Temples': Art and the Evolution of Kingship." *Artibus Asiae* 56, nos. 1–2: 33–66.

Karashima, Noboru. 1984. *South Indian History and Society*. New Delhi: Oxford University Press.

Lefebvre, Henri. 1991. *The Production of Space*, trans. Donald Nicholson-Smith. Oxford: Oxford University Press.

Lorenzen, David N. 1972. *The Kapalikas and Kalamukhas, Two Lost Saivite Sects.* Australian National University Centre of Oriental Studies, Oriental Monograph Series, no. 12. New Delhi: Thomson Press.

Mauss, Marcel. 1967. *The Gift: The Form and Reason for Exchange in Archaic Societies*, trans. W. D. Halls. New York: Norton.

Morillo, Stephen. 2008. "Autonomy and Subordination: The Cultural Dynamics of Small Cities." In *Secondary Cities and Urban Networking in the Indian Ocean Realm*. ed. Kenneth R. Hall, 17–37.

Nagaswamy, R. and Abdul Majeed. 1979. *Tiruttani and Velanceri Copper Plates*. Madras: State Department of Archeology, Tamil Nadu.

Nilakanta Sastri, K.A. [1935] 1955. *The Colas*. Madras: University of Madras.

———. 1963. *Development of Religion in South India*. Madras: Orient Longman.

Ogura, Yasushi. 1999. "The Changing Concept of Kingship in the Cola Period: Royal Temple Constructions, c. AD 850–1279." In *Kingship in Indian History*, ed. Noboru Karashima, 119–41. Delhi: Manohar.

Orr, Leslie C. 2001. "Women in the Temple, the Palace, and the Family: The Construction of Women's Identities in Pre-Colonial Tamilnadu." In *Structure and Society in Early South India*, ed. Kenneth R. Hall, 198–234.

Polanyi, Karl, Conrad M. Arensberg, and Harry W. Pearson, eds. 1957. *Trade and Market in the Early Empires*. Glencoe, IL: Free Press.

Prasad, Om Prakash. 1989. *Decay and Revival of Urban Centers in Medieval South India (c. AD 600–1200)*. New Delhi: Commonwealth Publishers.

Raman, K.V. 1959. *The Early History of the Madras Region*. Madras: Amudha Nilayam Private Limited.

Sahlins, Marshall. 1972. *Stone Age Economics*. Chicago: Aldine.

Skinner, G. William. 1964. "Marketing and Social Structure in Rural China: Part I." *Journal of Asian Studies* 23, no. 5: 3–43

Stein, Burton. 1977. "Circulation and the Historical Geography of Tamil Country." *Journal of Asian Studies* 37: 7–26.

———. 1980. *Peasant State and Society in Medieval South India*. Delhi: Oxford University Press.

Trautmann, Thomas R., Richard D. Saran, Peter A. Granda, and Armgard Ruckert. 1985. "The Study of South Indian Inscriptions." In *Studies of South India: An Anthology of Recent Research and Scholarship*, ed. Robert E. Frykenberg and Pauline Kolenda, 1–29. Madras: New Era.

Wright, Gwendolyn and Paul Rabinow. 1982. "Spatialization of Power: A Discussion of the Work of Michel Foucault." *Skyline* (March): 14–20.

14

Will the Winner Please Stand Up

Conflicting Narratives of a Seventeenth-Century Philosophical Debate from Karnataka

MADHAV M. DESHPANDE

In medieval times, the competing traditions of Advaita Vedānta and Dvaita Vedānta in South India produced a plethora of works rejecting the claims of the opponents. The titles of such works containing violent descriptions like breaking, smashing, uprooting and denouncing the views of the other give us a sense of how hot these debates/disputes became. Some detailed accounts of particular debates have come down to us. In this essay, I will discuss the multiple accounts of a philosophical debate that occurred in Ikkeri at the early seventeenth-century court of the Nāyaka king Veṅkaṭappā between the Advaitin court scholar Raṅgojibhaṭṭa (younger brother of the well-known grammarian Bhaṭṭoji Dīkṣita) and his opponent, a Dvaitin scholar named Vidyādhīśa. The disputants and their followers produced varying accounts, each claiming to have won the debate and defeated the other. Though we ultimately remain in doubt as to who the "real" winner was, the material shows how such debates were represented by the various schools to their own audiences.

The Sanskrit grammarian Bhaṭṭoji Dīkṣita and his family as well as his scholarly lineage were engaged in some hot disputes raging between the Advaitins and the Dvaitins in the region of Karnataka. Bambardekar (1939: 161) says that, at the beginning of a work titled *Tantrasiddhāntadīpikā*, Bhaṭṭoji offers salutations to his guru Appayya Dīkṣita:

> *appayyadīkṣitendrān aśeṣavidyāgurūn ahaṃ vande /*
> *yatkṛtibodhābodhau vidvadavidvadbhājakopādhī //*

[I salute the great Appayya Dīkṣita, my Guru in all the branches of learning. Knowledge and ignorance of his works determines who is learned and who is ignorant.]

The virulent disputes between Advaitins and Dvaitins seem to have begun with Appayya Dīkṣita's critique of the Mādhva Vedānta in his works *Madhvatantramukhamardana*, "Smacking the Face of the Mādhva System," and *Madhvamatavidhvaṃsana*, "Demolishing the Views of Madhva" (Appayya Dīkṣita 1940). Appayya's criticisms were answered by his contemporary Mādhva scholar Vijayīndra in his work *Madhvādhvakaṇṭakoddhāra*, "Removing Thorns from the Path of Madhva." Vijayīndra is also said to have composed another work critical of Appayya Dīkṣita, namely *Appayyakapolacapeṭikā*, "Slap on the Cheek of Appayya." Similarly, Vijayīndra's *Bhedavidyāvilāsa*, "Beauty of the Doctrine of Difference," is a critique of Nṛsiṃhāśrama's *Bhedadhikkāra*, "Denunciation of the Doctrine of Difference." The anti-Appayya trend continues in the Mādhva tradition with works like Nārāyaṇācārya's *Advaitakālānala*, "Deadly Fire for Advaita," and Satyanātha Yati's *Abhinavagadā*, "New Mace [to Crush Advaita]." Describing this last work, B.N.K. Sharma (1961: 233) says, "The work has five chapters designated 'yuddhas' (battles) with an obvious allusion to the Gadā-yuddha between Bhīma and Suyodhana. The intensely bellicose attitude of the author is reflected even in the opening verse."[1]

At the beginning of his *Madhvatantramukhamardana*, Appayya Dīkṣita's says:

madhvatantramukhamardanam mayā yat kṛtaṃ
prakaraṇaṃ mitākṣaram //
padyarūpam anatisphuṭāśayaṃ tat sukhāvagatayevivicyate /

[I composed the text *Madhvatantramukhamardana* as a short treatise in verse. The significance of that text was not self-evident, and hence I am clarifying its meaning in the present work *Madhvamatavidhvaṃsana.*]

Appayya's disciple Bhaṭṭoji Dīkṣita composed an Advaitic work titled *Tattvakaustubha*, "The Jewel of Truth," where, following his teacher, he severely criticizes the Mādhva Vedānta.[2] Bhaṭṭoji Dīkṣita, in his grammatical work *Prauḍhamanoramā*, also disagreed with the views of Śeṣakṛṣṇa, his teacher in grammar, who happened to be a Mādhva Vedānta scholar. Enraged by Bhaṭṭoji's disrespect for his teacher Śeṣakṛṣṇa, Jagannātha, another disciple in the tradition of Śeṣakṛṣṇa, severely attacked Bhaṭṭoji's *Prauḍhamanoramā* in his commentary titled *Prauḍhamanoramākucamardinī*, "Crushing the Breasts of *Prauḍhamanoramā*" (included in the 1934 edition of *Prauḍhamanoramā*, Haridas Sanskrit Series, no. 23). Jagannātha was also an opponent of Bhaṭṭoji's Vedāntic teacher Appayya Dīkṣita. Jagannātha's use of "*mardinī*" in the title of his work is a direct rebuke to Bhaṭṭoji, but by evoking Appayya Dīkṣita's *Madhvatantramukhamardana*, it is an indirect rebuke to Appayya as well. It is pay back using the same abusive language.

More details are provided by Kauṇḍabhaṭṭa, son of Bhaṭṭoji's brother Raṅgojibhaṭṭa, at the beginning of his [*Bṛhat*] *Vaiyākaraṇabhūṣaṇa* (1900: 1, verse 4):

pāṇinyādimunīn praṇamya pitaraṃ raṅgojibhaṭṭābhidham /
dvaitadhvāntanivāraṇādiphalikāṃ puṃbhāvavāgdevatām //
ḍhuṇḍhiṃ gautamajaiminīyavacanavyākhyātṛbhir dūṣitān /
siddhāntān upapattibhiḥ prakaṭaye teṣāṃ vaco dūṣaye //,

[I salute Pāṇini and the other Munis, my father Raṅgojibhaṭṭa, who is none other than the Goddess of Speech (Sarasvatī) in male form who rewards with the removal of the darkness of the doctrine of Dvaita Vedānta, and Gaṇeṣa. I will expound with justification the established grammatical theories that were found fault with by the commentators on the works of Gautama and Jaimini, and I will indicate problems in their arguments.]

Kauṇḍabhaṭṭa gives a full account of what is happening in the world of the Navya grammarians, who their immediate opponents are, and what they must do in order to keep their own head high in the midst of this free-for-all philosophical debate. Tensions were particularly high between the Bhaṭṭoji-family and the followers of Rāmacandra's *Prakriyākaumudī*, according to Kauṇḍabhaṭṭa. Bhaṭṭoji's brother Raṅgoji, his nephew Kauṇḍabhaṭṭa, as well as scholars in his scholastic tradition like Nāgeṣabhaṭṭa, were staunch defenders of the Advaita-Vedānta, while the Śeṣa family, to which Rāmacandra and Bhaṭṭoji's teacher Śeṣakṛṣṇa belonged, remained a staunch defender of the Dvaita-Vedānta. Rāmacandra himself composed a Dvaita work titled *Vaiṣṇavasiddhāntasaddīpikā*, and his lineage remained committed to the Dvaita Vedānta.

On the contrary, the final verses of Kauṇḍabhaṭṭa's *[Bṛhad] Vaiyākaraṇabhūṣana* (1900: 325) offer a salutation to his father Raṅgojibhaṭṭa and say that he defeated a Mādhva scholar named Vidyādhīśavaḍeru and that he demolished the *siddhānta* of the Mādhva Vedānta. P.K. Gode (1956: 210) says, "We have to presume that Veṅkaṭappa Nāyak or Keladi Veṅkaṭayya who ruled at Ikkeri in AD 1623–24 may have continued his rule up to AD 1629. Very probably Raṅgojibhaṭṭa defeated in a debate the Mādhva ascetic 'Vaḍeru' at the court of this Veṅkaṭappa Nāyak of Ikkeri sometime prior to AD 1629." A lost work titled *Madhvasiddhāntabhañjanī* is attributed to Raṅgojibhaṭṭa, and it is possible that this work may have dealt with his debate with the Mādhva scholar at Ikkeri. Kauṇḍabhaṭṭa describes his father Raṅgoji as being at the helm of those scholars who are in full control of the systems of grammar, Mīmāṃsā, and Nyāya.[3] Kauṇḍabhaṭṭa says that, having defeated the Mādhva scholar Vidyādhīśa at the Ikkeri court of king Veṅkaṭa, Raṅgojibhaṭṭa received a gift of a palanquin from the king, and that he demolished the doctrines of the Mādhvas.[4] If only the works of

Bhaṭṭoji, Raṅgoji, and Kauṇḍabhaṭṭa are consulted, one gets a clear sense that they were the winners in the debates against the Mādhva scholars, and one would never think that others might believe they were defeated by the Mádhvas.

In contrast, B.N.K. Sharma (1961: 268–69) refers to Mādhva sources that describe this encounter of Raṅgoji with Vidyādhīśa, saying the "Mādhva sources, on the other hand, state that the victory was on the side of Vidyādhīśa. There is no doubt that there was a meeting between the two." The hagiographical work *Śrīvidyādhīśavijaya* of Janārdanasūri (1926: 63ff.) describes the three-month long debate between the two. Janārdana describes Raṅgoji as a demon (*danuja*) born in the garb of a Brahman, barking like a dog at his opponent. They hurled many weapons at each other during the debate. Sharma (1961: 268–69, 271, 297) also refers to the existence of a short tract titled *Raṅgojibhaṭṭadhikkāra* in the possession of K.T. Pandurangi, which indicates the heat of the debate between the parties involved, as well as a work titled *Bhaṭṭojikuṭṭanam* by Kuṇḍalagirisūri that refuted Bhaṭṭoji's *Advaitakaustubha*. These interactions indicate the intensity of Bhaṭṭoji's debates on Vedāntic topics. R. Nagaraja Sarma, in the introduction to his edition of Raghūttamayati's *Bhāvabodha*, interestingly refers to three distinct Mādhva works with the same title, i.e., *Bhaṭṭojikuṭṭana*, composed by Vijayīndra, Kuṇḍalagiri, and Calāri Narasiṃhācārya. Sarma remarks (1956: xxxvii), "It is transparent that Vijayīndra's *Bhaṭṭojikuṭṭana* should have been the first and supplied necessary inspiration to all subsequent attempts made by others under the same title. The latest reply to Bhaṭṭoji Dīkṣita has been written by Mahāmahopādhyāya Vyākaraṇa Setumādhavācārya (Retd. Principal, Tirupati Venkateswara Sanskrit College)." This last work of Setumadhavācārya (1957), an extensive refutation of the *Tattvakaustubha* under the title *Tattvakaustubhakuliśa*, was edited by Ramamurti Sarma and published from Tirupati.

Regarding the identity of Raṅgoji's opponent in debate, P.K. Gode (1956: 110) says, "Possibly this Mādhva ascetic named

'Vaḍeru' belonged to the Vaiṣṇava Maṭh of the Sārasvata Brahmins at Partagali in the Cancon division of Goa." Here is what we know about Vidyādhīśa from traditional hagiographies. Vidyādhīśa was the sixteenth pontiff of the Uttarādi Maṭha of the Mādhva tradition, where his image is still enshrined, from 1619 to 1631. He was born in a small town called Punatambe in Maharashtra in the Pandurangi family. His original name was Narasiṃhācārya, son of Ānanda Bhaṭṭāraka. He studied the śāstras under his father. He became a great young scholar in Nyāya, Mīmāṃsā, Vyākaraṇa and Vedānta when he was just sixteen years old. He started teaching these śāstras at the Trivikrama temple in Puṇyastambhapura (Punatambe). He defeated Śivapaṇḍita and Viśvapaṇḍita in a debate in Vyākaraṇa. Similarly he defeated Goliṅgapaṇḍita in Nyāya and Tānabhaṭṭa in Śrautasūtras. There are many stories of his travels and debates with different scholars of various scholarly backgrounds. He was given Sannyāsa by Vedavyāsatīrtha, made his successor for the position of abbot at Uttarādi Maṭha, and named Śrī Vidyādhīśa Tīrtha. With the blessings of his Guru, Śrī Vidyādhīśa Tīrtha undertook a tour of various parts of north and south India, and afterwards went to Uḍipi. From Uḍipi he is said to have gone to Ikkeri and defeated Raṅgojibhaṭṭa in a philosophical debate. The event of this debate is recorded by Kauṇḍabhaṭṭa in his work [*Bṛhat*] *Vaiyākaraṇabhūṣaṇasāra* in the closing verses as referred to earlier, although Kauṇḍabhaṭṭa claims that it was Raṅgoji who won the debate. On the other hand, the Mādhva tradition has preserved a text ascribed to Vidyādhīśa titled *Raṅgojibhaṭṭadhikkāra*, where Vidyādhīśa provides some first-hand details about his debate with Raṅgojibhaṭṭa.

RAṄGOJIBHAṬṬADHIKKĀRA, "CONDEMNATION OF RAṄGOJIBHAṬṬA"

In my communication with Professor K.T. Pandurangi of Bangalore, I learned that he had a copy of *Raṅgojibhaṭṭadhikkāra* in his personal collection, and during my visit to him in January

2007 he gave me a photocopy of his manuscript. I also learned that Professor Pandurangi belongs to the same family as Vidyādhīśa, the author of this rare work, and that he had edited a collection of narrative texts describing the life and encounters of Vidyādhīśa with Raṅgojibhaṭṭa and others (Pandurangi 1987). In the *Raṅgojibhaṭṭadhikkāra* manuscript we have a unique view of the debate between Raṅgojibhaṭṭa and Vidyādhīśa, both in the words of Vidyādhīśa himself, as well as in the words of his followers and opponents. While the first folio of the manuscript is unfortunately missing, on the existing folio (1) we find the following colophon:

> *iti śrīmad-veda-vyāsatīrtha-pūjyapādānāṃ śiṣyeṇa śrī-vidyādhīśa-yatinā viracite raṅgojibhaṭṭadhikkāre prathamaḥ paricchedaḥ* ||

[Thus ends the first chapter in the Rejection of Raṅgojibhaṭṭa composed by the ascetic Vidyādhīśa, the disciple of the highly honored Vedavyāsatīrtha.]

Folio (1) also gives us some idea of the first topic of debate between these two individuals. Apparently, Raṅgojibhaṭṭa claimed that dying in Banaras was sufficient in itself to lead to Mokṣa for a person (*kāśīmaraṇamātreṇa mokṣaḥ*). Vidyādhīśa on the other hand, rejected Raṅgojibhaṭṭa's view, and asserted that only true knowledge leads to Mokṣa (*jñānasya eva mokṣasādhanatā*). Vidyādhīśa claimed that while his view was supported by passages from Śruti (Vedic texts) and Yukti (logic), Raṅgojibhaṭṭa's claims, on the other hand, were contradicted by such "evidence" and were merely based on his own imagination. For this reason, Raṅgojibhaṭṭa's first claim was based purely on a complete misunderstanding of the position of others as well as of his own position.[5]

The text of *Raṅgojibhaṭṭadhikkāra* continues in this vein till the end of the fourth chapter. Such a debate in itself would not be uncommon in the history of sectarian debates, and we can find many dozens of similar instances. However, what follows the end of the fourth chapter in the manuscript (folio 7) is an account from Vidyādhīśa of the actual events of his debates and disputes with Raṅgojibhaṭṭa. This portion, for me, is historically the most significant part of the manuscript:

> *svaśiṣyajanāvalokaneccchayā ikkerigrāme prasthinān asmāṃs tatratyanāyako vidvattvābhimāne sati raṅgojībhaṭṭena saha prasaṅgārthaṃ bhavadbhiḥ prasthāya matsamīpam āgantavyam ity āhvayat* |

[When we [Vidyādhīśa] had set out to go to the town of Ikkerī to visit our disciples, the ruler of that locality issued the following invitation, "If you have pride in your learning, then you should come to me [my court] for a debate with Raṅgojibhaṭṭa."]

> *vijigīṣuvādiprativādyupanyastasvasvābhimataprameya-sādhakayuktisadasattvaniraṇyakartrūbhayasiddhāntābhijña-prāśnikābhāve prasaṅgasya kolāhalamātraparyavasānena svābhimataphalāsiddhyā bhavatsamīpe tādṛśaprāśnikā-bhāvāt bhavadviduṣaḥ prasaṅge lālasatve tādṛśānekaprāśni-kopetacolamaṇḍalādideśaviśeṣaprasthānam eva āvayor nyāyyam iti svakīyavidvān api asmatsahāyena deśāntaraṃ preṣaṇīya ity asmābhiḥ sūttarite 'pi bhavadasmadīyavidvat-saṃskṛtaprayogacāturīnibhālanajanyakautukamā-trecchuṃ prati naitādṛśaparyanuyogaḥ samucita iti naḥ pralobhya samīpam upāyatān sambhāvya asmadupakṣiptaprameye svakīyaviduṣo dūṣaṇa-bhūṣaṇāśaktisambhāvanayā svayam eva ādau kāśīmaraṇamātrasya na mokṣasādhanatvam api tu brahmajñānasyaiva ity eteṣām matam ity upākṣipat* |

[We responded to the king saying, "in the absence of a competent judge to preside over the debate, a judge who is expert in both the competing doctrines and one who is fully capable of deciding the right and false arguments offered by the contenders in the debate desiring to win such a debate, a mere occasion of debate is likely to result in just a shouting match, and this will not lead to what we desire to achieve. Since at your court there [is] no such judge for the debate, if the scholar at your court [Raṅgojibhaṭṭa] does indeed desire such a debate, he should be sent along with us to the Chola region, where many such judges are available." Even after we properly responded like this, the king said, "Please, such a rejection of my request is not appropriate. I am merely interested in watching the intellectual skill in the Sanskrit debate between you and our scholars." Having thus lured us into his court, when we got there, realizing the inability of his own court scholars to find faults with the position presented by us, he himself said that the position of the visiting scholar is that death in Kāśī alone does not lead to Mokṣa, but that knowledge of Brahman alone leads to Mokṣa.]

The manuscript relates some discussion of this question of the effect of death in Kāśī, then proceeds onward:

> *etat prameyam parityajya asmadudbhāvitām asaṅgatim api nāyakapakṣapātabalena avagaṇayya utkrānter jñānaphalatvābhāvarūpam prameyāntaram pratijñāviṣayatvena agrahīt* | *tadīyabalātkāravaśena tatraikoktayuktijātasvarūpaṃ tanmudritapatrapratinidhipatrād avagantavyam* | … *ity asmābhir ukte 'pi* … *ity ārabhya svayam eva likhitaṃ svakīyāsmadīyayuktijātabodhakalipikulaṃ svanāyakānumatim āpādya asmadananumatāv api kuṇḍalikākāreṇa vyatītaśat* | *tadanantaram uttaradivase* … *pūrvāṅgīkṛtavādakathātvaṃ parityajya jalpakathātvam aṅgīkṛtya nāyakapakṣapātena samayabandham akārayat* |

[Then having abandoned this first position, and after disregarding the contradictions pointed by us, with the support of the ruler, he [Raṅgojibhaṭṭa] moved on to another position as the topic for debate—is transmigration a result of knowledge, or not? The nature of the arguments we presented there under these forced circumstances can be seen from the documents with the ruler's seal and other representative documents (*pratinidhipatra*?).... Even after we objected, with the consent of the ruler and without our consent, he [Raṅgojibhaṭṭa] falsified the arguments presented by us and by him in writing by circling those portions. Then, next day, with the support of the ruler, Raṅgojibhaṭṭa abandoned the (honest) Vāda mode of debate, and entered into a (destructive) Jalpa mode of debate, and appealed for a time-bound debate (*samayabandha*?).]

Vidyādhīśa's personal account of the debate with Raṅgojibhaṭṭa ends with this information, though the manuscript continues with the work of Keśava, a disciple of Vidyādhīśa, who persists in rejecting the claims of Raṅgojibhaṭṭa. In the colophon on folio 17, we see how Vidyādhīśa was perceived by his successors within his own tradition:

> *iti śrīmatsakalavidvaccakracūḍāmaṇīnāṃ śrīmadvidyādhīśatīrthapūjyapādānāṃ nijaśiṣyakeśavaviracitaḥ raṅgojīśiṣyavādīndra-bauddhadhikkāraḥ samāptaḥ*

[Thus ends the Condemnation of the [Crypto-] Buddhist, Vādīndra, disciple of Raṅgoji, composed by Keśava, a direct disciple of His Holy Feet, honorable teacher Vidyādhīśa, the crest jewel of the entire assembly of learned scholars.]

We have two subsequent narratives of the same event, found in the *Śrīvidyādhīśavijaya* of Janārdanasūri (1926), and in the *Śrīvidyādhīśacarita,* part of the larger work *Śrīpūrṇabodhaguruvaṃ-śakathākalpataru* composed by Daivajña Bhīma. The sixth sarga of Janārdanasūri's *Śrīvidyādhīśavijaya* (verses 32–49) contains poetically embellished accounts of Vidyādhīśa's debates with Raṅgojibhaṭṭa and Vādīndra. While Vidyādhīśa's own account seems to reflect a perception that the king Veṅkaṭappā of Ikkerī was already in favor of Raṅgojibhaṭṭa and ill-disposed toward Vidyādhīśa, the narrative of Janārdana seems to simply say that Vidyādhīśa was honored by the king of Ikkerī who was impressed with his fame, and that Vidyādhīśa stayed in Ikkerī happily,[6] until the debate with Raṅgoji came up. Raṅgoji is described as being a true demon dressed as a Brahman (*danujo 'vanidevaveṣabhṛt*), who acquired a deceptive form of language by worshipping the Ucchiṣṭa Gaṇapati (verse 34). In the king's assembly he would bark like a dog. But his logic was defeated by Vidyādhīśa, whose own logic seemed like the fierce dance of Tāṇḍava. Janārdana says that for three months the debaters kept on sending each other various written notes (verse 42; *likhitānyonyavicitrapatrikam*). This seems to be supported by Vidyādhīśa's own account in his *Raṅgojibhaṭṭadhikkāra*. Finally, Raṅgojibhaṭṭa is said to have run away, seeing the weakness of his own arguments (*ślathapakṣatayā adravat kṣaṇāt*, verse 44). Verse 45 of Janārdana clearly says that Raṅgojibhaṭṭa was defeated by Vidyādhīśa (*raṅgābhikhyaṃ nirjitya*). The next verse says that Raṅgojibhaṭṭa was caught by the soldiers of the king and brought to the village of Muṅgī to meet Vidyādhīśa (*narapatibhaṭakḷptākarṣaṇam*). There he fell at the feet of Vidyādhīśa (*pādanamram*), and was let go out of compassion (*yatipatir anukampāklinnacittaḥ atyajat tam*). After that Raṅgojibhaṭṭa is said to have left the region, with his pride shattered (*atyajat ... sapadi galitamānaḥ so 'pi taṃ deśam eva*, verse 46).

In the second account of Vidyādhīśa's encounter with Raṅgojibhaṭṭa, found in the *Śrīvidyādhīśacarita* (part of *Śrīpūrṇabodhaguruvaṃśakathākalpataru* composed by Daivajña Bhīma), we find a few further details of interest. An abbreviated version of this text is included in the *Aṇuvidyādhīśavijaya* edited by K.T. Pandurangi (1987). In Bidrur or Bednur (referred to in this text by the name Veṇupurī[7]), Vidyādhīśa had a debate with Raṅgojibhaṭṭa who had come from Kāśī (*kāśyāḥ samāgatam*). Here we have a location of debate different from Ikkeri, though still within the Keladi kingdom. After stating that Raṅgoji was defeated by Vidyādhīśa (*so 'tha vidyādhīśaiḥ parājitaḥ*), this account says that the scared Raṅgoji had run away to the town of Paiṭhaıa (*bhītyā palāyanaparāyaṇaḥ jagāma paiṭhaṇam*). Vidyādhīśa chased him to Paiṭhaṇa.[8] There, having defeated him, Vidyādhīśa took from Raṅgoji a jayapatra, a "document of victory" (*tatra jitvā māyivaraṃ jayapatram pragṛhya*). Vidyādhīśa's own account does not provide the details that Raṅgojibhaṭṭa ran away and was forced to yield a jayapatra to Vidyādhīśa. Conversely, Daivajña Bhīma's account does not say that this debate went on for three months. Vidyādhīśa's own account tells us that he was rather dissatisfied with the king constantly showing his favor to Raṅgojibhaṭṭa, and felt cheated by the invitation and the way the debate itself was conducted. Furthermore, he seems to indicate that the written reports and documents were falsified with the support of the king, and so finally Vidyādhīśa comes across more as an angry person, rather than someone who was accepted by everyone as a winner. Vidyādhīśa's followers, on the other hand, gradually changed the narrative conclusively in his favor and declared him a winner of the debate, a win certified apparently by the jayapatra extracted from Raṅgoji who was on the run.

The description of the debate provided by Kauṇḍabhaṭṭa stands in stark contrast with the one provided by Vidyādhīśa and his followers. Did Raṅgoji win the debate, and was he honored with a palanquin by the king of Ikkeri, as Kauṇḍabhaṭṭa reports, or did he run away from debate and was finally made to yield a jayapatra to Vidyādhīśa, as the accounts of Janārdana and Daivajña Bhīma seem to say? We have no conclusive way of deciding what exactly happened at the debate. However, the first-hand account coming from Vidyādhīśa himself expresses his misgivings about the invitation for debate and the way the debate was conducted, and claims that the king was in favor of Raṅgojibhaṭṭa from the very beginning and that written documents were falsified with the express support of the king. This would suggest that the debate probably ended in a stalemate of sorts, with each party claiming victory, and finding fault with the claims seen in written documents like the jayapatras. With the charge that the written documents were falsified, probably both sides were free to make statements that were contrary to what one might have found in the written documents, as the probative value of such documents was already discounted by the imputation of falsification. Thus, any possibility of verification is rejected out of hand, as all sources of information are tainted in some way, except one's own perception of what happened as seen in Vidyādhīśa's own words, and the perception of the followers about what must have happened. For the followers it is inconceivable that their hero could have been defeated at a debate. Positives from the received information are accentuated, and the negatives are discounted with disbelief. As we move away from the actual historical event to which we have no direct access, subsequent narratives coming from subsequent generations clearly depict the leading figures of their own lineage as the absolute victors in the debate, leaving no room for doubt. This evolving direction of the narratives away from the nuts and bolts of the historical happenings and into a realm of projected perfect victories is fascinating and instructive in helping us make a realistic assessment of all such received accounts.

NOTES

1. Sharma cites the verse (1961: 233):

   sadāpeye dīkṣitasya mṛdhe durabhimāninaḥ /
   pātayāmi śirasyadya gurvīm abhinavāṃ gadām.

2. I have consulted a manuscript of the *Tattvakaustubha* of Bhaṭṭoji Dīkṣita (Bhandarkar Oriental Research Institute ms. 319-A/1899–1915). Karl Potter's *Encyclopedia of Indian Philosophies*, Vol. I, p (1970: 283), cites Bhaṭṭoji Dīkṣita's *Tattvakaustubha* as being published by P. P. S. Shastri in *the Journal of the Sri Sankara Gurukulam, Sri Rangam*, vol. 3.10 (1941–42). However, this edition does not contain the complete text.
3. *iti śrīmatpadavākyapramāṇapārāvārīṇadhurīṇaraṅgojibhaṭṭātmajakoṇḍabhaṭṭakṛte vaiyākaraṇabhūṣaṇe* (Kauṇḍabhaṭṭa 1900: 325)
4. *vidyādhīśavaḍerusaṃjñakayatiśrīmādhvabhaṭṭārakaṃ /*
   jitvā kevalaveṅkaṭayyasavidhe 'py āndolikāṃ prāptavān //
   yaś cakre munivaryasūtravivṛtiṃ siddhāntabhaṅgaṃ tathā /
   mādhvānāṃ tam ahaṃ gurūpamaguruṃ raṅgojibhaṭṭaṃ bhaje //
   (Kauṇḍabhaṭṭa 1900: 325)
5. *śrutiyuktibādhitatvena ca svotprekṣitamātrasya asādhakatvāt |*
   tasmāt prathamam prameyaṃ tāvat
   svaparamatānavabodhavijṛmbhitam iti sthitam ||
6. *mahipena sa mānito 'nvahaṃ śravaṇāgantukitātmakīrtinā /*
   mudamāracayan manīṣiṇāṃ nyavasat tatra dināni kānicit //
   (Janardana 1926: verse 33).

7. For identification of Veṇupurī with Bidrur or Bednur, see B.N.K. Sharma (1961: 268). Sharma says that this place is within the territory of the Keladi kingdom.
8. The previous account (which claimed that Raṅgojibhaṭṭa was apprehended in Muṅgī village) may not be contradictory to this one. There is a village named Muṅgī very close to Paiṭhaṇa, just south of Aurangabad in Maharashtra. A treaty between the first Bajirao Peshwa and the Nizam was signed at Mungi-Paithan on March 6, 1728. So both accounts are likely to contain some grain of truth.

REFERENCES

Appayya Dīkṣita. 1940. *Madhvatantramukhamardana*, with commentary [*Madhvamata*] *Vidhvaṃsana*, ed. Ramacandra Sastri. Anandashrama Sanskrit Series, no. 113. Pune: Anandashrama Press.

Bambardekar, Vasudeo Anant. 1939. *Bhaṭṭojidīkṣitajñātiviveka*. Mumbai: published by the author.

Bhaṭṭoji Dīkṣita. 1928. *Prauḍhamanoramā*, with *Laghuśabdaratna* by Nāgeśabhaṭṭa (ascribed to Haridīkṣita on the title-page). 3 vols. Benares: Chowkhambha Sanskrit Series Office.

———. 1934. *Prauḍhamanoramā, Avyayībhāvānta*, with *Laghuśabdaratna* by Haridīkṣita, *Jyotsnā* by Jagannātha Śāstri, and *Kucamardinī* by Paṇḍitarāja Jagannātha, ed. Sadashiva Sharma Shastri. Banaras: Haridas Sanskrit Series, no. 23.

———. 1964. *Prauḍhamanoramā*, with *Bṛhacchabdaratna* by Haridīkṣita and *Laghuśabdaratna* by Nāgeśabhaṭṭa. *Vol. I, Avyayībhāvānta*, ed. Sitaram Shastri. Banaras: Hindu Vishwavidyalaya Nepal-Rajya Sanskrit Series, No. VIII.

———. 1966. *Prauḍhamanoramā* with commentary [*Bṛhat*]*Śabdaratna*. Vol. I., ed. V. L. Joshi. Deccan College Monograph Series, no 31. Pune: Deccan College.

Deshpande, Madhav M. Forthcoming. "Bhaṭṭoji DīkṣitaŸs Perceptions of Intellectual History: Narrative of Fall and Recovery of the Grammatical Authority." Professor Ashok Aklujkar Festschrift, Japan.

Gode, P.K. 1956. "The Chronology of the Works of Koṇḍabhaṭṭa." In *Studies in Indian Literary History*, Vol. 3, 207–11. Pune: Prof. P. K. Gode Collected Works Publication Committee

Janārdanasūri. 1926. *Śrīvidyādhīśavijaya*, ed. Rangacharya Reddi. Pune: Hanumanamudranalaye.

Kauṇḍabhaṭṭa. 1900. [*Bṛhat*] *Vaiyākaraṇabhūṣaṇa*, ed. Rama Krishna Sastri (alias Tatya Shastri Patavardhana). Banaras: Benares Sanskrit Series.

Lakṣmīnṛsiṃha. 1955. *Ābhogaḥ – Kalpataruvyākhyā*, ed. Polgam Rama Sastri and S. Subrahmanya Sastri. Madras Government Oriental Series, no. 128. Madras: Government Oriental Manuscripts Library.

Pandurangi, K.T., ed. 1987. *Aṇuvidyādhīśavijaya*. Sri Vidyadhisha Granthamala No. 1. Bangalore: K.T. Pandurangi.

Pollock, Sheldon. 2001. "New Intellectuals in Seventeenth-Century India." In *Indian Economic and Social History Review* 38, no. 1: 3–31.

———. 2002. "Introduction: Working Papers on Sanskrit Knowledge Systems on the Eve of Colonialism." *Journal of Indian Philosophy* 30: 431–39.

Potter, Karl H. 1970. *Encyclopedia of Indian Philosophies, Vol. 1: Bibliography*. Delhi: Motilal Banarsidass.

Raghūttamayati. 1956. *Bhāvabodhaḥ – Tattvaprakāśikāvyākhyā*, ed. R. Nagaraja Sarma. Madras Government Oriental Series, no. 142. Madras: Government Oriental Manuscripts Library.

Raṅgojibhaṭṭa. 1920. *Advaitacintāmaṇi*, ed. Narayana Sastri Khiste. Princess of Wales Sarasvati Bhavana Texts, no. 2. Benares: Govt. Sanskrit Library.

Sharma, B.N.K. 1961. *A History of the Dvaita School of Vedānta and its Literature*, Vol. 2. Mumbai: Bookseller's Publishing Co.

Setumadhavācārya, Srimushnam. 1957. *Tattvakaustubhakuliśa*, ed. Ramamurti Sarma. Tirupati: Tirumala Tirupati Devasthanam.

Swaminathan, K.D. 1957. *The Nayakas of Ikkeri*. Madras: P. Varadachary & Co.

Vidyādhīśa. n.d. *Raṅgojibhaṭṭadhikkāraḥ*. Photocopy of a manuscript in the personal collection of K.T. Pandurangi, Bangalore.

Tributes to Trautmann

15

Trautmann's Gift

Dravidian Kinship as Dana

TOM FRICKE

"The Dravidian kinship system has long exercised a special fascination on anthropology." One could say the same for the author of that sentence, appearing on the first page of a book straightforwardly named after the object of fascination itself and followed by an additional 468 pages of empirical investigations into kinship, linguistics, ethnography, and history, coupled with dense argument, two appendices, a comprehensive bibliography, and an index. Thomas Trautmann's "special fascination" began with a series of articles and chapters on the topic of consanguineous or cross-cousin marriage, in the early 1970s. It continued beyond the publication of *Dravidian Kinship* to an exploration of Lewis Henry Morgan, to whose work Tom was led as the first scholarly study of Indian kinship systems altogether. *Lewis Henry Morgan and the Invention of Kinship* appeared in 1987 to extend and make "good the shortcomings of my analysis of Morgan's kinship project in an earlier book," writes Tom in that later preface.

Among the pleasures of such threads and comment is evidence for the workings of a first-rate scholarly mind. Problems encountered by happenstance take hold. A trial essay or two emerges and before long, a sustained treatment. In Tom's case, two books and a large number of essays add up to a serious contribution to the study of kinship, a subject once occupying pride of place, since Morgan's "invention" in 1871, in history's sister discipline of anthropology. Tom's contributions, coming a century or so after Morgan's death, are a large part of his legacy and have brought him a significant reputation in his adopted discipline.

And yet, to all appearances, the 1981 publication of *Dravidian Kinship* could not have occurred at a more inauspicious moment in anthropological kinship studies. Where much of the energy and a better part of the élan of kinship studies until the 1970s had been either in the study of terminologies or the study of kinship as a way of organizing groups, the allure of these approaches had begun to fade. This was a moment of searching and reflection in anthropology perhaps best exemplified by the title of a 1984 book intended by its author David Schneider to put paid to these old approaches: *A Critique of the Study of Kinship*. To exaggerate just a bit, a good many of the problems in kinship studies had to do with the increasing move to abstraction, the formulation of universalizing and inevitably ethnocentric systems, and an attenuated concern for concrete and local meanings.

One of the little remarked upon features of *Dravidian Kinship* is how it, perhaps unintentionally (after all, the primary argument is concerned to show that those Indian and Sri Lankan kinship systems called Dravidian are all descendents of a single ancestral system that can be reconstructed using the combined resources of anthropology and history), anticipates so many of the features of the renewal of kinship studies. Little remarked upon but not so surprising since that renewal was another ten to fifteen years in the future. Still, a look at Tom's "massive work" (as Adrian Mayer wrote in his review) in the light of hindsight shows how the rejuvenation of a field may find its sources in classic problems.

Tom's book is certainly "massive," if by massive we also mean demonstrating an unnerving breadth and expertise in domains seldom combined in one intellect. It is also an unusual book that elicits an appreciative comment from even its most argumentative of reviewers, as Anthony Good finished with the confession "that I enjoyed it thoroughly, felt constantly challenged and compelled to make explicit my reasons for disagreement." Nearly all reviewers were quick to note its several contributions in such areas as method and the repairing of the rupture between anthropology and history. Sylvia Vatuk's summary comment may have said it best when she called it "a book that in its field is certainly one of a kind—in terms of scope, depth, and overall conception—and [one that] deserves to be widely read by historians, Sanskritists, linguists, anthropologists."

Or maybe it was the author himself who elicits the appreciation since all this good and true commentary leaves out those pleasures of the text found, for example, in such wry footnotes as the one on page 76 that summarily dismisses Jan Garret Held's 1935 *The Mahabharata: An Ethnological Study* as "a case of conjectural history run amok" and a book with "an influence quite astonishing in the face of its (richly deserved) obscurity." It's worth being reminded by Tom that erudite works like his own are not cheapened for making the reader smile.

To my own mind, the many specific contributions, such as the methodological, celebrated in those early reviews are overshadowed by the pervasive and underlying attitude that animates *Dravidian Kinship*. As I mentioned, kinship studies in anthropology was in a torpor of its own devising at about the time that Tom became engaged with these themes. Part of that torpor was the retreat from history initiated by A.R. Radcliffe-Brown, whose attacks on Morgan and all "conjectural history" lead "to a denial of the possibility of historical anthropology" (p. 74). The return to historical problems brought two significant contributions that intersect with later movements in the renewal of kinship studies.

First, by shaking loose the restrictions imposed by Radcliffe-Brown's orthodoxy, Tom liberated Lewis Henry Morgan's work from the antiquarian box to which it had been consigned. Instead of a remote ancestor, Morgan becomes a contemporary interlocutor deserving of the complex argument one would accord a contemporary. *Dravidian Kinship* is not to be taken as "a new departure. It is, rather, in the nature of taking up unfinished business" (p. 90). A part of that "unfinished business" was to return to kinship as a system of meanings—the semantic sense that was always a feature of Morgan's thinking, that is a central contribution in Tom's book, and that was to become a defining feature of the soon to come renewal in kinship studies.

That concern for meaning leads to the next contribution, that tonic return to concreteness that is so much a feature of *Dravidian Kinship*, distinguishing it from so much of the dreary abstraction to which kinship analysis had fallen. The book abounds with examples, but my favorite comes with the pivotal discussion of gift and exchange in the context of marriage. Tom's discussion fully merges what he calls the "sociology of reciprocity as [in] Marcel Mauss's masterwork on the gift" with what he calls the soteriology found in the Dharmashastra theory of the gift (p. 279). In so doing, it clarifies the conundrum of "two pairs of contrasting modes of exchange, sacred versus profane and noble versus ignoble" (p. 285) which, in their extension to marriage, go a long way toward explaining the paradox of hierarchies embedded within exchange systems that in the abstract structure lean toward reciprocity.

Here is where Tom's grasp of the empirical evidence and the theoretical models that help to make sense of it are fully displayed. When he writes that "The fourfold conceptualization of exchange implicates the social contract, the polity, religion, even the law of property. It implicates marriage as well" (p. 288), he anticipates subsequent developments that will reintegrate kinship as the study of relationship with other domains of social life. The ultimate concreteness is to bring kinship to its grounding in cultural conceptions of personhood and the moral as is accomplished in *Dravidian Kinship*. These are precisely the animating orientations of the new kinship studies that began its institutionalization in edited collections nearly twenty years later (for example, Janet

Carsten's *Cultures of Relatedness* in 2000 or Sarah Franklin and Susan McKinnon's *Relative Values* in 2001).

There are times in serious scholarship when the work produced becomes its own illustration of the examined subject. We can take comfort in seeing *Dravidian Kinship* as one of those works. Devoted in pivotal portions to the nature of "the gift" it becomes its own gift to its source disciplines of history and anthropology by using the concrete materials of India to breathe new life into old questions. These concrete materials enjoin us to look for "the peculiar Indianness of the *dāna* doctrine," as Tom writes in his discussion on page 280. As he extends that enquiry into Indianness, he addresses the six motives for gift-giving found in the *smṛti* of Devala—piety (*dharma*), material or political interest (*artha*), desire (*kāma*), shame (*vrīḍā*), pleasure (*harṣa*), and fear (*bhaya*). Although lost, these six motives are regularly quoted in medieval manuscripts and help to offer a distinctly Indian taxonomy for the purity and excellence of a gift. It's safe to say that Tom's motivation was of the highest quality, that of piety or *dharma*. But I would not be surprised to hear that he took great pleasure, too, in the giving.

16

The *Paramparas* of Trautmann

RICHARD H. DAVIS

Conferences and volumes of academic celebration lead me always to consider questions of intellectual lineage, or *parampara*. Through his decades of work with graduate and undergraduate students at the University of Michigan, and his mentoring and collegial work with faculty there, Thomas Trautmann has established a formidable *parampara*. I am not part of that direct lineage. The closest genealogical link I can claim is a kind of academic nephewship. Trautmann's adviser at the School of Oriental and African Studies, A.L. Basham, was advisor also to my first graduate advisor in South Asian history at the University of Toronto, Narendra Wagle. My primary lineage, however, runs through Ronald Inden at the University of Chicago, and I consider myself a *sisya* of the Chicago school of South Asian studies.

Intellectual currents do not only follow such neat streambeds, of course, and Trautmann's research and ideas, from his early work on Kautilya up through his recent investigations of the colonial-era Madras school, have exerted far-reaching influence generally within South Asian studies, and on me. This is particularly so with his study of the early British Orientalists based mostly in Calcutta and their successors, *Aryans and British India* (1997), a major exploration of the *parampara* that stands, for better or worse, at the foundation of all modern study of early Indian civilization. Dedicated to Trautmann's own *guru*, Basham, this intellectual history retraces the early work of William Jones and other late eighteenth-century enthusiasts for ancient India and the harsh response of evangelical and utilitarian critics like Charles Grant and James Mill in the early nineteenth century, and it explores the lingering consequences of their constructions of India. (Trautmann notes that Basham died in India, holding a fellowship from the Asiatic Society named for William Jones.) Trautmann frames his historical narrative around the antitheses of "Indomania" inspired by the discoveries of Jones and his cohorts at the Asiatic Society, and the "Indophobic" reactions of Grant, Mill, and their followers. In this narrative, Trautmann also traces the genealogy of what he calls the "racial theory of Indian civilization."

Lineage is relevant to my reading of *Aryans and British India*. When Trautmann's book first appeared, I read it in conscious juxtaposition to the work of my *guru*, Ron Inden, whose *Imagining India* (1990) had come out a few years earlier and had dealt with many of the same figures and issues. Rereading them both now, from the not-very-distant vantage of 2008–9, I can see both studies as significant, but very different, statements in the late twentieth-century rethinking of the history of Indology as an intellectual enterprise.

Imagining India was written shortly after the appearance of Edward Said's *Orientalism* (1978). I was a beginning graduate student at Chicago when *Orientalism* came out, and I can recall the excitement it provoked, with its lurid cover and its seeming promise to expose the underside of the academic discipline to which I was just committing myself. Inden's work owes part of its critical stance and its polemical style to Said and his redirection of a Foucaultian approach to the area of non-Western studies. Inden acknowledges this lineage in his introductory discussion of "Orientalist Discourse:"

> The discourse of orientalists, according to Edward Said (1978), presents itself as a form of knowledge that is both different from, and superior to, the knowledges that the Orientals have of themselves.... The knowledge of the orientalist is, therefore, privileged in relation to that of the Orientals, and it invariably places itself in a relationship of intellectual dominance over that of the Easterners. It has appropriated the power to represent the Orientals, to translate and explain his (or her) thoughts and acts not only to Europeans and Americans, but also to the Orientals themselves (1990: 37–38).

Inden goes on, in a Saidian manner, to argue that this claim to special knowledge is enmeshed in the operations of power: "to gain trade concessions, conquer, colonize, rule, and punish in the East" (1990: 38). The major portion of Inden's study consists in a thoroughgoing critique of the representations of India that the discourse of orientalists has generated, from the time of William Jones up to the present.

In one respect Inden's work should be seen in dialectical relation to an earlier generation of studies in the history of Indian studies that developed a celebratory narrative. The British Orientalists (here in the more narrow *soi-disant* usage) "discovered" India's great classical civilization and made it available as an object of knowledge and field of study both to the West and to modern Indians. If studies like Garland Cannon's *Oriental Jones* (1964) and David Kopf's *British Orientalism and the Bengal Renaissance* (1969) exemplify this thesis, Inden's study forms the antithesis. Inden saw his critique of Indology not as an end in itself, however, but as a necessary step to clear the way for a new historiography of India. We graduate students at Chicago referred to this, with both admiration and anxiety, as a "slash and burn" procedure. By shifting the presuppositions and assumptions of Indological discourse, Inden argued, it would become possible "to construct a picture of Hindu India that differs greatly from the ones we have inherited" (1990: 3), and one that would be better. The final section on the Rashtrakuta dynasty, entitled "Reconstructions," was intended to demonstrate how this different picture might appear, but this important coda has unfortunately been neglected by most readers.

If the celebratory and the deconstructive are the two poles of this Indological dialectic, I think of Trautmann's *Aryans and British India* as occupying the position of a synthesis. He values the scholarship of historians like Cannon and Kopf, but he does not seek to rehabilitate the narrative of pure discovery. He is certainly engaged with the issues raised by Said and Inden, and devotes a substantial portion of the Introduction and Conclusion to discussions of what he labels "Orientalism-2," but he shows no indication to continue their discursive agenda. Rather, Trautmann situates himself at a point where a new critical historiography of our Indological genealogy might begin. The result is a much more nuanced and contextual intellectual history of late eighteenth- and early nineteenth-century lineages of thought. In this account we hear about the crankier side of William Jones's scholarly agenda, such as his allegiance to the "Mosaic ethnology" which he adopted from the work of Jacob Bryant, along with his undoubted contributions to linguistic and Sanskritic learning. We see how the works of Indophobes developed in relation to other intellectual and political trends in England, and we even develop a measure of sympathy for James Mill, the hard-working journalist supporting a large family while working away at his mammoth *History of British India* on the side, angling for a better job with the East India Company.

I do not mean to imply that *Aryans and British India* occupies some toothless middle ground. Trautmann's work is also driven by an ideological agenda, and as with Inden's work there is a disciplinary reform in the field of South Asian studies behind it. His study aims to trace the etiology of a pernicious intellectual construct, and to remove it:

> By [nineteenth] century's end a deep and lasting consensus was reached respecting India, which I call the racial theory of Indian civilization: that India's civilization was produced by the clash and subsequent mixture

of light-skinned civilizing invaders (the Aryans) and dark-skinned barbarian aborigines (often identified as Dravidians). The racial theory of Indian civilization has proved remarkably durable and resistant to new information, and it persists to this day. It is the crabgrass of Indian history, and I should like to uproot it. (1997: 4)

This is a different approach than the ground-clearing in *Imagining India*. If the lawn of Indian historical study is infested with the intricate roots of racial crabgrass, then it requires the more careful, close-up activities of disentangling and yanking out roots to eradicate the problem. One hopes that the valuable grass will not be pulled out in the process. This is the kind of scrupulous, critical, and fair-minded narrative that Trautmann has produced in *Aryans and British India*.

When this book appeared in 1997, Trautmann was already deeply involved in another project, which forms a pair with his study of the scholarship on the Aryan idea. After several articles, the new work appeared in book form as *Languages and Nations: The Dravidian Proof in Colonial Madras* (2006). If *Aryans* is set largely in Calcutta, *Languages and Nations* takes place primarily in Madras, in the early nineteenth century. Both works explore the early historiography of language, race, and social distinction in India, but they do so through two paired representations: the "Aryan" and the "Dravidian." The early history of the Calcutta Orientalists was relatively well-known, but in *Languages and Nations*, Trautmann reconstructs the work of a distinctive and largely neglected south Indian school of "Orientalism." This group of British and Indian scholars carried out the foundational work of the "Dravidian proof," establishing the Dravidian language family to go alongside the more famous establishment of the Indo-European language family for which Jones is usually given credit.

Languages and Nations gives us another way to situate *Aryans and British India*. The earlier work makes its path through the better-known field of the Calcutta Orientalists and their opponents; the later work seeks to restore the lesser-known Madras Dravidianists to a rightful place in the history of the study of South Asia. The two books together trace the formative moments and key ideas (both generative and pernicious) that the founders left for us. As Trautmann reminds us at the close of *Aryans and British India*, even those crabgrass-like ideas like the "Aryan" racial concept are not inherently nefarious, like a "hidden virus or all-determining genetic code" that vitiates all Indological scholarship (1997: 228). But this does not excuse us from the labor of weeding. It is valuable, always, to re-explore critically our own intellectual *parampara*, and Trautmann has done so magnificently in these two books.

17

Excavations of British and Indian Intellectual Traditions in Thomas R. Trautmann's *Languages & Nations*

RAMA SUNDARI MANTENA

BRITISH ORIENTALISM AND PHILOLOGY

Thomas R. Trautmann's work on British Orientalists in India is monumental. His most recent publications, *Aryans and British India* (1997) and *Languages & Nations: The Dravidian Proof in Colonial Madras* (2006), charted the progress of philology in the late eighteenth and early nineteenth century when the British colonial state was just beginning to take shape in India. His command of the material is breathtaking as he undertakes to explain the distinct traditions of language study in both Britain and India. His unique perspective brings clarity to the complex traditions of language study in both places. Previously, Hans Aarsleff argued in *The Study of Language in England* that the origins of philology lie in the convergence of two ways of studying language in eighteenth-century England: the Cartesian legacy of universal grammar and Lockean probings into the origins of language. Aarsleff suggests that both were joined by a renewed interest in national origins and the study of old texts and distant languages. Trautmann makes two important interventions to the discussion of philology at this critical juncture: one is the centrality of the colonial dimensions of the emergence of historical philology and second that language study at the time was not a purely linguistic enterprise. Rather, Trautmann argues, language was an instrument of knowledge—primarily knowledge about the historical relations between nations. This important understanding underlies both *Aryans* and *Languages & Nations*. In the latter work, Trautmann investigates precisely how and why the historical relations between nations as embedded in language became a primary preoccupation in British India.

The burgeoning field of philology in late eighteenth-century England relied on the expansion of British imperial rule into South and Southeast Asia. Orientalist scholar-administrators stationed in India, such as Sir William Jones, Francis Ellis and John Leyden, found its diverse languages a treasure trove for philology. Coupled with the historical expansion of the British Empire into southern Asia, the time was ripe for the kind of discoveries that British Orientalists made. They believed that the study of language could potentially aid in efforts to reconstruct early historical relations of nations. And they knew that British imperial expansion occasioned this opportunity to investigate Indian languages. Trautmann notes that John Leyden was acutely aware of the critical role of the British Orientalists in preserving Indian languages. Leyden declared (before Max Mueller did in the latter part of the nineteenth century): "India is as it were the literary property of the English nation" (Trautmann 2006: 40). He went on to say "The peculiar advantages therefore which the English enjoy, render them responsible to the general commonwealth of letters and pledged to all posterity as long as civilized men shall exist in this earth" (2006: 40). The convergence of British imperial interests and the growth of philology at the turn of the nineteenth century was not coincidental. Trautmann asks whether the European languages and nations project as it was being transported around the globe through imperial expansion was especially fruitful in British India. What did British India provide that contributed to its growth? The languages and nations project clearly predated European imperial expansion but experienced an unprecedented growth during the early colonial period in British India. It was in British India, Trautmann argues, that the languages and nations project found the most productive interlocutors. Indian traditions of language analysis provided British philology the necessary tools to unlock the knowledge contained in languages—especially regarding historical relations between peoples.

COLONIAL KNOWLEDGE AS CONJUNCTURAL

Trautmann argues that the languages and nations project was elaborated in British India precisely due to the convergence of the following critical elements: Mosaic ethnology of the Bible, the study of word lists in Europe, the expansion of the British Empire, and finally Indian vocabularies and grammars. However it was the last element, Indian traditions of language analysis, that leads Trautmann to propose the concept of conjunctural knowledge. He defines it as a process in which Indian forms of knowledge encountered Western forms to produce something significantly new. Trautmann's argument about historical philology—that it relied on Indian forms of knowledge and thus developed only after contact with knowledge from the colonies—is an excellent illustration of the ways in which conjunctural knowledge works. This view is quite radical for understanding knowledge production at this important juncture at the end of the eighteenth century. It is radical in that it locates the production of knowledge in India itself. Furthermore, the proposal is that historical philology itself would not have emerged (as an European intellectual contribution) had it not been for British Orientalists' reliance on Indians and Indian forms of knowledge. What is the meaning of this? That historical philology—which we have always thought of as Western—was in fact reliant on indigenous knowledge systems in India: the traditions of language study in India such as *vyakarana*. Trautmann shifts the locus of intellectual production to British India so that the center of intellectual production and innovation is shifted to the so-called "periphery." Trautmann's extensive work on British Orientalists in both Calcutta and Madras has demonstrated to us that, rather than how Max Mueller viewed India as important from the perspective of Europe's past and future, we can now rightly view historical philology as emerging and taking shape in India itself. Most importantly *Languages & Nations* restores Indian contributions to the conversation about the historical relations between nations through language study.

Trautmann proposes another idea about how we do intellectual history. He argues that in the field of intellectual history there is a tendency to attribute an idea or concept to a nationalist tradition. Rather than think of knowledge formation as a static process, Trautmann suggests that in fact there are certain fields of knowledge that rely on a "progressive accumulation of knowledge (2006: 3)." The idea is that an area or field of study coheres into a body of knowledge only after a series of intellectual breakthroughs achieved by a number of individuals and communities of scholars. And finally, Trautmann suggests that a body of knowledge as monumental as language study in England and India can only achieve the advances that it achieved in both traditions as a result of an "anonymous collective effort (2006:4)." In other words, Trautmann seems to be saying that rather than be concerned about who authored the so-called discoveries of the British Orientalists, let us not forget that their achievements (for instance the Madras School of Orientalism) only came about because of the convergence of two traditions of language study: British and Indian. In this sense, Trautmann's notion of conjunctural knowledge acknowledges the forms of knowledge that Indians were shaping.

CONCLUSION: INDIVIDUALS AND COLLECTIVE KNOWLEDGE

Thomas Trautmann has been an early pioneer in the field of Indian intellectual history. He not only charted a path for the intellectual history of Colonial India with his last two books (more are on their way) but his body of work represents a distinct field that opened up fields of inquiry within Indian intellectual history. Trautmann's unique style of doing intellectual history is exemplified in *Languages & Nations*. He gives coherence to a group of interlocutors in Madras at the College and he gives coherence to the lives of intellectuals both Indian and European working and residing in Madras. He takes careful interest in individuals and their unique contributions. There are a few particular figures that Trautmann singles out in *Languages & Nations*: Francis Ellis and John Leyden. Through Trautmann's careful reading of their body of work we get a sense of the intellectual differences between a figure like Ellis and one like Leyden. Trautmann also tries to communicate their personalities along with their intellectual contributions. I still remember when Trautmann returned from a summer trip to the British Library with a copy of the literary autobiography of Charles Phillip Brown for me, since I had expressed an interest in looking at his papers. He told me that Brown was an interesting figure but did not sound like a very nice man. Trautmann came to this conclusion because of the description of him provided by Robert Caldwell. Only then did it occur to me that the personalities of historical figures that we as scholars inevitably become intimate with do in fact matter to us, especially in the way we end up narrating their stories. Readers of Trautmann's work get a good sense of the individuals themselves and their intellectual ambitions and motivations. However, over and beyond that, Trautmann's unique methodology brings them all into conversation with each other and their working towards common intellectual goals. Trautmann's unique approach to intellectual history then is to excavate the lives of British Orientalists and their monumental intellectual achievements, all the while bringing into light the forgotten Indian lives that became intertwined with their patrons. Trautmann excavates the interconnected lives and traditions of British and Indian scholars in Colonial South India and restores the complexity of their intellectual pursuits, which often gets lost in intellectual histories that are narrowly construed and limited by the political boundaries of the modern nation-state (and often embedded in triumphant narratives of national and civilizational achievement).

List of Trautmann Publications

I. BOOKS

Kautilya and the Arthashastra, A Statistical Investigation of the Authorship and Evolution of the Text. Leiden: E.J. Brill, 1971.

Dravidian Kinship (Cambridge Studies in Social Anthropology). Cambridge: Cambridge University Press, 1981. Reprinted, with new preface, New Delhi: Vistaar Publications/Sage, 1995.

Lewis Henry Morgan and the Invention of Kinship. Berkeley: University of California Press, 1987. New edition, Lincoln, NE: University of Nebraska Press, 2008.

With Karl Sanford Kabelac. *The Library of Lewis Henry Morgan and Mary Elizabeth Morgan*. Philadelphia: American Philosophical Society, 1994.

Aryans and British India. Berkeley: University of California Press, 1997. Reprinted in paperback, New Delhi: Yoda Press, 2004.

Languages and Nations: The Dravidian Proof in Colonial Madras. Berkeley: University of California Press, 2006. Tamil version, *Dravida Chandru* (The Dravidian Proof), tr. R. Sundaram, ed. A.R. Venkatachalapathy. Nagercoil: Kaalachuvadu Pathippakam, 2007.

With Karl Sanford Kabelac. *The Library of Lewis Henry Morgan and Mary Elizabeth Morgan: The Pamphlets*. Rochester, NY: Department of Rare Books and Special Collections, Rush Rhees Library, University of Rochester, 2008.

The Clash of Chronologies: Ancient India in the Modern World. New Delhi: Yoda Press, 2009.

India: Brief History of a Civilization. New York: Oxford University Press, forthcoming.

II. EDITED VOLUMES

Kinship and History in South Asia. Michigan Papers on South and Southeast Asia, No. 7. Ann Arbor: Center for South and Southeast Asian Studies, University of Michigan, 1974.

With Diane Owen Hughes. *Time: Histories and Ethnologies.* Ann Arbor: University of Michigan Press, 1995.

With Maurice Godelier and Franklin Tjon Sie Fat. *Transformations of Kinship.* (Papers of the Round Table on Dravidian Kindship, Maison Suger, Paris, 3–5 June 1993.) Washington, D.C.: Smithsonian Institution Press, 1998.

The Aryan Debate. New Delhi: Oxford University Press, 2005.

The Madras School of Orientalism. New Delhi: Oxford University Press, 2009.

III. ARTICLES

"A Metrical Original for the Kautilya Arthastra?" *Journal of the American Oriental Society* 88 (1968): 347–49.

"Length of Generation and Reign in Ancient India." *Journal of the American Oriental Society* 89 (1969): 563–77.

"Alexander and Nandrus in Justin 15.4.16." *Annals of the Bhandarkar Oriental Research Institute* 60 (1971): 240–42.

"Licchavi-dauhitra." *Journal of the Royal Asiatic Society* (1972): 2–15.

"The Use of Electronic Computers in Sanskrit Authorship Problems." *Proceedings of the XXVII International Congress of Orientalists*, Wiesbaden: Otto Harrassowitz, 1972. (Abstract of paper presented to the Congress, 15 August 1967).

"Consanguineous Marriage in Pali Literature." *Journal of the American Oriental Society* 93 (1973): 158–80.

"Cross-cousin Marriage in Ancient North India?" In *Kinship and History in South Asia*, ed. Thomas R. Trautmann, pp. 61–103. Ann Arbor: Center for South and Southeast Asian Studies, University of Michigan, 1974.

"Traditions of Statecraft in Ancient India." In *Tradition and Politics in South Asia*, ed. R.J. Moore, pp. 86–102. Bombay: Vikas Publishing House, 1979.

"The Study of Dravidian Kinship." In *Aryan and Non-Aryan in India* (Michigan papers on South and Southeast Asia, No. 14), ed. Madhav

M. Deshpande and Peter E. Hook, pp. 153–73. Ann Arbor: Center for South and Southeast Asian Studies, University of Michigan and Karoma, 1979.

"Marriage and Rank in Bengali Culture." In *Journal of Asian Studies* 39 (1980): 519–24.

"Elephants and the Mauryas." In *India: History and Thought. Essays in Honour of A.L. Basham*, ed. S.N. Mukherjee, pp. 254–81. Calcutta: Subarnarekha, 1982.

"Decoding Dravidian Kinship: Morgan and McIlvaine." *Man* (n.s.) 19 (1984): 421–31.

With Richard D. Saran, Peter A. Granda and Armgard Ruckert. "The Study of South Indian Inscriptions." In *Studies of South India, An Anthology of Recent Research and Scholarship,* ed. Robert E. Frykenberg and Pauline Kolenda, pp. 1–29. Madras: New Era Publications, 1985.

"*El regalo* en la India: Marcel Mauss como Indologo." *Estudios de Asia y Africa* 21 (1986): 644–57.

"In Memoriam Arthur Llewellyn Basham 1914–1986." *Journal of the International Association of Buddhist Studies* 11 (1988): 131–35.

"Dravidian Kinship and the Anthropology of Lewis Henry Morgan." *Journal of the American Oriental Society* 108 (1988): 93–97.

"Whig Ethnology from Locke to Morgan." *Journal of the Anthropological Society of Oxford* 22 (1991): 201–18.

"Morgan, Lewis Henry." In *International Dictionary of Anthropologists*, comp. Library-Anthropology Resource Group (LARG), ed. Christopher Winters, pp. 481–84. New York & London: Garland Publishing, 1991.

"The Revolution in Ethnological Time." (The Marett Memorial Lecture 1991.) *Man* (n.s.) 27 (1992): 379–97.

"La revolución en el tiempo etnológico." *Estudios de Asia y Africa* 88 (1992): 232–61. (Spanish version of the preceding).

"Marriage Rules and Patterns of Marriage in the Dravidian Kinship Region." In *Family, Kinship and Marriage in India,* ed. Patricia Uberoi, pp. 273–86. Delhi: Oxford University Press, 1994. (Reprinted extracts from *Dravidian Kinship*).

"The Study of Dravidian Kinship." In *Family, Kinship and Marriage in India,* ed. Patricia Uberoi, pp. 74–90. Delhi: Oxford University Press, 1994. (Reprint of 1979 article).

"Dravidian Kinship as a Cultural Type and as a Structural Type." (In Russian translation) In *Algebra rodstva*, ed. V.A. Popov, pp. 43–57. St. Petersburg: Rossinskay Akademiy Nauk, 1995.

"Indian Time, European Time." In *Time: Histories and Ethnologies*, ed. Diane Owen Hughes and Thomas R. Trautmann, pp. 167–97. Ann Arbor: University of Michigan Press, 1995.

"An Improbable Conjuncture." In *D. School: Reflections on the Delhi School of Economics*, ed. Dharma Kumar and Dilip Mookherjee, pp. 74–79. Delhi: Oxford University Press, 1995.

With R.H. Barnes. "'Dravidian,' 'Iroquois,' and 'Crow-Omaha' in North American Perspective." In *Transformations of Kinship*, ed. Maurice Godelier, Thomas R. Trautmann and Franklin E. Tjon Sie Fat, pp. 27–58. Washington, D.C.: Smithsonian Institution Press, 1998.

With Maurice Godelier and Franklin E. Tjon Sie Fat. "Introduction." In *Transformations of Kinship*, ed. Maurice Godelier, Thomas R. Trautmann and Franklin E. Tjon Sie Fat, pp. 1–26. Washington, D.C.: Smithsonian Institution Press, 1998.

"The Lives of Sir William Jones." In *Sir William Jones 1746–94: A Commemoration*, ed. Alexander Murray, pp. 91–121. Oxford: Oxford University Press, 1998.

"Inventing the History of South India." In *Invoking the Past: The Uses of History in South Asia*, ed. Daud Ali, pp. 36–54. New Delhi: Oxford University Press, 1999.

"Constructing the Racial Theory of Indian Civilization." In *Aryan and Non-Aryan in South Asia*, ed. Johannes Bronkhorst and Madhav M. Deshpande, pp. 277–93. Harvard Oriental series, Opera Minora, vol. 3. Cambridge, MA: Department of Sanskrit and Indian Studies, Harvard University, 1999.

"Hullabaloo about Telugu." *South Asia Research* 19.1 (1999): 53–70.

"La parentī comme langage." In *La production du social: autour de Maurice Godelier*, ed. Philippe Descola, Jacques Hamel and Pierre Lemonnier, pp. 433–43. Paris: Fayard, 1999.

"Lewis Henry Morgan." In *American National Biography*, vol. 15. ed. John A. Garraty and Mark C. Carnes, pp. 848–51. New York and Oxford: Oxford University Press, 1999.

"India and the Study of Kinship Terminologies." Invited contribution to a special issue on kinship (Question de parentī). *L'Homme* 154–155 (2000): 559–71.

"Kinship, Language, and the Construction of South India." In *Structure and Society in Early South India: Essays in Honour of Noboru Karashima,* ed. Kenneth R. Hall, pp. 181–97. New Delhi: Oxford University Press, 2001.

"The Whole History of Kinship Terminology in Three Chapters: Before Morgan, Morgan, and After Morgan." *Anthropological Theory* 1.2 (2001): 268–85.

"Dr Johnson and the Pandits: Imagining the Perfect Dictionary in Colonial Madras." *Indian Economic and Social History Review* 38.4 (2001): 375–97.

With Carla M. Sinopoli. "In the Beginning was the Word: Excavating the Relations between History and Archaeology in South Asia." *Journal of the Economic and Social History of the Orient* 45.4 (2002): 492–523.

"Die Entdeckung von 'arisch' und 'dravidisch' in Britisch-Indien. Eine Erzālung zweier Stādte." ("The Invention of 'Aryan' and 'Dravidian': A Tale of Two Cities.") In *Kunstructionen der Vergangenheit als Grundlage für Selbst- und Fremdwahrnehmungen Sūdasiens*, ed. Michael Bergunder and Rahul Peter Das, pp. 14–39. Neue Hallesche Berichte. Quellen und Studien zur Geschichte und Gegenwart Sūdasiens. Halle: Franckeschen Stiftungen, 2002.

"Patterns of Marriage." In *The Oxford India Companion to Sociology and Social Anthropology*, ed. Veena Das, pp. 1104–26. New Delhi: Oxford University Press, 2003.

"Foreword." In *The Origins of Himalayan Studies: Brian Houghton Hodgson in Nepal and Darjeeling 1820–1858*, ed. David M. Waterhouse, pp. xiii–xix. Royal Asiatic Society Books. London and New York: Routledge Curzon, 2004.

"Discovering Aryan and Dravidian in British India: A Tale of Two Cities." In *Historiographia Linguistica* 31.1 (2004): 33–58. (English version, slightly revised, of "Die Entdeckung....", 2002).

"Foreword." In *The Wonder That Was India: A Study of the History and Culture of the Indian Sub-continent before the Coming of the Muslims*, 3rd edn, by A.L. Basham, pp. vii–xii. London: Picador, 2004.

"Francis Whyte Ellis." In *Oxford Dictionary of National Biography*, vol. 18, ed. H.C.G. Matthew and Brian Harrison, pp. 221–22. Oxford: Oxford University Press, 2004.

"Sir Charles Wilkins." In *Oxford Dictionary of National Biography*, vol. 58, ed., H.C.G. Matthew and Brian Harrison, pp. 973–75. Oxford: Oxford University Press, 2004.

"The Case against Ancient Indian History." *Biblio: A Review of Books* 11, no. 3–4 (March–April 2006), pp. 18–21.

"Explosion in the Grammar Factory." In *Ancient India in its Wider World*, ed. G. Parker and C. Sinopoli, pp. 165–181. Ann Arbor: Center for South Asian Studies, University of Michigan, 2008.

"The Missionary and the Orientalist." In *Ancient to Modern: Religion, Power, and Community in India*, ed. Ishita Banerjee-Dube and Saurabh Dube, pp. 236–58. New Delhi: Oxford University Press, 2008.

"Riot over *Ryotwar*." In *The Madras School of Orientalism*, ed. Thomas R. Trautmann, pp. 310–32. New Delhi: Oxford University Press, 2009.

Notes on Contributors

RICHARD H. DAVIS is Professor in the Religion and Asian Studies programs at Bard College. He is the author of *Ritual in an Oscillating Universe* and *Lives of Indian Images*, as well as two forthcoming publications, *A Priest's Guide for the Great Festival* (Oxford University Press) and *Global India, ca. 100 CE: South Asia in Early World History* (Association for Asian Studies).

MADHAV M. DESHPANDE was originally trained in Sanskrit in Pune, India, and later received a PhD from the University of Pennsylvania. Since 1972, Deshpande has been on the faculty of the University of Michigan as Professor of Sanskrit and Linguistics. He has published widely on the linguistics of Sanskrit and Indo-Aryan languages and Indian philosophical and religious traditions.

MICHAEL S. DODSON is Associate Professor of South Asian and British Imperial History at Indiana University Bloomington, and author of *Orientalism, Empire, and National Culture: India 1770–1880.*

TOM FRICKE is Professor of Anthropology at the University of Michigan. He has, since 1981, conducted his field research among Tibeto-Burman language speakers in Nepal where he specializes in kinship, social transformation, and marriage exchange.

KENNETH R. HALL (PhD Michigan), Professor of History at Ball State University, specializes in pre-1500 Southeast Asia and South Indian history. His publications include *An Economic History of Early Southeast Asia (Cambridge History of Southeast Asia), Maritime Trade and State Development in Early Southeast Asia*, and *Trade and Statecraft in the Age of the Colas*. Among his edited works are *Structure and Society in Early South India, Maritime Diasporas in the Indian Ocean and East and Southeast Asia (960–1775)*, and *Secondary Cities and Urban Networking in the Indian Ocean Realm, c. 1400–1800*. He is associate editor of the *Journal of the Economic and Social History of the Orient*.

SHAH MAHMOUD HANIFI received a PhD from the University of Michigan and now teaches the history of the modern Middle East and South Asia at James Madison University in Virginia. His book *Connecting Histories in Afghanistan: Market Relations and State Formation on a Colonial Frontier* appeared in 2008 in Columbia University Press' Gutenberg-e series of digital publications and is accessible at http://www.gutenberg-e.org/hanifi/index.html

ANNE HARDGROVE is Associate Professor of History at the University of Texas San Antonio. Thomas Trautmann along with Nicholas Dirks served as her dissertation co-chairs in the University of Michigan PhD Program of Anthropology and History. Hardgrove's first book is entitled *Community and Public Culture: The Marwaris in Calcutta c. 1897–1997* (Columbia and Oxford University Presses). She is currently completing a book manuscript entitled *Close your Eyes and Think of India: Translating the Kama Sutra*.

JUDITH T. IRVINE is the Edward Sapir Collegiate Professor of Anthropology at the University of Michigan, Ann Arbor. She received her doctoral degree from the University of Pennsylvania in 1973. Her work has primarily concerned language, culture, and history in sub-Saharan Africa, with field research in Senegal since 1970 and linguistic and archival research on other parts of the continent. Many of her recent papers focus on linguistic research in the colonial era.

DAVID N. LORENZEN has been a professor and researcher at the Center of Asian and African Studies of El Colegio de Mīxico since 1970. He has written many books and articles on the history of Hindu religious movements in India. His books include an edited volume, *Religious Movements in South Asia 600–1800* (Oxford University Press, 2004), and a collection of essays, *Who Invented Hinduism?* (Yoda Press, 2006). His current research project is on Capuchin missionaries in eighteenth-century Bihar. Yoda Press published his biography of a Capuchin friar of the Bihar Mission, *The Scourge of the Mission: Marco della Tomba in Hindustan* in 2010.

RAMA SUNDARI MANTENA is Assistant Professor of History at the University of Illinois at Chicago and is currently completing a book manuscript on the making of colonial archives, the forging of a new historical method, and the emergence of new practices of history in Colonial South India, 1780–1880.

BHAVANI RAMAN is Assistant Professor of History at Princeton University. She is currently working on a book manuscript on record-keeping practices and Company office culture in early nineteenth-century Madras.

PARNA SENGUPTA was a PhD advisee of Thomas Trautmann and is currently Associate Professor of History at Carleton College. She has completed a book manuscript on missionary education and religious identity in colonial Bengal for University of California Press. Her current project is on astrological almanacs and models of temporality in colonial India.

CARLA M. SINOPOLI is Director and Curator in the Museum of Anthropology and Professor in the Department of Anthropology at the University of Michigan. She has been conducting research in the Tungabhadra region of Karnataka since 1983 and is co-director of the Vijayanagara Metropolitan Survey project (1988–1997) and the Late Prehistoric/Prehistoric Landscapes Project of the Tungabhadra Corridor (2003–present). Among her publications are *Pots and Palaces: The Ceramics of the Nobleman's Quarter of Vijayanagara* (Manohar Publishing, 1993); *The Political Economy of Craft Production: Crafting Empire in South India, c. 1350–1650* (Cambridge University Press, 2003), and *The Vijayanagara Metropolitan Survey Project, Vol. 1* (with Kathleen D. Morrison, 2007, University of Michigan).

CYNTHIA TALBOT is Associate Professor of History and Asian Studies at the University of Texas at Austin. She earned her BA and MA at the University of Michigan under Thomas Trautmann's supervision, and her PhD from the University of Wisconsin-Madison. She is author of *Precolonial India in Practice: Society, Region, and Identity in Medieval Andhra* and co-author (with Catherine B. Asher) of *India Before Europe*. Her current research focuses on historical traditions and memories relating to Prithviraj Cauhan, as well as on early modern Rajput narratives in general.

ROMILA THAPAR is Emeritus Professor of History at the Jawaharlal Nehru University in New Delhi. She is currently working on historical writing in early India.

SYLVIA VATUK is Professor Emerita of Anthropology at the University of Illinois-Chicago. She received her PhD from Harvard University; her doctoral dissertation, based on field research in Uttar Pradesh, was later published as *Kinship and Urbanization: White Collar Migrants in an Indian City*. She has carried out research in both north and south India and among Muslims as well as Hindus. She has published extensively on the family and family histories, kinship and marriage systems, gender, and intergenerational relations in India. Most recently her work has focused on issues of Muslim women and personal law.